BLOOD SPORT

*The President
and
His Adversaries*

JAMES B. STEWART

SIMON & SCHUSTER

SIMON & SCHUSTER
Rockefeller Center
1230 Avenue of the Americas
New York, NY 10020

SIMON & SCHUSTER and colophon are
registered trademarks of Simon & Schuster Inc.
Designed by Edith Fowler
Picture research by Natalie Goldstein
Manufactured in the United States of America

10   9   8   7

Library of Congress Cataloging-in-Publication Data
is available.

ISBN 0-684-80230-9

CONTENTS

FOREWORD

HILLARY RODHAM CLINTON is called to testify before a grand jury, the first time a first lady has ever been subpoenaed in a criminal probe. On the Senate floor, Lauch Faircloth, conservative North Carolina Republican, calls her a liar. After vowing not to, President Bill Clinton invokes attorney-client privilege in an attempt to prevent disclosure of notes of a White House meeting to discuss his investment in Whitewater. A memo is discovered in the files of a White House aide suggesting that contrary to her lawyers' statements, it was the first lady who ordered the firing of White House travel office employees. Subpoenaed billing records from the Rose Law Firm, long described as missing, are suddenly found in a closet in the family quarters of the White House. They reveal that the first lady was far more involved in work for a failed Arkansas savings and loan than she has admitted.

It is January 1996, the beginning of a presidential election year. An independent counsel investigation probes the Clintons' Arkansas dealings, their activities in the White House, and the still-mysterious death of White House lawyer Vincent W. Foster, Jr. Numerous people connected to Whitewater have pleaded guilty to felonies, have been indicted, or remain under investigation. The Arkansas contingent working in the administration has been decimated. A Senate committee under the leadership of Alfonse D'Amato, Republican of New York, continues its Whitewater hearings, generating a steady flow of front-page stories and network news broadcasts. Yet polls indicate that much of the American public remains mystified.

This book begins in Arkansas in 1978, when the Whitewater investment began and Clinton was first running for governor. It covers events through the 1992 presidential campaign and into Clinton's presidency to the spring of 1994 just after the appointment of an independent counsel, and after the president and the first lady gave press conferences intended to put the scandal behind them. It is this period that is now under investigation. An epilogue summarizes developments between then and January 1996. Recent revelations all relate to incidents during the time described in these pages. By the spring of 1994, the Clintons' strategy for dealing with the scandal had been established, and so had that of their political opponents.

In the absence of the full report of the independent counsel, which is not expected until after the next presidential election, I believe this to be a comprehensive account of these events. In my view, it is this information that permits us to make sense of what is unfolding now. I hope readers will find that this book makes clear what is happening, and why. And I trust they will agree that this story isn't as arcane and confusing as those involved would have us believe.

JAMES B. STEWART
January 1996

CAST OF CHARACTERS

MARCH 1994

AT THE WHITE HOUSE

Bill Clinton, *President*
Hillary Rodham Clinton, *First Lady*

Thomas F. "Mack" McLarty III, *Chief of Staff*
     Bill Burton, *McLarty's Staff Director*
Bernard W. Nussbaum, *Counsel to the President*
     William H. Kennedy, *Associate Counsel*
     Steven Neuwirth, *Associate Counsel*
     Clifford M. Sloan, *Associate Counsel*
George Stephanopoulos, *Senior Advisor*
Bruce R. Lindsey, *Senior Advisor*
Harold M. Ickes, *Deputy Chief of Staff*
David Gergen, *Presidential Counselor*
John D. Podesta, *Staff Secretary*
Mark D. Gearan, *Communications Director*
Dee Dee Myers, *Press Secretary*
W. David Watkins, *Assistant to the President for Management and
     Administration*
Patsy Thomasson, *Director of White House Administration*
Margaret Williams, *Chief of Staff to the First Lady*
Lisa Caputo, *Press Secretary to the First Lady*

THE FOSTER FAMILY

Vincent W. Foster, Jr. (deceased), *former Deputy Counsel to the President*
Elizabeth (Lisa) Braden Foster, *his wife*
Sheila Foster Anthony, *his sister*
Sharon Bowman, *his sister*
James Hamilton, *the family lawyer*

FRIENDS AND ADVISORS TO THE CLINTONS

Harry Thomason *and his wife,* Linda Bloodworth-Thomason, *television producers, in California*
Susan Thomases, *Manhattan lawyer*
Betsey Wright, *former Clinton campaign official, in Washington*
David Kendall, *the Clintons' personal lawyer, in Washington*

AT THE JUSTICE DEPARTMENT

Janet Reno, *Attorney General*
Webster L. Hubbell, *Associate Attorney General*
Philip B. Heymann, *Deputy Attorney General*

THE INDEPENDENT COUNSEL

Robert B. Fiske, Jr.
Kenneth W. Starr, *successor to Fiske*

AT THE TREASURY DEPARTMENT
AND RESOLUTION TRUST CORPORATION (RTC)

Lloyd M. Bentsen, *Secretary of the Treasury*
Roger C. Altman, *Deputy Secretary of the Treasury and acting head of the RTC*
Joshua L. Steiner, *Altman's former assistant and Bentsen's Chief of Staff*

Jean Hanson, *General Counsel, Treasury*
Jack R. DeVore, *former Treasury spokesman*
William H. Roelle, *former RTC Senior Vice President*
Ellen Kulka, *RTC General Counsel*
L. Jean Lewis, *RTC criminal investigator, Kansas City*
L. Richard Iorio, *RTC investigative supervisor, Kansas City*
Julie Yanda, *head of the Professional Liability Section, Kansas City*
April Breslow, *lawyer in the RTC Professional Liability Section*

AT THE UNITED STATES PARK POLICE

Charles W. Hume, *Captain*
Peter W. Markland, *Sergeant*
John C. Rolla, *Investigator*
Cheryl A. Braun, *Investigator*

IN ARKADELPHIA, ARKANSAS

James B. McDougal, *former Chairman of Madison Guaranty Savings and Loan*
Susan McDougal, *his former wife, now living in California*

IN LITTLE ROCK, ARKANSAS

Jim Guy Tucker, *Governor*
Paula Casey, *U.S. Attorney*
Charles A. Banks, *former U.S. Attorney*
Sam Heuer, *lawyer for James McDougal*
John Latham, *former Chief Operating Officer, Madison Guaranty Savings and Loan*
David L. Hale, *head of Capital Management Services*
C. Joseph Giroir, *former partner, Rose Law Firm*
Ronald M. Clark, *managing partner, Rose Law Firm*
Richard N. Massey, *partner, Rose Law Firm*
Edward M. Penick, Jr., *former Chairman, Twin City Bank*
Terry Renaud, *President, Twin City Bank*

Margaret Davenport Eldridge, *Executive Vice President, Twin City Bank*
Roger Perry, *state trooper formerly assigned to governor's security*
Larry Patterson, *state trooper*
Danny Ferguson, *state trooper*
Buddy Young, *Captain in charge of governor's security, now in Denton,*
    Texas
Paula Corbin Jones, *former state employee, now living in California*
Clifford Jackson, *lawyer*
Sheffield Nelson, *former head of Arkla and former Republican*
    gubernatorial candidate

IN FAYETTEVILLE, ARKANSAS

Jim Blair, *General Counsel, Tyson Foods*
Diane Kincaid Blair, *his wife*
Robert L. "Red" Bone, *former commodities broker, now in Missouri*
Thomas Dittmer, *head of Refco Inc. commodities brokerage, now in*
    Chicago
Steve Smith, *former Clinton political advisor and business partner of James*
    McDougal
Beverly Bassett Schaffer, *former head of Arkansas Department of*
    Securities and Savings and Loans
Archie Schaffer, *her husband and a Tyson Foods executive*

IN FLIPPIN, ARKANSAS

Chris Wade, *realtor*
Rosalee Wade, *his wife*
J. Wesley Strange, *President, 1st Ozark National Bank*
Ronald A. Proctor, *Vice President, 1st Ozark National Bank*
Vernon Dewey, *former loan officer, 1st Ozark National Bank*

AT THE NEW YORK TIMES

Max Frankel, *Executive Editor*
Joseph Lelyveld, *Managing Editor*
Howell Raines, *Editorial Page Editor, former Washington Bureau Chief*

Jeff Gerth, *reporter, Washington Bureau*
Stephen Engelberg, *reporter, Washington Bureau*

AT THE WASHINGTON POST

Leonard Downie, Jr., *Executive Editor*
Robert G. Kaiser, *Managing Editor*
Michael Isikoff, *reporter*
Susan Schmidt, *reporter*

AT THE LOS ANGELES TIMES

Shelby Coffey, *Editor*
Jack Nelson, *Washington Bureau Chief*
William C. Rempel, *reporter*
Douglas Frantz, *reporter, Washington Bureau*

AT NBC NEWS

Ira Silverman, *producer*
Tim Russert, *Washington Bureau Chief*

AT ABC NEWS

Chris Vlasto, *producer*

AT THE AMERICAN SPECTATOR

David Brock, *staff writer*

AT THE NEW YORK POST

Eric Breindel, *Editorial Page Editor*
Christopher Ruddy, *reporter*

IN FAIRFAX, VIRGINIA

Floyd G. Brown, *Founder and Director, Citizens United*
David N. Bossie, *Communications Director, Citizens United*

FINANCIAL INSTITUTIONS

Formerly controlled by James and Susan McDougal
Madison Guaranty Savings and Loan (formerly Woodruff County
    Savings and Loan Association), main office in Little Rock
Madison Financial Corp., subsidiary of Madison Guaranty Savings
    and Loan
Madison Bank and Trust Co. of Kingston (formerly Bank of
    Kingston), Kingston

Lenders to the Clintons and McDougals
Citizens Bank and Trust Co. of Flippin, renamed 1st Ozark National
    Bank. Primary lender of Whitewater funds.
Twin City Bankshares Corp., holding company for Twin City Bank of
    Little Rock, acquired Citizens Bank. Subsidiary of Frank Lyon
    Company. (Twin City and its subsidiaries, including 1st Ozark,
    have since been acquired by Mercantile Bank Corporation of St.
    Louis.)
Union National Bank of Little Rock. Lender of Whitewater down
    payment.
Security Bank of Paragould. Lender of funds to build a model home.
Bank of Cherry Valley. Lender to Clinton campaign.

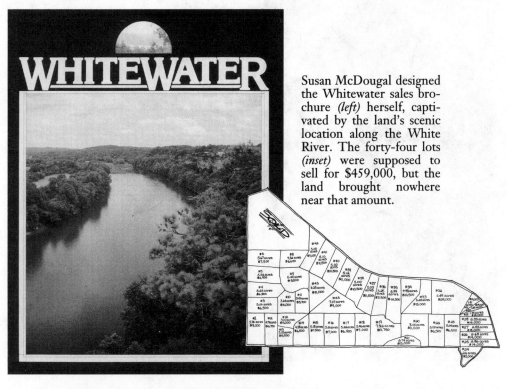

WHITEWATER

Susan McDougal designed the Whitewater sales brochure *(left)* herself, captivated by the land's scenic location along the White River. The forty-four lots *(inset)* were supposed to sell for $459,000, but the land brought nowhere near that amount.

Susan was a nineteen-year-old beauty queen contestant at conservative Ouachita Baptist University when she met Jim McDougal, a professor fifteen years older and a former aide to Senator J. William Fulbright.

Bill Clinton and Hillary Rodham attended Susan and Jim McDougal's wedding in 1978, which was a gathering of Arkansas's political elite. Jim McDougal is at left with his friend Claudia Riley.

Vincent W. Foster, Jr., was deputy counsel to the president when his body was found in Fort Marcy Park, just outside Washington, on July 20, 1993. His death stunned the White House and became a topic of nationwide speculation.

Foster was Hillary Clinton's mentor and confidant in the Rose Law Firm, and functioned as her advocate in the White House counsel's office. Lisa and Vincent Foster are shown with the Clintons at a Little Rock gala.

Linda Bloodworth-Thomason and Harry Thomason, Hollywood producers, numbered the Clintons among their closest friends and helped produce the inauguration. Thomason had the run of the White House.

The White House inner circle appeared at Senate hearings during the summer of 1994. *Left to right:* Cliff Sloan, Neil Eggleston, Bruce Lindsey, George Stephanopoulos, Maggie Williams, Mack McLarty, Harold Ickes, John Podesta, Mark Gearan, Lisa Caputo.

In and around the White House, *clockwise from top left:* Webb Hubbell, associate attorney general; Bernie Nussbaum, counsel to the president; Manhattan lawyer Susan Thomases; David Watkins, head of White House management; Roger Altman, deputy secretary of the treasury; David Gergen, counselor to the president.

With multiple Whitewater investigations underway, independent counsel Robert Fiske *(above left)* was abruptly replaced by Kenneth Starr *(above right)*, a former judge with prominent Republican credentials. The Clintons retained their own lawyer, David Kendall *(right)*. Testifying before Congress were L. Jean Lewis *(below left)*, an RTC investigator who claimed interference from "higher-ups," and Beverly Bassett Schaffer *(below right)*, the Arkansas regulator who oversaw Madison Guaranty.

With their real estate empire in ruins, Jim and Susan McDougal *(above)* faced new charges. Every false step by the Clinton administration and every new allegation was seized upon by the openly partisan but highly effective Citizens United team of Floyd Brown *(below left)* and David Bossie *(below right)*.

TWO PHOTOS: SPENCER TIREY / GAMMA LIAISON

In the wake of Foster's death, Clinton's accusers went public with their charges. Two Arkansas state troopers, Roger Perry and Larry Patterson *(above)*, recounted their experiences in Governor Clinton's security detail. David Hale *(above right)*, a lender to the McDougals, claimed he'd been "pressured" by then-Governor Clinton. Paula Jones *(right)* filed suit against the president, claiming she'd been sexually harassed during the time that he was governor and she was a state employee.

Jim Blair *(below left)*, general counsel to Tyson Foods, handled Hillary's commodities trading.

Blair persuaded Chris Wade *(below right)*, the Whitewater realtor, to pay off the balance of the original Whitewater loan.

FRED PROUSER / SIPA PRESS

TOM EWART / SYGMA

STEVE KEESEE / *ARKANSAS DEMOCRAT-GAZETTE* / SIPA PRESS

In the spring of 1994, the Clintons held separate press conferences to try to put Whitewater behind them. The president said he intended to "get on with the business of the country." The first lady, dressed in a pink jacket, explained her commodities trading and, as to Whitewater, said, "Every document that we have obtained has been turned over to the special counsel."

PROLOGUE

"WE'VE GOT A DB IN FORT MARCY PARK."

John C. Rolla, criminal investigator for the United States Park Police, suddenly looked up as the call came in over his shortwave radio. "DB" meant dead body. It was just after 6 P.M., July 20, 1993. After five years of undercover work in the war against drugs, posing as a busboy in Shenandoah National Park, a drug dealer in Glacier, the athletic thirty-one-year-old Rolla had graduated to the major crimes unit—robberies, rape, homicide—that month and had just returned from a stint at "death investigation" school. This might be his first homicide.

He hurried to his car and drove from his office in the District of Columbia to Virginia, where he turned north on the George Washington Memorial Parkway. Fort Marcy Park, the site of a Civil War fortification built to protect Washington from Confederate attack, was part of the federal park system. Despite its historic significance, the presence of two Civil War–era cannon, and several footpaths, it is now little more than a wooded roadside rest stop. Rolla had patrolled the park a few times before, and he knew it as a gay meeting place and cruising area convenient for commuters, the site of romantic trysts and an occasional assault.

As Rolla pulled into the parking area, emergency medical technicians were driving out. He noticed a blue Mercedes with its hazard lights flashing, a white Nissan, and a white or light gray Honda Accord. Several officers were already on the scene. Officer Franz Ferstle told Rolla that a body had been located up near the second cannon, and that he thought the Honda might belong to the deceased. A man and woman were in the Nissan, and the owner of the Mercedes had called for a tow truck. They looked in through the Honda's window. A dark blue suit jacket was neatly folded over the back of the front seat. Ferstle thought it matched the fabric on the corpse's slacks. A blue silk tie dotted with swans was draped over the jacket.

Using his car phone, Rolla phoned in the number on the Honda's Arkansas license plate to check the car registration on the National Crime Information Center computers. The response: Vincent Foster, Little Rock, Arkansas. The name meant nothing to Rolla or the other investigators.

Rolla walked uphill a fair distance to reach the cannon. It had been a hot day, 90 degrees, and the dirt was dry and packed. The body lay about ten feet from the cannon, the head near the crest of the embankment with the legs extending downhill, the feet resting on some exposed roots. There was no sign of a struggle, nor any indication the body had been moved. Rolla walked over and stood directly above the head, looking down into Foster's open, now lifeless eyes.

Blood, some of it still wet, ran from the right nostril and the right side of the mouth onto the dirt. Flies were crawling over the face. Rolla noticed how big the man was, probably six foot four. He was wearing a long-sleeved button-down white shirt, tucked in, but no tie. Rolla had to move the foliage of a small bush to see what looked like a .38 caliber revolver in the right hand, which was marked by powder burns. On his belt was a paging device, turned off, suggesting he didn't want to be disturbed. Rolla lifted the body's left hand. It was still warm.

When the medical examiner arrived, around 7 P.M., Rolla rolled the body over, struggling to keep it from slipping down the hillside. There was a small hole in the back of the head. Blood stained the back of the shirt. Wearing gloves, Rolla felt inside the wound. He noticed that the skull and brain were largely intact, though "mushy," and mixed with blood and hair. After taking several Polaroid snapshots, he searched the pants pockets, which seemed empty. He removed a watch, a ring, and the beeper. The beeper was marked with the letters "WHCS."

When Rolla got back to the parking lot, he opened the door of the unlocked Honda. The suit jacket did indeed match the trousers.

Inside the jacket was a wallet, with $282 in cash and an Arkansas driver's license identifying the owner as Vincent W. Foster, Jr. As Rolla searched the jacket, his colleague, Cheryl Braun, noticed a plasticized identification card attached to a chain that must have been lying under the jacket. She looked at it closely. "Uh oh, he has a White House ID here," she said.

Rolla reached for the card. It had a photo of Foster, his name, and the phrase "White House Communications." "This looks like the guy, it must be the guy, it looks like him," Rolla said. He knew that plenty of people worked in the White House, many at relatively menial tasks. Still, this could be significant. Braun thought she recognized the name, and that Vincent Foster might be somebody important.

"We'd better notify the Secret Service," Rolla said.

There was an air of excitement at the White House as the president's staff checked final preparations for an interview with Larry King. The talk show impresario was interviewing the president that evening, broadcasting live from the ground-floor library of the White House. It was Clinton's first appearance on Larry King since the inauguration, and the president and his staff saw it both as an opportunity to relive some of the talk show triumphs of the campaign and to put the recent snafus—gays in the military, the White House travel office—behind them. King himself seemed to be reveling in his access to the president and the unusual opportunity to broadcast his show right from the White House. He'd brought his wife along, and, assuming the interview went as expected, the couple was going to get a tour of the executive mansion after the broadcast.

Thomas F. "Mack" McLarty, the president's chief of staff, stopped in to make sure everything was set for the interview, then joined senior advisor George Stephanopoulos, counselor to the president Bruce Lindsey, and communications director Mark Gearan in the residence to watch the interview on television. But once it seemed to get off to a good start, McLarty excused himself and walked out into the broad corridor on the ground floor of the White House, planning to join his wife at home. He noticed Bill Burton, his staff director, hurrying toward him.

"Mack, I have tragic news," Burton began. "There's a body at

Fort Marcy Park that appears to be Vincent Foster. It appears to be suicide."

McLarty was stunned. He'd known Foster practically all his life. They'd grown up together in Hope, Arkansas, Clinton's birthplace. Tall and thin as a teenager, Foster was still known to McLarty by his high school nickname, "Pencil." Though Foster wasn't much of an athlete, he and McLarty had played football together in junior high. Foster was president of the student body in high school; McLarty was vice president. McLarty had gone on to be elected governor of Arkansas Boys State,* and Foster had called McLarty "Governor" ever since. McLarty had gone on to head Arkla, the big Arkansas gas utility, and Foster had become a partner in Little Rock's Rose Law Firm. As chairman of the Arkansas Democratic party, McLarty had become close to Bill Clinton, and Foster had forged a closer relationship with Hillary Clinton, his fellow litigation partner and soul mate at the Rose firm. They'd often bump into each other at Sunday buffets at the Country Club of Little Rock and at the Clintons' birthday parties.

It seemed impossible that Vince was dead. McLarty had gone over to chat with Foster that morning in the Rose Garden, when Louis Freeh was sworn in as the new FBI director. Vince had chuckled at something McLarty had said, as he often did. Surely there was a mistake, or at least the possibility of a mistake?

Burton allowed that the body hadn't yet been positively identified. Bill Kennedy, one of the White House lawyers and another former Rose partner, was on his way to the Fairfax County Hospital morgue to identify the body. Still, there was little likelihood that the identification by the Park Police had been mistaken. David Watkins, an Arkansas native who was head of White House management, was heading over to the Foster home.

Even as he continued to talk with Burton, McLarty found himself pushing his own thoughts and reactions out of his mind. Whatever had happened to Foster, his job now was to serve the interests of the president, who was being televised, live, down the hall. Was news of Foster's death about to go out on the news wires? Surely it was only a matter of time. Should he interrupt the Larry King interview?

---

* Boys State is an American Legion civics program for high school students organized in each state. Delegates may go on to Boys Nation in Washington, D.C.

Just then Stephanopoulos and Gearan noticed McLarty in the hall and came out from the room where they were watching the interview on television. McLarty broke the news, and the two men gasped. McLarty asked for their views on whether the interview should be interrupted; they agreed that it was better to wait. But they asked that incoming calls to the show be screened, so the president didn't learn the news on live television.

McLarty's next priority was to reach the first lady. He stepped into an adjacent room and asked the White House operator to locate her, saying it was urgent. Moments later McLarty was connected to the Rodham home in Little Rock, where Hillary was visiting her mother and father, who was ill, after a trip to the Far East and the West Coast. The first lady's press secretary, Lisa Caputo, answered the phone in the kitchen.

"I need to speak to Hillary right now," McLarty said. He wanted to make sure she heard the news from him, and not from a news bulletin. He knew that Foster was probably Hillary's best friend in the White House. Caputo was struck by the urgency in his voice.

"I have some tragic news," McLarty began when Hillary took the phone. Then he told her that Foster was dead, an apparent suicide.

There was silence. Then, "I can't believe it's true," Hillary said. "It just can't be true." She began to cry.

McLarty said there hadn't yet been a positive identification of the body, but that it most likely was true. "All we can do is hope and pray that there's been some mistake," he said.

"What about Bill, does he know?" she asked. The first lady hadn't been watching TV, and didn't seem to know that the president was being broadcast live at that very moment. McLarty explained the situation, and said he'd be told at the earliest opportunity. He told her he'd keep her apprised of developments, and the two hung up. The conversation had lasted just a few minutes.

While McLarty spoke to Hillary, Stephanopoulos called Webster Hubbell, another former Rose partner, now associate attorney general. He knew the Hubbells and Fosters had been best friends. McLarty also spoke to Hubbell, urging him to join Watkins at the Foster home. Just then, Stephanopoulos came rushing up with the news that Clinton had spontaneously agreed with Larry King to continue the interview for a half hour beyond its scheduled conclusion. "You've got to stop him," Stephanopoulos urged, anxious that the Foster news would break at any moment. "You're the only one who can stop this."

McLarty hurried into the library during the commercial break. Clinton looked ebullient, pleased with the interview.

"Mr. President, we need to quit while we're ahead," McLarty said, trying to appear grave without alarming King. "We've done the hour interview. It's been a fine interview."

"Oh, Mack," King replied, "it's going great." Clinton, too, resisted the idea of interrupting.

"Larry, I agree with you," McLarty continued, more firmly, "but the president has to conclude the interview at this point."

Clinton sensed that something must be amiss. "Mack is right," he said to King. "I'll be back in a few minutes."

As the two men walked into the hall, Clinton could barely contain himself. "Mack, what's wrong? What's up?"

"It's not a national emergency or crisis, but it's a very serious matter," he said. "Let's go upstairs where we can sit down." Clinton continued to press McLarty as they walked down the hall, but he held off until they were seated upstairs in the living quarters.

"Mr. President, Vince Foster has committed suicide."

"Oh, no," Clinton cried. Tears welled up in his eyes. "I want to call Hillary. Have you told Hillary? Does she know?"

After a few moments to collect himself, Clinton said he would call Hillary and then visit the Foster home himself. While Clinton got on the phone to the first lady, McLarty arranged with the Secret Service to get the president to the Foster residence safely while attracting minimal attention. No press were notified. They set out from the White House without the usual motorcade, traveling in a Chevy Suburban van, accompanied by two unmarked cars.

Leaving the other investigators at Fort Marcy Park, Rolla and Braun got into their car and phoned headquarters to get Foster's address. This would be Rolla's first death notice to the next-of-kin, and he was a bit apprehensive. As they drove to the Foster home, a three-story townhouse at 3027 Cambridge Place in Georgetown, Rolla got a call from his office asking him to phone someone named Bill Kennedy. Rolla reached him, and Kennedy said he was a personal friend of Foster's and worked at the White House. He wanted to see the body, and Rolla said he could go to the morgue at Fairfax County Hospital and help with the identification. Rolla was barely off the phone with Kennedy when he was told to contact another White House official, David Watkins, who was described as an even closer friend of Foster's. Watkins had grown up with Foster in Hope, and Watkins had dated Foster's sister Sharon. Watkins's wife had played tennis with Lisa Foster, Foster's wife, that morning, and the Watkins house was close to the Fosters' in Georgetown. Watkins asked if he could join Rolla in breaking the news to the Foster family. Rolla agreed to pick up Watkins first; Watkins's wife would follow in their car.

Rolla was glad to have a close family friend on hand, but as word spread at the White House, things threatened to get out of control. First Watkins had wanted to wait until Foster's sister could join them; Rolla had said no. Then, as they pulled up at the Foster home, several other people converged, introduced to Rolla as Sheila Anthony and Sharon Bowman, Foster's sisters, and a tall heavyset man who seemed to be always talking into a cellular phone. He, too, was introduced as a close friend of Foster's from Arkansas: Webb Hubbell. Rolla didn't want a crowd standing on the porch when a family member came to the door; he asked them to stand back.

Rolla, accompanied by Watkins, knocked on the door. Twenty-one-year-old Laura Foster answered. "I'm John Rolla, with the United States Park Police . . ." Before he could finish he saw Laura looking behind him at her aunts, Hubbell and his wife, Watkins's wife, Braun, all of them looking stricken.

"What's the matter?" she cried. "What's wrong? Mother," she yelled. Then, screaming, "Mother! Something's wrong."

Lisa Foster, clad in a bathrobe, her dark blond hair carefully coiffed, looking tanned and slender from her frequent tennis outings, hurried down the stairs. She paused on the third step as she saw Watkins and Rolla. "What's wrong?" she asked. "Is it something about Vincent?" She meant her son, Vincent III.

"Sit down," Rolla urged her, taking a deep breath. "I am very sorry to tell you that your husband, Vincent, is dead."

Lisa Foster screamed and slumped to the stairs, clutching her arms around her and sobbing. Watkins's wife rushed to comfort her. Laura, too, was crying uncontrollably.

"He shot himself," Rolla added. Laura screamed and ran upstairs.

Lisa, between sobs, managed to ask: "Did he put it in his mouth?"

"Yes," Rolla replied. He was startled by the question. Had Lisa had some indication, some premonition, that Foster planned to shoot himself? Lisa rose and rushed up the stairs after her daughter.

Everyone now pressed into the living room, and Rolla and his colleague, Braun, began trying to gather some information from the distraught members of the group, now talking quietly among themselves, many still fighting back tears. He knew this was the time when people were least likely to have their views of events colored or tainted by exchanges with others. This was still an open investigation. Though suicide seemed by far the most likely cause of death, murder remained a possibility that would have to be investigated. "Did you see this coming?" he asked. "Were there any signs of this?" Everyone insisted no. Hubbell declined to answer questions, spending his time on the cellular phone. Rolla called headquarters and said Foster's White House office should be sealed. Braun told Watkins the same thing.

After about fifteen minutes, Lisa returned, dressed and looking more collected. Braun tried to ask a few questions, but Lisa wouldn't answer. Rolla seemed to manage a better rapport with her. "Were there any indications of depression?" Rolla asked her.

"No, nothing," she said, her eyes brimming with tears. "He was so happy."

"Did he own a gun?"

"I don't know," she replied. "What kind was it? What did it look like?"

"It was a .38 caliber revolver . . ."

Suddenly she seemed agitated, even angry. "How would I know? I don't know what guns look like." She turned and stalked into the kitchen, terminating the interview. She and Hubbell began searching the house, looking in vain for a suicide note.

Neither Rolla nor Braun, who was also working the room, made much headway with any of the others. The phone began ringing off the hook. The investigators felt Hubbell, in particular, was discouraging people from saying anything; as Braun tried to question Sheila Anthony, the heavyset Hubbell pushed Braun out of the way and led Sheila out of the room. Some people seemed more concerned with publicity than with what had happened. Watkins asked Rolla and Braun not to issue any press release until Foster's elderly mother in Hope could be notified in person. A devout Catholic, Lisa worried that if it were known her husband had committed suicide, he couldn't be buried in a Catholic cemetery. The officer said they'd hold off as long as they could, but that they'd have no choice but to make a statement fairly soon.

The group's collective denial that anything was upsetting Foster didn't ring true to Rolla and, in any event, flew in the face of the apparent suicide. Lisa Foster's insistence that her husband had been "so happy" seemed forced. Was she in some kind of denial, brushing any problems under the rug to put a more acceptable face on the tragedy? Was she withholding information? How did she know to ask whether Foster had shot himself in the mouth?

Any hopes for further progress were soon dashed. At 10:50 P.M., the front door suddenly opened and a Secret Service agent walked in, followed by the president and McLarty. "Oh my God," Rolla thought, as the realization finally sank in that Foster was a member of the White House inner circle. Clinton looked haggard, his eyes red, visibly upset. He glared at Rolla, giving him the impression that Clinton thought it inappropriate for a law enforcement officer to be intruding on their privacy. The president hurried toward Lisa. Clinton put his arms around her, then sat between her and Laura on the sofa in the living room. He spoke quietly with Lisa and her daughter.

Rolla hovered in the background, trying fitfully to ask a few more questions, and was reduced to handing out his business card. "Please call me if you learn of anything . . ." More people poured into the Foster home: David Gergen, a White House advisor; Vernon Jordan, the Washington lawyer and close friend of Clinton's; Arkansas senator David Pryor and his wife. Rolla felt shunted aside. He'd never sensed that President Clinton was much of a friend to law enforcement, and this experience didn't change that impression. Finally Braun turned to him. "John, we might as well come back tomorrow, because we're not going to get any more information tonight."

Rolla stayed another ten minutes. No one seemed to pay him any attention. All eyes were on the president.

•

Vincent Foster, deputy White House counsel, lifelong friend, confidant, and counselor to the president and first lady, was the highest ranking White House official ever to die under suspicious circumstances while in office. The only comparable incident seems to have been James Forrestal, secretary of the navy under Truman, who leaped to his death from a military hospital. Foster had led a sheltered life in Little Rock, a partner in Arkansas's leading law firm, a pillar of the state bar, chairman of the local repertory theater. He married his college sweetheart and raised three children. His world was pretty much bounded by the attractive white-columned home in Little Rock's Heights neighborhood, the Country Club of Little Rock, a modest walk down the street, and his office downtown at the Rose firm. He rode to work each day with Rose partners who lived nearby, often remaining silent during the ten- to fifteen-minute drive. He lived quietly, with dignity, with a reputation for integrity that meant everything to him. With minor variations, it was the life he'd chosen years before, when he opted to attend Davidson College, a highly regarded Presbyterian liberal arts college in North Carolina, and then returned to Arkansas for law school.

It is impossible to know how Foster himself would have reacted to the events his death set in motion. Given the pain he suffered at the attention of the *Wall Street Journal* editorial page, given his idealism and naïveté about politics and government service, he would surely be horrified. His friends believe that had he had any idea at all of what was going to happen, he would still be alive. Or perhaps in the hours and days before his death he saw his destiny as a political liability only too clearly, a realization that, in deepening his despair, made his death all but inevitable.

What is clear is that Vincent Foster's death has festered like an open wound on the body politic. To the extent the Clinton administration ever enjoyed a honeymoon, it ended on July 20, 1993. Among the confidential matters Foster was working on when he died was the Clintons' ill-fated investment in Whitewater, an Arkansas land development. A minor footnote to the 1992 presidential campaign, Whitewater was suddenly resurrected in the national press, and soon was as familiar a synonym for White House scandal as Watergate or Iran-contra. To a degree that left them stunned and at times depressed, the president and his wife were buffeted by what seemed an unending succession of scandalous allegations, from the first lady's profitable commodities trading to sexual harassment charges filed by Paula Jones.

These matters arose not in a vacuum, but in an environment of bitter partisan conflict primed by years of seething resentments lingering from past scandals. Republicans in Congress predictably fell with glee upon every allegation that could damage the Clinton presidency and legislative agenda, calling successfully for legislative hearings and the appointment of an independent counsel. Partisan members of the media, from conservative populist radio hosts to influential columnists, had a field day, keeping the scandals alive in the public mind and all but forcing the mainstream media to devote resources, print space, and airtime to exploring the most unsavory questions surrounding the Clinton presidency.

Yet, despite all these efforts and the attention, the mysteries surrounding Vincent Foster and the White House seemed only to deepen. In a climate of apparent obfuscation and half-truths, conspiracy theories abounded among a population jaded and skeptical from years of scandalous revelations at the highest levels of power. Was Foster murdered? If he did commit suicide, why? Do the answers lie in what Foster knew about the president and first lady? Were documents hidden or destroyed? Did top officials tell the truth? Was there a conspiracy to obstruct justice? If the Clintons had nothing to hide, why did they so often act as though they did?

As events unfolded, the mystery of Foster's death became inextricable from the Clintons' own lives, especially a past that, apart from the president's tortured effort to avoid being drafted and his relationship with Gennifer Flowers, has proven surprisingly elusive. It was only after Clinton's election and Foster's death that Whitewater was explored in any detail or gained a foothold in the American consciousness, that the first lady's handling of the couple's personal finances caused any suspicion, or that Arkansas troopers surfaced with disclosures that corroborated allegations of marital infidelity by the president. Mystery begot mystery. Apart from hardened conspiracy theorists and partisan zealots both for and against the president, most Americans were left to wonder: Where does the truth lie?

•

This, in any event, was my state of mind in March 1994, shortly after the appointment of Robert Fiske as an independent counsel to investigate Whitewater, the death of Vincent Foster, and related matters, a time when media interest in these events was at a peak. On March 25, Susan Thomases, the Manhattan lawyer who played an important role in the Clinton campaign and transition, came to my office about a matter she had said she couldn't discuss over the phone. I knew Thomases slightly. A friend of mine had been a partner and close friend of hers at her firm, Willkie, Farr & Gallagher. When he became ill and died some years ago, I knew that Susan had been extraordinarily supportive in caring for him and helping make arrangements after his death. On this occasion, I suspected that she hoped I might be interested in a story involving one of her clients.

Why else would Thomases be calling me? I was at work on another book, writing for *The New Yorker* and *SmartMoney* magazines. As someone who often wrote about financial matters, the intrigues at Madison Guaranty Savings and Loan, the failed thrift at the heart of the Whitewater affair, were especially interesting to me, but I had done no reporting or writing on the subject. Nor had I ever done any political reporting. Although in my former capacity as page one editor of the *Wall Street Journal* I had nominally overseen front-page stories written by reporters in the Washington bureau, including coverage of the 1992 election, it was the paper's bureau chief, Al Hunt, who directed the paper's political coverage. With what seemed like an army of journalists from other news organizations already deeply enmeshed in these matters, I was content to be a reader, albeit an increasingly mystified one.

But after some pleasantries, Thomases began discussing the Clintons. Somewhat to my surprise, I realized that she had remained a close friend and advisor to both the president and first lady even though she had no position in the administration. (Her phone records, later produced in congressional hearings, show nearly constant calls to the White House, even at odd hours of the night and early morning.) She described a White House besieged by allegations ranging from the murder of Vincent Foster to irregularities in Whitewater's finances to obstruction of justice. Relations between the White House and the media had soured to the point that they seemed irreparable. The president and first lady had all but despaired of receiving fair coverage from the mainstream media. They had concluded that the best way—perhaps the only way—to clear their names was to open themselves to a reputable journalist. There would be no conditions and they would make available themselves and others they were in a position to influence.

For this project, Thomases continued, they wanted a journalist who was well known and would command national attention for his work; who had no ties to major media institutions; who was not a Washington insider beholden to other sources and organizations; who had financial and legal expertise; who had no known partisan leanings; who would be willing to investigate the Clintons' enemies; and whom they liked and felt comfortable with. Thomases never said explicitly that I was to be this person, but when I asked if this were the case, she seemed delighted that I might consider undertaking such a project.

Of course I considered it. The prospect of unfettered access to the president and first lady, on subjects of national controversy, overwhelmed all my thoughts the following weekend. I felt that an extraordinary opportunity had been laid in my lap. The closest I'd ever been to a president was a distant table at a White House correspondents' dinner. I'd never been to the White House, even as a tourist. I grew up in Quincy, Illinois, a town that still talks about the time Richard Nixon landed at the local airport during the 1960 campaign. I was awed at the prospect of meeting and getting to know the Clintons, fantasizing about long afternoons of interviews at Camp David.

I told a few people of this turn of events, and swore them to secrecy. I was a bit deflated by their reactions. For the most part, they were skeptical. I chalked that up to pervasive cynicism about our elected officials, though I recognized that there were plenty of potential pitfalls ahead.

I was told the next step would be to meet the Clintons. Several dates were proposed, then canceled. Finally I was told I would meet the first lady. On April 13, I flew to Washington and was escorted into the Map Room on the ground floor of the White House, where Hillary Clinton was wrapping up an interview with Bob Woodward of the *Washington Post*. She was wearing a brilliant turquoise suit and a colorful scarf pinned to her jacket. As many people had told me, she was much more attractive in person than on television or in pictures. She had a vitality, a liveliness that I hadn't anticipated.

We talked about our respective backgrounds in Illinois, the perspectives a Midwestern upbringing had given us. Then she turned to the project at hand. There were a few flashes of anger as she described her and her husband's treatment by the media. She seemed especially upset by recent coverage of Paula Jones's sexual harassment lawsuit, mentioning that people had no idea how painful it was for her to endure public reports of her husband's alleged infidelity. She railed against the tactics of the right-wing media and think tanks, wondering how they were being financed. A recurring theme was that she couldn't understand why reporters would publish allegations by people of questionable integrity and motives in the face of denials by her and her husband. She seemed shocked that when the president and first lady made assertions of fact, they were not accepted at face value. On the contrary, they seemed to be greeted with scorn and skepticism.

I felt compassion for her obvious distress, but nonetheless found her views to be somewhat naive. The days when journalists accepted presidential pronouncements without question—or even covered up the truth—were long gone. And after the many ways past presidents have misled the American public, how could it be otherwise? Journalists routinely check the assertions of presidents and their wives, as they do anyone else.

The first lady freely conceded that mistakes had been made, and that she, in particular, had put too much emphasis on privacy, leading to perceptions that the White House had something to hide. This was not true, she insisted.

When she paused, I asked if she had any questions for me. She didn't respond, as if she hadn't given this aspect of our meeting much thought. So, in part at the urging of my skeptical friends, I volunteered that there were some things I thought she and the president should be considering. I stressed that there could be no conditions attached to their cooperation and that I would be fully independent. I said that while surely she and the president had far more expert public relations advice than I could provide, the openness she and her husband were thinking of offering me, especially in the midst of pending criminal investigations, was unprecedented in my experience as a reporter. While it was wholly admirable from my point of view—and might forcefully make the point that they had nothing to hide—it flew in the face of conventional public relations wisdom. If this were to go forward, I hoped they would consider the implications now rather than later.

The conversation lasted about an hour and a half. In the ensuing weeks I had extensive discussions with the first lady's chief of staff, Maggie Williams, and her press secretary, Lisa Caputo. I met with George Stephanopoulos in New York on May 19, where we sat unnoticed in the lobby of the Algonquin Hotel. I was asked to write a memo for the president, and I did. I was told by various people connected to the White House that the president was having trouble making up his mind; that the first lady had written a memo outlining why they should cooperate in my project (point one was that someone was bound to do it, I was told); that Stephanopoulos had turned against the idea.

By late June, having received no definitive answer from the White House, I broached the possibility that I didn't feel comfortable with the notion that I needed the Clintons' permission to undertake this work, and might well begin it on my own. As I had told Mrs. Clinton, I was drawn to the story as much for what it would say about our culture, values, and political processes as for what it would reveal about the president and his wife. And I've learned from experience that too much cooperation can get in the way of thorough, objective reporting.

Maggie Williams called me on July 6. She said that after lengthy discussions, the first lady had concluded that she would cooperate with me, as would people in her entourage and people she was in a position to influence. She could not speak for the president, but she said she thought he would cooperate once the project was underway. Susan Thomases further assured me that I would have her cooperation, and said she, too, felt the president would want to participate. With that, I began my work.

It now seems ironic that it was the Clintons themselves who set this book in motion. For the promised cooperation never materialized. I believe that Susan Thomases and Maggie Williams, in particular, did their best. I believe that Hillary Clinton, when we met in the White House, genuinely wanted to speak openly to someone she deemed to be fair-minded. But in the final analysis, the Clintons themselves proved no different than their predecessors, deeply enmeshed in a Washington culture so inured to partisan distortion and spin that truth is the most frightening prospect of all.

Why that would be the case will become clear, I believe, in the story that unfolds in these pages. I am just one reporter and writer, and I don't have the enormous resources of the FBI or congressional investigators at my disposal. I cannot claim to have solved every mystery surrounding the Clinton presidency. But most, I believe, have yielded their secrets.

PART ONE

THE ROAD TO SCANDAL

ONE

Susan McDougal stretched her legs in the ample passenger space of her husband, Jim's, light green Mercedes 280-S as it cruised north along the winding Route 65 to the resort town of Eureka Springs, Arkansas. It was a mild, brilliantly sunny winter day in early 1978. Susan was wearing bell-bottom pants and a tight white tank top. She knew her husband liked the impression she made along Arkansas's rural highways. Susan gazed out on the rugged hills of north-central Arkansas and thought how pretty it was. They passed occasional signs advertising campgrounds and raft trips down the White River. With the mild winters and scenery, McDougal was convinced that real estate in the area would be attractive to growing numbers of retirees. Jim and Susan McDougal were always on the lookout for real estate deals.

The big Mercedes was one of her husband's few indulgences. Given the money they were making, the McDougals didn't live lavishly. They lived in a modest, $74,000 house on Shadow Lane in Little Rock. Jim seemed indifferent to most of the trappings of wealth, but he loved clothes and cars, especially Mercedes. He'd had one of the first diesel-powered Mercedes in Arkansas. He also had a Jeep, which he abandoned after backing hard into a gas pump, smashing both the car and the pump, spewing gasoline. The gas station attendant had been apoplectic when McDougal got out of the car and casually lit a cigarette. Then he'd gotten a yellow 450-SL convertible. While driving to work with one of his close friends, future Arkansas governor Jim Guy Tucker, he managed to beach the car on the dividing strip of North University Street in

Little Rock, stopping traffic during rush hour. McDougal was unfazed, chatting with Tucker as though nothing had happened. "Don't get out and look around, giving everyone the satisfaction of seeing what an idiot you've been," he told his passenger. "Don't worry. Somebody will come and take care of this." (Someone did.)

It was one of the many ways in which McDougal seemed to live on a higher plane than ordinary mortals, and it was one of the qualities that had dazzled Susan when, as a sheltered nineteen-year-old student at Ouachita Baptist University in Arkadelphia, she first met McDougal, fifteen years her senior, who was teaching political science there, an interlude in a career that had included stints as an aide to Arkansas senators John McClellan and J. William Fulbright. McDougal had all but run the state of Arkansas with his closest friend, Bob Riley, a decorated Marine Corps veteran who was blinded during World War II. Riley was Arkansas's lieutenant governor under Dale Bumpers, and when Bumpers defeated Fulbright in 1974 and went to the U.S. Senate, Riley served as governor for two weeks until Bumpers's elected successor was inaugurated. McDougal was his only staff. Riley was now chairman of the Political Science Department at Ouachita, and persuaded McDougal to join him on the faculty. McDougal's experience made him one of the most respected professors in the department, even though he was actually completing his own bachelor's and master's degrees while he taught.

Even people who wouldn't call the balding, slender McDougal handsome had to admit his appearance was striking. With his Savile Row suits, straw hats, and aristocratic accent, McDougal cut quite a swath in remote Arkadelphia, a town of ten thousand people about an hour's drive southwest of Little Rock that still had a few dirt streets and houses without indoor plumbing. McDougal sprang from equally humble origins. His grandfather had owned a pear orchard outside tiny Bradford, Arkansas, and operated a fruit stand. McDougal's father ran a dime store and restaurant near Bradford, where McDougal was forced to work in high school (he hated it). By the standards of Bradford, the McDougals were well-off; they were the first family in town to have air-conditioning. The young McDougal was a precocious student who was obsessed with politics. When he was sixteen he heard Adlai Stevenson speak in Little Rock, and came home with reams of campaign literature, thrilled by the experience. He dazzled family and peers with his vocabulary and even as a child could recite from memory speeches by Thomas Jefferson and Andrew Jackson. He was a fervent admirer of Franklin Delano Roosevelt, Woodrow Wilson, and Winston Churchill.

At the age of eighteen, McDougal was named an assistant "reading clerk," the person who reads the title, numbers, and contents of proposed legislation in the Arkansas House of Representatives. Though he left to return to the University of Arkansas, his attention was already focused on the State House. He dropped out and at age twenty, even before he could vote, he managed to get himself elected to the state's Democratic party central committee, the youngest member ever. He worked on the Kennedy campaign and then landed a job on McClellan's staff in Washington. He later joined Fulbright's staff and ran the senator's successful 1968 campaign. Fulbright liked McDougal, the senator once said, because he could write a good speech and "buy three watermelons at a good price." In the process McDougal acquired a storehouse of Arkansas political lore. It seemed he knew everybody who was, had been, or wanted to be a figure in Arkansas politics.

McDougal didn't hesitate to embroider his own legend. Despite his upbringing in rural Arkansas, he liked to boast that he had inherited royal blood: he was a direct descendant of an early Scottish lord, Somerled, who married a Norwegian princess. The McDougals, he claimed, once owned a third of all the land in Scotland, and it was to those roots that he ascribed his affinity for real estate.

No one questioned the literal accuracy of such claims. In Arkadelphia, such tales added welcome romance to a world that seemed far removed from the glamour and excitement people read about elsewhere and saw on TV. Susan Henley, in particular, who grew up in rural Camden, Arkansas, with her six brothers and sisters, was swept off her feet by McDougal. Susan's father had been an army motorcycle policeman and career officer. During World War II he rescued an attractive Belgian medical student during an air raid. He later married her, and Susan was born in Germany, where the couple was stationed at the time. The family moved back to Camden, her father's hometown, while Susan was a child. He owned and ran several service stations there with military efficiency. At Henley's stations, before a customer even turned off the motor, an attendant would be standing stiffly at the window. By the time the gas had been pumped, the attendant was expected to have completed an inventory of the tires, the oil, the underside of the car, and to have washed the windscreen. Susan was a precocious, imaginative child, and loved acting in school plays. She dreamed of someday moving to New York and becoming an actress like Ethel Barrymore.

During the summer before her senior year, Susan got a job as a researcher for another political science professor, who decided that his attractive but naive young employee should be introduced to a more worldly man. His first candidate was Cliff Harris, who played football for the Dallas Cowboys. That was perhaps too worldly for Susan, who was tongue-tied on their date. Next he introduced her to his colleague in the department, Jim McDougal, who asked Susan for a date. She was busy. "I only ask a girl once," McDougal warned, then walked away. So Susan asked him for their first date.

Later that summer, McDougal invited Susan to join him for an afternoon with Bob Riley and his wife, Claudia, on the Rileys' pontoon houseboat at De Gray Lake. Susan looked gorgeous in her bathing suit. McDougal prided himself on his unblemished skin, which he took care to shield from the sun's rays. He had a year-round pallor that somehow added to his genteel appearance. But this afternoon, he shed his clothes, donned a bathing suit, threw himself into the water, and even water-skied—all, Claudia Riley felt certain, to impress Susan.

McDougal was a Southern gentleman of the old school, and he treated Susan with elaborate courtesy, as if she were Scarlett in *Gone With the Wind*. One afternoon Susan had forgotten her keys, and was locked out of an office where she needed to finish some work. McDougal simply knocked the door down.

Susan was dating another student at the time, but she found McDougal hard to resist. Soon they were seeing each other regularly, even though Susan was still a senior in college. At conservative Ouachita, she was required to be in her room in the women-only dorm every evening by 10 P.M., which cramped McDougal's courtship. It would have been a minor scandal for a prominent professor to be found dating a student. The university president once warned McDougal against corrupting the morality of a student. Still, it all lent a certain illicit excitement to the affair.

One afternoon that fall Jim called, sounding excited. "Bill Clinton is coming down with an advance guy, and he needs a crowd. See what you can do." It was 1975, and the young politician was in the midst of his campaign for Arkansas attorney general.

McDougal and Clinton were already close, even though McDougal was six years older and considered himself vastly more experienced. He still tended to think of Clinton as the twenty-one-year-old "boy" he'd met in 1968 during Fulbright's Senate campaign. It was the first time in three elections that Fulbright faced any opposition, from Jim Johnson, a segregationist supporter of Alabama governor George Wallace. McDougal was running the senator's Arkansas campaign office, and had asked for some help. Lee Williams, then Fulbright's administrative assistant, had called McDougal and said, "I'll send this Clinton boy out to help you."

Clinton, who'd just finished his senior year at Georgetown, had been working for two years on the Senate Foreign Relations Committee staff. He had met Fulbright while attending Boys Nation years before, and the powerful chairman of the Senate Foreign Relations Committee, a former Rhodes Scholar, had encouraged Clinton to apply for the coveted scholarship and had intervened to help assure that Clinton was named as one. Clinton would be heading for Oxford that fall. For the campaign, McDougal assigned Clinton to the post of Fulbright's driver. Clinton took advantage of the long, hot trips out of Little Rock and Hot Springs into the small, impoverished towns of the Delta to talk at length with the senator. One afternoon Fulbright called McDougal and Williams at campaign headquarters from Nashville, Arkansas. It was about 100 degrees and humid. "Something is wrong with our car," Fulbright reported. "We've got the goddamn air-conditioner on," he drawled. McDougal turned to Williams. "Two goddamn Rhodes Scholars in one car out there and they can't figure out why they're making rain." Clinton, it turned out, had been running the air-conditioner with the vents closed.

Shortly after, Fulbright and Clinton pulled into the Arlington Hotel in Hot Springs where Clinton parked the car blocking the main entrance, then left with the car keys. When Fulbright located Clinton he found him arguing about the Vietnam War with a constituent—the editor of the *Hope Star*. Fulbright was furious. "This is not going to happen again," he told McDougal, adding that he was tired of listening to Clinton's incessant chatter about politics and foreign affairs in the car. Clinton was dismissed as Fulbright's driver, though he continued lending a hand in the campaign.

Despite the inauspicious beginning, McDougal liked Clinton. He saw him, as he later put it, "as an amiable fuck-up who needed help." For starters, Clinton needed to learn how to dress. On campaign swings through Fayetteville, McDougal took Clinton to his favorite clothing store, which was holding a going-out-of-business sale, and insisted that he buy a suit and a decent shirt. The two would have long conversations about politics, with Clinton subtly flattering McDougal with his attentiveness and eagerness to please. And the two discussed their personal lives. McDougal confided in Clinton that he was enrolled in Alcoholics Anonymous, where he was now sponsoring another member. McDougal had long been a hard drinker, but few had realized how serious his problem had become. Now, in keeping with AA strictures, McDougal didn't touch a drop of liquor. Clinton seemed fascinated; he told McDougal that his stepfather had been an alcoholic, and he seemed eager to know more about alcoholism as a way to better understand his own family background. They also talked about women. McDougal made it a point to hire attractive young women for the campaign staff. Clinton was constantly flirting with them.

That fall, as Clinton was en route to Oxford, he and McDougal were in Washington, and met Fulbright in the Senate dining room for lunch. Despite McDougal's efforts, Clinton had long hair and was wearing a checkered shirt and sloppy clothes. Even McDougal, in a nod to the times, had let his sideburns grow out. Fulbright, deeply traditional despite his antiwar political views, was incensed. "God damn," he said to Clinton. "If I'd known you were going to look like some god-damned hippie, I wouldn't have gotten you this appointment." Then he turned to McDougal. "And look at you. You always had a crease in your trousers. Now you look like a footman to Henry VIII." The senator turned away and refused to eat with them or talk to them any further.

Since then Clinton had finished his stint at Oxford, graduated from Yale Law School, and returned to Arkansas to launch his political career. Susan had never met Clinton, and barely knew who he was. She knew from Jim that he'd recently run for Congress in another district, lost, and was now campaigning for attorney general. Susan could tell that Clinton had struck a chord with Jim.

Since McDougal was something of a political kingmaker in Arkansas, most aspiring Democrats made the pilgrimage to Arkadelphia to seek his support. Few displayed the combination of brains, energy, and ambition that McDougal looked for. But Clinton, Jim told Susan, was a young man with dreams. McDougal, a man who still harbored many dreams of his own, had a weakness for young men with dreams. There were too few of them in Arkansas, he'd often say.

That afternoon, Susan happened to have a speech class at Ouachita's neighboring school in Arkadelphia, Henderson State University. After class, she managed to drag virtually the whole class, about forty-five students, and their professor to the Henderson cafeteria. Clinton arrived looking younger than she expected and delivered a short talk. Jim seemed thrilled by Susan's efforts: apart from the speech students, the "crowd" consisted of Jim and four other people. They all laughed with Clinton about it later that evening, when Susan met him for the first time. That evening McDougal wrote Clinton a check for $1,500, the legal maximum for individual political contributions. Shortly after, Clinton sent McDougal a thank-you note. "I really liked that pretty girl," Clinton wrote, referring to Susan.

About a month later, McDougal told Susan he'd been invited to Hot Springs for a party to celebrate Clinton's engagement to a fellow Yale Law School graduate, Hillary Rodham. Did Susan want to join him?

Hot Springs! Susan was thrilled. It could have been Monte Carlo and she wouldn't have been any more excited. She'd never been farther away from home without her family than Arkadelphia, an hour's drive from Camden. In her mind, Hot Springs, the most prominent resort in Arkansas, was synonymous with glamour, excitement, sophistication. Jim bought her a new dress for the occasion. She wanted to look good for him and his high-powered friends.

The party was held at the home of a friend of Clinton's in Hot Springs, where Clinton's mother, Virginia Dwire, lived and where Clinton had grown up. When Susan and Jim arrived, the party was in full swing, and Susan was hardly prepared for the experience. She'd grown up in a home where smoking and drinking and dancing were strictly prohibited. Here, rock music was throbbing, a pall of smoke hung over the room, there was an open bar, and as far as she could tell, most of the guests seemed drunk. When she went to the bathroom, one woman had passed out on the floor. "My God, where am I and what have I gotten myself into," Susan thought. "This is hell."

The evening took on a slightly surreal quality. Susan was introduced to Hillary Rodham, and it just didn't add up. This was Clinton's fiancée? The party was filled with people who were Bill's old friends. The women all seemed to be tall, blond or brunette, wearing lots of makeup and jewelry. Susan thought they were nearly all beautiful and sophisticated. Hillary looked nothing like them. She seemed to pay little or no attention to her appearance. She wore almost no makeup, and it looked like she hadn't even been to the hairdresser the day of her own engagement party. She wore big, unattractive glasses that made her look bookish, which was poison when it came to men as far as Susan was concerned. Susan thought she would rather die than stick out the way Hillary did, especially in a place like Hot Springs. In Hot Springs, Susan had always been told, women cared about their appearance. Hot Springs was a city where people put on airs.

Hillary and Susan spoke briefly; Susan took note of Hillary's harsh Yankee accent. Bill Clinton seemed in high spirits, working the crowd, throwing his arm around friends, flattering the women. Susan thought Clinton was attentive to his future bride. But at one point he sidled up to Susan, and pointed out an attractive woman he'd just been talking with. He leaned in close to Susan's ear. "See that older woman?" he said. "Older women are really sexy, hot." Susan pulled back, startled. She was shocked by the remark. Yet she was also excited by it. Clinton looked amused by her obvious discomfort.

Unlike Susan, McDougal spent quite a bit of time talking to Hillary, discussing Arkansas politics and Clinton's campaign. Hardly anyone else seemed to be talking to her. Afterward he couldn't stop talking about Hillary: her great education, her intellect, her poise. McDougal was very friendly with Clinton's mother, Virginia, who'd made no secret of her own disapproval of Hillary. As Virginia Kelley (she married Dick Kelley in 1982) wrote in her autobiography, "Hillary . . . was different. No makeup. Coke bottle glasses. Brown hair with no apparent style. . . . She was quiet, cool, unresponsive." But McDougal told Susan that Virginia had it all wrong. Her son was attracted to intelligent women, and so was he. It all made Susan a little uncomfortable. She was just a Southern country girl. She'd never known anyone like Hillary. She'd certainly never heard that these were qualities that men looked for in a woman. Why was McDougal interested in her if he could be with women like Hillary? Was this what men looked for in places like New York and Washington?

Susan needn't have worried. McDougal seemed to court her single-mindedly. He showered her with flowers and gifts. He proposed to her on a student trip to Washington, D.C. She told her parents about McDougal, and they were horrified. McDougal was not only fifteen years older, he was divorced. "You'll ruin your life," her mother warned her. Susan introduced Jim to her brother Bill Henley, who also had a negative reaction. Not only was McDougal too old, in his view, but he pontificated. Bill thought he might be the smartest person he'd ever met, but he was no conversationalist. He preferred to hold court. Susan didn't care. She was in love.

On the morning of her graduation, McDougal pulled up in his yellow convertible. When Susan reached the car, he said, "I'm taking you away."

"I'll miss graduation," she protested. But she got in. McDougal drove her to the small bungalow he still owned in Little Rock, which he'd freshly decorated with French wallpaper. "Either you marry me now or I'm taking you back and I'll never want to see you again," he said. They called Susan's parents to break the news. "I have to do it," Susan told them.

They were married in May 1976, in an afternoon ceremony on the lawn of the bungalow decorated with a flower-entwined arbor. It was a beautiful afternoon. Bob Riley, who also happened to be a licensed minister, officiated, and one of Susan's sisters was a bridesmaid. Bill Clinton and Hillary Rodham were there, arriving late after Bill gave a campaign speech. Bill and Hillary had been married in Fayetteville the year before, and Hillary had kept her own name, another thing Susan had trouble understanding. She couldn't wait to be Susan McDougal rather than Susan Henley. Also attending were Betty and Jim Guy Tucker. Among Arkansas Democrats, it was like an extended family gathering.

Susan's parents overcame their disapproval and showed up.

They'd never fully reconciled themselves to the idea of Susan marrying Jim, and they were especially upset that the wedding ceremony wasn't held in a church. They felt out of place among Jim's political cronies; none of their friends were there. A modest reception with punch and cookies followed. Many of the guests, including the Rileys, had dinner at McDonald's afterward. Jim and Susan left immediately for New York City, prior to embarking on a honeymoon tour of Europe. Jim borrowed $3,000 for the trip. Susan could hardly believe she would be seeing places she'd always dreamed of. To Claudia Riley, it was like something out of Camelot: Jim and Susan were the perfect couple with the world at their feet.

Susan had assumed life with Jim McDougal would be interesting. But it had proven even more of an adventure than she anticipated, in ways large and small. One afternoon she was in the bungalow when she heard a chain saw. When she went outside, Jim was leaning out of a freshly cut diamond-shaped hole in the hayloft of the barn. "This is the window of the new guest cottage," he called down to her. "I'm roughing it in." McDougal had scant skills as a carpenter, and someone else had to finish the work. But eventually the barn was transformed into a guest cottage. It was typical of McDougal's style. He'd have a big, imaginative idea, and somehow he'd get others to carry it out, or rescue him when he ran into trouble.

Despite his entrepreneurial energies and instincts, McDougal paid no attention to managing money, leaving the family finances to Susan, and he was generous to a fault. Susan had redecorated the bungalow, and the first piece of furniture she bought was a small glass-topped table. It held considerable sentimental value for her. When the McDougals decided to sell the house, a young couple agreed to buy it. McDougal liked them, and when they admired Susan's table, he gave it to them on the spot. Susan was furious, but when they moved, McDougal insisted it stay behind. Susan never quite got over the loss of that table.

Now, as McDougal sped the Mercedes through some hairpin turns in the foothills of the Ozark Mountains, Susan wondered where this expedition to northwest Arkansas was likely to lead. Apart from politics and his growing real estate deals, McDougal had virtually no interests or hobbies. Specifically, in sports-crazy Arkansas, he liked to reinforce his iconoclastic reputation by boasting that he wasn't interested in "anything that involves a ball." That ran the gamut from football to golf. His idea of a good time was to drive along remote roads around Little Rock, looking for parcels of real estate that he could clean up, carve up, and resell at a profit.

Susan loved real estate, too—up to a point. This weekend was supposed to be a quiet getaway to Eureka Springs, a quaint Ozarks tourist town just south of the Missouri border. But after they arrived and checked into their hotel for the night, they awoke the next morning to discover that a freak snowstorm had blown in overnight, making driving difficult. Jim wanted to stay in, and in no time, Susan noticed, was scanning the real estate ads in the local paper. Suddenly he looked up with a gleam in his eye. "Look at this," he told Susan. "Twelve hundred acres in Marion County for less than $100 an acre." He paused thoughtfully. It struck him as an amazingly good deal. "Is there any land in America that could be worth less than $100 an acre?" Susan looked at the ad. Echoing what she knew her husband already thought, Susan said no.

They bought the land within a week, sight unseen.

Flippin, population one thousand, is located in the far northern part of Arkansas in the foothills of the Ozarks, about an hour east of Eureka Springs and a three-hour drive from Little Rock. Though the area is popular with anglers and white-water rafters, it has never developed into a major tourist area, and remains far overshadowed by the Missouri Ozarks, with attractions like country music capital Branson. Flippin doesn't even have a motel. The town is little more than the intersection of two state highways, and the main street has vacant lots on it. Ozarks Realty is located just past the intersection, just down the street from the Citizens Bank and Trust Co. of Flippin.

Chris Wade, the owner of Ozarks Realty, didn't expect much walk-in trade. Still, he'd showed up at the office the weekend after the McDougals bought the land in Marion County. There wasn't much else to do anyway, and he liked to shoot the breeze with his agents, his heavyset frame settled in his chair, feet propped up on his desk, glancing out the picture window of the former barber shop that now served as Ozarks's office. His wife, Rosalee, usually came along. She handled the bookkeeping and kept the office running. It was a nice, small-town operation.

Wade had every reason to look with satisfaction on his life and career there. He'd grown up poor; his father had been driving through the area en route from New Mexico to Florida, and liked the terrain and scenery. On impulse, he stopped to go fishing, then traded the family station wagon for a piece of land, and the family settled down.

From such modest beginnings, Wade had become one of the area's leading citizens. He got his real estate license at age seventeen and began selling in the Flippin and Yellville area. In addition to his real estate operation, he was president of the local chamber of commerce, a post that brought him into contact with most of the state's political figures. He'd helped found the Citizens Bank along with other local businessmen concerned that the area's existing bank, located in the nearby town of Yellville, was favoring Yellville customers at the expense of Flippin. Wade was on the bank's board. True, there was some grumbling about Wade at the bank, where some referred to him as "fifty-cents-down Wade." Many of Wade's real estate customers were poor, and bought property with little down and financing provided by Wade. Many defaulted, Wade would repossess, and sell the property again, all with a speed that some found unseemly.

About midafternoon, Wade looked out and saw a large Mercedes pull into his adjoining parking lot, parking next to his pickup. Hardly anyone in Flippin drove an import, let alone a Mercedes. Out walked Jim McDougal, impeccably dressed in a dark suit even though it was the weekend, and Susan in her tank top. The two came in and announced they had just bought 1,200 acres nearby. Wade pointed out that the acreage consisted of scattered parcels, some of them lacking road frontage or access. McDougal was impressed that Wade seemed to know what he was talking about; he knew land, he knew the area, and he knew the customer base. The two chatted a little, and Wade was impressed by the fact that McDougal was a professor with political connections. They drove out to a few of the parcels, but most of them McDougal never saw. He listed the land with Wade for immediate resale.

As McDougal saw it, there was little risk. He had a half-dozen real estate developments underway, and he needed an outlet for the growing cash flow they were generating. He and Susan had formed Great Southern Land Co. to invest in land, and had already developed three parcels around Little Rock. They needed inventory, and McDougal thought the Flippin area held promise as a retirement and vacation haven. In any event, McDougal didn't expect to own the property for very long. Even as he reached an agreement to list the parcel, he told Wade to divide it up and sell the individual pieces. As events turned out, Wade was able to sell all of them by the time McDougal closed on his own purchase, netting McDougal a handsome profit without ever having put his capital at risk. For his part, Wade was delighted at the commissions.

McDougal had never expected to get into real estate until he was persuaded to invest by his own sponsor in AA, Doyle Rowe. Rowe was a big believer in land, and owned twenty-two parcels around Little Rock. McDougal had mentioned he wanted to make some money, and one day Rowe took him out to a parcel that was for sale. "Buy it," he told McDougal. "If you don't make money I'll pay you back." McDougal took a $500 cash advance from his credit card for the down payment and borrowed the rest of the $40,000 purchase price from the seller. The property was overgrown with weeds and bushes and looked like a mess. McDougal rented a brush hog and cleared and groomed the parcel. The broker sold it six months later for $80,000. McDougal was thrilled. It was the easiest money he'd ever made.

Soon after, another broker called him. "I've got eight hundred acres at $140 an acre," he said, "but half of it doesn't have road access." McDougal went out to see the tract and calculated that the land with the frontage alone was worth the purchase price. He bought it, cleaned it up, obtained easements for the plots lacking frontage, and sold it again in six months. This time his profit was more than $180,000.

McDougal occasionally mentioned his ventures to Senator Fulbright, who had inherited considerable wealth and had a net worth of several million dollars. One day Fulbright asked, "How'd that land of yours do?" When McDougal told him, Fulbright exclaimed, "Jesus Christ! Inflation is eating away everything I inherited. I could use something like that." McDougal said he'd see what he could do.

Soon after, in 1973, McDougal heard about a tract near Benton, a cash deal for $150,000. Fulbright had been a mentor, a father figure for him, and McDougal liked the idea of being able to somehow repay him. He asked Fulbright if he'd like to come in on the deal, and Fulbright agreed. The two formed a partnership, Rolling Manor, and they co-signed a note for the property. Fulbright was campaigning at the time, and was too busy to be involved. He never saw the property and showed little interest until it was subdivided and sold within a year, more than tripling Fulbright's investment.

Fulbright was thrilled, and word soon spread among the senator's circle of McDougal's financial acumen. For McDougal, the name Fulbright was also magic in Arkansas banking circles. Borrowing was easy, often at below-market rates offered the senator.

Soon after Clinton's visit to Arkadelphia, McDougal had his eye on another small plot near Little Rock, and, almost offhand, mentioned it one day in a conversation with Clinton. "You ought to buy this, Bill," McDougal said. Clinton knew of McDougal's success with Fulbright, and was interested. He was still paying off student loans he'd taken to finish Yale Law School and he was $24,000 in debt from his unsuccessful 1974 campaign for Congress. Still, Clinton knew next to nothing about real estate, mortgages, or finance. McDougal was amazed that a Rhodes Scholar and Yale law graduate seemed to know so little about business and money. After McDougal walked him through it, Clinton went in on the five-acre investment, paying $500 down and sending a monthly payment of $75, which he did conscientiously.

McDougal's motives in this instance were the reverse of his ventures with Fulbright; here McDougal was the mentor, the father figure, and Clinton the neophyte. McDougal was a professor still harboring some political ambitions; Clinton was a young man with a future, but hadn't yet been elected to office. McDougal included Clinton because he liked him and wanted to remain a player in the Arkansas political world. From Clinton he expected gratitude and respect, but little more. He took satisfaction in helping him, much as he did the people he helped in AA. And McDougal simply liked having a partner. An only child, it helped satisfy the longing he'd always felt for a brother or sister.

Soon after Clinton's first investment with McDougal, in 1976, Clinton won the race for Arkansas attorney general, and he and Hillary moved to Little Rock into a house at 5419 L Street just west of the State Capitol. While small and unpretentious, the house was located in the older, comfortable Hillcrest neighborhood, and its purchase took all the financial resources the couple could muster.

Hillary went to work for the Rose Law Firm, arguably the state's most prestigious, at an associate's salary of $24,500. As attorney general, Clinton earned a meager $26,500. Their combined salaries in 1978 were $51,000. The McDougals were among the new circle of friends the Clintons cultivated, and they often dropped by each other's houses or bumped into each other at the Black-Eyed Pea, a blue-plate restaurant with country atmosphere featuring Southern food located just minutes from each of their homes.

Clinton liked to use nicknames for Susan that he'd coined: either "Child Bride" or "The Kid." They all discussed their political ambitions, including Jim Guy Tucker's interest in the Senate seat held by former governor David Pryor, and Clinton's own decision to seek the governor's mansion rather than run for Pryor's seat himself. Susan was thrilled that Clinton, somebody she and her husband knew personally, was becoming so powerful and had moved to Little Rock with Hillary. Susan considered Hillary and Betty Tucker to be her best friends. Still, Hillary continued to both intrigue and mystify Susan. Not long after the Clintons' marriage and after Bill's election as attorney general, on one of her first visits to the Clintons' home, Susan and Hillary were chatting, and Susan said, "Your parents must be really proud of you."

"Not really," Hillary answered. Susan was perplexed. If she'd married the attorney general, her parents would have been delighted.

"My parents didn't even know where Arkansas was," Hillary continued, a trace of bitterness in her voice. "I had to get out the map and show them. They thought I'd end up in Washington, D.C., doing something with my life."

The comment made an impression on Susan. She herself still hadn't thought of having an identity beyond that of her husband. Yet obviously Hillary longed for a career of her own.

During their frequent visits, McDougal and Susan would sometimes mention their successful real estate operations; Susan had even obtained a real estate license and was working as a broker. The Clintons, by contrast, complained that they could barely make ends meet. But at least Clinton's small land investment worked out well. In 1978, just as Clinton was starting to mount his campaign for governor, McDougal was able to sell the tract for $5,000, a 75 percent return on their initial investment of $2,850.

That transaction had closed just two months before. So that

summer, when Wade happened to mention that he had a new listing he thought might interest McDougal, the Clintons' finances were on McDougal's mind. He mentioned to Wade, "I'd like to do something to help Bill Clinton. He's starving to death as attorney general. I'd really like to see him make a little money." McDougal said he'd jump in the car with Susan and come up and take a look.

Wade was delighted at the mention of Clinton's name. He'd first met Clinton when he was running for Congress from the Third District, which included Flippin. Clinton had not only visited Flippin personally; he'd walked down the streets, going door-to-door and visiting with voters. Not long before McDougal's visit, Wade had been astounded by Clinton at a chamber of commerce lunch in Flippin. Clinton, as attorney general, was the featured guest, and sat with Wade at the head table. During lunch, Clinton asked Wade to tell him the name of every chamber of commerce member and that of their wives, about thirty people, which Wade did. After Clinton spoke, he greeted every member of the audience by their first name, without any notes or further prompting. Wade thought the feat not only demonstrated a prodigious memory, but showed that Clinton really cared about people in Flippin. That spring, Clinton had easily won the Democratic nomination for governor, which in Arkansas at the time was tantamount to election. Just about everybody in Flippin had voted for him. Wade was flattered that any future governor of the state might be interested in investing in his area, but especially flattered that it was Bill Clinton.

"Take a look at this," Wade said when the McDougals arrived in Flippin after the three-hour drive from Little Rock. A group of local businesspeople, shareholders of the 101 Development Corp., had just listed a parcel of 230 acres along the White River, about a twenty-minute drive from Flippin. The group had bought the property, known locally as part of the Ranchettes development, after the prior owner, a company called Horseshoe Bend Development Corp., had fallen into bankruptcy. The group had named their company after Arkansas Route 101, which runs to the tract the group acquired. Route 101 is a remarkably broad, well-paved thoroughfare for such a rugged and sparsely populated area of the state, especially given the poor condition of many of the other, more heavily traveled state roads in Arkansas. Indeed, Route 101 is one of the many legacies of former Democratic governor Orval Faubus, whose administration built Route 101 after Faubus received generous contributions from local land owners. Asked by a reporter how he could afford a $200,000 home when he retired from his $10,000-a-year job as governor, Faubus replied, "I was frugal."

McDougal was intrigued, especially because the acreage had a lot of frontage on the White River. The river descends through the rugged terrain of north-central Arkansas and has stretches of white water, making it popular for rafting expeditions and with fishermen. There was only so much river frontage available, McDougal figured, and given his vision for the area as a retirement and vacation haven, he thought a premium could be charged for access to and views of the river. Like his previous investments, the large tract seemed ideal for subdividing and reselling as individual lots. Jim and Susan joined Wade in his truck and they drove to the property.

The last mile or so was over a pretty rugged road, but as they reached sight of the river the McDougals were captivated. The land was hilly, lightly forested, descending fairly steeply to the rushing water of the river. No houses were visible on the other side, and the place felt remote and unspoiled. There was already a public boat landing on some adjoining property. Susan, in particular, accustomed to the flat, scrub properties McDougal had been buying near Little Rock, thought it was beautiful and had a certain romance. She could almost see the marketing brochure she could create.

The McDougals told Wade they were interested, and wanted to talk to the Clintons and maybe some other potential investors about it. They weren't told that the price per acre of nearly $900, a total of $203,000, was more than double what the 101 group was paying for it in a deal that hadn't even yet closed, or that they were the buyers in a deal where the seller was breaking up and reselling a large parcel. As Wade pointed out, they would be getting the most desirable acreage, with most of the river frontage. That was worth a large premium to the average price that 101 had paid for a lot of undistinguished land. Wade said he'd do a rough subdivision plan for the McDougals so they could get a sense of how the land could be resold. As with his earlier deal with Wade, McDougal wanted to move quickly, listing the individual lots for resale as soon as possible, even before closing. He didn't see the investment as more than a two- or three-year venture.

The McDougals were excited by the prospects. Later Jim invited Nancy Pietrafesa and John Danner, a married couple who were among the Clintons' closest friends at Yale, to see the property. Independently well-off and idealistic, originally from California, they'd come down that summer to help the Clintons plan a transition to the governor's mansion and were thinking of moving to Arkansas after the general election to work in Clinton's administration. They were living with the Clintons in the Hillcrest bungalow that summer and had met the McDougals. Jim saw them as practically the Clintons' closest friends. He suggested they drive up for the weekend, look at the property, and arrange a rafting trip on the river. Danner and Pietrafesa had barely gotten out of sweltering Little Rock, and they liked Jim and Susan, so they accepted.

"Are these low-income housing projects?" Nancy asked as they drove north and passed rows of dilapidated wooden structures. "No," McDougal replied. "They're chicken coops."

When they got to the Flippin area, Danner went into a local grocery and ordered sandwiches for the raft trip. "You all aren't from around here, are you?" the man behind the counter said.

"No," Danner replied.

"Well, let me tell you a little joke, boy. Do you know the difference between a Yankee and a damn Yankee?"

Danner had learned to answer "No, sir" in all such circumstances.

"The damn Yankee stayed."

To Danner and Pietrafesa, the raft trip was a sweltering bore. The tract of land for sale, which Jim and Susan eagerly pointed out as they drifted by at an all too leisurely pace, was undistinguished, second-growth scrub forest in the middle of nowhere. But they didn't have the heart to share their real feelings. Jim and Susan had the impression they loved it.

The couple's reaction hadn't had any effect on the Clintons. The Sunday after their trip to Flippin, Jim and Susan had bumped into Bill and Hillary having dinner at the Black-Eyed Pea. Jim started telling them about the great piece of property he'd just stumbled upon near Flippin. "You'll want to go in with us on this," McDougal confidently predicted.

"What do you have to do?" Bill asked.

"I'll take care of it," McDougal said. "You may have to sign a mortgage." McDougal explained that the investment would involve little or no cash—they'd borrow the full amount and flip the land as quickly as possible. While they would have to borrow the purchase price, he could easily borrow the full amount on the strength of his own financial position and track record. McDougal didn't want to emphasize the point, but the Clintons' own personal finances were so precarious that they would add little or nothing to the borrowing power of the enterprise.

Both Bill and Hillary seemed excited at the prospect of making some money and agreed on the spot to join in the venture. McDougal was pleasantly surprised, given how uninterested the two had generally seemed on the subject of making money. Maybe the prospect of becoming governor had caused a change of heart. But McDougal didn't dwell on the question very long. McDougal might never be a politician himself, but he had a knack for making money. Every politician he'd ever known had needed money, and that meant they'd need him.

Given that Wade was a founder and director of the Citizens Bank and Trust Co. of Flippin, it wasn't surprising that McDougal turned there first to finance the purchase of the 101 tract, with Wade's encouragement. The loan officer was a young senior vice president, Frank Burge, who was soon to be named president of the bank. The president then was James Patterson, who happened to be one of the investors in 101 Development Corp., which was selling the land.

Given the incestuous relationships (prohibited under current banking laws), it's surprising the application didn't breeze through the approval process. Despite its small asset base and remote location, the bank in Flippin was conservatively run. By its standards, a $200,000 loan was a big deal. Even Wade acknowledged that the price was a little rich (but he was, after all, the agent for the seller, with an obligation to get the highest price possible). The McDougals and the Clintons couldn't borrow 100 percent of the purchase price, which violated the bank's guideline requiring a 10 percent down payment. Burge was also concerned that the small bank had too many loans outstanding in this single area around the White River, since the bank had also financed some of the 101 Development Corp.'s purchase of the larger parcel from which the 230 acres were being carved. Along with several other neighboring land deals the bank had financed, it represented what Burge considered an unhealthy geographic concentration of credit.

Burge discussed his concerns with the bank's board members. They were, of course, aware that Clinton was likely to be the state's next governor. They were flattered that he was interested in investing in their part of the state, and even more flattered that, as McDougal informed them, Bill and Hillary were planning to use one of the lots for their own vacation home. Burge, in particular, thought the presence of Clinton in the deal made it all but a sure thing, assuming Clinton did become governor. He assumed that wealthy Clinton supporters would simply buy the lots at highly inflated prices as a clandestine means of funneling money into the governor's pockets, thereby gaining influence. That, at least, was how he'd always assumed these deals worked in Arkansas. The bank's board members were also aware that one of the sellers was the bank's president, the agent was also a fellow board member, and both obviously wanted the profitable deal to go through.

Under the circumstances, it's probably remarkable that the bank insisted on any conditions for granting the loan. It decided it could live with the credit concentration problem, but insisted that the McDougals and Clintons come up with a 10 percent down payment. It also insisted that all the owners, including both Bill and Hillary, be jointly and severally liable for the mortgage. The terms were easily enough satisfied. McDougal and Bill Clinton simply borrowed the down payment from another bank, Union National Bank of Little Rock, where McDougal had been borrowing since 1970.

McDougal and Harry Don Denton, Union Bank's chief loan officer, were friends, Union having handled most of McDougal's earlier ventures with Senator Fulbright, financed at below-market interest rates "as an accommodation" to the senator, according to the bank's records. Referring to an earlier financial statement submitted by McDougal, the bank cited McDougal's assets as $975,245, liabilities of $424,054, for a net worth of $551,191; for Clinton it listed only unsecured liabilities of $27,211. The bank sought no security for the loan.

The McDougals and Clintons didn't tell Citizens Bank that they were borrowing the down payment. The Clintons agreed to co-sign the mortgage and appear at the closing. The risk seemed minimal given the speed with which McDougal expected to resell the property and pay off the mortgage. The loan would be short-term—principal and interest due in six months—and the interest rate would be 10 percent. As Union Bank noted when it agreed to take a half-participation in the Citizens Bank mortgage, "Due to the individuals and the collateral involved, the risk is minimal."

The closing was set for August 2, 1978, at 10 A.M. Despite bank policy requiring the attendance of all borrowers, the Clintons didn't attend. With a flurry of checks, documents, and signatures, the closing was soon over, with Jim and Susan, Bill and Hillary equal owners of the 230 acres, jointly and severally liable for the mortgage debt and interest. Susan christened the property White Water, and produced the marketing brochure she'd dreamed of: eight pages, with over a dozen full-color photographs.

"Now this is what most folks think of as White Water," the brochure concludes over a photo of sun-dappled water and babbling falls:

"Clean rippling water and stepping stones—but it's really so much more. More than a place to live, it's a way to live . . . quiet, peaceful, serene, simple and honest. One weekend here and you'll never want to live anywhere else."

TWO

SUSAN MCDOUGAL's sense of Hillary's estrangement from Arkansas was, if anything, an understatement. Hillary, after all, had been at the center of national events as a member of the staff of the House Judiciary Committee exploring the possibility of the removal from office of Richard Nixon. She'd had her picture in *Life* magazine as the commencement speaker at her Wellesley College graduation. She was a Yale Law School graduate with friends in the most prestigious judicial clerkships and most powerful law firms in the country. Now she was in Arkansas, known primarily as Bill Clinton's wife.

Susan was among a group of Arkansas women whom Hillary befriended largely because of proximity and expedience, but her confidants remained few, mostly friends from Yale and Washington. In Arkansas she had John Danner and Nancy Pietrafesa, who'd now moved to Arkansas to work in Clinton's new administration, but they always remained more a part of the world from which Hillary came. Among local Arkansans, her best friends by far were Diane Kincaid and Jim Blair, a couple dating at the time who were perfectly at home in the rural South or in sophisticated East Coast dinner parties.

Kincaid had known Bill Clinton since 1972, when she was vice chairman of the Arkansas delegation to the Democratic National Convention and Clinton was working in the McGovern campaign. One day that year Clinton called her and asked if he could visit her at her office at the university in Fayetteville, where she taught political science. The two launched into a lively political conversation that spanned lunch at the student union and lasted for several hours. Clinton made no secret of his own political ambitions. Kincaid liked a lot of what Clinton had to say. Originally from Washington, D.C., Kincaid was attractive, bright, worldly, politically savvy, and had come to Arkansas to be with her first husband. "You remind me so much of the woman I'm in love with," Clinton interrupted to say at one point. He then went on to extol the virtues of Hillary Rodham.

"Why don't you go ahead and marry her and bring her back to Arkansas?" Kincaid asked.

"Nothing would please me more," Clinton replied. But if she married him and came to Arkansas, he continued, he was concerned it would be his life, his state, his political future. He thought she had the potential for a brilliant political career of her own. The comment impressed Kincaid. Not many women had political careers then, and not many men would have encouraged them.

Kincaid met Hillary briefly when she came to Fayetteville to help Clinton in his failed bid for Congress. But they became close when Hillary moved to Arkansas and joined Bill on the law faculty at the university. Hillary and Diane liked to play tennis, sometimes joined by Jim Blair, a prominent lawyer who'd also been a delegate to the 1968 and 1972 Democratic conventions. (Hillary and Blair won a mixed doubles tournament at the Fayetteville Country Club.) Like Clinton, Blair had grown up in a troubled family and was raised by his grandparents. He'd been something of a prodigy, graduating from college at nineteen and receiving a law degree at twenty-one. Blair had been a student guide at the university, where he showed a young Jim McDougal and his parents around campus. He and McDougal belonged to the same fraternity—Acacia—and he tried, unsuccessfully, to persuade McDougal to attend law school. Blair was now, in 1978, general counsel to fast-growing Tyson Foods, headquartered in nearby Springdale, and had been a fund-raiser for Clinton's campaign for attorney general. He also taught at the law school and was an ordained Baptist minister, though he'd fallen out with the church over its support for segregation. Handsome and debonair, ten years older than the Clintons, he was firmly ensconced in business and political circles of influence in Arkansas.

When Jim and Diane had divorced their respective spouses and began dating, they and the Clintons became even closer; each couple considered the other their best friends. The Clintons often spent weekends at Blair's house on Beaver Lake. Jim and Diane had Thanksgiving dinner at the Clintons'. Jim had his own plane, and would fly Hillary and Bill from Little Rock to Fayetteville for Razorback games and other events. They shared books and spent hours in conversation, usually, in Bill's case, about politics, but sometimes about deeper personal and philosophical matters. One of the most important of these for Hillary was children, and she and her close friends spent hours discussing the pros and cons of motherhood. In the Southern world where Hillary now lived, the idea that a married woman would choose not to have children was heresy. Yet in the Ivy League feminist circles that helped shape Hillary's thinking, it was increasingly accepted, even lauded. Between these poles, Hillary's thinking was always steadfast: she wanted children. Simone de Beauvoir, the feminist thinker and author of *The Second Sex*, was one of the women Hillary said she most admired. Yet she found inexplicable that Beauvoir opted not to marry or have children. "You can't be a woman if you don't have children," she opined. "It's the central mission of women. It's too great, it's too important not to experience it." It was a conviction that led her to take a job and remain involved with the Children's Defense Fund, a child advocacy group, and to help found Arkansas Advocates for Children and Families.

Since her marriage, Hillary's desire to have a child had hardened into determination, and during that summer of 1978, with Clinton all but certain to be the state's next governor, she and Bill were trying to conceive. It seemed to be a subject of considerable anxiety for Hillary, who worried out loud to a few close friends that she might find it impossible to become pregnant because of a medical condition. Especially for Hillary, having a child was inextricably entwined with paying for education and other expenses. It was one thing for her and Bill to live simply; it was another to provide the things she would want for a child.

Hillary's views on money had been in an almost constant state of transformation since she graduated from high school. She grew up in a Republican family in a comfortable suburb of Chicago, Park Ridge, where they lived in a spacious Georgian home. Her father, Hugh Rodham, was a local manufacturer who drove a Cadillac. He taught her to read the newspaper stock tables, and she earned money baby-sitting. But membership in her Methodist church youth group exposed her to problems in the inner city and triggered the development of an active social conscience. By the time she graduated from Wellesley, she seems to have embraced the contempt for capitalism and its institutions, especially large corporations, that had swept America's campuses during the late 1960s. One of her boyfriends at the time told Clinton biographer David Maraniss that Hillary had "grown up and out of the conservative materialistic mind-set which is typical of affluent suburbs. She was not interested in making money or being affluent." This attitude was echoed in her Wellesley graduation speech: "There are some things we feel—feelings that our prevailing acquisitive and competitive corporate life, including, tragically, universities, is not the way of life for us. We're searching for more immediate, ecstatic and penetrating modes of living."

It's not clear how deeply these newfound convictions took root. During the summer between her first and second years at Yale Law School she worked in Oakland, California, for Robert Treuhaft, who ran a public interest law firm that took on cases for the Black Panthers, Vietnam Veterans Against the War, conscientious objectors, and miscellaneous leftist causes. His wife is the writer Jessica Mitford. But many of Hillary's Yale classmates who expressed similar rhetoric nonetheless easily made the transition to highly paid jobs at law firms, discovering that money not only provided a more comfortable existence, but could help realize their social and political ambitions. Even at Yale, Hillary would buttonhole John Danner for conversations about making money. While neither Bill nor Hillary had followed the route into high-paid law firm jobs, they had managed a reasonably comfortable living in low-cost Fayetteville while both taught on the law faculty at the University of Arkansas and they had only themselves to support. At the university, faculty discussions often turned to academic salaries, with pride that scholars worked for a nobler cause than money mixed with anger over the low salaries and resentment that so many people with lesser credentials made so much more. Hillary would sometimes speak with some passion about the hypocrisy of a society that paid lip service to education and public service but was so miserly with salaries in those fields.

At the same time, people in Fayetteville were keenly aware of the possibilities for making money because of the stunning success of two area companies: Wal-Mart Stores, headquartered in nearby Benton, and Tyson Foods. Many local people, even of modest means, had bought stock in those companies because they knew people who worked there. A small investment in either company had multiplied many times over; Wal-Mart was one of the top ten performing stocks of the decade, and Tyson became the largest chicken producer in the world. The Blairs and the Clintons would sometimes chat with a woman who worked as a cashier in the checkout line at the local Safeway supermarket, who had bought stock in Wal-Mart and Tyson and was thrilled by her growing wealth. Some faculty members, too, had invested successfully.

The strongest evidence that Hillary's ideological reservations about capitalism were co-existing with an increasingly pragmatic need to make money was her decision to join the Rose Law Firm in Little Rock. She could have continued to pursue a career in public service or teaching, as she had in the past. She had considered working for the large firm of Williams & Connolly in Washington one summer, but opted instead to work in San Francisco for Treuhaft. But now Hillary spent considerable time talking to Jim Blair about the demands and rewards of private practice, seeming to consider the prospect in a fresh light. She could have pursued a position in Little Rock with a lawyer like Phil Kaplan, who, while in private practice, directed most of his energy to public interest cases.

By contrast, Rose, which boasted of being the oldest law firm west of the Mississippi, was the closest thing to a blue-chip corporate firm in Arkansas, numbering among its clients the brokerage firm Stephens, Inc., the Stephens family's Worthen Bank, Tyson Foods, and Wal-Mart. While firms in Little Rock didn't tend to attract graduates of the top national law schools, it numbered three Rhodes Scholars among its all-male partnership as well as civic and professional community leaders. Significantly, it prided itself on its professional skills rather than its political ties, in contrast to a firm like Wright, Lindsey & Jennings, which, in addition to its professional skills, often served as a way station for aspiring or retired state politicians. At the Rose firm, Hillary's marriage to the state's attorney general was, if anything, mildly unsettling to many of the partners, even though they liked her high profile in the community.

The firm offered the highest-quality practice in town and its partners earned an average income of more than six figures, more than that at any other firm.

Even before the investment in Whitewater, Hillary had sought out a highly regarded financial advisor in Little Rock, William Smith, a broker with Stephens, Inc., the state's leading brokerage firm, controlled by the powerful Stephens family, and the nation's largest investment firm outside Wall Street. The Clintons didn't have much to invest, but Smith agreed to take them on because Bill was the state's attorney general, they seemed an up-and-coming young couple, and he was flattered they would choose him. Hillary handled all the details, and set up a joint investment account over which Smith would have discretionary investment authority. She also had her own account, separate from that of her husband. She explained that she knew little about financial markets and didn't have time to monitor specific investments. Nonetheless, it was clear she wanted to make money, and earn a return greater than what was available from simple savings accounts or Treasury bonds.

By now, it must also have been obvious that Hillary couldn't count much on financial contributions from her husband, given his earnings prospects and lack of interest in making money. In his campaigns, Bill typically didn't even carry any money, leaving it to aides to pick up the tab when necessary (an approach he'd learned from McDougal and Fulbright). At semiannual meetings with Smith to discuss the discretionary account, it was Hillary who asked nearly all the questions and wanted explanations for various investment strategies. Bill, by contrast, showed little interest in the account's growth and would ramble on about political developments, comments that left Smith puzzled as to their financial relevance.

According to friends of the couple, it was also at this time that Hillary expressed doubts about the future of her marriage, and, as a result, whether she could count on Bill to support her and a child. Their marriage, now in its third year, was, by the Clintons' subsequent admission, at a low point. If Gennifer Flowers's account can be believed, she and Bill were in the passionate, early stages of their affair that summer. People close to the Clintons were aware of other women in Bill's life, too. They believed Bill had been unfaithful to Hillary even during their engagement, and moving to Little Rock as attorney general had only broadened his opportunities with other women. They were suspicious of Bill's "jogging" expeditions, especially on days improbably hot and humid for athletic activity. On one such occasion, an Arkansas state trooper assigned to Clinton's security detail, Roger Perry, asked Clinton how far he'd run that day. "Five miles," Clinton replied.

"Well, sir. You need to see a doctor," Perry replied. "There's something wrong with your sweat glands." Later, Perry noticed that Clinton would sometimes use the troopers' bathroom to splash water on his face and shirt before he entered the governor's mansion.

To many of their friends, the situation seemed especially painful for Hillary. Bill seemed to flaunt his interest in certain women. One summer he liked to run with Pat Wyatt, who was locally renowned as a founder of the Marquis de Sade running club and who had helped carry the Olympic torch across the country in preparation for the 1980 Winter Games in Lake Placid. She later worked in Clinton's first administration as governor. When he'd return from their runs, he couldn't stop extolling her virtues to Hillary, with comments like "Isn't that Pat terrific?"* Hillary would typically say nothing then. But later there would be arguments, shouting matches, a thrown shoe or two. Both Bill and Hillary had volatile tempers, which they didn't hesitate to inflict on each other. To longtime observers, it was an essential dynamic of their relationship, and the fights were often followed by reconciliations that seemed loving and tranquil. But privately, Hillary expressed pain and dismay. She sought out the husband of one close friend, trying to understand why Bill would be so unfaithful. Did he cheat on his wife? Did he know other men who did? How should she react? How should she feel? Hillary seemed in equal parts puzzled and hurt.

Bill and Hillary's move to the governor's mansion in January 1979 did little to ease these anxieties. If anything, Bill's greater celebrity status opened up more opportunities. He confided in Susan McDougal that he loved being governor: "This is fun. Women are throwing themselves at me. All the while I was growing up, I was the fat boy in the Big Boy jeans." Women treated Bill like

---

* Wyatt, now Torvestad, denies having any romantic involvement with Clinton. She confirms their jogging outings. "He can still sprint and drop me," she says.

he was a rock star. When a group of Girl Scouts visited and Bill came out to greet them, they shrieked and screamed as though they were meeting the Beatles. Susan wasn't surprised that women seemed to be hurling themselves at him. Her brother Bill Henley had been elected to the State Senate. He had women around all the time, and he was just a state senator. Still, Susan felt bad for Hillary. At an inauguration party, Susan had seen Bill Clinton disappear from the party with a tall blond woman in tow. Hillary was putting on a brave face, but the incident was stirring up a buzz and Susan could tell she was upset. She went over to commiserate with the state's new first lady, sharing an observation she'd gotten from Betty Tucker, wife of Congressman Jim Guy Tucker. "Betty told me," Susan confided, "that it doesn't change from the local, to the state, to the federal level. The girls just get prettier."

In the Clintons' thinking about money, Jim Blair was probably as much an influence as anyone. Politically active, sympathetic to their values and goals, loyal and supportive, he had also made considerable money, not just from his law practice, but from shrewd investments. Blair had grown up poor, living in a small apartment above a grocery store in Fayetteville. Even as a student, Blair was fascinated by the markets. He made his first investment in the stock market when he was twenty, and during his first few years of practicing law he was making far more money trading stocks than he did from his practice. He had the natural instincts of the trader: an appetite for risk, a keen mind for information, a willingness to bet against the tide. He often thought he could easily have become a stockbroker or trader, and he counted several among his friends and clients.

One of these, Robert L. "Red" Bone, was something of a legend in and around Fayetteville. Bone was orphaned at age seven, raised in tiny Pineville, Missouri, on a chicken farm, and never attended college. Heavyset, often red-faced (hence the nickname), Bone is sometimes described as an ex-prizefighter or, as one friend put it, "a real razorback," who always wore cowboy boots. He started working in the area as a truck driver for Tyson Foods, rising through the ranks of the rough-and-tumble operation to become head of the company's fleet. According to local legend, Bone worked for a time as the personal bodyguard for Donald J. Tyson, the company's chairman, and lived with Tyson while both men were between marriages. When the head of Tyson's egg department retired, Bone was named a vice president and took over the egg operation. There he discovered the commodities market.

Bone had found his life's calling. Bone is an inveterate gambler who loves to play in high-stakes poker games and has been a frequent visitor to Las Vegas. (Bone played regularly in the World Series of Poker and made the finals in the 1979 million-dollar Amarillo Slim Poker Classic, only to lose the $150,000 top prize in the last hand.) One of Bone's poker buddies was Blair. Bone had discovered that the commodities market was as close a thing to legalized gambling as anyone was likely to find. The commodities market involves the purchase or sale of futures, meaning the right to buy or sell at a future date a given amount of whatever is being traded for a fixed price. Such contracts fluctuate in price constantly until the date specified in the contract, at which time they expire and the quantity is delivered. Obviously, most traders in commodities never own the herds of cattle or bushels of corn specified in the contract; they are simply betting on movement in price of the option, hoping to sell at a profit. Unlike the stock market, tame by comparison, commodities investments are highly leveraged, more like trading in stock options. The amount of money needed to buy or sell a contract—10 percent—is only a small fraction of the total value of the commodities covered by the contract. Selling a contract short—betting that the price will fall—exposes an investor to unlimited loss. Unlike call options in the stock market, where loss is limited to the amount invested, buying commodities contracts can lead to losses many times that of the initial investment, since the buyer is obligated to deliver the full amount of the contract at the contract price even if prices rise precipitously. In such cases, investors may be required to post margins—a financial guarantee that they can honor their contract obligations.

As the *Almanac of Investments* cautions, "Leverage is a two-edged sword. Losses are leveraged. In fact in commodities futures, losses are much more common than profits. How can a person tell if commodity futures is worth trading? First, investors need the proper emotional make-up. Early-morning margin calls can play havoc with nervous systems, destroy sleep, and encourage ulcers. Cautious, indecisive, or highly emotional people should steer clear.

Only those with cast-iron nerves need apply." Or, as a federal judge in Fayetteville later wrote succinctly in an opinion involving Bone's operation, "Commodities speculation is a form of gambling condoned by our society because it stabilizes the farm markets, an important function in the economy."

Risk-loving investors have long been drawn to the commodities markets, often with disastrous results. It is dominated by large institutions, agribusiness, farmers, and feed-lot owners, all of whom have an edge over the average investor because of their knowledge of market conditions. There are no insider trading laws in the commodities field. There are rules prohibiting cornering the market and market manipulation, but such schemes require enormous market power and are notoriously difficult to prove.* While regulated by the Commodities Futures Trading Commission, the commodities markets do not offer investors the safeguards of the stock exchanges, regulated by the Securities and Exchange Commission, and have long fought to maintain their regulatory independence. While the commodities markets have been an efficient and vital mechanism in the American economy, there isn't even the pretense that they offer individual investors a level playing field, as is the case with the stock exchanges.

That was all fine with Bone. As head of Tyson's vast egg operations and an active player in the egg market, Bone was uniquely positioned to anticipate movements in the egg market based on Tyson's own supplies and information he could glean from, or trade with, other major market participants. Bone traded for the company and for his own accounts, embarking on a roller coaster in which he made and lost millions but managed to end up flush. He loved to splash his newfound wealth around. Arriving just after closing time, he once paid a pizza shop employee $500 to reopen the shop for him and a friend. On a visit to a Springdale nightclub, when the band played one of Bone's favorite country-and-western tunes, Bone offered the band $100 to play it again. He repeated the offer, paying cash, eleven times, driving the other patrons away. But Bone's enthusiasm for commodities trading appears to have crossed the line even by the standards of the commodities industry. Commodities regulators alleged that Bone (represented by Blair) at

---

* The Hunt brothers' attempt to corner the silver market remains a prominent exception.

Tyson had manipulated egg futures by cornering the market, and Bone was suspended from trading for a year. Told by Tyson that he'd either have to stop trading commodities for himself or give up his job, Bone asked, "How long do I have to clean out my desk?"

Perhaps inevitably, Bone soon surfaced as a commodities broker himself, eventually running an office of Refco (Ray E. Friedman & Co.), one of the world's leading commodities brokerages, in Springdale, just outside Fayetteville. Bone knew people at Refco from his days at Tyson, including Thomas Dittmer, the enormously wealthy chairman and nearly sole stockholder of the firm. Dittmer built Refco almost single-handedly, using intimate knowledge of the cattle markets gleaned from his position as one of the country's largest cattle owners. Dittmer's self-made style, trading instincts, and success appealed to Bone, and the two struck up a relationship. Bone became even closer with Ed Apel, Refco's chief trader on the floor of the Mercantile Exchange in Chicago, one of the top traders in the pit. Bone was soon on the phone with Apel ten to twenty times a day; Bone was legendary for placing hundreds of calls a day.

Bone was soon on another roll. Now that he was a broker, he called Blair, who among other things had handled two divorces for him, eager to enlist him as a customer. Bone later told Blair that he'd run up a fortune of $15 million, which meant he could finally pay Blair's bills. "This time, I'm not giving it back," Bone said of his new wealth. He added that he had some interesting new information and theories about the cattle market, so why didn't Blair come down and visit with him? Bone's "theory" about the cattle market, he explained when Blair arrived, was based on information from Dittmer and other Refco traders on the dwindling size of the nation's cattle herds, information that Refco was uniquely positioned to obtain because of its own cattle business and its contacts among other cattle operations. Given the time required to raise cattle for slaughter, Bone was convinced that a long-term bull market in cattle futures was in the offing.

As Blair put it in later testimony, Bone "convinced me that Refco knew more about the cattle market than anybody alive, and that they had inside information about the cattle market, and there was a great fortune to be made in cattle." Blair began by funding a joint account with Bone. The investments were an instant success. Blair opened his own account. The money poured in. Soon, Blair was visiting Bone in person nearly every day. He installed his own commodities ticker in his office along with a Radio Shack computer to keep track of moving averages. Blair was deemed such an important customer that he accompanied Bone to a lavish party and business meeting hosted by Dittmer every year at the Union Plaza Hotel in Las Vegas, which Dittmer owned. For his part, Bone was generating so many commissions that Dittmer bestowed a gold Rolex watch on him at the event.

These were heady days for Bone, Refco, and their customers, as Refco's predictions about a long-term bull market proved accurate. But Bone's theory of a long-term bull market in cattle hardly accounts for the success, especially since many of the most lucrative trades during the period were short sales—bets that the prices of cattle would decline. In the context of a long-term bull market— a phenomenon increasingly obvious to market participants—the spreads were much higher, and the opportunity for profit correspondingly greater, in selling short. Successfully selling short in a bull market takes far more precise information.

Each trading day, Bone participated in a crucial conference call usually originated by Dittmer at Refco's headquarters in Chicago. On many days, Blair was allowed to listen in. Participants in the call might vary, but typically included Dittmer himself; Ed Apel; one of the country's largest cattle feed operators; Cactus Feeders and Cactus Growers, Dittmer's own cattle raising operations; and a buyer for one of the country's largest meat packing operations. Among them, the participants pretty much represented both sides of the demand and supply equation for beef cattle.

This quality of information alone would have given Bone and his clients an enormous edge. (By contrast, information about a company's plans to buy or sell stock is supposed to be a closely guarded secret, and buying or selling stock based on the exchange of such information would almost certainly be considered insider trading.) But in addition, commodities trading, especially the smaller markets, is peculiarly susceptible to squeezes—forcing traders to cover positions by withholding stock or by flooding the market. The bull market in cattle that began in 1978, or any commodities bull market for that matter, could easily become overbought, making it ripe for a squeeze by owners willing to release more stock. In such instances, there could be a sharp drop in price before the bull market trend reappeared, and a corresponding opportunity to profit by anyone who foresaw the correction.

Anything as large and liquid as the American cattle market, of course, isn't easily subject to manipulation, and not even Bone represented that anything was a sure thing. But he did tell Blair that his information and Refco's clout in the market could lead to extraordinary gains, and they did discuss the dynamics of the market in detail. And there's certainly every indication that Refco brokers tried to move the market and thought that they could. Because of Dittmer's ownership of cattle, he actually could flood the market or withhold stock, and was in a position to share that information with his network of brokers. Over the Refco hotline connecting the Springdale office to Refco headquarters in Chicago, Bone and other brokers would be routinely exhorted to get their clients to "go long in the cattle," "load the boat," or "mortgage the farm." One broker later testified that Dittmer himself told him that "he was going to drive the cattle market low." There were findings that on some days Dittmer and those he controlled accounted for well over half the total deliveries of cattle made. In October 1979, for example, Dittmer's cattle deliveries in the first three days of the month accounted for 58 percent of the month's total deliveries.

Bone didn't always follow orders from Chicago, nor was his trading always the same as Dittmer's. On some days the group on the conference call could come to no particular consensus on what the market was likely to do. But on many other occasions, they knew, or felt they knew, almost to a certainty, and bought and sold with corresponding confidence. By contrast, Bone kept a bronze plaque on his desk that read, "Don't Fuck With The T-bills." Asked by a client what that meant, Bone said he'd gotten burned trading in the highly liquid Treasury bill market, where his information didn't yield the kind of edge he had in cattle. "One time I thought I was smart enough to trade in the money market, and then I made that same mistake again, and so I put this plaque on my desk so I wouldn't forget and try again," he explained.

It didn't take Blair long to realize that he was on to an extraordinary opportunity. His trading volume was so high that he was generating an average of $50,000 a month in commissions. He opened commodities trading accounts for his children. He was spending so much time away from his law firm that, to compensate, he opened an account for his partners. Then he opened an account for the firm's associates, nicknamed the "pups" account. He opened an account for his future wife, Diane Kincaid. And, perhaps inevitably, one day that fall he called Hillary Clinton at her new office at the Rose firm to tell her of his success in commodities.

"Hillary, these opportunities don't come along very often," he said. "It's a chance to make a lot of money. You've got a chance to make some substantial leverage on some investments. Why don't you let me give you some advice?"

Hillary was interested, but admitted she knew little about the commodities markets. She was learning about leverage—that had been one of McDougal's selling points in the no-money-down Whitewater investment. And most important, she trusted Blair. If he said this was a rare opportunity that would make her money, she believed him. The conversation soon shifted from the nature of the proposed investment to how the earnings might finance a child's college education.

While Hillary apparently didn't make any concrete decision in that conversation, she seemed sufficiently inclined to go ahead that Blair called Bone and had him open an account for Hillary Rodham. The papers for her to sign, misspelling her name "Hilary," soon arrived at her office, and she called Blair in some confusion. "What's going on?" she asked.

Blair reminded her of their earlier conversation about commodities trading and argued once again that it was a rare opportunity she should take advantage of. He assured her that he'd keep her posted about developments in the account, but that she could rely on him to handle the trading decisions. Just as McDougal, a real estate specialist, would handle day-to-day management of Whitewater, she could count on Blair's expertise in commodities and, most important, his access to Bone. Hillary signed the papers, not bothering to correct the spelling of her name, made the $1,000 initial payment asked for, and began trading on October 11, 1978.

Technically, Hillary's account was a nondiscretionary account in which Bone handled the trading but Hillary retained all the decision-making authority. In practice, this was not how Refco's Springdale office handled Hillary's account under Bone's management. Essentially, Bone decided what his clients' trading strategy would be, and he and his brokers executed it, sometimes making large block trades and only later carving them up and allocating them to individual accounts. One of Bone's big clients, a wealthy banker named Hayden McIlroy, was out of town when Bone simply opened an account for him and began trading. When he received a statement in the mail, McIlroy called Bone. "Are you crazy?" he asked.

Don't worry, Bone assured him. "I'll take care of everything."

"If I lose money in this account, I'm not going to pay it."

"You won't lose money," Bone replied.

Blair had more clout with Bone than just about any other customer, but even he had to contend with Bone making trades in his accounts without his knowledge or authorization. That was one reason why Blair spent so much time in Bone's office, where he could keep an eye on his activities. Blair would also devise his own sell points to lock in gains and limit losses, which he insisted Bone execute even when Bone disagreed. Still, as Blair later testified, "Most of the brokers ran most of their accounts like they were discretionary accounts, although the proper documents to technically qualify them as discretionary accounts were never authorized."

Like other clients in Blair's orbit, Bone never spoke to Hillary about the trades, and was hardly aware she was a client. They did run into each other at Blair's Christmas party, and Bone had bought a tract of land adjacent to Whitewater after learning from Blair of the Clintons' investment. Bone could not have cared less that Hillary was married to the attorney general; all that mattered was that she was a friend of Blair's. Blair, after all, placed orders for Hillary, as he did for others in his circle of investors. Blair would keep Hillary abreast of the trading, and share his and Bone's thinking with her. But she rarely countermanded his suggestions. For all practical purposes, Blair traded Hillary's account, with her acquiescence.

In Bone's operation, margin calls were also lax. In the prevailing bull market, Bone seemed to assume that any losses would soon be recouped, so why bother with margin? Indeed, Bone himself had been disciplined just the year before, 1977, when the Chicago Board of Trade ordered Refco to remove Bone from any position with supervisory duties. As a result, others in the office were designated "office manager." Soon after, he was further sanctioned by the Chicago Mercantile Exchange for "repeated and serious violations of record-keeping functions, order-entry procedures, margin requirements and hedge procedures." But Bone was allowed to trade, to function as a broker, and in practice, he continued to hold unchallenged sway over the office.

Bone himself was unapologetic about the sanctions and sacrificed none of his swagger. As Blair put it in one suit where he defended Bone, "You might observe there's a difference between the Ozark hills and the big urban cities as to how people do business." Asked by regulators about his lax, even chaotic, approach to record keeping and running the office, Bone replied, "Well, you're saying it's lax but it's not your nickel and it is mine and if I'm satisfied with it, then I don't think it's lax."

As the money rolled in, none of Bone's customers complained. On the contrary, as word of Bone's exploits spread around Fayetteville, customers flocked in precisely because they thought Bone was handling the accounts. Bone's operation is estimated to have earned profits of from $20 to $30 million for its customers in 1979. And many of those customers knew the source of Bone's success—the information that flowed in the daily conference calls, some of which they, like Blair, were allowed to listen in on. As one such customer testified, "I told Mr. Bone that if—that Refco could trade that account for me as long as they were trading it the way they were trading it . . . as long as the officers were trading in unison, as long as the information—as long as [the] Refco Chicago office was giving the advice, as long as they were establishing their positions, everybody was establishing their positions together and this information was given to the Springdale office and I was, you know, I was certainly willing to go along with it." Given what Blair told her, Hillary certainly knew that Bone had superior information and contacts.

Hillary's first investment appears to have been the short sale of ten live cattle contracts with a value of $220,000 on October 11, 1978. The sale was covered, or closed out, either the same day or the next day, after cattle prices declined a cent and a half per pound, yielding a profit on the contracts of $5,300. Two days later she sold short five more contracts, a position she held until October 23, when she cashed out at a profit of nearly $8,000. At that point she withdrew $5,000 in cash. Thus, in less than two weeks, she was able to recoup five times her original investment. It was just what Blair had predicted.

It wasn't always so easy or surefire. Of Hillary's next six trades, half were losers, including her worst loss of over $17,000 on a short sale of live cattle closed out on November 22. That brought her account balance to a precariously low $5,401, at a time when she had forty open soybean contracts, a situation likely to have triggered a margin call in any office less chaotic than Bone's. Refco's superior information and market power gave its customers an edge, something that significantly shifted the odds in their favor, but was no guarantee. Blair discussed these setbacks with Hillary, and she was upset by the losses. But with his assurances, she was willing to keep trying. She ended the year with net profits of over $26,000, and was able to withdraw another $15,000 in cash for the holiday season. Hillary was thrilled. "Blair can turn anything into money," she confided to Nancy Pietrafesa.

During the new year, with the Clintons in the governor's mansion, Hillary's trading, while continuing steadily, slowed somewhat. While she'd executed eleven contracts the previous November, she did just three in January and none in February. The January trades all proved highly profitable, but later results were desultory, leading up to a $16,000 loss in a short sale of feeder cattle for October delivery, a position closed out in July. Worse, on June 27 Blair had sold live cattle short aggressively, a total of over forty contracts for August delivery in Hillary's account. All of those contracts were still open, exposing her to even greater losses. According to calculations by James Glassman in *The New Republic*, Hillary's position was so precarious in July 1979 that she should have received a margin call demanding payment of $117,500—that is, in just about any office but Bone's.

About that time, Hillary and Bill spent a weekend with Jim and Diana at their lake house, memorable for the fact that Hillary succeeded in getting up on water skis. It was a welcome break for the new governor and his wife, who was simultaneously struggling with the enormous demands of helping her husband organize the new administration, launching her career in private practice at the Rose firm, and becoming pregnant. The last, in particular, was cause for growing despair, to the point where the Clintons had contemplated a visit to a doctor at the University of California at

San Francisco after they returned from a planned trip to London. The additional stress of the commodities trading was hardly welcome. Even though it had yielded cumulative gains of over $50,000, it hadn't made the Clintons rich, certainly not on the scale of Blair. The open contracts, which exposed Hillary to hundreds of thousands of dollars in risk, could easily wipe out all those gains, not to mention all their assets. Not much was said during what was supposed to be a carefree weekend, but Hillary did mention her concerns to Blair. She said it was making her nervous, she wasn't sure she had the temperament for such trading, and she was thinking maybe she should stop. What did Blair think? Blair said it was her decision, but told an anecdote attributed to J. P. Morgan. A friend confided that he couldn't sleep because of his stock positions and asked the legendary financier what he should do. "Sell until you start sleeping," Morgan had replied. Hillary said she'd think about it.

Once again, however, Bone's and Dittmer's predictions that the live cattle market had become overbought proved correct. Just days after covering one short sale at a loss, the market plunged. On July 20, it dropped the legal limit. Hillary was able to cash out the open short positions with the biggest gains of her trading experience, a total of more than $40,000, bringing her total gains to just under $100,000.

Blair was ecstatic over the news. Hillary, while pleased and relieved, had a different reaction. "I think it's enough for me," she said. On July 23, she withdrew $60,000, and shortly after closed the account. With her bank account flush and her commodities worries behind her, it was an auspicious beginning for their trip to England. They visited Oxford and Bill's former haunts as a Rhodes Scholar and took in the sights of London. It was there one aprocryphally sunny morning that, as the Clintons strolled through the neighborhood of Chelsea, Bill spontaneously burst into the Joni Mitchell song "Chelsea Morning." He and Hillary had just learned she was pregnant.

No one was more delighted by the news than the Blairs, who now realized that Hillary had actually been pregnant during the weekend they prodded her onto water skis. They were relieved that the physical strain had had no adverse consequences. Hillary's spirits obviously soared. The trip to the doctor in San Francisco proved unnecessary. Hillary's deep-seated fears of not being able to conceive a child had evaporated. Her cherished dream of motherhood was to be fulfilled. Thoughts of leaving Bill were banished. The change in Hillary was noticeable to everyone.

In the months since closing Hillary's account, Bone and Blair had continued to trade successfully, relying on the information flow to conclude that the bull market would continue. At the beginning of October, Dittmer, Refco's chairman, held an extraordinary three hundred open long positions for October delivery in his personal trading account—an extremely bullish position.

On October 2, Blair was out of the market, his Radio Shack computer having tracked the moving averages to a point where he felt the market was in equilibrium, offering no real profit potential on either the long or short side. That morning, however, an unusually excited Bone called him, exhorting him to go long in live cattle. Ed Apel had spoken with Dittmer that morning, and Dittmer told him he "favored the long position," Apel later testified. Blair agreed to go long; his and other Refco clients' buying helped push the October futures up the limit that day.

Then something extraordinary happened. Even as he was apparently spreading the word to customers to go long, Dittmer flooded the market with live cattle. And as Refco customers, exhorted by brokers like Bone, loaded up on long positions on October 2, Dittmer liquidated his three hundred long contracts and replaced them with three hundred short contracts. So did hedge accounts in Dittmer-controlled companies like Cactus Feeders and Cactus Growers. As the impact of the sudden influx of cattle and Dittmer's short sales spread, the market abruptly reversed course and closed down the limit. Dittmer closed out his short positions that day with immense profits, a trading coup that has become legendary.

Bone, meanwhile, still in the dark about Dittmer's actual trading, was on the phone to Blair and other customers, reassuring them that Refco's position was still bullish, that they shouldn't liquidate their positions, that the market would turn again in their favor the next day. But on that day, October 3, Dittmer again liquidated cattle stock. Cattle futures sank again, marking the end of the long bull market. The losses for Bone and his customers were devastating. Having vowed never again to lose the $15 million, Bone was ultimately forced to declare personal bankruptcy. Blair watched his own account plunge from just under $4 million to about $1.5 million.

Bone, Blair and his customers were apoplectic. Not only had they lost their fortunes practically overnight—their losses had come at the hands of their erstwhile ally, Dittmer. Even by the often cutthroat norms of the commodities markets, they felt this to be a betrayal of historic proportions. To this day, they don't know why Dittmer acted as he did; why Refco's chairman would turn on his own brokers and best customers. There has been speculation that his own immense exposure to the cattle market had led to growing losses that could only be recouped in a spectacular reversal of the market. His move may also have coincided with his decision to get Refco out of the retail commodities brokerage business. After the debacle, Refco focused almost entirely on trading for its own account and large institutional clients. The days of the cozy conference calls were over. The Springdale office, and others catering to individuals, were closed.

Dittmer has offered no explanation for his change of heart. Bone, Blair, and other customers all sued Refco and Dittmer; Dittmer and the other defendants denied any attempt to manipulate or corner the market (though the essential facts were uncontested). The Eighth Circuit Court of Appeals, holding the plaintiffs to a nearly impossible standard of proof, reversed several jury verdicts finding that Refco and Dittmer were guilty of market manipulation, ruling for Refco in every case. Alone among the plaintiffs, Blair sued in state court, ultimately settling with Refco. The Chicago Mercantile Exchange investigated charges of market manipulation as well; Refco settled the matter, admitting record-keeping violations and denying all other allegations, and paid $250,000, at the time the largest fine ever levied by the commodities regulators.

Like so many information-sharing arrangements, the Dittmer-led group was vulnerable to betrayal from within. But its collapse was an inverse measure of its success; it provided dramatic evidence of how great an edge Dittmer's information gave the participants at the expense of other traders in those markets. Betrayed by Dittmer, Bone and his colleagues faced the same brutal odds as everyone else. The Eighth Circuit ruled that nothing illegal occurred. Still, Jim Blair and Hillary Clinton were beneficiaries of a scheme that, on the face of it, came precariously close to collusion to manipulate the market. Hillary was briefly retained to represent McIlroy, so she must have known his views of what happened (citing other commitments, she referred him to another Rose partner).

For Hillary, the turmoil at Refco and Blair's losses had little impact. Later that same month, despite Blair's setback, she resumed trading in commodities, this time through her financial advisor at Stephens, Bill Smith. Smith, in Little Rock, had heard nothing of the turmoil in Springdale, and when he raised the possibility of investing a modest amount—$5,000—Hillary gave no indication she'd heard anything about Blair's losses, who was hardly eager to boast about it. Smith told Hillary he sensed a market move in gold in the offing. Hillary mentioned her previous success in commodities, and authorized Smith to go ahead. All the trades were in commodities other than cattle (though not, curiously, gold). Hillary told Blair nothing of her return to commodities speculation.

Without the Refco edge, Hillary and Smith's trading produced solid if not spectacular returns. In five and a half months of often volatile price moves, Smith doubled the account to just under $10,000.* On February 27, 1980, Hillary gave birth to a daughter, whom she and Bill named Chelsea Victoria. The next month, Hillary called Smith and closed her commodities account, this time for good. She moved her assets into U.S. Treasury bonds. She confided to Blair that she'd finally decided she couldn't handle the stress. Even while she was in labor with Chelsea, she said, she was worrying about her sugar contracts.

---

* The Clintons failed to report the gain on their 1980 tax returns. They voluntarily paid the taxes and penalties in 1994, after news reports of the trading.

THREE

LIFE IN GOVERNOR CLINTON'S office was chaotic but—most of the time—fun. Clinton and his even younger staff would talk politics and policy all day, sometimes until ten at night, and then roll into a local bar like the Gumbo Ya Ya. Jim McDougal joined the new administration as an economic advisor, specifically, liaison for industrial development, banking, insurance, and the highway department. He worked for a nominal salary. But as the oldest member of the administration, he served as its éminence grise and minister without portfolio, spending hours with his feet propped on his desk holding forth on the subject of the day. He loved to sprinkle his comments with anecdotes like "This reminds me of the time James Madison entertained the ambassador to France . . ." While the youthful staff tended to dress in open-collar shirts, jeans, and loafers, McDougal elevated the tone of the office by appearing in a neatly pressed seersucker suit and straw Panama hat. Once again, he was very much a player in the political scene.

Besides McDougal, Bill relied on Rudy Moore, Jr., his chief of staff; Steve Smith, his political advisor; and John Danner, his chief policy advisor, to run the office. But Bill's penchant for seeing people, often followed by impromptu invitations to the governor's mansion, often wreaked havoc with the schedule. To many, it was Hillary who managed to impose what semblance of order there was, often attending meetings, interrupting her husband when necessary to get things back on course. Another formidable presence from time to time was Bill's outspoken, colorful mother, Virginia Dwire, who'd drive up from Hot Springs and drop in unannounced.

With her skunk-stripe hair, thick makeup, and eyeliner, she would charge through the office, on one occasion all but bumping Rudy Moore out of the way. "Get the hell out of here," Dwire said. "I want to talk to this little brat." From behind the closed office door, the staff could hear her yell at her son, "I'll be god-damned if you can pull this shit on me." Dwire considered herself an expert on the opinions of the common man.

Susan McDougal was in and out of the office constantly, hanging around, chatting with everybody, flirting. In her miniskirts and low-cut blouses she was hard to miss. "Susan, you ought to be able to sell some real estate in that outfit," commented Julie Baldridge, Clinton's press secretary, one day, eyeing Susan's three-inch heels and all-but-unbuttoned blouse. Susan loved the excitement of being around the governor, and she loved all the parties—the Peanut Growers of America, the Cotton Council—some organization was always coming to town, and it seemed there was a party practically every night. Bill loved all the hoopla. One day Miss America visited, and all work came to a halt. The governor personally escorted her around to practically every cubicle in the office.

Dana Farr, a gorgeous young secretary, had been stationed right outside the governor's office, but at Hillary's insistence had been moved to a desk in the basement. On hearing the news, Bill Wilson, married to one of Clinton's aides, commented to Hillary and Susan that "I guess we'll be having to make quite a few trips to the basement." Susan shot back, "You know, there's a guy down there with the cutest butt," referring to an intern who was the Razorbacks' quarterback. Eyeing Hillary, she said, "I think we'll be making quite a few trips to the basement." Hillary and she laughed and laughed, though the comment, Susan felt, was a little risqué for the first lady.

Susan liked the way Hillary would stick up for other women. North Little Rock had been rocked by a sensational killing, in which a lover had shot a woman's husband. When Bill Clinton and others in the office suggested that the woman must have done something to egg on the killer, Hillary was furious, arguing that it was typical for men to blame the victim. Susan was impressed that she stopped Bill and the other men in their tracks.

Susan had initially been taken aback by Jim's decision to leave their burgeoning real estate business for the governor's staff. Since their marriage, she had become increasingly involved in the business; the two shared an antique partners desk in the office. One day he'd simply said, "I'm joining the governor's staff. I'll see you later."

"Excuse me?" Susan had replied, incredulous. But she thought it was so like Jim to just walk into a new job, leaving her to pick up all the pieces. Jim was swept into the governor's immediate circle, traveling often with him and joining him for frequent meetings at the governor's mansion. Later, when Susan complained that she was overwhelmed by the amount of work, and was lonely without Jim there, he became angry, telling her she was too "clinging" and that it was time for her to grow up. Her reaction was to spend even more time at the governor's office, where at least she had other people to talk to.

Among the real estate responsibilities largely ceded to Susan was management of Whitewater. Despite McDougal's hopes for fast returns on the investment, by the end of the summer in 1979, more than a year after the closing, not a single lot had been sold. Unlike McDougal's earlier investment in the area through Chris Wade, the Whitewater property had never been surveyed, and without a survey, the new individual lots couldn't be sold. McDougal commissioned a survey, but the results were inexplicably slow in materializing. Distracted by the move to the governor's office, neither Jim nor Susan, and certainly neither of the Clintons, had bothered to look into the matter for nearly a year, and then the McDougals discovered that the survey was faulty and had to be redone with a new team of surveyors. That held up clearing of trees and grading of a road to provide access to the individual plots. Despite the glossy photos and rosy promises of the sales brochure, Whitewater remained remote, inaccessible, and unimproved.

Whitewater also surfaced as a possible political headache. In October 1979, an *Arkansas Democrat* reporter, Mike Rothenberg, wrote, "Political ties and possible conflicts of interest surround the purchase of 230 acres of land along the White River in Marion County by Gov. Bill Clinton, one of his aides and their spouses." The article focused on the possible conflict of having the bank president, James Patterson, functioning as both lender and seller, not on any conflict on the Clintons' part. Still, it quoted board member Steve Sanders as saying the board was concerned about the "ethicalness" of the situation. The article caused few ripples.

When the reporter had called the bank, Frank Burge had contacted Bill Clinton about what he should say. "Tell them the truth," Clinton said. "I've got nothing to hide."

Though nobody focused on it at the time, the economic prospects for the Whitewater development were rapidly fading. Essentially an impulse purchase from the outset, the returns were never likely to be all that high, even if events had unfolded as McDougal had hoped. The original tract of 230 acres, for which they paid $203,000, was carved into forty-four lots, whose combined list prices (which in practice would never have been realized) amounted to $459,000. With estimated development costs and interest of $93,000, less commissions and closing costs of 15 percent of sales revenue, the net proceeds would have been a maximum of $95,000 to be divided between the Clintons and McDougals. Even that return is hard to calculate, since most of the lots would have been sold on an installment plan with just 10 percent down. Any profits would have flowed in over a lengthy period of time as buyers made their monthly payments.

But the McDougals, in all their real estate ventures, rarely bothered with profit projections. All that mattered was cash flow—cash flow sufficient to cover all the costs of the project, hopefully with a surplus that funded further ventures and contributed to their living expenses. So far, however, Whitewater had been a cash drain. For some of the improvements to the property, McDougal had simply written a check on the account of his and Susan's Great Southern Land Co. But he'd asked the Clintons for payments during the first year that totaled $22,620, a negative cash flow for the Clintons of nearly $2,000 a month.

The whole thing was deeply embarrassing to McDougal. Here he'd brought the Clintons in as a favor from a mentor to his protégé based on a successful track record, and the investment was turning sour. From his AA training, McDougal felt he had to make amends for the trouble he'd gotten the Clintons into. Thus it was with considerable excitement that McDougal told Bill and Hillary of the project's first sale, one of the lots bordering the river, in September 1979. Within six months, they'd sold five more lots, and each sale was unveiled with even more enthusiasm. To the Clintons, McDougal exuded confidence that the project had turned a corner and was finally on its way to profitability.

Susan suspected the truth to be otherwise. As was increasingly the case, however, she could say nothing to dampen Jim's enthusiasm. He didn't want to hear the details, which were anything but reassuring. "This is what I want done, and you take care of the details," he said. The down payments on the lot sales barely covered Wade's real estate commissions and the closing costs. At the end of May 1980, with the Citizens Bank loan up for renewal and the next quarterly interest payment of $4,352 due, Whitewater Development Co.* had less than $2,000 in cash. By this point, the McDougals had invested nearly twice as much as the Clintons.

While the Clintons may have been unaware of the financial details of the venture, they were keenly interested in whatever tax breaks they could extract from it. One afternoon in the governor's office, Bill mentioned to Jim that he should "talk to Hillary about taxes because she and Jim Blair have made some money in commodities."

The next time Hillary dropped in, Jim asked her about it, and she told him both she and Blair had been quite successful and she was looking for some kind of tax shelter. She complained that she and Bill didn't have any deductions to speak of, not even a home mortgage now that they were in the governor's mansion. Jim did some research and came up with a scheme involving a gold mine that promised five-to-one write-offs. Even he was dubious, however, and a partner of Hillary's at the Rose firm said he doubted it would survive scrutiny by the IRS. That plan was abandoned, but Hillary pressed Jim to see how much in interest payments from Whitewater she could deduct from their taxes, arguing that she and Bill were entitled to a full half of the interest payments. But it was McDougal who was making a disproportionate share of the interest payments and was thus entitled to the deduction. Jim finally burst out, "Goddamn it, Hillary, didn't they teach you in law school that you can't take a deduction for something you didn't pay?"

McDougal might have added that you can't take a deduction for everything you do pay—only for payments of interest and legitimate business expenses. Yet, in a pattern that would continue, the

---

* *Whitewater was incorporated in 1979 as Whitewater Development Company, Inc. It appears in many references and documents, however, as Whitewater Development Corp. Participants also sometimes refer to the development as "White Water."*

Clintons deducted $10,131 on their 1978 tax returns, describing it
as an itemized interest expense, to shelter some of the commodities
profits. The Clintons had written a personal check in this amount
to the McDougals' Great Southern Land Co. on December 28, and
the payment was reflected in the Whitewater accounting ledger as
an "adjusting entry." But Whitewater apparently didn't pay anywhere near that much interest in 1978, and no documentation from
the banks was offered to support such a claim.*

While the 1978 deduction might be characterized as a misun-
derstanding, the Clintons were even more aggressive in 1979. They
made Whitewater payments totaling $12,490 that year, and de-
ducted all but $500 of it as itemized interest expenses described
as "bank loans" and "Jim McDougal." Of their payments, $2,900
consisted of an advance and paid-in capital, which would not be
deductible. Another payment of $4,600 went to Great Southern
Land Co., ostensibly for reimbursement of interest payments.†

Over time, the Clintons had fewer and fewer payments to
deduct. With the next interest payment due, McDougal didn't want
to ask the Clintons for their share. It wasn't that he thought the
Clintons didn't have the money; he knew, after all, of Hillary's
success in commodities trading. But after his boasting that
Whitewater's prospects were improving, he was simply too embarrassed to ask the Clintons for another payment. Without telling the
Clintons, he wrote a personal check for $4,000 to cover the short-
fall, depositing it in the Whitewater account the day the interest
payment had to be made.

As the summer of 1980 unfolded and the date of the next
interest payment drew closer, Whitewater lot sales came to a halt.
Interest rates were soaring. No buyers could be found.

---

* As most taxpayers recognize, deducting interest payments ordinarily requires documentation from the bank. In this case, the payment wasn't even made to a bank; the ledger
adjustment suggests that the money was actually used to reimburse Great Southern Land
Co. for payments it made for capital improvements to Whitewater, such as roads. Those
deductions would have to be capitalized—not claimed in full the year paid. Though the
White House later defended the deduction, saying McDougal told the Clintons it was an
interest payment, and while the amount does appear to correspond to interest payments
made in 1978 and 1979, it is doubtful the payment would pass IRS muster as prepaid
interest.
† The Clintons' 1979 tax return was audited by the IRS and was approved without
change, indicating the agency accepted the Clintons' explanations. The White House
maintains that the 1978 and 1979 deductions were proper.

•

The fun was wearing off in the governor's office as the 1980 campaign loomed. People were up in arms over a license plate tax Clinton had imposed to raise money for highways. The timber industry was angry over a task force Clinton had launched to investigate clear-cutting practices. President Jimmy Carter's decision to lodge thousands of Cuban refugees at Fort Chaffee, near Fort Smith, leading to a melee after refugees fled the base, had left Arkansans infuriated. A recession was unfolding. The weather was unusually hot. Clinton bore the brunt of people's frustrations. Unaccustomed to such resentment, Bill was often dispirited. As Hillary said to Julie Baldridge, Clinton's press secretary, one day, "If I didn't kick Bill Clinton's ass every day, he wouldn't be worth anything." Bill and Hillary seemed to be arguing constantly, and everyone's temper was short.

Clinton's staff became increasingly disgruntled. John Danner and Nancy Pietrafesa were among the first to go. Though Danner percolated with innovative policy ideas, the couple had never really fit in in Arkansas, and were thought to be too liberal and idealistic rather than pragmatic. Both left to join the Carter administration in Washington.

Steve Smith, one of Clinton's chief political advisors, now married to press secretary Julie Baldridge, had become similarly disillusioned. Clinton had placed Smith at the head of the timber industry probe, and for Smith, curbing practices in the industry would be environmentally sound, strike a populist stand against big business, and be a political coup. But before the task force report was released, Clinton, alarmed by the hostility of the timber industry, insisted that criticism of the industry be watered down and called for voluntary measures rather than state regulation. Smith was furious, and resigned from the task force. As Smith told David Maraniss, his philosophy is, "You win, you do what you can for your side, you screw the opposition. Then if the other side wins, you take what's coming." By contrast, Clinton's philosophy was, "You can reach a satisfactory compromise of polar positions that is superior to either side." In Smith's view, Clinton's approach usually succeeded only in alienating both sides.

Another attempt at compromise involved the trucking and poultry industries, which lobbied vigorously against Clinton's efforts to pay for highway improvements by raising license fees. Clinton responded by easing the burden on heavy trucks and shifting it to passenger cars, which seemed only to further anger the general population (including Clinton's mother), yet failed to assuage big companies like J.B. Hunt Trucking and Tyson Foods. This controversy was raging, moreover, at the very same time that Jim Blair, officially Tyson's general counsel, was so generously assisting Hillary with her commodities trading. There's no indication of any actual conflict of interest—Hillary didn't get much involved in the matter, nor did Blair press Tyson's case through the first lady. In any event, Tyson didn't get all it wanted, and what was significant was that Clinton did anything to alienate a company as important to Arkansas as Tyson Foods. Still, it was an appearance of a conflict, one likely to resurface in any of the myriad dealings between the governor's office and Tyson.

Appearances of conflict weren't much of an issue in Arkansas, where real conflicts had been all too common in administrations prior to Clinton's. The issue never seemed to occur to Bill or Hillary or Blair or even McDougal, who knew about the trading and was involved in the highway issue. But the compromises did upset McDougal. He worked closely with Smith in the office—they'd gotten to be best friends—and he shared his frustration. But McDougal was even more upset by what he considered to be Hillary's meddling. Like Danner, he had lots of ideas, and he'd gotten some favorable press from the *Arkansas Democrat* for his highway development efforts. But McDougal viewed change from an Arkansas perspective, which meant things should happen slowly. Increasingly, Hillary was demanding action, and she wanted it now, in time for the election campaign. Jim was left wondering: just who did he work for—Bill or Hillary?

One day during this period, Jim was outlining some new ideas he'd had when Hillary interrupted him. "Ideas are great, Jim," she said, "but it's time for you to do something for a change. There's too much fun and games around here." Jim was seething when he told Susan about the exchange. Jim considered it a favor that he was even working for the state, at a nominal salary, and he expected some deference in return. Hillary was trying to control him, he complained, and no one could treat Jim McDougal like that. It was true, Susan thought, that no one ever questioned her husband. She certainly didn't.

About the time he was souring on his job in the governor's office, McDougal drove through tiny Kingston, fifty miles east of Fayetteville, and admired the distinctive architecture of the town's bank, the Bank of Kingston. He mentioned this to Steve Smith, who grew up in the area and knew the bank was for sale. Suddenly McDougal began hatching a new plan, bigger than any of his real estate deals: he'd buy a bank. He and Susan would become bankers. In his position in the governor's office, he'd learned something about the banking business and had met nearly every prominent banker in the state. Moreover, the people he met in Kingston reminded him of the folks who'd shopped at his father's store.

McDougal prided himself on his "country road populism," as he put it, and he'd always mistrusted bankers. He'd even tried to start a bank at age twenty-two, but he couldn't get a charter. As he saw it, the banks in Arkansas had taken people's money, paid them scant interest, invested their capital in U.S. Treasury bonds, and refused to lend. They'd been ripping off people in the state and plowing nothing back into economic development. No wonder, he often railed, that Arkansas was so backward economically. One of his motives for taking his job in the Clinton administration had been to inject some competition into the Arkansas banking industry, heavily protected by state laws limiting branch banking. Nothing he'd experienced there had done anything to change his views of Arkansas bankers. All they did was whine: "We're going broke."

As usual, McDougal liked the idea of having a partner in this new adventure, so he took his Bank of Kingston plan to Steve Smith, who'd earlier represented Madison County in the Arkansas legislature. McDougal's populist spin to the project appealed to Smith, who had wanted to leave the office since the flap over the timber investigation. "This deal can work for both of us," McDougal argued. "There's no reason to keep this up," referring to their work for the Clintons. The two agreed to buy the bank (future governor Jim Guy Tucker also came in for a small percentage of the deal, as did Fulbright). The McDougals sold their house in Little Rock, using the proceeds for part of the bank's purchase price. McDougal borrowed $270,000 from Union Bank, the source of the Whitewater down payment, and Union loaned the money for the Smiths' interest as well. In the fall of 1980, the McDougals packed up for Kingston. It was another bewildering change for Susan. What would become of all the real estate deals? What about all their friends in Little Rock? But as usual, she was swept along by McDougal's enthusiasm and confidence. He promised her the past would sort itself out. Now he could think only of the Bank of Kingston.

When Susan finally arrived in Kingston, she thought she'd been exiled. The day she arrived, a cow dung–throwing contest was in progress. Kingston is a tiny, old-fashioned town of two hundred people built around a dusty central square to which area farmers still brought their livestock for sale on weekends. She and Jim moved into a glorified mobile home on McCracken Hill. The bank itself, located on the square, occupying a series of turn-of-the-century storefronts with pressed tin ceilings, had been founded in 1911 and was still run by the same family. It had a single phone lacking even a hold button. Its assets were a paltry $1.4 million. When Susan showed up at the bank wearing high heels, makeup, and a short dress, overall-clad customers gawked. For Jim McDougal, the primitive aspects of the place only meant greater opportunity.

He and Smith rechristened the bank Madison Bank and Trust Co. of Kingston, named for the Ozarks county where Kingston is located and after James Madison. He had a new logo designed for the bank incorporating a likeness of the nation's fourth president. That was just the beginning. McDougal decided that the bank building should be restored to its original splendor, which meant, among other projects, rebrassing the original teller cages and re-gilding the old barrel safe. People were stopping in just to marvel at the transformation. For the bank's seventieth anniversary, in April 1981, McDougal threw a one-day festival on the square, with rides in a massive hot-air balloon, bluegrass music, and a "millionaire for a day" contest, where the winner got one day's interest on one million dollars. Senator Fulbright was among the guests.

On the business side, McDougal and Smith launched an aggressive advertising campaign to promote new higher rates on deposits. Assets swelled to $3.6 million in the first five months after the takeover. The one phone line was replaced with a modern phone system, computers were installed, and Kingston boasted an automated teller machine even before one had appeared in Little Rock. Still, the bank remained so down-home that Smith and McDougal would handle transactions on the sidewalk. McDougal lent aggressively. Among other ventures, he offered low-interest loans to other businesses on the square willing to renovate and restore their buildings. McDougal had visions of turning Kingston into a quaint tourist town. All in all, the bank was turning out to be the fantasy that McDougal had dreamed of living—at least, for a while.

It isn't clear at exactly what point McDougal went too far, but it wasn't long before the people of Kingston—his customer base— were grumbling. Inexplicably to the McDougals, they had pretty much liked Kingston the way it was before they and the Smiths blew into town and started redecorating. When the McDougals bought a big barn just off the square and had it repainted, they complained that they had liked the old barn the way it was. There were rumblings that the McDougals and Smith and his wife, Julie Baldridge, thought they were big-city know-it-alls who put on airs. Worse, the aggressive interest rates and marketing may have been great for expanding the bank's asset base, but they were devastating to profits. As McDougal's loan officer at Union Bank later observed, "substantial expenditures on modernization of banking house, internal systems and advertising have not resulted in profits, however, officer is not concerned with absence of profit at this point."

McDougal's preoccupation with his new bank hardly made Susan's efforts to maintain the real estate empire any easier. Whitewater, in particular, required one stopgap measure after another to keep the venture out of default, all of which had the net effect of making things worse. At the end of June, the loan from Union Bank used for the down payment had come due, and the bank had become uneasy about continuing the loan. It had originally been a six-month note, and now two years had elapsed. None of the principal had been repaid. At the same time, McDougal was applying for more credit at Union Bank, this time with Jim Guy Tucker, to purchase an apartment building, renovate it, and resell the units as condominiums. Harry Don Denton, the loan officer in charge of McDougal's affairs at the bank, told McDougal that the bank wouldn't extend him and Tucker credit for another land deal unless he cleaned up some other matters, including the Whitewater loan.

So McDougal went to the Bank of Cherry Valley, whose chairman, W. Maurice Smith, was a friend of his and a big supporter of

Governor Clinton. Smith came from a wealthy east Arkansas family and had played an active role in Clinton's election. The governor had named him his liaison to the State Senate, but Smith's real interest was the highway department. Since McDougal's portfolio included highways, he and Smith were in frequent contact and had gotten to be good friends. McDougal knew Smith would lend him and Clinton the money to retire the Union Bank loan, which he readily agreed to do. McDougal, not wanting to bother the governor just as he was quitting his staff, took the new loan out personally, which relieved Clinton of liability for it.

Later that summer, however, when the Citizens Bank mortgage had to be retired or refinanced, McDougal wasn't in a position to bail out the Clintons. He'd had to borrow to buy his Bank of Kingston stake, and the year of working with little pay had eaten into his and Susan's cash reserves. Frank Burge, the loan officer at Citizens, had now replaced James Patterson as the bank's president, and he was determined to crack down on some of the sloppier lending practices at the bank. Whitewater was a case in point. Thus far, interest payments had often been late and none of the principal had been repaid. He insisted that the McDougals and Clintons pay down 10 percent of the outstanding principal and agree to a repayment schedule that would eventually retire the principal (something resembling a conventional mortgage). McDougal broke the news to the Clintons that they had to pay their share: $9,000 in principal and an interest payment of $4,350. (The Clintons, apparently at McDougal's instructions, left the "payee" line blank on the check and gave the check to McDougal. He never bothered filling in the line, and the check was deposited directly into Citizens Bank and applied to principal.) As they had in the past, the Clintons deducted all the payments on their 1980 tax returns, including the $9,000 payment of principal. (Only interest, not payments of principal, is deductible.) The latest payments brought the Clintons' total cash payments in the venture to just under $36,000.*

McDougal may have been disillusioned by his tenure in the governor's office, but he still felt close to Clinton and he was still

---

* *The White House maintains that the $9,000 deduction was proper because the McDougals told the Clintons it was interest. But an internal White House memo concludes "This would not be a proper tax deduction."*

acutely embarrassed by the worsening prospects for Whitewater. Property sales had stalled. Susan's glossy brochure had not had the impact he'd hoped for, and he recognized that something had to be done to spur sales. A tactic that had worked in other developments once initial enthusiasm faded was to build and sell a house on a lot conspicuously near a development's entrance. This tended to reassure potential buyers that someone else was living there and helped people visualize what their future dream home might look like. Such a strategy might work at Whitewater, he thought, though it also required a further investment of capital just when all the partners were strapped. The Clintons agreed with the plan to build a model home; to pay for the house, McDougal simply loaned Whitewater some funds from another of his real estate investment concerns. McDougal arranged the purchase of an exceedingly modest two-bedroom prefabricated house for a little over $20,000; installation on Lot 13 brought the costs to over $28,000. Whitewater had its first home.

Other than occasional calls and the need to sign papers, the McDougals and the Clintons had little contact once Jim left the governor's office. The McDougals paid little attention to the 1980 campaign that fall; they gave Clinton's challenger, Frank White, a savings and loan executive and former Democrat, little chance in what was still pretty much a one-party state. Distracted by his new bank, McDougal had fallen uncharacteristically out of touch with the mood of the electorate, which had become deeply disenchanted with Clinton over everything from the Cuban refugees to the license plate fees to Hillary's use of her maiden name.

The morning after the election, Jim McDougal was in the shower when the phone rang. Susan answered. It was Hillary Clinton, and she was croaking, her voice barely recognizable.

"Let me talk to Jim," Hillary said. Ordinarily Susan wouldn't have interrupted her husband's shower, but Hillary sounded like it was urgent.

"It's Hillary Clinton," Susan called out. "She sounds terrible." Dripping wet, Jim got on the line.

Hillary said they'd lost the governor's race. Bill was too depressed to get on the phone. "You need to send us money," Hillary said, sounding desperate. "We need it now, and we need all you can send." Jim said he was sorry and stunned by the news, and he'd see what he could do. Hillary hung up; Jim assumed he was the recipient of one of many similar calls she was making that morning.

Jim told Susan the news. She was even more shocked. She and the Clintons used to make fun of White, calling him a "bozo." They were contemptuous of his wife's Junior League primness, such a contrast to Hillary. Susan was sympathetic to the Clintons' plight. They didn't even own a house, and she knew Whitewater was a strain.

But Jim vowed he wasn't going to send the Clintons any money beyond subsidizing them on Whitewater. He thought Clinton had blown it, and deserved to lose. Clinton had spurned McDougal's advice. He thought Clinton should never have alienated Steve Smith, who knew how to run an Arkansas campaign. He shouldn't have let Hillary run things.

More to the point, the McDougals were strapped for cash themselves. They'd increased their holdings in the bank at Kingston by borrowing more, raising their debt at Union Bank to just under $400,000. With Ronald Reagan newly installed in the White House, the country settled into recession and interest rates rose. Sales slowed at all the McDougal developments, even as loans had to be renegotiated at much higher rates. At the same time, Arkansas's usury law restricted to 10 percent the interest Whitewater could charge buyers who financed their purchases of plots.*

These same factors continued to hurt the Whitewater operation, increasing the pressure to generate some sales and reduce the crushing debt burden. Lot 7, the largest and most desirable of the plots along the river, had been marked "sold" on the original plans of the property, and was the parcel being held for the Clintons' eventual use. It was unlikely that the Clintons ever seriously intended to use the parcel, which they'd never seen, but McDougal now decided it was a perk the development couldn't afford, and would have to be sold. Eager to raise cash by the date of the next payment to Citizens Bank, he agreed to sell the land to Chris Wade, the broker for the development, for $33,000.

Wade insisted he wanted the land for his own use and thought he'd paid a fair price. But soon after, he was showing the purchaser

---

* Under federal legislation, federally insured lenders were exempt from state usury laws; individuals and private lenders, like Whitewater, were not.

of the adjoining plot, Dr. M.T. Bronstad, around the development and mentioned that they would be neighbors now that Wade had bought Lot 7. This was the first Bronstad had heard that Lot 7 had been on the market, and he pressed Wade to sell the more desirable lot to him. Just two days after paying Whitewater $33,000, Wade sold Lot 7 to Bronstad for $45,000 in cash. However much Wade may have wanted the land for his own enjoyment, the maneuver shows a willingness on Wade's part to profit at the expense of his clients.

McDougal was happy to get an infusion of cash, nearly all of which was used to pay down the outstanding principal of the Citizens Bank loan. Then, to replace the advance he'd made to finance the construction of the modular home, McDougal arranged for Hillary to borrow $30,000 from Madison Bank and take title to the property. The loan would be repaid, he assured her, using proceeds from the sale of the house. She agreed, and henceforth the modular home on Lot 13 became known as the Hillary house.

Though McDougal didn't intend this to be the effect, the transaction exposed Hillary to considerable personal liability on the loan, which carried an interest rate of about 20 percent. For McDougal, however, using Hillary to buy the house using a loan from his bank was convenient for several reasons: It avoided the appearance of blatant self-interest had the Kingston Bank loaned him the money or loaned it to Whitewater, of which he was a principal. It also avoided his having to reveal to the bank the precarious financial state of Whitewater; Hillary, as a Rose firm partner, was a far better credit risk. At the same time, it avoided bothering her husband, the soon-to-be ex-governor.

But the underlying economics of the venture could hardly be disguised. The house was soon sold to Hilman Logan for $27,500 for $6,000 in cash and a $21,500 note receivable. Commission and closing costs to McDougal were $3,000. The prefab house alone had cost McDougal over $28,000 and the land was carried on Whitewater's books for $3,000. On its face, the sale triggered a loss of $7,000. Since the interest that could be charged for Logan's note was 10 percent, while Hillary's loan was at 20 percent, Logan's monthly payments weren't nearly enough to cover the interest payments due.

Though all this information was available to the Clintons had they asked, they remained oblivious, no doubt encouraged by McDougal's occasional references to lots being sold and his reluctance to ask them for their share of payments due. The Citizens Bank loan was routinely renewed in August 1981, again at a higher interest rate, and a month later McDougal was still collecting signed copies of the renewal documents. In what appears to be a reply to such a request from McDougal, Hillary wrote him on her personal letterhead:

"Enclosed is our signed copy of the Extension and Modification Agreement. You will have to have it notarized before sending it on to Flippin.

"If Reagonomics works at all, Whitewater could become the western hemisphere's mecca.

"Give our regards to Susan and we to hope to visit soon."

But that extraordinarily optimistic view of Whitewater's prospects (given that she'd never even seen the property, what can have inspired her to draw an analogy to the pilgrimage city of Mecca?) was soon drawn into question. In August 1982, the Kingston loan officer in charge of the loan wrote a disturbing letter to Hillary:

"Your note and mortgage with Madison Bank & Trust in the amount of $28,000 matured on June 1, 1982. We have been receiving payments in the amount of $285.13 per month which has been applied to accrued interest. However, interest is accruing at $373.33 every 30 days and the $285.13 payments received each month are not satisfying the interest that is accruing."

Evidently eager to distance herself from the matter, she wrote back:

"I ask that you speak with either Mr. or Mrs. McDougal who have made all the arrangements for this loan. It has been my understanding that the loan has been paid out of proceeds from sales by the White Water Development Corporation."

The letter suggests that Hillary was woefully out of touch with the true financial condition of the venture. Whitewater itself couldn't even manage its own interest payments to Citizens Bank without increasingly frequent infusions of cash from McDougal and McDougal-controlled entities. Indeed, Whitewater itself had also borrowed $30,000 from McDougal's bank to meet its debt obligations. The loan fell into default at Kingston. The Federal Deposit Insurance Corporation, concerned by losses at Madison Bank and Trust, had launched an investigation in September 1982, and it had specifically cited the Whitewater loan as "unsound." Thus, for all practical purposes, the bank couldn't again extend Hillary's loan. Eventually Bill Clinton himself borrowed over $20,000 from the Security Bank of Paragould, whose former president, Marlin Jackson, had been named bank commissioner by Governor Clinton, and applied the proceeds to reduce Hillary's debt. (That amount, however, did not wipe out her debt entirely. It isn't clear who paid off the several thousand dollars remaining, but Madison Bank retired the loan.)

Jackson was aware of McDougal's questionable activities. As bank commissioner, he had warned McDougal during the FDIC examination to discontinue loaning money for projects remote from the bank's home territory. He had also warned Clinton that McDougal might be running afoul of the state's banking laws. But Clinton apparently ignored the warning. Though the Arkansas Bank Commission participated in the FDIC investigation, no further steps were taken to curb McDougal's lending activities. Nor did Clinton terminate his relationship with McDougal.

By this point, surely even the Clintons realized that Whitewater was proving to be a disastrous investment. They had to borrow another $20,000 from Citizens Bank (a note the Clintons and the McDougals signed personally) at 14.5 percent just to cover interest payments on the original Citizens loan. Lot sales had stalled. Existing revenues weren't nearly sufficient to cover interest expenses, which kept rising as notes were renewed at higher rates and new notes taken on. Yet, in the financial statement the Clintons submitted to both the Security Bank of Paragould and the Bank of Cherry Valley in 1983 to obtain their loans, they listed assets of $505,000, valuing their one-half interest in Whitewater at $200,000.

So far, the partners had kept their fingers in the dike by continuing to borrow from friendly bankers or the bank controlled by McDougal. But this was little more than pouring good money after bad. If the lending dried up, and all the notes were called at once, the Clintons and McDougals faced a financial crisis—just as Clinton was plotting a political comeback. McDougal was desperate to find a new source of funds.

Jim McDougal was never a Charles Keating, whose plundering of Lincoln Savings and Loan came to symbolize the savings and loan disaster of the 1980s. But the Charles Keatings of the industry

account for only a tiny fraction of the more than $100 billion in
taxpayer losses that flowed from the deregulation of the savings and
loan industry. McDougal was far more typical of the kind of person
who generated such losses: a real estate entrepreneur for whom
leverage was an article of faith with scant experience in banking
who ended up controlling an S&L.

In late 1981, as some of McDougal's initial enthusiasm about
his bank in Kingston was wearing off, he got a call from Harvey
Bell, who had been Governor Clinton's securities and savings and
loan commissioner and was now acting as a broker for struggling
financial institutions looking for buyers. Having just emerged from
his tenure as savings and loan commissioner, Bell was intimately
familiar with the new laws that allowed S&Ls, hitherto restricted
to residential real estate loans, to create wholly owned subsidiaries
that could invest in anything from junk bonds to resort developments and apartment complexes. Better yet, they could do it with
their federally insured deposits, meaning the federal government
rather than depositors ultimately bore the risk of loss.

The sudden rise in interest rates that had so devastated
Whitewater and other developments had left scores of S&Ls in
weakened condition, looking for buyers. Naturally, brokers like Bell
gravitated to the biggest borrowers, people like McDougal.
McDougal was immediately excited by the prospects. He'd been
frustrated at Madison Bank and Trust in Kingston by two restrictions: the bank wasn't allowed to invest directly in real estate, and
he couldn't establish branches in more populated, lucrative centers
to raise funds. These were the main reasons he believed he hadn't
yet been able to turn a profit. He'd even gone so far as to hire Vince
Foster at the Rose firm after he tried to take over a nearby bank,
which sued him to derail his effort. He lost the case, and was
furious about it. A Rose associate—not Foster—had tried the case.
McDougal refused to pay the full amount of his Rose firm bill.

Bell told McDougal that Woodruff County Savings and Loan
Association in Augusta, Arkansas, was for sale, and, as a newly
deregulated S&L, would face neither obstacle that had hobbled him
in Kingston. As McDougal put it to Harry Don Denton, his loan
officer at Union Bank, the S&L—as opposed to a bank—was a
"candy store." Even better, the S&L for sale was located just across
the White River from Bradford, McDougal's hometown. McDou-

gal's romantic imagination was soon fired up. He'd return to his hometown a conquering hero, his pockets bulging with cash, lavishing higher interest rates and loans, liberating his fellow citizens from the stodgy stranglehold of the entrenched bankers. Susan recognized all the symptoms she'd seen when they bought the Bank of Kingston: her husband was now obsessed with the Bradford deal. He was bored with the bank at Kingston.

The McDougals had no trouble borrowing even more money, this time from the Worthen Bank, the large Little Rock bank controlled by the Stephens family. They borrowed $70,000, then an additional $142,000 to pay for a controlling interest in Woodruff, and filed for state approval of a change in control at the savings and loan.

As if McDougal didn't have enough to occupy his attention, in 1982 he decided to launch his own long-dreamed-of entry into politics by running for Congress in the Third Congressional District against Republican John Paul Hammerschmidt, the same opponent who'd defeated Clinton in 1974. McDougal called Susan from a pay phone in Fayetteville, telling her to "turn on the TV." He was on-screen making the announcement. Suddenly Jim and Susan were thrown onto the campaign trail with Bill and Hillary, who were trying to regain the governor's mansion. The two candidates often appeared at rallies together throughout the state. It was politically awkward during the primary: Clinton was running against McDougal's good friend Jim Guy Tucker, trying to mount his own comeback after losing the Senate race in the last election. Even so, Hillary was happy to offer McDougal advice on his campaign strategy, all of which McDougal ignored.

Now that McDougal was finally running his own race, he had distinctive ideas for how a campaign should be conducted. He loved the stump speech, where he could wax eloquent with old-fashioned rhetoric drawn from his political hero, Franklin D. Roosevelt. In his standard speech, and despite his aristocratic accent, he always inserted a reference to the neglected interests of the state's "widder women and orphans." Finally a supporter asked why McDougal kept mispronouncing "widow." It turned out that when FDR came to Arkansas, he had used exactly the same phrase and pronunciation. McDougal liberally borrowed from FDR. The district had a significant Irish population, and despite his claims to have descended from Scottish royalty, McDougal now claimed his family had lived in Ireland before 780 A.D. He festooned his campaign appearances with four-leaf clovers and used the color green whenever possible. In contrast with his opponent's German origins, he liked to say that "My ancestors were over here farming this country when my opponent's ancestors were rutting with the wild hogs in the forests of Silesia."

None of this seemed to make an impression on the electorate, and no one accorded McDougal much of a chance. Indeed, a staff memo warned Clinton to distance himself from McDougal, saying Jim was "turning off voters rapidly." McDougal's emphasis on the working poor and the underprivileged seemed out-of-date in increasingly prosperous northwest Arkansas. He had no grassroots organization and scant funding, nor was he much interested in such matters. But even his critics had to admit that his speeches were, in their own way, mesmerizing.

Clinton's campaign, by contrast, was a model of professional organization, thanks largely to the efforts of Hillary and Betsey Wright. At the Clintons' urging, Wright had come to Little Rock in the dark days immediately after the humiliating loss, living in the basement of the governor's mansion until the Clintons moved out, then setting up shop with Clinton at his new law firm, Wright, Lindsey & Jennings. A Texas native and an earthy feminist with a broad mother-hen streak, Wright knew Clinton from the McGovern campaign. She was herself out of a job, and she loved the idea that the Clintons needed her. She devoted herself to Clinton's comeback, organizing his files of supporters and contacts to the exclusion of any personal life of her own. Like Hillary, she was the kind of woman who could argue with Bill, discipline him from time to time, keep him focused and on course. She also had an instinctive kinship with Hillary, and she was no romantic threat. Indeed, some people in the campaign assumed that one of her functions was to keep Bill's amorous impulses in check and to protect his political future.

Susan McDougal was amazed by the transformation of Hillary Clinton on the campaign trail. Suddenly she was being introduced, and even referred to herself, as "Mrs. Bill Clinton" rather than Hillary Rodham. Susan assumed Hillary had gotten the message that Arkansas voters didn't like women to flaunt their independence, but still she was bewildered. Hillary had always been so militant about keeping her name, and it had made such an impression on her. Equally surprising, Hillary had acquired a new, tastefully conservative, even ladylike wardrobe. She had contact lenses now. She was even wearing makeup, and had had her hair styled. She looked much more attractive, Susan thought, far more like the conventional politician's wife.

Still, the new facade didn't entirely suppress Hillary's nature. Much like Bill, Susan loved campaigning—all the hugging and glad-handing and getting to know people from all over the state. Hillary, by contrast, usually looked slightly pained by the experience. On one occasion when the McDougals and Clintons appeared together, a woman came rushing up to Hillary. "I made these for you, honey," she said. "I just think so much of your husband." Beaming, she handed Hillary a pair of earrings in the shape of hogs —the Arkansas Razorback mascot. Susan thought they were so cute she would have put them on then and there and worn them for weeks. Hillary mustered a thank-you, then the woman asked her to put them on. Hillary wouldn't. With the woman out of earshot, she turned to Susan. "This is the kind of shit I have to put up with."

In a tough race, Clinton ousted Tucker in the primary by attacking Tucker's congressional record. In a runoff with the other candidate, a nondescript former lieutenant governor, the campaign organization put together by Wright proved decisive, and Clinton won the nomination. In the general election that fall, Clinton ousted Frank White handily, successfully portraying him as the captive of business interests and the electric utilities. The election was a triumph for the sheer willpower of the Clinton forces, especially people like Betsey Wright and Hillary. Clinton's political future, strengthened by the crucible of defeat, was alive again.

McDougal was swamped.

There was soon more bad news for the McDougals. Madison Bank and Trust at Kingston reported a 1982 net loss of $100,000. The FDIC concluded its investigation in January, finding the bank had engaged in so many unsafe and unsound lending practices that it considered barring McDougal from making further loans. The report accused Madison of excessive poor-quality assets, excessive lending outside its trade area (Whitewater was a specific example), improper transactions with affiliates (Whitewater again), inadequate loan loss reserves, and insufficient capital. McDougal had to agree to a cease-and-desist order that so curbed Madison's lending flexibility that, for all practical purposes, it rendered the bank worthless for McDougal's grander ambitions.

Despite the election loss and the sobering situation at Kingston, Jim experienced a new burst of energy and enthusiasm over the new savings and loan venture. He and Susan were undeterred by the precarious operating condition of Woodruff, which, caught between the high rates necessary to attract deposits and the low interest rates being earned on loans, was losing money at a rate that would have bankrupted the institution within a matter of months. The McDougal acquisition was approved by state banking authorities in October 1983 and the deal closed a month later. Including their debt for acquiring the bank at Kingston, the McDougals had now borrowed a total of $548,000 to finance their foray into banking.

The McDougals plunged into their new venture with characteristic enthusiasm, beginning again with a name change. Dispensing with the parochial Woodruff County Savings and Loan, they christened it Madison Guaranty Savings and Loan, turning again to James Madison for inspiration (and introducing a certain amount of confusion for those who failed to distinguish it from Madison Bank and Trust in Kingston). McDougal embarked on another aggressive campaign to increase capital, advertising higher rates and buying brokered deposits from other institutions. Within a year, total assets swelled from $6.7 million to $17 million. Despite the romance of serving his hometown, McDougal had no intention of limiting the S&L's operation to Woodruff County. He and Susan had already moved back to Little Rock.

For the new flagship office of Madison Guaranty, the McDougals settled on a large old laundry building in a run-down area of Little Rock's Quapaw quarter. Conveniently located on South Main Street, just to the south of downtown and Interstate 630, which intersects Little Rock, it is an old part of the city with some large older homes and the governor's mansion. But like much of central Little Rock, it had fallen into steep decline, pockmarked by abandoned buildings, vacant lots, houses falling into disrepair, and a growing black population. In much the way that Kingston appealed to McDougal's liberal imagination, so did the Quapaw laundry site. McDougal saw it as the linchpin of development that could revive the whole area.

Under Susan's design direction, the old laundry was transformed into a vaguely Art Deco fantasy, painted light purple with a new faux marble floor, new windows with purple awnings, lots of glass block accents and new lighting. McDougal's own glass-enclosed office was suspended above the boiler, affording him a panoramic view of the aqua- and purple-painted banking floor. Susan won a design award for the transformation and the building did help trigger something of a revival for the area, which now boasts Juanita's, Little Rock's most popular Mexican restaurant, and a bakery and café that attracts a more bohemian and sophisticated crowd.

Now that he was in Little Rock, McDougal could run Madison in his own inimitable style. He hired the night watchman to oversee the thrift's new computer system. He promoted another armed guard to loan officer. He made a point of hiring people who were going through Alcoholics Anonymous. Salesmen from the real estate developments would bring in clients and get them loans on the spot. McDougal carried business records to his accountant in a brown paper bag. Susan was able to bring three of her brothers into the Madison operation as real estate salesmen, as well as her sister and brother-in-law. (Her other brother, Bill, had successfully run for the State Senate and become a backer of Governor Clinton in the State Legislature.) Others at the bank complained that the Henleys were constantly squabbling among themselves.

McDougal wasted no time in taking advantage of the new opportunities for S&Ls. In late 1982, even before he'd gotten formal approvals for the takeover of Woodruff, he incorporated a subsidiary of Madison Guaranty, Madison Financial Corp., as his vehicle for direct business investments, especially real estate. As Madison Guaranty's assets swelled through brokered deposits, higher rates, and advertising—at their peak Madison's assets reached nearly $100 million—McDougal had a nearly limitless source of funds to invest, as long as he could earn a greater return than he was paying in interest and other costs. With the easing of the recession and the gradual accompanying decline in interest rates, some of McDougal's new ventures were undeniably successful, such as Flowerwood Farms and Pembroke Manor, developments that quickly sold out.

It was also true, however, that McDougal's flights of fancy were now even less restrained by the need to borrow money from someone other than himself. Indeed, whenever he and Susan were now pressed for cash, they simply borrowed it from their own savings and loan. In 1984, the once-generous but increasingly restless Union National Bank insisted that the McDougals pay off at least $100,000 of the debt taken on to buy the bank at Kingston and pay all interest due, a total of nearly $150,000. To make the payment, the McDougals took out two loans from Madison Guaranty, one for $85,000 and one for $59,000. This practice became all but routine whenever the McDougals faced demands from other banks, including Whitewater's lenders. However unsound and self-interested these loans were—no one at Madison Guaranty dared to challenge the practice, for fear of McDougal's volatile temper—the McDougals were obligated to repay the loans at prevailing interest rates. They never simply took the money.

McDougal's dream was to finance ever bigger real estate ventures. In this vein, Madison Financial's most grandiose real estate venture may have been the purchase of Campobello Island in the remote Atlantic province of New Brunswick, Canada. McDougal had been reading the *Wall Street Journal* one morning when he spotted an ad in the real estate listings for Campobello, a summer resort where McDougal's hero, Franklin D. Roosevelt, had had a house. It was four thousand mostly wilderness acres with thirteen miles of ocean frontage, with an asking price of $825,000. McDougal loved the play and the movie version starring Ralph Bellamy as FDR, *Sunrise at Campobello*. McDougal's imagination was once again fired up: imagine the appeal to investors of being able to own a piece of land where the great president himself had once vacationed!

The project violated every rule of prudent lending: it lay far outside the geographic area served by Madison; it was located in a foreign market where McDougal knew little about prices and trends; it would be aimed at a national, upscale market with which he had no experience; and it was expensive, representing too substantial a commitment given the risks. While undeniably pristine wilderness, its location meant it was cold most of the year and even in summer was often shrouded in fog. The normally ebullient Susan loved the idea, but had reservations about taking on such a big new project. None of this fazed McDougal. Refusing to acknowledge how far from favor FDR liberalism had fallen—let alone the passing of a generation for whom FDR remained a national hero—he was convinced the Roosevelt connection would hold irresistible marketing appeal. He and Chris Wade, the Flippin broker, flew up to see the property. It was a project he shopped to many Little Rock businessmen and friends, including Jim Guy Tucker, now an attorney in private practice representing McDougal, and Sheffield Nelson, head of Arkansas-Louisiana Gas Co. (Arkla), and he soon put together a group to buy the property.

With the piggy bank flush, Jim and Susan were able to live better than they ever had before. The constant pressure to refinance loans coming due that couldn't be paid without additional borrowing was now relieved. This didn't mean they lived lavishly—when he paid attention, Jim was still relatively tightfisted with his own money. Still, Susan was finally able to remodel the house of her dreams, a Cape Cod fantasy in Little Rock's fashionable Heights area that was featured in the home design section of the local paper.

Everywhere she went these days, people recognized Susan as "the lady in the hot pants." They weren't exactly hot pants, but Susan was appearing on local television throughout Arkansas to promote Maple Creek Farms, one of the McDougals' latest real estate ventures, wearing very short cutoff bluejeans, a tight work shirt, and boots, leading a horse. By the still-conservative standards of Arkansas, the ads were a minor sensation. People tended to remember Susan, with her flowing dark hair and gorgeous figure, much better than they did the name of the development. Still, lots were selling briskly.

With plenty of money for campaign contributions, the McDougals were soon reestablished socially in influential political circles, and began seeing more of the Clintons. Bill liked to drop in on McDougal's office at Madison Guaranty during his morning jogs; the office was just four blocks from the governor's mansion. The two would shoot the breeze for a half hour or so, usually about politics.

Perhaps inevitably, McDougal got a call from someone involved in fund-raising for the Clinton campaign, asking if McDougal would be willing to help reduce Clinton's outstanding campaign debts by hosting a fund-raiser at Madison Guaranty's newly renovated headquarters. Even though McDougal had been telling Susan and his friends that his interest in politics had waned since his own defeat, he readily agreed. Indeed, he seemed pleased to have been asked. A March 26 memo to Governor Clinton reported a call from McDougal: "Wants you to come by for 30 minutes on either April 3 or April 4 for a fund-raiser for you. He said it has to be one of those dates because that is when Fulbright can come."

The date was set for the fourth. With the help of John Latham, Madison Guaranty's chief operating officer, he rounded up a group of contributors, including various Madison clients, Susan's brothers, and other people who did business with McDougal. Though McDougal had hoped to use Fulbright as a draw, the former senator didn't show up and later claimed to have known nothing about the event, even though he was listed as a $3,000 donor. McDougal himself also gave $3,000, the legal maximum. At one point Latham had mentioned to Jim that he thought he'd found a "loophole" in the election financing law that would allow them to exceed the $3,000 limit by having different entities give $3,000, but McDougal brushed that aside. "Haven't we done enough for the Clintons as it is?"

It wasn't much of a party. Clinton and Betsey Wright dropped by, staying for less than the promised thirty minutes. McDougal was more interested in talking to Maurice Smith than to Clinton, whom he was seeing frequently anyway. The two bankers retired to McDougal's office, from which McDougal saw Charles Peacock, a wealthy Madison borrower who McDougal thought was a Republican, hand over some checks to Wright. All told, the event raised $35,000, deposited in a Clinton political account at the Bank of Cherry Valley.

FOUR

BEHIND THE NEWLY RENOVATED red-brick facade of the oldest law firm west of the Mississippi, a distinctly modern rift was developing between the firm's corporate lawyers and its litigators. Like many such old-line firms, the Rose Law Firm had long prospered on the strength of its corporate practice for clients like banks, insurance companies, utility companies, and corporations. The firm was named for U.M. Rose, one of the founders of the American Bar Association and President Theodore Roosevelt's chief envoy to the 1902 Hague Peace Conference (a distinction that earned him a place in Statuary Hall in the U.S. Capitol). Rose's son, George, also practiced in the firm, all the while writing and publishing a work of art history, *Renaissance Masters*.

Despite its cultivation of scholar-lawyers like Rose, the firm had developed a tradition of a strong senior partner, beginning with Gaston Williamson, a former Rhodes Scholar who worked at a large New York firm before returning home to Little Rock after World War II. A courtly Southern gentleman, a pillar of Little Rock society and the Country Club, Williamson cemented the Rose firm's ties to Worthen Bank by marrying a member of the Worthen family.

Williamson was also responsible for introducing a compensation formula for partners at the Rose firm that he adapted from his experience in New York. Most firms in Little Rock still operated like small-town law firms. Partners earned what they brought in, usually through a combination of retainers, contingency fees, flat fees, and hourly billings. But Rose's practice was large enough that work was farmed out by a handful of dominant partners—those who burnished client relationships and brought in the business—to other lawyers who did most of the actual work. Williamson's formula rewarded the rainmakers by giving credit for generating business as well as for hours of work billed, based on a five-year average. The Rose firm prided itself on this merit-based system rather than that at many big-city firms, which rewarded partners strictly on seniority, regardless of their performance. At the same time, the system recognized implicitly that Little Rock was still a town where even Rose partners had to hustle for clients.

When he retired, Williamson was succeeded by C. Joseph Giroir, Jr., a corporate lawyer who continued to run the firm in Williamson's paternalistic manner. Rose lawyers tended to be involved in bar activities and the American Bar Association conventions, using them as an opportunity to stay in touch with trends in the profession beyond Arkansas's borders, and the early 1980s was the beginning of a period of considerable upheaval in the profession. Even as profits surged, the old order of tenured partners and seniority-based compensation was crumbling. Firms raided each other for partners and business, clients shopped aggressively for the best results and fee structure, old-line firms plunged into once-unsavory areas like bankruptcy and hostile takeovers. Not much of this had reached Arkansas, but Giroir came to believe that such trends inevitably would, even if not for some years.

One of the trends Giroir focused on was the rising importance of litigation at other firms like Rose that had once relied heavily on their corporate practices. As the 1980s unfolded, the traditional corporate practice in Arkansas seemed mature. Growth was in commercial litigation—environmental, tax, antitrust cases. Rose's litigation department, a small group headed by Philip Carroll, existed primarily as a service to corporate clients, handling insurance defense work, industrial accidents, the odd private dispute. The practice was neither high-powered nor particularly lucrative. Unlike personal injury firms, the firm's litigators billed strictly on an hourly basis, rarely accepting the more speculative but potentially much more lucrative contingency fee case. Most cases were referred by corporate partners, so under the firm's compensation system, the corporate partners tended to get the finder's fees. But in anticipation of change, Giroir concluded the litigation department had to be beefed up. He asked another Rose partner, Vincent Foster, to head a team of litigators that would expand the firm's commercial litigation practice.

Like many of the senior partners in the Rose firm, Giroir held Foster in high regard, even viewing him as the probable successor to himself as the firm's chief executive. Foster had joined the firm in 1971, just after graduating first in his class from the University of Arkansas Law School. Foster had further burnished his reputation by logging the highest score on the Arkansas bar exam. Foster, just twenty-six years old at the time, made partner in two years. He was tall, slender, good-looking, with a sober demeanor and naturally judicious manner that inspired confidence in his judgment and discretion. In his legal work he was thorough almost to a fault, scholarly, and hardworking; at the firm he was businesslike, strictly professional, rarely making any reference to his personal life or outside interests. Indeed, he and Phil Carroll, neighbors in the Heights section of Little Rock, often rode to the office together each morning—in silence.

Like Bill Clinton and Mack McLarty, Foster was born in Hope and attended kindergarten with them. But his early life was far removed from Clinton's turbulent upbringing. Foster's father, Vincent Sr., was a self-made real estate developer and salesman, one of Hope's most successful businessmen. Despite his growing wealth, Foster Sr. never lost the rough edges of his own rural upbringing. He was a sportsman, a gun collector who loved to hunt and fish, often described as a "man's man." He was a colorful raconteur who salted his narratives with off-color language and anecdotes. He was gregarious and loved parties. He had a reputation as a womanizer.

By contrast, Foster's mother was a genteel Southern lady, tall and beautiful, outwardly serene, much more reserved than her husband. Vince had two older sisters, Sharon and Sheila, who inherited their mother's good looks. In high school they were popular and social. Boys clamored after them, often dropping by the Foster home to listen to the elder Foster's stories, toss a football around with young Vince, and court his older sisters. The family lived in a sprawling Victorian home, the biggest in town.

People remember an amber-tinged, almost postcard-perfect picture of life in the Foster family. Like most families, this was only partly true. Vince took more after his mother than his father; she seemed to develop a special relationship with her youngest and most sensitive child, often shielding him from a father who could at times seem overbearing and crass. Despite his many appealing qualities as a child, Vince did not seem to be the kind of son and namesake that Vincent Sr. had expected, and, in a rare moment of introspection, Vince would later confide that he had always felt like a disappointment to his father. Vince was not much of an athlete, and he dreaded the hunting trips with his father. Foster was embarrassed by his father's affairs, angry on his mother's behalf. In high school, he often sought refuge in Mack McLarty's family.

Despite being reserved, almost introspective, Vince was a leader and an overachiever in high school. He was elected president of the student body. He belonged to the Key Club (a junior branch of the Kiwanis Club) and was a delegate to Boys State, a breeding ground for future Arkansas politicians and business leaders, Bill Clinton among them. His grades were good. Though he didn't earn a letter in sports, he wrote about them for the student newspaper.

Vince could probably have gone anywhere to college, and he later told friends he had fantasized about attending an Ivy League college. This prospect got scant support in the Foster family. Indeed, Vince's father made no secret of the fact that he wanted his son to return to Hope and follow in his footsteps in the real estate business. Vince ended up choosing Davidson College in Davidson, North Carolina, then a highly regarded men's liberal arts college founded by the Presbyterian church. Davidson forms part of a cluster of liberal arts colleges in the Southeast that includes two women's colleges, Randolph-Macon Woman's College and Sweet Briar College, and Washington and Lee, then a men's school. Though less well known outside the South, these schools had long catered to the Southern aristocracy. Academically respectable while never aspiring to Ivy League pointy-headedness, they bred future business and political leaders and, at the women's colleges, their well-groomed wives. Their reputations appealed especially to Vince's mother, and both of Vince's sisters had attended Randolph-Macon. For Vince, Davidson satisfied his desire to live outside Arkansas while conforming comfortably to his parents' expectations.

Vince promptly joined a fraternity, Sigma Alpha Epsilon, but appears to have engaged in none of the usual pranks; he often seemed concerned that he not appear "silly." His fraternity brothers describe him as steadfast, reliable, quiet, private, emotionally guarded. He was interested in politics, a Democrat—at a national Sigma Alpha Epsilon fraternity convention in Chicago he argued vociferously with young Republicans—but he was hardly a radical. He never mentioned running for political office, but it wouldn't have surprised his friends if he eventually did. Other than occasional intramurals, he didn't participate in college sports. He had a succession of girlfriends from neighboring colleges, all charming, pretty, conventional, but nothing terribly serious until he showed up with Elizabeth Braden, a Sweet Briar student from Nashville, whom everybody called Lisa. Vince met Lisa at a Sweet Briar party weekend his sophomore year, though they didn't seem serious until he was a senior. As Lisa later described it, to *New Yorker* writer Peter Boyer, "I just went head over heels in love with him." She, too, was charming and pretty, compared by some to actress Doris Day, sheltered, largely oblivious to the social upheaval of the late 1960s. Her father was a prosperous insurance broker from Nashville, she'd attended a Catholic girls' school, and made a society debut. Her goals were simple, straightforward, and traditional: she wanted to be a wife and mother.

After graduation from Davidson, Foster enrolled in Vanderbilt University Law School in Nashville, another traditional breeding ground for Southern leaders, which was located in Lisa's hometown. Both Vince and Lisa moved to Nashville, Lisa to her parents' home. But with the Vietnam War raging, Foster maneuvered himself into the Arkansas National Guard to avoid the draft, which meant he had to attend law school in Arkansas. He married Lisa and the two moved to Fayetteville. There's no evidence that Vince had harbored any deep ambition to be a lawyer, but for someone as cerebral, cautious, and ordered as he was, it must have seemed appealing, especially compared to the rough-edged, high-pressure, sales-oriented real estate business of his father. In Fayetteville, Vince's natural aptitude for the legal profession first surfaced. A fellow student there, Doug Buford, once got a paper back from a professor who told him it was so good he wanted to keep it to use as an example. "But," he added, "I want you to know that I've got one paper that yours doesn't even come close to: Vince Foster's."

Despite his academic success, no one thought of Vince as especially intellectual. Thorough and analytically sound, his work was competent but not provocative; he wasn't the kind to make waves in the classroom. He practically lived in the library, studying so compulsively that, at the end of a term, when most students were cramming, he had so thoroughly memorized the material that he had little left to do.

Socially, Vince and Lisa fell in with a crowd that surrounded Claude Pruette, a potbellied married student who, by all accounts, was the class card and center of social life, much of which revolved around Razorback games. Foster remained a lifelong Razorback fan, once traveling to San Antonio for a basketball conference championship on a trip organized by Pruette. All the Razorback fans wore pink shirts, and Pruette had gotten permission to have a party on barges on the San Antonio River in the center of town, as long as there were no more than twenty people per barge. Foster had been typically cautious, warning Pruette that he'd never pull it off. In the event, the barges nearly sank under the weight of the Hog Wild band, the Razorback and Texas Tech cheerleaders, the pink-shirted Razorback fans, and what seemed like hundreds of others—all invited by Pruette. Yet the party went on, Foster joined in the revelry, and Pruette emerged unscathed. About the wildest anyone can remember Foster was on one occasion when, after a few drinks at a party, he got down on the floor and leg-wrestled with Bill Wilson's wife (she flipped him).

Foster was so eager to begin work at the Rose firm, which had asked him to join as an associate, that he skipped his law school graduation. Rose, dignified, stable, old-line, and prestigious, must have seemed the ideal firm to Foster. Indeed, it was really the only firm in Little Rock that aspired to the standards of national law firms elsewhere. It was the road to respectability, bar association officerships, and, perhaps, a judicial appointment. Foster's decision to stay in Little Rock also reflected a sense of personal obligation to stay in Arkansas and do something to better the state. While hardly worldly or well-traveled, Foster seemed embarrassed by the legacy of governors like Orval Faubus, and Arkansas's enduring reputation as an opponent of desegregation and a state that perennially ranked last or near-last in measures of well-being like per capita income and public education standards. A college friend of Foster's recalls him arguing that as a bright son of Arkansas he had a duty to return home and help elevate the state. In addition to his legal work, Foster plunged into an array of civic and professional activities, such as various bar associations, but much of his passion seemed reserved for the Arkansas Repertory Theater, where he served as chairman.

Foster's civic-mindedness extended to the Rose firm itself, which he considered an important Arkansas institution, one whose traditions and standards needed to be nurtured and built upon. He led an effort to research the firm's history, trying to get senior partners to record their recollections, and he helped compile a slender pamphlet, *The Rose Firm*. He served on various firm committees, and was the partner in charge of recruiting new lawyers.

When Foster joined the Rose firm, it wasn't divided into formal departments, but Foster had gravitated to the litigation work under Carroll. Not many of Foster's cases ever went to trial; they tended to be settled during or after the discovery process. Foster especially liked appellate work, with its extensive legal research, its careful drafting of briefs, and its carefully orchestrated oral arguments. In contrast to trial work, there are few surprises in appeals: the facts are already determined. There is limited interaction with witnesses and clients. Success turns on the force of arguments that can be carefully rehearsed. Colleagues say that Foster, in particular, left nothing to chance, spending hours practicing his appellate presentations. He'd often rewrite a brief seven or eight times before he was satisfied. His research, as it had been in law school, was legendary. An associate recalls leaving for home one evening after failing to discover a kind of case that Foster was seeking for a legal brief. When she got into her office at nine the next morning, a copy of the case was lying on her desk, compliments of Foster.

Given his skills and experience, Foster was a logical choice to head a newly constituted litigation department. But Giroir recognized that for all his abilities, Foster wasn't very outgoing, and attracted clients mostly by virtue of his reputation. Trying to attract clients is a role with which many lawyers feel uncomfortable, requiring as it does many of the instincts of the real estate salesmen whom Foster disdained. Rainmakers tend to be outgoing, involved in business circles, and, at least in Little Rock, sportsmen and golfers. Foster did not golf. It was a game for which he had little natural aptitude, and rather than risk something at which he didn't excel, he preferred not to play at all. Giroir asked Webster Hubbell to join the litigation team, and Hubbell turned out to have many of those qualities Foster lacked.

Hubbell had joined the firm just two years after Foster. Also a graduate of the University of Arkansas Law School, he hadn't known Foster at the university, and on the surface the two had little in common. Hubbell was big—at six foot five even taller than Foster—burly, a former Razorback offensive lineman, very much in the Arkansas good-old-boy mold. He'd grown up in Little Rock, where his father, a building contractor, had moved the family when Webb was a boy. Hubbell had also attended Boys State, where he'd gotten to know Mack McLarty, and harbored some political ambitions of his own. He was elected to the Little Rock City Board in 1978, and was named Little Rock's mayor the next year, serving a two-year term. (Day-to-day management of the city is in the hands of a professional city manager, and Hubbell remained a Rose partner during these stints in public service.) From the City Board he was named by Clinton to the Arkansas Supreme Court, serving there for a brief six months. Hubbell had ample political and business contacts; he was a Country Club member and a golfer. He seemed a natural for attracting litigation business. And once he started working closely with Foster, he discovered that they got along very well.

In 1977, Herb Rule, a bankruptcy partner, former state legislator, and political supporter and friend of Bill Clinton, had asked Hubbell to interview an intriguing prospect: Hillary Rodham, the wife of the state's newly elected attorney general and a lawyer with impressive credentials in her own right. Rule had begun recruiting Hillary as soon as her husband mentioned to him that they'd be moving to Little Rock and Hillary would be interested in a law firm job. Foster was another booster of Hillary's: he and Hillary had worked together in some matters dealing with the Legal Aid Society. There was mild concern on the part of some of the partners about Hillary's being the spouse of an elected official, both because of possible conflicts of interest and because of the firm's wariness about politics generally. But enthusiasm for Hillary easily carried the day. Giroir had recently handled a merger in Texas with a woman attorney, and he said, "Let's get ourselves a woman, too." Hillary's high visibility and political connections, it went without saying, might also help attract clients.

After arriving at the firm, Hillary did impress the partners, and

she was made a partner by unanimous vote in just two years—
almost as fast as Foster had been—becoming the first woman partner in the firm's history (an earlier woman associate had gone on to
become a federal judge). To ease the concerns about her marriage
to an elected official, Hillary agreed that her share of the firm's
earnings would be reduced by the percentage of revenue generated
by work for state agencies, and she personally would do no work
for state agencies. In practice, however, this was a small sacrifice,
since the Rose firm traditionally preferred private clients, and was
usually only ranked seventh or eighth among firms doing work for
state agencies. Significantly, Hillary wasn't barred from earnings or
from doing work for clients in matters before state agencies—a
large part of the firm's work. These steps assuaged what concerns
there were within the firm.

Giroir assigned her, too, to the new litigation unit. Hillary's
work at Rose, however, seems a curious mix. She took on some
family law matters and domestic issues, mostly on a pro bono basis;
these were issues that had long held her interest but contributed
little to firm profits. She developed an expertise in intellectual property law working for a Little Rock–based computer client, but
demand for such an esoteric area was limited. She took time off to
have Chelsea and also to help her husband campaign. Her ceremo-
nial duties as the state's first lady obviously ate into the time she
could devote to the office. Her feelings about the firm seem somewhat ambiguous: when Nancy Pietrafesa wanted to throw a small
party to celebrate Hillary's partnership, she flatly refused. It isn't
clear what, if any, lure Hillary was for clients attracted by her
connection to the governor, but it can't have been much, since she
was consistently the lowest-paid partner in the firm. Had she been
generating more clients, that would have been reflected in her partnership draw. It seems that she hadn't made all that much of an
impression on at least some of her fellow partners. Jim Blair was
working on a case with a Rose senior partner, whom he compli-
mented for having Hillary Rodham as a partner at the firm. "She's
a good lawyer," the Rose partner replied. "I just wish she wasn't
involved in politics and I wish she wasn't married to Jim Guy
Tucker." Blair didn't bother to correct him.

As the core of a new department, Hillary, Foster, and Hubbell
became close colleagues and friends. This may have been in large
part due to circumstance and proximity; Hillary's first office was

directly across the hall from Webb's, and she later moved into
an office adjacent to Vince's. The Rose firm had always operated
collegially, beginning most days with a meeting where partners
spoke briefly about their work and plans. But now meetings were
by department, which in litigation meant essentially Vince, Webb,
and Hillary. Building the fledgling department took constant attention, and there was always something to talk about. When they
were at the firm and not otherwise involved with clients, Webb,
Vince, and Hillary tended to have lunch together—so often that
Webb's wife, Susie, and Lisa Foster got calls intimating the possibility of an affair between their husbands and Hillary. Foster and
Hubbell laughed off such rumors, deeming them the inevitable
result of women joining the profession.

The three became professionally and personally close, especially by the standards of the Rose firm. Hubbell and Foster had
never really dealt with a woman like Hillary, so different from
their own wives. She was smart, forceful, and articulate. She was
analytical and decisive, Foster was methodical and judicious, so they
complemented each other. Hubbell was their emissary to greater
Little Rock. The Rose firm, self-consciously proud of its reputation, was a stuffy place that in its concern for appearances of propriety hadn't changed since Williamson's heyday; Hillary was a breath
of fresh air. As she exclaimed once after taking on a pro bono case
involving sexual assault, "How in the world am I going to handle
this case around here where I can't even use the word 'penis' in
public?"

Colleagues describe Foster, with his good judgment and discretion, as the kind of person Hillary and others at the firm could
confide in. People at the Rose firm noticed how close Vince and
Hillary were becoming; when they mentioned something to Foster,
he'd reply, "I was talking to Hillary about that . . ." and when they
brought something up to Hillary, she'd say, "I was discussing that
with Vince . . ." They could practically finish each other's sentences.
At firm outings, held in places like Eden Isle and Hot Springs
beginning in 1978, Vince and Hillary were often together while the
others played golf, though the two usually joined in the volleyball
tournament, and Hillary, a Cubs fan, played softball.

No one saw anything untoward in this. It's not possible to
prove that Foster and Hillary never had an affair, but no one among
their closest friends believes it, emphasizing that even if both had

wanted such a relationship, neither would have acted on it. Indeed, given their personalities, the possibility seems almost ludicrous. Foster never joked about other women, flirted, or repeated even mildly off-color stories. As the occasional object of an even slightly flirtatious remark, Foster would blush and brush it aside. Socially, Vince and Lisa were part of a group of Country Club members that gave formal, multicourse dinner parties, invariably cooked by the wives. Vince was a wine aficionado who carefully chose the correct wines for each course. His idea of leisure was sitting around the pool in his backyard reading legal briefs and research. He took his kids to soccer games and made videos of them. Given his emphasis on propriety and reputation, it seems Foster would never have risked an intraoffice affair and the accompanying gossip, let alone one with the state's first lady. As for Hillary, however fond she was of Foster, she never expressed anything beyond friendship and professional respect. Emotionally, Foster must have seemed the opposite of her husband, in ways she may have found reassuring and comforting. But for all his admirable qualities, Foster was simply not the kind of man to inspire romantic passion in most women. As one woman who knew him well put it, "Vince was just born middle-aged."

In that regard, too, Hillary and Vince may have felt a rapport. Clinton had once described Hillary in much the same way. During family counseling triggered by his half-brother's arrest for dealing in cocaine, the therapist mentioned that each person is born a certain age. Clinton replied, "I was born at sixteen and I'll always feel I'm sixteen. And Hillary was born at age forty."

Foster, Hubbell, and Hillary didn't generate all that much business for the litigation department. The firm's litigation practice remained pretty much the same as it had before the group was started—referrals from the firm's existing corporate clients. The high-profile environmental, antitrust, and tax litigation that was flourishing in places like Los Angeles and New York simply wasn't showing up in Arkansas yet. And that was reflected in the Rose firm's compensation structure: as Giroir's own pay soared into the $500,000 range, Carroll, still the litigation head, was taking home $160,000, and the others less. The litigation triumvirate complained to Giroir about the inequity of the pay. Indeed, mirroring Hillary's ongoing efforts to boost her income, the partners formed their own investment pool, each contributing $5,000 to a fund to

invest in stocks. They also complained that the litigation department lacked a "book"—Rose parlance for the kind of regular business generated by corporate clients, with their predictable,
recurring needs for debt offerings and tax returns. Litigation tended
to come and go, which required constant hustling for new clients.
And when they did land clients, their fees were limited to hourly
rates, unlike corporate, which often charged by transaction or per-
centages of the money involved. While these views were more often
conveyed to Giroir by Foster, Hillary seemed to some partners to
be the intellectual force behind them.

Giroir acknowledged that they made some reasonable points,
but he had no intention of embroiling the firm in an inevitably
controversial change in the firm's compensation system. Backed by
the paternalistic wisdom of years of practice, delivered with the
polished diplomatic charm that had made him so effective as the
firm's leader, Giroir counseled patience, arguing that their day
would come, although not as soon as they had initially predicted.
He never told them, in so many words, that the solution was for
them to generate more litigation clients. But under the firm's compensation system, that was the only alternative. The litigation partners may have been muted in expressing their displeasure to Giroir,
but inwardly they seethed.

Given the firm's emphasis on generating new business, and
Madison's increasing visibility, it's not surprising that Rose lawyers
eyed it as a potential client. Rose hadn't done any work for McDougal since the ill-fated 1981 suit involving Madison Bank and Trust,
when McDougal had been so annoyed that he refused to pay Rose's
bill. Hillary thought a direct appeal to McDougal would work,
which prompted a 1983 letter from Giroir himself: "Pursuant to
your discussion with Hillary Rodham Clinton, I am enclosing here-
with a copy of our firm statement, dated December 23, 1981, covering services rendered. . . ."*

---

* Despite the letter from Giroir, the accompanying statement cannot, in fact, have been a
copy of the December 1981 invoice. Though the document is dated December 23, 1981, it
refers to "legal services and professional advice" rendered "subsequent to our billing dated
December 23, 1981 through May 15, 1982," and refers further to costs advanced
"through July 31, 1982." A line across the copy suggests that an updated statement may
have been pasted onto the original December invoice. Rose firm managing partner Ron
Clark said he has no explanation for the anomaly.

Though Hillary herself hadn't worked on the 1981 matter—Vince Foster was the partner in charge—the letter indicates she tried to collect the $5,893 account receivable. Despite Hillary's ties to the McDougals, the effort hadn't resulted in any payment.

Despite this, Richard Massey, an associate at the Rose firm who specialized in securities law, and a corporate partner at Rose, David Knight, had had lunch in the spring of 1985 with John Latham, whom McDougal had hired as Madison Guaranty's chief executive officer, hoping to land Madison business. Latham was a certified public accountant who'd worked for the Arkansas Public Services Commission before deciding to go to law school; Knight was one of his professors; and Massey had functioned as a teaching assistant in the same class. Latham often sought him out after class for free legal advice. Latham was just thirty, still a student with no banking experience, when McDougal met him through an executive recruiter and hired him to run Madison Guaranty in 1984. But the lunch proved fruitless: Latham said Madison already had outside counsel—McDougal's friend Jim Guy Tucker, now in private practice—and didn't plan to hire others. Knight may have written Latham a follow-up letter, but otherwise gave up on Madison.

But there was another route to McDougal: Hillary. The previous August, one particularly hot morning, Bill had dropped in on McDougal during one of his jogging sessions, and conversation had shifted to Hillary and her situation at the Rose firm. Hillary had been complaining to her husband that she was under pressure from her partners to generate more business, which was hard for her because she had so many duties as the state's first lady. Hillary had been griping about this, which was getting on his nerves, he told McDougal.

During this conversation, the fastidious McDougal noted with mounting distaste that the governor, drenched from his short run over to the office, was dripping sweat all over the chair. It was a new chair, in light blue leather, that Susan had just given him as a birthday present. McDougal had been suffering from lower back pain, and the chair was orthopedically designed to support his back.

"If we send some business to the Rose firm, will that help Hillary?" McDougal asked, wondering what else he could say to get Clinton moving before his sweat did any more damage to the upholstery.

"Yes," Clinton replied.

McDougal rose at that point, as did Clinton, and McDougal gently steered him out of the office. Susan's brother Bill Henley was standing nearby. With the governor safely out of earshot, McDougal turned to Henley. "I don't mind the fat little son of a bitch coming by and taking up my time. I just wish he wouldn't ruin my chair."

Soon after Clinton's visit, Jim mentioned to Susan that "Bill was here, and Hillary seems to be having problems. She doesn't get along well with people, you know. She's a Yankee. Let's send her some of the S&L business."

Rose records don't indicate any Madison Guaranty payments in the immediate months after the meeting between McDougal and the governor, but the following spring, Hillary scheduled a visit with McDougal, arriving late in the morning of April 23. After his experience in the governor's office, McDougal wasn't nearly as enamored of Hillary as he had once been, but they were still cordial. After some pleasantries, Hillary mentioned that her husband had suggested she stop by. "Fine," McDougal said. Honoring his commitment made earlier to Bill, he said, "I'm sending you some work."*

Some Rose partners were evidently still miffed about McDougal's earlier failure to pay the firm's bill, so Hillary suggested Madison Guaranty pay the firm a monthly retainer. McDougal seemed surprisingly amenable. "Two thousand a month should cover it," he suggested, and Hillary agreed. The details he'd leave to Latham, McDougal added, though he assumed Hillary would be the partner in charge and would get credit within the firm for the business. As he saw it, the whole matter was a favor to the governor. He remarked to Susan that "One lawyer's as good as another, so we might as well help Hillary." McDougal didn't know what, exactly, Hillary would be doing for Madison. He was only vaguely aware of Latham's plan to raise capital through a preferred stock offering. "I'm not interested in those paper machinations," he said.

---

* Clinton has denied visiting McDougal and asking that he send business to the Rose firm to help Hillary. But it seems almost certain that some such visit did take place. McDougal insists he was solicited by the governor, and Henley, who was present outside the office during the visit, remembers the incident and McDougal's remark when Clinton left. In repeated interviews, McDougal has insisted that he began paying a retainer to the Rose firm shortly after that meeting, but available firm records indicate no payments until the following spring.

The turn of events came as a surprise to Massey, the Rose associate who ended up doing most of the work. Latham called Massey shortly after to discuss the stock offering. It was the first Massey knew of Madison Guaranty's having become a client.*

McDougal's bravura in tossing a $2,000-a-month retainer to the Rose firm and hosting a fund-raiser for the governor, both in April 1985, in fact masked a growing sense of desperation on both his part and Susan's. As long as McDougal could expand deposits at Madison Guaranty and borrow from the S&L to cover his own cash needs, the ever-growing demands of his debt burden could be satisfied. But should any aspect of his ability to borrow be jeopardized, what was essentially a real estate version of a Ponzi scheme would come crashing down. As it was, it was a strain having to constantly shuffle funds from one account to another in stopgap efforts to prevent overdrafts in accounts for developments that

---

The precise circumstances of Hillary's retainer by McDougal are much disputed. In response to a written interrogatory in the Resolution Trust Corporation's investigation of Madison, Hillary Clinton testified:

"To the best of my recollection, the president of Madison Guaranty, John Latham, who was a friend of an associate at the Rose Law Firm, Richard Massey, became interested in having Madison Guaranty issue some kind of preferred stock to raise capital. Latham had spoken to Massey about doing the related legal work. In the spring of 1985, Massey came to see me because he had learned that certain lawyers at the law firm were opposed to doing any more legal work for Jim McDougal or any of his companies until he paid his bill and then only if Madison Guaranty agreed to prepay a certain sum to the firm once a month to cover fees and expenses. Under such an arrangement, the firm could be assured that Madison Guaranty was staying current with regard to paying for the new work that the firm might do for it.

"I believe Massey approached me about presenting this proposal to Jim McDougal because he was aware that I knew him. I agreed to go see McDougal. I visited him at his office on April 23, 1985. . . ."

That version, however, is contradicted by every other firsthand participant. Massey denies that he had anything to do with procuring the business, and says he got involved only after Hillary met with McDougal and he received a call from Latham. He says he was never aware of any concern on the part of firm partners about McDougal's earlier bill and that he didn't ask Hillary to approach McDougal about it.

McDougal recalls nothing about any Rose concern about his earlier failure to pay or their need for a retainer, recalling that he offered the retainer to help Hillary. It defies common sense that Hillary would have shown up at his office purely by coincidence. Surely the governor did suggest she drop by, as McDougal recalls her saying. Moreover, it is hard to understand why Hillary, a litigator, would have been the billing partner on a securities matter, as opposed to Latham's friend David Knight, a securities lawyer, unless the retainer was initiated by McDougal as a favor to the Clintons. As will be seen, the manner in which this incident became public lends further credence to McDougal's recollection.

weren't generating enough cash to make their interest payments, let alone any reduction of principal.

There were also signs that McDougal was growing disenchanted with his foray into banking. One day, McDougal had lunch with Pat Harris, another young man in whom he had shown a paternal interest. Harris had worked for McDougal in his 1982 congressional campaign, and then McDougal had hired him to work at Madison Guaranty and sent him to real estate school. At lunch, McDougal seemed uncharacteristically wistful and nostalgic, saying he just wanted to buy and cut up parcels of land, that he'd "get out of the savings and loan" and "get back to the good old days of just buying real estate and selling it," doing it "the old way we used to do it before we got involved in Madison." About the same time, Susan noticed that Jim occasionally seemed withdrawn, silent, moody; that he would sit in a chair staring silently into space. But then he'd snap out of it, and the essential optimism of the real estate entrepreneur would reassert itself. Success was always just around the corner: interest rates would decline, lot and home sales would pick up, buyers would make their installment payments, and the debt could be retired with plenty of cash left over for new ventures.

As financial demands on the McDougals continued to increase, a dreaded event occurred: the Federal Home Loan Bank Board, the S&L equivalent of the FDIC, launched an investigation of Madison Guaranty, the first since it had been acquired by McDougal. McDougal and Madison's board members received the FHLBB's report in June 1984, and it was reminiscent of the FDIC's scathing report on Madison Bank. It cited another litany of bad banking practices: poor appraisal practices, loan documentation problems, loans to affiliates, too much concentration in real estate development, loans to borrowers without any equity, excessive reliance on brokered deposits, and questionable accounting practices. In the latter regard, it specifically faulted Madison for recognizing over $560,000 in unrealized gains, requiring an adjustment that would have wiped out the institution's entire net worth. As the confidential report summary concluded in no uncertain terms:

"The viability of the institution is jeopardized through the institution's current investment and lending practices in real estate development projects.

"There is a concentration of assets and loans in land and development type properties. Prudent investment practices have not been utilized in development projects and poor loan underwriting is characteristic on loans originated. These long-term investments and loans have been funded with short-term brokered deposits.

"Substantial profits from the service corporation on the sale of the real estate owned have been improperly recognized. Such profits were recognized as a result of contract sales and submarket interest rates. Correcting entries will adversely affect net worth and result in an insolvent position."

A month later, Madison had to agree to a cease-and-desist order that specifically prevented Madison Guaranty from, among other things, making loans to the McDougals and entities they controlled. At Madison Bank, a similar provision had brought such lending to a halt; indeed, it had helped prompt the search for a new source of funds that resulted in the purchase of Madison Guaranty. Now the McDougals had nowhere else to turn. With demands for various principal and interest payments continuing to mount, in February 1985 the McDougals borrowed an additional $360,000 from Madison Guaranty, in defiance of the cease-and-desist order. Moreover, their loan application stated that the use of the loan proceeds would be to "remodel"—precisely what was going to be remodeled and to what extent remained unexplained. Instead, nearly all the money was used almost immediately to pay off other loans, leaving the McDougals with less than $70,000 in their Madison Guaranty account just two months before the fund-raiser and Madison's retainer agreement with Hillary.

While McDougal scrambled to prop up his own debt-mired empire, he left it to Latham to salvage Madison Guaranty. As part of its cease-and-desist order, the FHLBB required Madison to raise additional capital to meet minimum capital standards. Obviously, every lending institution needs a capital base to provide for withdrawals by depositors and payments of interest; once Madison's books were restated to comply with FHLBB requirements it was woefully short. The options were limited: the McDougals themselves clearly couldn't commit more capital or borrow elsewhere. Madison needed new investors, a prospect McDougal didn't really want to face, because it would have, at the least, diluted his control. Nonetheless, Latham began to explore the possibility of an offering to investors of preferred stock. Such stock would have limited voting control, but would still be considered equity, and thus capital, Latham reasoned.

It wasn't at all clear how Madison would find the investors for such a stock issue, or even whether savings and loans were authorized under Arkansas law to issue such securities. For that, Madison needed the approval of the Arkansas Securities Department, where it was already seeking approval to buy and sell securities as a brokerage. Unlike many larger states, in Arkansas the jobs of regulating securities and savings and loans were lodged in the same office, presided over by the securities commissioner and savings and loan supervisor. Despite the broad scope of its activities, it was a relatively sleepy, low-profile office. There were only two full-time staff members assigned to overseeing S&Ls, and they tended to get involved in something only if their attention was called to it by the FHLBB. There was only one lawyer on the staff.

The commissioner since 1985 was Beverly Bassett, appointed to the post by Governor Clinton. Among the nation's securities commissioners, Bassett was an anomaly: a young woman, attractive, with flowing dark blond hair. Bassett had worked for then–Attorney General Clinton as a second-year law student, and he'd written her a note praising her work. She'd gone on to the Mitchell firm with Jim Guy Tucker, where she focused on banking and securities law. Tucker was doing a lot of work for Madison Guaranty and McDougal at the time, as well as investing in many of McDougal's deals, and Bassett helped on one matter. But she didn't know McDougal, had never even met him or Susan, whom she nonetheless recognized from TV ads. In 1984 Bassett had just made partner but was becoming bored with private practice. When she learned the securities commissioner was resigning, she volunteered for the position. At her interview with Clinton, he did most of the talking, focusing on his concerns about some of the go-go securities firms that had sprung up in Arkansas and how inevitably the next few years would bring some failures. Neither Clinton nor Bassett had any idea that the whole savings and loan industry was about to collapse.

It isn't clear that Bassett was the most qualified person for the post—the Rose firm and most of the Little Rock establishment lobbied for Bob Eubanks, who was named insurance commissioner instead—but Betsey Wright lobbied Clinton to name a woman, and Bassett got the job. There wasn't all that much competition for the post.

After securing the retainer with McDougal on April 23, Hillary and Massey began work on the matter of Madison's preferred stock offering. Hillary had very little experience in securities law, and Massey did nearly all the research. Rose's billing records indicate that during 1985 Hillary billed less than $1,500 against the Madison retainer; Massey's billings were considerably more. Massey, with Hillary's concurrence, concluded that under Arkansas law a savings and loan had the authority of any corporation to issue preferred stock. Hillary called Bassett on April 29 and mentioned that she'd be sending her a letter. It arrived at the Securities Department the next day. It concluded, "should you require further information or assistance, please advise Hillary Rodham Clinton or Richard Massey of this firm." It was signed collectively by "the Rose firm."

That the name of the governor's wife appeared in the letter made no particular impression on Bassett, who knew nothing of any connection between McDougal and the Clintons. In any event, the Rose firm's position was not especially controversial, though it was apparently a matter of first impression in Arkansas. Although the staff attorney disagreed with the Rose position, Charles Handley, Bassett's top assistant, told her that he found nothing to contradict the Rose firm's position. After all, they weren't yet being asked to approve a specific securities offering—disclosure materials would still have to be submitted to them for review—nor were they asked to approve the wisdom of such a course. Accordingly, Bassett replied two weeks later that "as the Savings and Loan Supervisor, I concur in your opinion that Madison's proposed capitalization plan is not inconsistent with Arkansas law."

That hardly cleared the way for the preferred stock offering, however. One of the reasons Madison was simultaneously seeking approval to acquire a brokerage business was so that it could market the preferred stock. Charles Handley, in particular, aware of the capital weakness at Madison, was reluctant to allow it into yet another potentially speculative business. Just several days after Bassett's letter, Handley sent Massey and Hillary a memorandum withholding approval to engage in brokerage activities, insisting,

among other requirements, that Madison meet the FHLBB minimum capital requirements. This put Madison in a difficult position,
since the whole point of the preferred stock offering was to raise
capital to the level demanded by federal regulators, and it couldn't
issue the stock without approval to engage in brokerage activities.
Despite a flurry of memos and meetings between Handley, Bassett,
and Massey (Hillary apparently remained minimally involved), Bassett remained firm on this point. In her final communication to the
Rose firm on the matter, in October 1985, she noted that brokerage
approval was "conditioned on Madison's meeting the Federal
Home Loan Bank Board's minimum net worth requirement by
December 31, 1985. Please keep us informed as to the progress of
Madison's efforts to achieve such compliance."

Had Madison really wanted to issue preferred stock, or had any
realistic chance of successfully marketing it, it could have turned to
another brokerage firm, like Stephens. But Madison wasn't about to
allow outsiders into its financial records. McDougal, in any event,
professed to be unconcerned, and vetoed the whole idea of preferred stock, which he said he'd never approved to begin with.
Bassett's deadline came and went, Madison's capital continued to
deteriorate, and the Rose effort ended in failure.

Though hardly the largest of the McDougals' headaches, in
microcosm the Whitewater venture illustrated all the major trends
troubling the McDougal empire. In 1983, no new lots had been
sold. Because of all the interest payments, negative cash flow that
year was nearly $51,000, all of it covered either by new borrowing
or payments from McDougal or his various ventures. One lot was
sold in 1984. Negative cash flow was over $20,000, all of it covered
by McDougal. With more interest and principal payments due,
1985 was even worse. Only one lot was sold. Negative cash flow
was over $75,000, requiring even more payments from McDougal.
At about the same time he was retaining Hillary and the Rose
firm, in April 1985, McDougal had Madison Financial, the S&L's
investment subsidiary, pay him a "bonus" of $30,000, payable to
Whitewater, according to minutes of a Madison board meeting.
The money was deposited directly in the Whitewater account, the
one instance where money went directly from Madison into
Whitewater. The Clintons weren't asked for, nor did they make,
any payments during these years.

McDougal recognized that this couldn't continue. In May 1985 he called Chris Wade, the Whitewater broker who already had bought and sold Lot 7. "I'm tired of messing with this," an uncharacteristically sober McDougal told him. He said he wanted to sell Wade all the unsold lots, none of them with river frontage, that had been carried on the books as inventory worth nearly $200,000. "Give me $70,000 or $75,000," McDougal pleaded.

Wade said he didn't have the money, but he smelled a distress sale and a deal. He happened to have a 1979 Piper Seminole airplane, which he and a partner had bought for a contemplated charter aircraft service. That venture, Ozark Air Service, had never proven profitable in an area as remote as Flippin, and Wade was looking to sell the aircraft, which he valued at $35,000. He offered McDougal the airplane and agreed that Ozark Air would assume $35,000 of Whitewater's debt to Citizens Bank in return for the unsold lots. McDougal agreed. He took the plane, and Wade began making at least some payments on the bank debt. (The bank itself, however, did not release either the McDougals or the Clintons from liability for the full amount of the loan.)

Whitewater's land was now all sold, for vastly less than had been anticipated. Its only assets were the payments due from the installment purchasers. There could never be a profit. Its remaining assets were worth far less than the outstanding debt, which meant it was insolvent. Still, with the last infusion of cash from McDougal to reduce the principal of the Citizens Bank loan and the assumption of $35,000 by Wade's company, the payments from the lot buyers should, in the future, cover the debt service, easing the drain on McDougal.

In September that year, Rosalee Wade, Chris's wife, who handled most of the bookkeeping at Ozarks Realty, had gotten the bill for the Marion County property taxes on the Whitewater property, due October 10. As usual, she had made the tax payments for the Clintons and McDougals, then was reimbursed by Jim McDougal. As with most aspects of the investment, the Clintons expected the McDougals to handle all such details. But Rosalee Wade had grown tired of the delays and repeated calls and letters it had been taking to get the payment. This year she decided they could pay the taxes themselves, and simply forwarded the bill, care of the McDougals, with a note reminding them that they should pay on time. Nonetheless, she wasn't surprised when the local paper, the *Yellville Mountain Echo*, published a list of delinquent taxpayers on November 14, 1985, and she saw the name of Whitewater Development Corp. The tax bill and her note had either been overlooked or ignored.

Flippin is the kind of town where just about everybody reads the list of delinquent taxpayers with a kind of morbid fascination. With the bank officers and people at Ozarks Realty well aware that Clinton was a partner in Whitewater, gossip soon spread that the governor hadn't paid his taxes, just a few months before the 1986 primary campaign would be heating up and just after *U.S. News & World Report* had cited Clinton as an up-and-coming national leader. (A later revelation that movie star Burt Reynolds was delinquent in paying taxes on some property bordering Bull Shoals Lake, just north of Flippin, set off an even bigger stir.)

Soon after the *Mountain Echo* story, Jim and Susan were in McDougal's office at Madison when Bill Clinton called. McDougal's secretary put him on the speaker phone. The governor sounded upset, wanting to know what was going on with Whitewater. Despite the venture's worsening financial straits, Jim tried to reassure him: "I've got my plate full and I know you do, too," he began. Clinton interrupted.

"My name is in the Marion County paper for overdue taxes!" Clinton complained. "You know that's political suicide. Hillary is mad as hell. This cannot happen."

Jim and Susan were taken aback. They were admittedly lax about such tax matters themselves, but they had an employee whose job was to make sure taxes on the developments got paid on time. But whatever the reason for the delinquency, in Clinton's anger McDougal saw a glimmer of opportunity. Perhaps he could extricate the Clintons from the deal while still saving face. "Let's just get you out of this," McDougal suggested. Whitewater will "break even," McDougal euphemistically said, but that was the best that could be hoped for. Bill and Hillary could simply sign over their interest to the McDougals, who would in turn assume the remaining liabilities and obligations.

"Fine with me," Clinton replied, sounding relieved. McDougal said he'd do the paperwork. "Just run it by Hillary, would you?" Clinton asked.

Then and there, McDougal had his secretary get a blank stock transfer certificate. He filled it out, and McDougal told Susan to take it over to Hillary so she could review and sign it. That afternoon, Susan dropped in at the Rose firm. She was in buoyant spirits, relieved that she and her husband could stop worrying about the Clintons. She breezed through the corridors, smiling and greeting lawyers and secretaries with her characteristic "Hi, guys."

She sat down across from Hillary at her desk, thinking how she might brighten up the office if it was hers, as Hillary read the proposed transfer of ownership. "What is this?" Hillary demanded, her tone cold. Susan's smile froze.

"It's just a stock certificate," Susan said, still trying to be cheerful. "Jim says you're going to get out of Whitewater. Jim talked to Bill. I know you don't want this to become a campaign issue. This is strictly for your and Bill's protection. You and Bill just sign it—"

"No!" Hillary angrily interrupted. Looking intently at Susan, she rose and leaned over her desk. "Jim told me that this was going to pay for college for Chelsea. I still expect it to do that!"

Susan was stunned. Obviously Bill hadn't told Hillary anything. And why was Hillary treating her like this? They were supposed to be friends. She laughed nervously, trying to lighten the mood. "You have a problem? Well, okay, no big deal." Susan took back the paper, rose stiffly and went straight back to Jim's office.

"There are problems," she said ominously. "Bill didn't tell Hillary."

McDougal was beside himself. "All these years of our paying for them. We paid the bills, Bill blasted us over the property taxes, and now Hillary is annoyed with me?" He shrugged. "Well, fuck them."

FIVE

FOR SUSAN MCDOUGAL, the honeymoon was over. She was no longer the innocent country girl. For years she'd done whatever McDougal told her, writing checks, keeping accounts, selling properties, remodeling the headquarters and their houses, working all the time. She laughingly referred to herself as Jim's "yes-girl." It had been exciting; she'd met people, been places; it had seemed like a big party.

But in the last few years, even Susan could see what was happening financially. The constant new loans, the shuffling of money. She owned nearly half the stock in Madison Guaranty; it represented her future, and she felt she had to assert herself more. She gently tried putting the brakes on some of Jim's extravagant gestures, like paying to fly in potential investors and opening elaborate field offices for new developments. John Latham, the young chief executive brought in by McDougal, had actually read the regulations governing federally insured savings and loans, and he and Susan began to worry about some of McDougal's tendencies. He seemed recklessly willing to lend to just about any real estate developer who walked through the door, as long as they were Madison Financial projects. "You can't do this with a federally insured institution," she argued to Jim. Such comments infuriated him, but Latham did get McDougal to agree to hire an experienced savings and loan executive, a former FHLBB investigator.

For all McDougal's professed admiration of smart, independent women, as soon as Susan began to assert herself, the marriage deteriorated. "You're such a downer," McDougal would complain as they drove home from the office. "You're a drag." Over the years, their relationship had evolved into more of a friendship than a romance, but they had stayed close. But now he told her she was awful to live with.

Susan was increasingly miserable. She had to be the "downer"—everyone else was afraid to contradict Jim. They'd come to her, telling her he had to be stopped, a decision had to be changed, and then it was up to her to confront her husband. She was becoming increasingly angry that it was always her burden, that no one else would say no. Increasingly, McDougal was avoiding her at the office, freezing her out of decisions. Latham had stepped in for a while, but now he was being shunned as her ally. They were both shut out once McDougal hired Seth Ward, Webb Hubbell's father-in-law and a locally prominent businessman. Among other things, Ward was on the board of the Little Rock airport, one of Hillary's clients at the Rose firm. Hillary appeared exasperated by many of Ward's ideas at board meetings. McDougal hoped Ward would attract other wealthy clients to Madison.

Professionally, McDougal was also becoming more erratic. He arranged a meeting with Governor Clinton and officials of the Arkansas Department of Health after several run-ins with department officials over sewage at his various real estate developments. Clinton was determined to mollify McDougal; he introduced him as "my friend of twenty years who has never asked me for a favor." Going beyond his usual hyperbole, McDougal accused department officials of "duplicity and trickery" in their dealings with him and singled out one official as "not sane, not qualified, not stable and psychotic." (A subsequent memo from his staff to Clinton said that the three people attacked by McDougal in the meeting had been "removed from those jobs.")

At home, the periods where McDougal seemed silent and withdrawn began occurring more frequently. In the past, he'd always arisen early, full of ideas and energy. Now he lingered in bed. He would sit silent and motionless in a chair. It was all Susan could do to get him to the office. Once there, he yelled and argued with her whenever she questioned his decisions, usually in full hearing of the staff. He would often work himself into a frenzy but then, in midafternoon, would abruptly leave for the day. When Susan later searched Jim's bedside table and drawers, she discovered bottle after bottle of prescription antidepressants.

With her husband obviously in worse shape than she'd suspected, and as her world seemed about to cave in around her, Susan felt it was up to her alone to salvage what she could. Schooled by McDougal, she thought that she could stave off the creditors by pulling off one more successful development. She felt she could complete sales in her Flowerwood Farms project, located about ten miles west of Little Rock, if she could get the money to finish improving the property with sewer and water service. In addition, for some time she and Jim had been eyeing a large tract south of Little Rock owned by International Paper Co. The idea was to divide the land and market the lots for mobile homes to a lower-income segment of the population, especially senior citizens. It was a big project—International Paper wanted more than $550,000— but on paper, the potential returns were high. In typical fashion, Jim had gone ahead just a few weeks earlier, in March 1986, and signed a contract with International Paper to buy the property.

Susan envisioned another television campaign like the one that had been so successful for Maple Creek Farms. But where were they going to raise the purchase price? Another loan from Madison Guaranty was no longer an option: the FHLBB had begun another investigation of the institution that same month, in part to see whether Madison was honoring the earlier cease-and-desist order, and examiners from the board had actually moved into Jim's office. Jim had moved to an office at his Castle Grande development. Just two days before the examiners arrived, Latham, the CEO, presumably at McDougal's behest, ordered that any reference to McDougal's bonus and Whitewater be deleted from the April 1985 minutes of the board meeting. (Despite a note to that effect, the minutes weren't altered.)

One evening, Jim and Susan were having dinner at the Black-Eyed Pea, the same restaurant where Whitewater had been spawned, when David Hale dropped in. McDougal had known Hale for years through their involvement in the Democratic party. Hale was a figure of some note in Little Rock. A lawyer, he'd been a state prosecutor for four years and had gone on to be national president of the Jaycees, a member of the U.S. Bicentennial Commission and the U.S. Council on Inflation. Short, pudgy, retiring, and soft-spoken, Hale was a devout Baptist whose father had been a poor farmer.

More recently, Hale had joined with cartoonist Al Capp to launch a theme park, Dog Patch, U.S.A., in the Ozark Mountains. It featured such figures as Li'l Abner and Shmoo and a hillbilly motif. While pursuing this and various other business activities, Hale was now a municipal court judge, appointed by Governor Clinton. Of more interest to the McDougals was his lending operation, Capital Management Services, Inc., which was licensed by the Small Business Administration in Washington to invest in disadvantaged small businesses. Susan had earlier been talking to Jim Guy Tucker about her financial plight and need to borrow money for the International Paper project, and he'd suggested she see Hale.

The idea probably wouldn't have occurred to Susan. She knew next to nothing about the SBA, and she'd never thought of herself as particularly disadvantaged. But since she was a woman, she might very well qualify, especially if she set up her own business entity. Susan had been contemplating opening her own advertising business, drawing on her experience in real estate sales.

At the restaurant that evening, Jim mentioned this, and Hale indicated he'd have no problem making a loan to Susan. Hale tended to take an extremely broad view of "disadvantaged." It was true that Congress had been vague in defining what disadvantaged meant, though the statute finally passed mentions "low income, limited education, or participation in the Armed Forces during the Vietnam era." Hale took that a step further. As he later told SBA examiners, "Arkansas is the poorest state in the United States with almost one-half of its area included in the Delta Development Region created by the United States Congress. This area has been determined by the Congress to be economically depressed in comparison with that of the Third World Countries," so *anyone* living in Arkansas was disadvantaged, Hale concluded.

The encounter gave Jim a glimmer of his old excitement. Jim and Susan went home that very evening and typed up a one-page proposal to borrow $300,000. Neither had any idea what was required for such a loan. "Does this look okay?" Jim asked. Susan signed it. It contained a generous estimate of $2.2 million as their net worth.

After playing tennis the next day, Susan took the letter into

Hale's office, dropping it off with his secretary. About a week later, on April 3, 1986, Hale called Susan. "The papers are ready. You can pick up your check." Susan could hardly believe she was getting the money this fast, with no further questions about her assets or how the money would be used. She hurried over to Hale's office and signed the documents. Despite an explicit SBA requirement that each such loan be accompanied by a verification that the borrower is economically or socially disadvantaged, Susan's papers contained only a boilerplate paragraph that Hale used for all his borrowers:

"The owner of the herein SBC [small business concern] because of her economic background and the social and economic system which [sic] she works has prevented her from obtaining financial and other assistance available to the average entrepreneur in the economic mainstream." Despite the large estimate of her worth, not to mention the extensive loans she and Jim had already obtained elsewhere, Susan signed the statement.

Hale handed over the check, made out to "Susan McDougal d/b/a Master Marketing." The loan was at an interest rate of 12 percent, with the first interest payment of $36,000 due a year later. "Can I come back again tomorrow?" she asked, teasingly. "This is too easy."

"These SBC's are gold," Hale confided.*

Whatever Susan's stated plans for the money, the money was simply deposited into the McDougals' joint checking account at Madison Guaranty, of which $25,000 was used almost immediately as a down payment on the International Paper property. Other amounts were used to stave off other lenders and creditors. Some did go to improvements in the Flowerwood Farms development. But "Master Marketing" seems to have existed only on Susan's loan application; it never even had a checking account.

The reprieve offered by the SBA loan was brief. Jim plunged back into depression and his quarrels with Susan continued. "Arguing is tearing us apart," McDougal finally told her. "We need a

---

* Exactly what representations Susan made to obtain the loan remains a subject of controversy, since two contradictory documents surfaced in Hale's files. One application is for Susan's "Master Marketing," which was supposed to be an advertising agency. The other, marked "confidential," indicated that the money would be used for the International Paper land and Flowerwood Farms.

break." Soon after, she arrived home to discover that Jim had packed most of her things into boxes. "These are your things," he said, indicating the boxes. "I'll help you pack them into the car. Why don't you take a trip."

Susan was dazed, but she realized that Jim couldn't wait to get her out of town. So she let him help her pack the car, and then she set out for Dallas. She knew no one there, but it was the nearest city of any size. It was a relief to get away. She spent the next four months at a condominium she leased there, holed up, talking to no one, working on her tan. She thought the separation would be temporary, but when she returned, she realized the marriage was over. She was no longer the protégé, no longer the ingenue. They agreed that Jim could stay in their apartment; they'd never moved into their newly remodeled home. Susan eventually rented an apartment in the same complex with Gennifer Flowers. The separation was a blow to Susan; she began seeing a psychiatrist at St. Vincent's Hospital for help in coping with being on her own for the first time in her life.

In Susan's absence, the FHLBB examiners had completed their report on Madison Guaranty, and it was prompting a crisis. Madison's board of directors received copies of the report on June 19. It concluded that "management blatantly disregarded numerous regulations," adding that aspects of the 1984 cease-and-desist order had been "ignored." "James McDougal, a major stockholder, with the help of others effectively controls the affairs of the institution and its wholly owned subsidiary. Among other things, this control enabled Mr. McDougal to use corporate resources to develop large land developments. It also enabled him to divert substantial amounts of funds from the projects to himself and others. . . . These developments have been determined to be of questionable economic worth and significant losses are apparent. . . . If recognized, losses associated with these projects could render the institution insolvent."

Just days after the letter arrived, Susan was visiting Jim at their former home when she noticed her husband begin to tremble. He had a seizure, then came to. He suddenly ran outside onto the hot pavement, blacked out, and collapsed. Within moments he'd gone rigid; he lost consciousness. Susan rushed to his side, looking for a pulse, convinced he'd had a heart attack and died. She called the paramedics, then, hysterical, called Jim Guy Tucker. McDougal was taken on a stretcher to Baptist Hospital; he was alive, but clearly had experienced a heart attack. Susan was so hysterical that Tucker took her first to her doctor, then the hospital.

When Susan arrived, the doctors told her that some abnormalities were evident in Jim's blood, and that they'd given him some blood-thinning medication. But they questioned her extensively about Jim's recent health. Susan said he'd been severely depressed, but said he always snapped out of it, often showing more energy and excitement than she did. The doctors called in a consulting psychiatrist, who diagnosed McDougal as manic-depressive. It was a revelation to Susan: much of the energy and drive, the "highs" that had been so much a part of his personality and that made him so appealing, could be attributed to the disorder.

After he'd regained consciousness and begun to feel better, the doctors told McDougal that he suffered from manic-depressive syndrome and should be taking medicine. Jim was furious, vehemently denying that he was manic. He refused to take the medicine, relenting only after several sessions with the psychiatrist.

While still tending to her husband's recovery, Susan tried to focus on the upcoming meeting with the FHLBB examiners. But since her separation from Jim, Madison employees were wary of talking to her. Finally she went to the bank's lawyer, John Selig, Jim Guy Tucker's partner, and said she had to be told what was going on. She and Jim wanted to attend the meeting in Dallas and they needed to be prepared. "Jim is not well," she said. "Please tell me what is going on."

Selig was obviously uncomfortable, saying he represented the board and the institution, not Susan and Jim. He finally said they would not be allowed to attend the meeting. "We have to," she pleaded, arguing they were the only ones who could convince the board that there'd been no "phantom" buyers or "land flips," the most notorious practices common at many Texas S&Ls. Finally Selig called in Tucker to make the point more forcefully. "Susan," Tucker said. "Preliminarily, if they have one thing they can prove Jim did wrong, he should not go to that meeting. There would be repercussions."

"You're making a big mistake," Susan said.

On July 11, Madison Guaranty board members, represented by Selig and one of his law partners, met with FHLBB officials in

Dallas. McDougal himself was in no condition to attend and Susan remained in Little Rock. John Latham was the highest ranking Madison representative. Beverly Bassett attended. Walter Faulk, the FHLBB supervising agent presiding over the meeting, made the case that Madison was insolvent and pressed the directors about operations of Madison Financial and the real estate developments. They acknowledged that they knew little about the subsidiary, and had always simply taken McDougal's word that the real estate developments were profitable. They argued that they thought "things were going well" at Madison Guaranty itself, and that the branches were flourishing, which made no impact on the examiners. The board's lawyer acknowledged that McDougal was willing to step down as chairman, but urged that he be kept on as a paid consultant. "No," Faulk interrupted, showing some anger. "McDougal is going to be out completely." Latham was allowed to stay on only for a two-month transition period. Bassett was silent for most of the meeting, and made no argument on McDougal's behalf.

It fell to Steve Cuffman, a Little Rock lawyer who had been on Madison's board since 1985, to assume the chief executive's responsibilities and break the news to McDougal. Cuffman hand-delivered a letter of resignation drafted by the board to McDougal's home. McDougal had gotten out of the hospital the day before and answered the door in his bathrobe. He read the letter over, and simply said "okay." Cuffman stayed around for about a half hour, and McDougal offered some suggestions about pending matters at the savings and loan. When Cuffman left, McDougal handed him the keys to his beloved light blue Bentley, an asset actually owned by Madison. Cuffman never saw McDougal again.

To Susan, however, McDougal expressed bitterness. When she tried to say how angry she was at their treatment by the board, at how little loyalty they'd been shown, and at how the McDougals were being blamed for everything that went wrong, he cut her off. "Do not discuss it," he ordered. Of Madison Guaranty, he said, "If they close it, fine. I never want to see those people again. I'm never going there again."

Madison Guaranty was hardly the only federally insured savings and loan to fall under government supervision in 1986. Indeed, the Dallas regional office in particular was besieged with failing institutions in its territory, which included all of Texas in addition to Arkansas. Of thirty-six state-chartered savings and loans in Arkansas in 1980, only four were still in business in 1992. By the end of the year, the situation was so dire that the Federal Savings and Loan Insurance Corporation (FSLIC) was itself insolvent, and Congress had to create a whole new regulatory apparatus, the Resolution Trust Corporation, to take over the assets of the failed institutions and try to restore or close them. Failures in the twenty-four states covered by the Kansas City office of the RTC alone eventually cost taxpayers an estimated $42 billion.

The crisis did have a silver lining for some: lawyers, especially litigators, who were hired by first the FSLIC, then the RTC, to pursue claims on behalf of the failed institutions whose assets now belonged to the government. Even a single failed savings and loan could generate dozens of lawsuits, as the government sued real estate developers and other creditors who had defaulted on their loans, instituted foreclosure proceedings, and pursued claims for fraud. As the full force of the S&L crisis began to make itself felt in Arkansas, the opportunity was not lost on the litigators at the Rose firm.

Since their earlier discussions with Giroir, not much had changed for Hillary, Vince, and Webb. Giroir had nominated first Vince, and then Webb to serve under him as the firm's chief administrative officer, but the post carried little real power. The compensation system had been modified slightly, allowing up to 20 percent of a partner's compensation to be based on "intangible" factors, such as board memberships and community service. This helped Hillary, who chaired the Children's Defense Fund and was tapped for several corporate boards, among them Wal-Mart and TCBY, the fast-food yogurt chain. But it hadn't helped litigators overall, and the pressure to generate business was still acute.

Suddenly the S&L crisis seemed like a godsend. In 1985, the FSLIC approached the Rose firm about representing the government agency in litigation involving one of the Arkansas S&Ls it had seized, Guaranty Savings and Loan in Harrison, Arkansas. Depending on how that case turned out, the agency might be interested in retaining the Rose litigators on a regular basis in connection with lawsuits involving failed thrifts. Here, at last, was a client that promised the "book" of business they had envied in the firm's corporate clients. It would be a steady stream of business, eliminating the need for hustling for other clients, and for which the litigators would get credit.

But the three partners were in for a shock when they sought approval from their partners in the firm. On principle, some of them were not interested in representing government agencies based in Washington. The Rose firm prided itself on its Arkansas ties and Arkansas clients. More to the point, many partners didn't like the idea of the Rose firm suing Arkansas institutions on behalf of outsiders. However badly they may have been run, many of the failed S&Ls had financed Rose corporate clients, and their officers and directors were friends of Rose corporate clients. Many of these people were potential targets of litigation as the failed S&Ls tried to recoup losses by suing their borrowers. As one influential corporate partner, Watt Gregory, put it, "Personally, I am not comfortable claiming that someone has committed fraud against my client and then sitting down next to him at the Country Club." Thus, the possibility of representing the FSLIC came to be seen not so much as an opportunity for the litigators, but as a positive threat to the rest of the firm's practice.

While Giroir, as the firm's chief executive, tried to keep above the fray, it was obvious that his sympathies lay with his corporate allies. He seemed cool to the idea of taking on the FSLIC, which angered Hillary, Vince, and Webb. The debate brought to the fore much of what Hillary most disliked about Arkansas: its provincial concern with not making waves, worrying about what people would think at the Country Club, favoring the good old boys at the expense of a national institution engaged in an important rescue mission. She was an articulate, zealous proponent of taking on the FSLIC; she and Webb tended to play the role of "bad cop" to Vince's "good cop." After a series of acrimonious firm meetings, Hillary's views prevailed, at least temporarily. The partnership agreed to let them take on the Harrison case. But the experience left an uncomfortable rift in the firm, even as it strengthened the alliance among Hillary, Vince, and Webb.

There remained some relatively minor housekeeping matters. Before retaining Rose, the FSLIC wanted the firm to certify it was free of any actual or potential conflicts of interest; one of the reasons the FSLIC was attracted to Rose in the first place was that it

was one of the few respected Little Rock firms that didn't have an
S&L practice. This didn't prove any problem in the Harrison case,
but the litigation partners recognized that it might if their relationship with the FSLIC blossomed, as they hoped it would. So they
decided to curtail their work for S&L clients.

Since the 1985 retainer agreement negotiated by Hillary with
Madison Guaranty, the Rose firm had taken on sporadic assign-
ments. Probably the most significant was a 1985 purchase by Madison Financial of a large tract of land destined to become Madison's
Castle Grande real estate development. Among other amenities,
Castle Grande was going to boast its own microbrewery, the only
one in the state, prompting some research by Rose into whether a
brewery could operate in a dry township. But a bigger problem was
that a regulation of the Arkansas savings and loan board prohibited
Madison Financial from buying the entire Castle Grande tract,
because, as a subsidiary of Madison Guaranty, it could hold total
investments of no more than 6 percent of Madison Guaranty's
assets. So Madison assigned the right to purchase part of the property to Seth Ward, Hubbell's father-in-law, for $1.15 million. Madi-
son loaned the entire purchase price to Ward, a loan for which
Ward was not even personally liable. McDougal also promised
Ward that as lots from his land were sold and the proceeds used to
repay the Madison loan, Ward would earn a 10 percent commission
on the sales, whether or not he generated the sales. As Ward later
told the *Arkansas Democrat-Gazette*, "I didn't try to sell anything,
really. Madison sold it all." Still, the sales generated over $300,000
in commissions for Ward. Madison subsequently obtained an option to repurchase 22 acres of the tract from Ward for $400,000,
even though the fair market value, the FHLBB later concluded, was
far less. The Castle Grande acquisition and sales were described in
the FHLBB report on Madison as "a series of flips and fictitious
sales," shams intended to disguise Madison Financial's control of
the parcel.

The Rose firm represented both Madison Guaranty and Seth
Ward in these transactions, with Ward's bills paid by Madison.
According to Rose firm records, Hillary Clinton had fourteen
meetings or conversations about Castle Grande for which she apparently billed Madison, many of these with Seth Ward. The work
apparently included drafting the $400,000 option agreement; one

Rose bill says "telephone conference with Seth Ward regarding option" and "prepare option."*

But now work for Madison had to stop, even though Hillary had also recently begun some additional Madison work, involving a loan participation agreement with a Texas S&L. On July 14, 1986, Hillary had a letter hand-delivered to Madison Guaranty, addressed to McDougal and Latham, who had both been ousted just days before at the meeting in Dallas.

"Dear Jim and John:

"When you requested the Rose firm represent Madison on a specific matter in April, 1985, I advised you that the firm would credit fees against a monthly retainer and then bill for whatever fees might be in excess of the retainer at the end of the month. Since that time, Madison has run a credit in its account at the end of every month."

Noting that Madison "has been relying and continues to rely on a number of other law firms," and that "our representation has been for isolated matters," she wrote that the firm was returning Madison's latest monthly check for $2,000 as well as its account surplus of $4,623.

"We do not believe it appropriate for us to take a prepayment of legal fees when there is only one matter we are representing

---

* The role of Rose firm lawyers, including Hillary Clinton, in the Castle Grande transactions is among the matters being examined by the independent counsel to determine if a fraud was committed and, if so, who was responsible. Mrs. Clinton has strenuously denied wrongdoing and has done everything possible to distance herself from Castle Grande. In response to an RTC interrogatory that mentioned Castle Grande and other McDougal real estate ventures, Hillary Clinton testified, "I don't believe I knew anything about any of these real estate parcels and projects, . . ." Her lawyer, David Kendall, has said that Mrs. Clinton was referring to Castle Grande Estates, a mobile home development within the larger Castle Grande tract, which she didn't work on. In a letter to the Washington Post, Kendall said that Mrs. Clinton worked for two hours on the option agreement, which dealt with a parcel some distance from Castle Grande Estates, and which she knew by the name of the prior owner, the Industrial Development Co. (IDC). He said, "Confusion may be created" by referring to the entire tract as Castle Grande rather than IDC. But nearly everyone involved appears to have routinely referred to the entire tract as Castle Grande, and the RTC interrogatory asked about Castle Grande, not Castle Grande Estates.

In a report dated Dec. 28, 1995, the RTC concluded that the Rose lawyers, including Hillary Clinton, were unaware that the Castle Grande transactions may have been shams intended to circumvent state regulation and disguise payments to Ward. However, the FDIC reopened this aspect of the RTC's investigation two weeks later, after it learned of the billing records indicating that Mrs. Clinton worked on the option agreement.

Madison on. . . . If you would like us to work on another specific matter, we would be glad to discuss it on a case-by-case basis.

"Sincerely yours,

"For the Rose Law Firm

"Hillary Rodham Clinton."

Blind copies of the letter went to Vince Foster and Herb Rule, who also received a short memo from Hillary suggesting they discuss the matter when he returned from vacation.

The letter was disingenuous on its face, since the whole purpose of the original retainer agreement had been to prepay legal fees for a single matter, the preferred stock plan. But it achieved its purpose, which was to withdraw essentially from representing Madison. After July 1986, there were only two minor billing entries for Madison in the Rose records.

McDougal was true to his word: he never again mentioned Madison to Susan. It was as if it had all been a bad dream that had never happened. In his medicated state, it was all McDougal could do to care for himself; Susan often came over to prepare meals. He was withdrawn and isolated; there were some months when Susan thought she was the only person he saw. For Susan, that meant all the lingering problems were on her shoulders. She couldn't vote her stock in Madison, which was likely to be worthless in any event. Ousted from her position there, she had no source of income other than her and Jim's floundering real estate developments. She had some assets, mostly notes payable from property buyers. She had to sell them at a deeply discounted price in order to raise cash.

News of the crisis at Madison had slowly spread through the Little Rock business community. Finally, on September 16, the *Arkansas Gazette* ran a story, headlined "Madison Has Shakeup":

"There has been a management shake-up at Madison Guaranty Savings and Loan, the Augusta-based institution with a very large branch at Little Rock, but Madison officials don't want to talk about it," the paper reported. "Steve Cuffman, a Little Rock lawyer, confirmed Monday that he is now Madison's board chairman, but he wouldn't comment further, even to say how long he had held the job. No one would say who is the institution's chief executive officer. . . . Efforts to determine the status of Jim McDougal, a major Madison shareholder and at least until recently president of the savings and loan's Madison Financial subsidiary, revealed only that he no longer has an office at Madison Guaranty's renovated building at Sixteenth and Main Streets." The cryptic responses did nothing to dispel rumors of Madison's troubles. The article turned Susan into a pariah in the Little Rock investment community.

Under the circumstances—McDougal's ouster from Madison, his nervous breakdown, his separation from Susan, his worsening financial prospects—it seems amazing that the deal to develop the International Paper land went forward. Yet Jim and Susan felt they had no choice; it seems typical that, under severe duress, they would look to yet another deal for salvation. This was to be Susan's deal, the first she'd done on her own. Jim encouraged her, and she wanted to prove she could make it on her own.

In October 1986, Jim and Susan closed on the property, using what was left of the Hale loan and financing most of it with a note payable to International Paper. As their vehicle for this transaction, the McDougals settled on Whitewater Development Corp., and to International Paper they represented themselves as Whitewater's officers and sole owners. No mention of this was made to the Clintons. Indeed, the reason Jim used Whitewater was because he still expected to extricate the Clintons from the project, despite Hillary's earlier rebuffs of the stock transfer, and then use the Whitewater losses to shelter profits in the new land deal.

To that end, McDougal had again tried to get the Clintons to transfer their interest to him and Susan, mailing a copy of the stock transfer dated October 1 to Hillary at the Rose firm. Hillary again refused, this time noting that there was no point in giving up their equity if she and Bill couldn't simultaneously extricate themselves from liability on the Citizens Bank loan, which the bank refused to do.

A year before, the McDougals would gladly have assumed the Clintons' liability, but now their financial plight precluded that. While Hillary was technically correct about the mortgage, from McDougal's point of view he didn't see that there was a problem. The mortgage interest was being paid by installment purchasers of the lots. McDougal had made most of the payments on the loan, after all, and if the Clintons stayed in Whitewater and he defaulted, they would still be liable. As he saw it, if the Clintons got out of the now doomed investment they could spare themselves political embarrassment. But if Hillary wanted to stay in, so be it.

That meant Whitewater couldn't be the owner of record of

the International Paper project. McDougal sought to cure this problem by having Whitewater transfer the International Paper assets to his and Susan's Great Southern Land Co. The note payable to International Paper, however, couldn't be unilaterally transferred and remained a liability for Whitewater and its partners. McDougal tried to solve that problem by signing an agreement providing that he and Susan would be liable in the event Whitewater defaulted on the note. No doubt he didn't mean to, but technically he increased Whitewater's liabilities without the Clintons' knowledge.

The International Paper tract was christened Lowrance Heights. Desperate to raise cash, Susan put in roads and began marketing lots at the new development almost immediately. She oversaw production of television ads, which emphasized leafy scenery, the country atmosphere, and low prices. But, given her recent notoriety, she stayed out of the footage. The development was a success—it practically sold out in the first month. But even that income stream couldn't meet Susan's debts. She sold her Jaguar. The bank began foreclosure proceedings on the blue clapboard New England–style house she and Jim had designed and remodelled.

In Flippin, Citizens Bank was now 1st Ozark National Bank, a new, wholly owned subsidiary of a much bigger bank. Citizens Bank had been acquired the year before by Twin City Bankshares Corp., the holding company for Twin City Bank, the largest state-chartered bank in Arkansas. Twin City Bankshares was in turn a subsidiary of the closely held Frank Lyon Company, owned by Frank Lyon, Jr., one of the state's richest men. (His net worth was recently estimated at $500 million.) An avid sportsman, Lyon had attracted unwanted publicity when, after being named by Clinton's Republican predecessor to the Arkansas Game and Fish Commission, he was arrested for shooting ducks over the limit. Twin City, headquartered in North Little Rock, had bought several small-town banks, and had converted them to national banks, reasoning that local depositors would be impressed by the word "national" in the bank's name.

As a result of the takeover by Twin City, there had been quite a few personnel changes at 1st Ozark. Chris Wade was no longer on the bank's board, nor was James Patterson, the former president. Several other of the founding directors had also resigned; they didn't really see it as a local bank now that it was being controlled from Little Rock. Frank Burge had moved on. Twin City chairman Ed Penick became chairman of 1st Ozark as well, and Terry Renaud, Twin City president, also joined the board, both driving in for Friday board meetings (which allowed them to stay into the weekend and fly-fish, as they often did). Senior vice president Ron Proctor, who had been the Whitewater loan officer for many years, was still there, though he'd turned much of the Whitewater file over to Vernon Dewey, a more junior loan officer.

Vernon Dewey didn't have a good feeling about the Whitewater loan. He was impressed that the governor was involved, but that didn't make his work any easier. It was up to Dewey to make sure that the monthly payments were applied to the loan and to collect the payment if it fell short or was past due, as was often the case. Under the last loan restructuring, in 1984, most buyers of the lots were making their payments directly into an escrow account at the bank, which was supposed to cover the monthly payments. It almost never did, however, and Dewey would have to call Rosalee Wade at Ozarks Realty to make up the shortfall. He didn't know where she was coming up with the payments, which were almost always late. The fact that Whitewater had had to borrow just to make the interest payments was another sign that the venture's cash flow wasn't adequate to meet the debt service.

With the Whitewater loan due to expire on December 3, Dewey would have liked to see the principal paid off and the loan removed from the bank's books before 1st Ozark was visited by auditors from the comptroller of the currency in Washington, a requirement now that 1st Ozark was a national rather than state-chartered bank. So the bank sent the Whitewater partners a letter, reminding them of the December 3 date and calling for payment in full of the principal and interest due—an amount over $100,000.

Susan felt a sense of panic after she opened the envelope and read the letter. In the past, the bank in Flippin had never demanded repayment of the note; it had always suggested a renewal. Was this a reflection of new management at 1st Ozark? Or had the bankers there heard of the McDougals' trouble at Madison Guaranty and decided they wanted to call the loan? Whatever the reason, Susan knew she was in trouble. She would have to try to renegotiate the loan. If she failed, and 1st Ozark insisted on calling the loan, she and Jim had no money to pay it off. That meant the Clintons would be liable for the entire amount.

Adopting her perkiest, most carefree tone—she was afraid that any hint of trouble would encourage the bank to call the loan—Susan called Ron Proctor, the Whitewater loan officer. "What's this all about," Susan began. "Can't we just renew the loan?" To Susan's dismay, Proctor indicated that their friendly, almost casual relationship with the bank would have to change. "The bank examiners are coming in," he explained, and from the tone of his voice, Susan wondered if they weren't standing behind him at that moment. He noted that the loan had never been structured with regular monthly payments of interest and a reduction of principal. He also seemed concerned that the loan involved the governor of the state. While once that might have seemed an asset, he suggested that in the current political climate, and dealing with federal bank examiners, any hint of favoritism could cause trouble, and prove an embarrassment for everyone. All in all, he thought simply paying off the note would be the best course.*

Susan said she'd get back to him with a proposal. She set to work, calculating what kind of monthly payment might be generated if all the lot purchasers made their payments directly to the bank. Given the reduced amount of the principal outstanding (just over $50,000 after several payments by McDougal, as well as some payments by Wade), she thought an amount could be generated that would cover the interest and provide some reduction in principal. Excited, she called back Proctor. "I think we have enough lots sold to make a good monthly payment" on a new loan, she suggested. She'd have Whitewater assign its rights to those payments to 1st Ozark. "That ought to make you secure," she said, adding that the arrangement would look good to the examiners: local purchasers would now be making payments on a loan for purchase of local land. "Local," she knew from her and Jim's experience, was a talisman for bank examiners.

* It's not clear that bank examiners were about to come in or were present, though 1st Ozark was now subject to federal audits. Dewey doesn't recall that being the motive for calling the Whitewater loan. A comptroller's examination "is a big bluff by bankers to get things done," he says. "We always used that as an excuse to get information. That's an old banker's trick."

Proctor had heard of the McDougals' troubles at Madison, and he was prepared to be sympathetic. Assuming the payments could be what Susan represented, he agreed that 1st Ozark would renew the loan and accept the assignment of payments. There was just one thing, he added. The bank would need current financial disclosure statements for the McDougals and the Clintons, routine documentation mandated by the comptroller for any loan from a nationally chartered bank. Susan was so relieved she barely thought about the disclosure statements. She did not want to have to admit that she couldn't pay back the bank.

Neither Susan nor Jim had spoken to Hillary or Bill since Jim had been in the hospital and been ousted at Madison Guaranty. But now Susan called the governor's office and got Bill on the phone. Again, she was doing her best to save face by sounding cheerful. The bank loan was up for renewal, she explained, assuring him that the payments by the lot purchasers would cover the new loan payments. "I'm just going to need current financials" for you and Hillary, she said. "Yeah, that sounds fine," he replied, as though he were barely focusing on the matter. "Would you just run it by Hillary?"

After their last encounter, Susan wasn't eager to talk to Hillary, but she called her at the Rose firm, explaining again that she needed the financial disclosure statements. As soon as Hillary started talking, Susan could tell from her tone that this was going to be difficult. Instead of simply agreeing to provide the form, Hillary began, in Susan's view, cross-examining her about Whitewater sales and income. Finally she said she wasn't inclined to give Susan any financial statement. "This isn't for me," Susan said, almost beside herself, "it's for the bank. The bank wants it." She felt she was practically pleading with Hillary. But she didn't want to say the obvious—that if she didn't get the form the bank might call the loan, and she and Jim couldn't pay. Susan felt so beaten down. She didn't know how long she could maintain the illusion that nothing was wrong. How could Hillary have been her friend and be treating her this way?

It was true that in the past, Citizens Bank had been lax about requiring the Clintons to submit a financial disclosure form, even though such documentation was clearly required by state and federal banking regulators. The earliest such form for the Clintons in the Citizens Bank files dated from 1981, two years after the initial loan, and the loan had since been renewed numerous times without requiring an update. State banking regulators had occasionally asked about the lack of a statement for the Clintons, but the bank officers always satisfied them by producing the McDougals' statement and reminding the examiners that Clinton was the governor. But two years before, in 1984, as the bank's activities were being scrutinized in anticipation of a takeover, the bank had been more scrupulous, insisting that the Clintons provide such a disclosure so the bank's records would be complete.*

It hadn't been easy getting it. In a November 21, 1984, letter to Ron Proctor, McDougal wrote that "I have asked Governor Clinton to mail his statement directly to you." By December 3, the bank hadn't received it; Proctor wrote McDougal that he was enclosing the renewal note, but "Please tell Mr. Clinton that the renewal will not go into effect until we receive his current personal financial statement. This means the loan will remain past due until we receive the statement." Finally it appears that McDougal himself prepared the financial statement for the Clintons based on information he got from their accountant; a December 12 memo from him to Hillary directs her to "Please sign your name and Bill's name to your financial statement which is enclosed. . . . The financial statement and note renewal should be forwarded immediately to Ron Proctor in the enclosed envelope. It is urgent that this be mailed immediately." At the same time, McDougal wrote Proctor: "I have been unsuccessful in trying to meet with Bill and Hillary to sign the note renewal. I have forwarded to them by messenger this morning the note and an envelope with which to forward it to you. . . . Thank you very much for your patience and tolerance in this matter."

Given that no further correspondence ensued, Hillary presumably followed McDougal's instructions and forwarded the statement and signed note. Both documents are in the files at the bank, dated December 17, 1985, and signed Bill Clinton and Hillary Clinton in what appears to be Hillary's handwriting. It isn't clear if this is the document prepared for them by McDougal. Under assets, it lists

---

* *Under federal law Title 18, section 1344, it is a crime to submit a false financial disclosure statement, but not to fail to submit one. To most bankers, however, it would be unthinkable not to obtain such a statement, since banks are required by regulation to have the statements on file.*

cash and securities of $130,000, which, if accurate, suggests the Clintons were better off financially than Hillary's oft-cited concerns about money and paying for Chelsea's education would suggest. The form also lists "accounts, loans, notes receivable" of $100,000 and real estate of $100,000. Whitewater isn't listed by name, though it appears to represent the only accounts receivable and real estate the couple owned at the time. If that is the case, the statement values their half interest in Whitewater at a ludicrously high $200,000.

Perhaps the 1984 delays could be ascribed to negligence, but now, in 1986, Susan felt that Hillary was being obstructionist. Susan was so upset by Hillary's recalcitrance that she called Charles James, the accountant who handled the Whitewater books and had handled the paperwork to incorporate Whitewater Development in the first place. Susan explained that Hillary was refusing to submit a financial statement, and she was desperate. "What can I do?" she asked. "This whole house of cards could come down." James recognized how upset Susan was and how important it was to get the financial statement. He said he'd bring the Whitewater records over to her house and they'd prepare some information to use with Hillary.

When he arrived, James and Susan sat down and James wrote down the various payments from the McDougals and Clintons on a yellow legal pad. Of the almost $200,000 that the Whitewater partners had had to contribute to cover shortfalls in income from the development itself, the McDougals had contributed just over $138,000; the Clintons just under $36,000. Before performing this exercise, James and Susan hadn't realized how large a discrepancy the payments reflected, and James was irate. "You tell her, by God, you've given all this money to this project and, by God, you want the statement!"

Thus armed, the next day Susan took the yellow pad, mustered her resolve, and went to the Rose firm's office without an appointment. "Can I see Hillary," she said. Once ushered into Hillary's office, she dropped her perky cheerleader facade. "Look at these numbers," she said. "This is a list of our contributions, and this is a list of yours. I really don't understand your attitude given these numbers. If you don't give the bank the statement, they're going to call the loan." She still couldn't bring herself to admit that, in that event, she couldn't pay it and it would fall to the Clintons. She continued, "This is really important. We have nothing to worry about if you give me the statement."

Hillary responded by saying she wanted to review the numbers Susan had provided. Exasperated, Susan left empty-handed.

By December 3, the loan expiration date, nothing had been resolved. But the next time Susan spoke to Proctor, he mentioned that he "just wanted you to know" that he was dealing with Hillary on the matter, and that he was sure there would be "no problems." In marked contrast to their earlier conversations, he seemed to be falling all over himself to be nice, asking her how things were going and telling her not to worry about the Whitewater bank loan. Yet Proctor himself was evidently still trying to get the financial statement from the Clintons. Susan Sisk, the senior lender at Twin City at the time, recalls chatting with Wes Strange, 1st Ozark's new president, who mentioned that Clinton had recently made a speech in the Flippin area. "I told Bill," Strange reported to Sisk, "we still need the financial statement."

"Well, I'm sure that whatever you need we'll get for you," he said Clinton replied. But no statement had been forthcoming.

Susan McDougal was aware that something was going on between Hillary, 1st Ozark, and officials at the parent, Twin City. One day Hillary called, asking Susan to get a copy of a Whitewater document and drop it off at the Twin City headquarters in North Little Rock, which Susan did. Then, soon after, Susan received a call from the governor himself. "Would you mind," he began, "Hillary wants to look at the documents" to support Susan and James's calculations on the yellow pad. So Hillary didn't trust her, Susan thought. Well, she'd be only too happy to give her the documents. She had more files than the bank. She was sick of the paperwork and the responsibility. Let Hillary take it on if she was suddenly so concerned that Susan might be cheating her.

Susan gathered all the documents she had and got them into a large box. She was preparing to load them in her car when the man she was dating at the time stopped by and wanted to know where she was going. "I'm taking these over to Bill Clinton," she said. "No you're not," he said. "You're not going over there, not within a mile of that guy." He seemed convinced that the governor might make a pass at Susan, given his increasingly widespread reputation as a womanizer. Susan thought it was ridiculous—she'd flirted with Bill for years, but nothing beyond that had ever happened—but he insisted. So she called her brother Bill Henley, the state senator, and asked if he would take the documents over. Bill agreed; he was on his way to the Capitol anyway, and dropped them off with a state trooper at the mansion's gate house.

Apparently the matter was temporarily patched over with the bank, which agreed to take the land purchasers' payments for the next six months. In a letter dated December 16, 1986, McDougal informed Bill and Hillary that three land buyers had defaulted, "thereby creating a shortfall of about $1,000 a month for our monthly payment to Citizens Bank of Flippin. We have negotiated an arrangement with the bank to accept the amount we are now receiving from customers as the monthly payment over the next six months. This will take us into the month of May 1987." Susan was never aware of such an arrangement, nor did she know that Jim had spoken with the bank. Almost immediately after writing the letter, Jim moved to California.*

Not everyone at the bank in Flippin was comfortable about what was happening. Dewey, in particular, thought it was imprudent and that the bank should call the loan. He'd written the Clintons repeatedly asking, then demanding, that they provide a financial disclosure. He couldn't understand why the Clintons wouldn't provide it. Surely they understood that no matter what the statements showed—even if the Clintons had a negative net worth—the bank was all but certain to renew the loan since he was the governor. Dewey didn't want to face the bank examiners over this; it would almost surely cause questions. The Whitewater loan was the only one in the bank's portfolio that had such irregular documentation. He insisted that the matter be brought to the bank's board of directors, and argued that the loan should be called.

---

*Citing his medical condition at the time, McDougal says he has no memory of any negotiations with the bank or writing such a memo to Hillary. Nor, he says, was he aware that Hillary was talking to anyone at the bank at the same time about an extension of the loan. Ron Proctor, the only person who appears to have been talking to Susan, Jim, and Hillary about the matter, says he has been instructed by the independent counsel to remain silent.

Dewey was right to be concerned. As Sue Winkley, the chief auditor for Twin City Bank, puts it, failure to provide a financial disclosure form "is a red flag. When the customer doesn't give the information when you ask for it, that's a red flag and it's a red flag to the investigators. There's something funny. Otherwise, why not share the information?" (Winkley was not, however, aware of the problem at the time, and later was surprised to learn that the Clintons had a loan from a Twin City subsidiary.)

Dewey's argument seemed to make the board nervous. Clinton was, after all, the governor. Penick, the Twin City chairman and ex-officio chairman of 1st Ozark, said he'd take up the matter personally. He knew Hillary somewhat; Hillary and the Rose firm had successfully represented Twin City in a complicated bond case, and the firm did other work for the Frank Lyon Company, which owned Twin City. Penick drafted the letter and sent it to Hillary at the Rose firm, rather than to both Hillary and Bill at the governor's mansion. The thought of raising such a delicate matter with the governor himself was too embarrassing to Penick.

Penick had a far more important matter pending with the state government: the extension of branch banking. As was the case in many rural states at the time, Arkansas's banking law, dating from Reconstruction, was a populist measure designed to encourage and protect small, local banks and their communities and prevent statewide domination by the bigger banks in Little Rock. Thus, state law prohibited bank branches anywhere beyond the city limits of the city where the bank was incorporated. This was the single most important issue on the Twin City political agenda, because the bank was incorporated in North Little Rock. All it could do was gaze enviously at its rivals across the river in richer and more populous Little Rock.

For years, Twin City had been trying unsuccessfully to gain support for loosening the restrictive statute. The small-town banks always howled in protest, as did some of Twin City's large rivals in Little Rock, which didn't want to see increased competition there, either. Politically, the measure seemed a long shot. Nonetheless, the bank had contributed generously to Clinton's campaigns, much to the displeasure of its major shareholder, Frank Lyon, who was a staunch supporter of Republican Frank White. When he questioned the contributions, he was reminded of the branch banking and other issues and the practical need to curry favor with the governor. Twin City president Terry Renaud was a Democrat who contributed to the Clinton campaigns.

But the bank's main link to the Clintons was Margaret Davenport, an executive vice president, a close friend of Hillary's, and generous Clinton campaign contributor. Margaret was the bank's principal line of communications to the governor, through Hillary, and Penick had been relying on Davenport to press the branch banking issue in her periodic lunches with the state's first lady. Davenport had gotten to know Hillary when she first came to town in the late 1970s; they were among the few professional women in Little Rock at the time. She was dazzled by Hillary ("one of the most tremendous human beings I have ever known," she says) and served as co-chairman of Clinton's first gubernatorial campaign in North Little Rock. As governor, Clinton appointed her to the Commission for Arkansas's Future and, more important, to the Arkansas Development Finance Authority Board, which provides long-term financing for businesses starting or expanding in Arkansas. While Twin City had rarely been a trustee for various bonds issued under the ADFA, it was named the trustee for four bond issues in 1988 and 1989, which brought in some lucrative fee income. Twin City, in turn, steered at least some legal work to the Rose firm, including the tax matter referred to Hillary. So when the unresolved issue of the Whitewater loan again arose at a 1st Ozark board meeting, Penick said, "Margaret and Hillary are close friends, so I'll have Margaret talk to Hillary about this."

At about that time, Hillary did evidently speak to Margaret Davenport about the Whitewater loan. "Notes of TK w/M. Davenport," handwritten notes on Hillary's personal note paper read. At the top right-hand corner is the date 1987. "56,623 balance. 2,303.78 Oct. 3." On the side is an arrow, then "5 yr amortization. w/2 yr balloon. 12/3. Note secured by mortgage recorded Aug. 3, 1978 on 171 acres known as Whitewater Estates. Original $100,121 note."

"TK" appears to be an abbreviation for "talk." And, in fact, $56,623 was the precise amount of the 1st Ozark loan outstanding as of October 3, 1986, and $2,303.78 was the interest then due on the Whitewater loan.*

At 1st Ozark, concern about the status of the Whitewater loan and the failure of the Clintons to produce a financial statement was such that in mid-December Ron Proctor made a visit to the Whitewater property to see the bank's collateral for himself. In a memo dated January 6, 1987, Proctor wrote, "In mid-December, 1986, I inspected the real estate securing the loan to Whitewater Development, Inc. in the current principal amount of $53,161.52. The property is located on the bank of White River approximately twenty-five miles from Flippin near Rea Valley. As the following analysis of the forty-four lots will show, several of the lots are sold, however, very few have improvements. I noticed two or three medium priced homes and about the same number of mobile homes which were in bad repair and trash and junk surrounded these mobile homes. This will curtail future sales of the remaining unsold lots."

Proctor concluded that the "realistic value" of the "remaining unsold property" was $43,500, and that contracts receivable for the lots already sold totaled $60,786. That meant the bank valued all of Whitewater at $104,000.

Two days later, on January 8, 1st Ozark's loan committee convened to consider, among other things, the Whitewater loan. Attending were Strange, Proctor, Dewey, documents clerk Barbara Carson, mortgage loan officer Wanda Felty, and cashier Twyla Hudson. Proctor reported on his recent Whitewater visit, and the committee gave the loan a risk rating of "3," meaning the bank should start preparing for a default, but still hoped the loan would perform. (Such loans might be called within the bank's discretion.) The committee attached several conditions to approving the loan

---

* *Margaret Davenport Eldridge said she doesn't recall discussing either Whitewater or the branch banking issue with Hillary Clinton, nor does she recall Ed Penick asking her to discuss the issue. "If Ed Penick—he's a good friend—if he'd asked me to make a contact, I would have told him no. I never tried to take advantage of a friendship. Our talks were personal, things that were interesting. We stayed away from business or politics. My opinion was, she had enough of that. Everybody knew we were friends, but no one ever tried to ask me to try to be influential. If I had something that needed to be said to the governor, I'd talk to him directly." Asked about Hillary's notes, Eldridge said that Hillary might have called her for information about the 1st Ozark loan, but she doesn't recall any such conversation.*

renewal, including obtaining the Clintons' personal financial statement for the bank's files. An internal bank memo dated January 8 lists "All financials in file before renewal" as a condition of the loan and is initialed at the lower right by the loan committee members.

The combined efforts of the loan committee, Strange, Proctor, Twin City chairman Penick and Davenport apparently had an effect. In March, Hillary Clinton finally produced the long-awaited financial statement, submitting a Twin City Bank form. At the top of the statement is the admonition: "NOTE: Any willful misrepresentation could result in violation of Federal law." The statement lists total assets of $290,000. The assets include cash and marketable securities of $170,000. Curiously, Whitewater is not mentioned by name as an asset. The statement lists $50,000 as "Real Estate—Partial Interest" and $50,000 in "Accounts/Notes Receivables." It isn't clear what assets these entries describe, but, presumably, they refer to Whitewater. The Clintons don't appear to have owned any other real estate at that time, and the only "investment or holding" identified on Governor Clinton's statement of financial interest, filed with the Arkansas secretary of state, is Whitewater. If the assets are meant to describe their interest in Whitewater, the value of $100,000 seems grossly inflated.

Even if the twenty-four unsold Whitewater lots hadn't already been conveyed to Chris Wade's Ozark Air, a half interest would only be worth $52,000. But those lots had been sold, and Wade had since reduced his obligation to repay $35,000 of the 1st Ozark mortgage by making payments of about $10,000. Thus, the Clintons' and McDougals' half interests of what remained in Whitewater Development would be valued at $30,000 (half the value of the contracts receivable) plus half the value of Wade's obligation to repay $25,500 of the 1st Ozark mortgage, or about $12,750. That would bring the total value of the Clintons' interest to about $42,750.

Surely at this point, with all the records and information at Hillary's disposal, it should have been obvious to the Clintons that a half-interest in Whitewater Development could not be worth anywhere near $100,000. Jim McDougal had told Hillary the previous summer that all the remaining lots had been sold to Chris Wade, as Hillary later acknowledged in a sworn answer to an RTC interrogatory. And Ron Proctor or Wes Strange could have provided an accurate valuation, since they were in regular contact with Hillary at the time.

There's no record the bank ever questioned the accuracy of the Clintons' disclosure form. The legal obligation to be accurate lay with the Clintons, not the bank. Strange and Proctor were happy just to have the statement, thus satisfying the bank examiners. The Whitewater loan was renewed on March 26, 1987.

That winter, 1st Ozark wasn't the only bank seeking the Clintons' financial disclosure statement. Security Bank of Paragould— the lender of the money for the Hillary house—had also written Hillary asking her to "complete the enclosed financial statement" in order to extend the Paragould loan. Such a document in Security Bank's files is signed by both Bill and Hillary Clinton. The form lists the same asset values as the one submitted to 1st Ozark, and carries the instruction, "Do not include assets of doubtful value." The statement concludes with the underscored admonition that "each undersigned represents and warrants that the information provided is true and complete."*

On April 1, 1987, just after the 1st Ozark Whitewater loan was finally extended, the Arkansas legislature passed Act No. 539, which was the first chink in Arkansas's restrictive banking law. The governor's friend and state banking commissioner, Marlin Jackson (the source of Clinton's loan from the Security Bank of Paragould) had, at about the same time, abandoned his opposition, throwing his support behind the new legislation. The statute, signed by Governor Clinton, provided for countywide branch banking in Arkansas counties with populations over 200,000.

There was no mention of Twin City by name in the legislation. But in fact, there was only one Arkansas county at the time with a population over 200,000: Pulaski County, which contains Little Rock and North Little Rock. And there was only one major bank chartered in North Little Rock: Twin City. The Little Rock banks had comparatively little to gain by expanding into lightly populated North Little Rock. Indeed, one of them, First Commercial,

---

* *The Clintons' lawyer, David Kendall, confirmed that the $100,000 refers to Whitewater. He offered no explanation for the asset values on the Clintons' disclosure forms other than to say that land values in northern Arkansas rose in the late 1980s, adding that the Clintons had used "their best estimate." Ron Proctor, citing instructions from the independent counsel, declined comment, as did Wes Strange.*

promptly sued Twin City, arguing that the new law was unconstitutional because it affected just one county. In practice, the statute benefited primarily one institution, and that was Twin City Bank.*

In Flippin, most of the bank employees, including Dewey, were only dimly aware of the new legislation and its impact on their parent company. Dewey recalls, "I knew that Twin City was trying to get the Clintons' support on getting into Little Rock. It was nixed, then it was approved after some calls were made. I don't know the inner workings." But he was still upset about the handling of the Clintons' loan. The "higher-ups," as he called them, didn't have the guts to stand up to the governor, and that offended him.

---

* *Jackson says Clinton never pressured him to change his view.* Arkansas Business *reported that Jackson's support for the bill drew some criticism of him as a "promoter of potentially divisive industry issues. One such issue concerns Jackson's stand on county-wide branch banking. Initially Jackson believed that county-wide banking would hurt the small banks, one of which was his own, Security Bank of Paragould. Today, Jackson sees restrictions on bank branching . . . as hindering banks. It follows a general attitude on regulation: 'I am convinced that the most serious impediment is the magic fences we build.'* " ("The Redneck from Paragould," Arkansas Business, *September 28, 1987.)*

SIX

IN APRIL 1987, SUSAN McDOUGAL's first payment of interest on the Hale SBA loan came due. She didn't have the money. She wrote Hale, "Because of the fluctuation between payment of media expenses and reimbursement, it will be 30 to 60 days before I can make this payment to you." No payment materialized then, either. Finally Susan assigned Hale her shares in Madison Guaranty as additional security for the loan. They were all but worthless, and in any event, had already been assigned by her and Jim to Worthen Bank. Ultimately Susan failed to make any payment of either interest or principal on the $300,000 loan, and Hale finally filed suit against her. He also considered joining a suit against Frost & Co., Madison's accountants, blaming them for Susan's default. He discovered Frost was already being sued by the FSLIC, in a case soon to be taken over by the Rose firm.

The Rose firm's work for the S&L regulators had continued apace, eventually involving numerous matters related to seventeen failed Arkansas thrifts, generating billings of well over $1 million. Giroir and his allies were now in open conflict with the litigators and, increasingly, the litigators' supporters from other parts of the firm. They were especially infuriated when they learned that Giroir's position might itself be motivated more by concern for his own personal finances than those of the firm. For Giroir, it turned out, was suffering from some of the same problems besetting McDougal.

Giroir had always been prominent in Arkansas banking circles; the Worthen Bank had historically been among the firm's most important clients and a link to many other clients in the business community. In the early eighties Giroir took a step that would have been prohibited in many firms: he invested his own money in banks, acquiring a controlling interest in four Arkansas institutions, while maintaining his own law practice at Rose. The investments proved lucrative: in 1984 he sold the four banks to First Arkansas Bankstock Corporation and joined its board of directors. Then he sold his 91 percent stake in First National Bank of Fayetteville to Worthen itself for $18.5 million in Worthen stock, making him one of the bank's largest shareholders. He was also a member of the Worthen board.

But not all of his investments had performed so well. Giroir had also acquired a small stake in an S&L, FirstSouth Federal Association in Pine Bluff, which was seized by the FSLIC in 1987. FirstSouth was in the process of making a $2 million loan to Giroir —and the FSLIC refused to honor the loan commitment. This caused Giroir to default on other loan obligations. Thus Giroir himself faced a conflict of interest with the very client the litigators were representing.

Giroir filed suit against the FSLIC, which had prevented FirstSouth from making his loan. Then the FSLIC countersued Rose for malpractice, producing an opinion by Giroir on Rose firm letterhead saying that a loan that benefited Giroir was legal. That was the last straw for Giroir's opponents within the firm. After rancorous debate, Giroir was forced to resign. The Rose firm (and its insurer) had to settle the FSLIC suit for a substantial sum. (Terms of the settlement remain under seal.) Giroir's cases were settled, too, largely in his favor. With another Rose partner, Giroir opened a new firm, taking many of Rose's prominent clients with him.

At first it seemed a clear-cut victory for the Vince-Hillary-Webb faction. Yet over time, partners realized that the business lost to Giroir was far greater than anything the firm gained by its now unfettered ability to pursue work for government regulators. The loss of Giroir's clients put even more pressure on the litigators to generate business from the FSLIC and other clients, just to meet the high overhead of the firm's newly renovated office building. Vince, Webb, and Hillary continued to be the driving force behind the litigation work, and in each case the Rose firm assured the

FSLIC and its successor, the RTC, that the firm was free of actual and potential conflicts of interest. Webb Hubbell served as head of the firm's conflicts committee. Curiously, when asked to sue Madison Guaranty's accounting firm, neither he nor anyone else at the firm mentioned Hillary's work for Madison, nor that Webb Hubbell's father-in-law, Seth Ward, was a Madison official involved in some of the S&L's questionable transactions. The firm's carelessness in this regard is especially surprising since the subject of conflicts of interest had plunged the firm into its leadership crisis. But the pressure to generate business may have caused Hubbell and others to come up with tortured rationalizations for explaining such conflicts away.*

Failure to pay interest on the Hale loan was just one event in the ongoing collapse of the McDougals' real estate empire. In October 1987 Susan and Jim similarly defaulted on the note from International Paper they'd signed to close the Lowrance Heights project. Susan had been panic-stricken that the default would cause the purchasers of the lots, most of them low-to-middle-income retirees, to lose title to their land. But when International Paper began foreclosure proceedings, it agreed to honor the sales agreements in return for Susan assigning the purchasers' payments to International Paper. That was an immense relief to Susan—she'd been having nightmares that people who'd trusted her would lose their homes. She felt she could leave Arkansas with a clear conscience. She moved to California, joining her brother Bill, who had moved there after giving up his political career in Arkansas.†

Whitewater was now part of an era in Arkansas that both McDougals wanted to put behind them. They were only too happy to let Hillary take over day-to-day management, as she had done

---

* Ironically, various investigators later concluded that the Rose firm didn't engage in any actual conflict, but that Hubbell's failure to disclose the work for Madison violated RTC rules and created an appearance of impropriety.
† In its foreclosure lawsuit, International Paper named as defendants Whitewater Development Corp. and the McDougals. Because Susan and Jim had signed the agreement providing that they would be personally liable in the event of Whitewater's default, International Paper's lawyers didn't sue the Clintons. The company eventually won a judgment against Whitewater in the amount of $478,000, which was more than satisfied by the fact that they kept the McDougals' down payment and regained ownership of the development. All told, the McDougals lost over $110,000 on the venture.

after successfully negotiating the 1987 loan renewal at 1st Ozark. When Hillary periodically needed the McDougals to sign something, they didn't even respond; in various tax returns, Hillary signed for Whitewater, using the title "president."

For a project that was yielding no profit, Whitewater was a constant headache. In the fall of 1987, Hilman Logan, the buyer of Lot 13, the site of the Hillary house, defaulted on his payments after filing bankruptcy. Those payments were servicing the Clintons' loan from Security Bank of Paragould, and Hillary had to find a way to keep that loan from being called. Chris Wade found another buyer. Hillary bought the lot back from Logan's bankruptcy estate for $8,000, then resold it to Wade's client for about $24,000.*

Hillary was eager to use the proceeds to dispose of the troublesome debt she and Bill had taken on at Security Bank of Paragould to buy the house in the first place. As recently as April 4, 1988, Marlin Jackson had written Hillary enclosing a past-due notice on their note asking for accrued interest of $665 and either the principal or an extension agreement. Despite being a close friend and political ally of the governor (though he had now resigned as state banking commissioner), Jackson proved more of a stickler than had 1st Ozark. "Time is of the essence," he wrote. "By statute the Security Bank must have an examination that begins prior to the end of this month. [There is a statutory provision for state banks to be examined no less frequently than once each twenty-four month period.]

"If you have any questions, do not hesitate to call me. . . ."

Presumably, Hillary complied; a check for the interest dated April 11 was received by the bank.

While waiting for the closing on the sale of the house, Hillary again wrote the McDougals, trying to secure authority to act independently with respect to Whitewater. Evidently unaware of the McDougals' separate moves to California, on November 28, 1988 Hillary wrote to Jim at the address in Arkadelphia where he had been convalescing after his surgery.

"I am enclosing a Power of Attorney for you to sign, authorizing me to act on your behalf with respect to matters concerning

---

*It seems remarkable that the lot was sold for $8,000 when the fair market value was obviously much higher.

Whitewater Development Corp.," Hillary wrote. "I am also enclosing a blank Power of Attorney for Susan to sign doing the same. ... We are trying to sell off the property that is left and get out from under the obligations at both Flippin and Paragould. Chris and Rosalee Wade have been a big help to us, and I hope we'll be able to get all that behind us by the end of the year. If you have any questions or suggestions, please give me a call.

"I hope things are going well for you in Arkadelphia and that you have a happy holiday season."

The letter went unanswered.

Toward the end of the year, the house sale closed, and in December Hillary used the proceeds to retire the Paragould loan. But her wish for Whitewater—to "get all that behind us by the end of the year"—went unfulfilled.

That April, 1st Ozark again contacted Hillary about renewing the Whitewater loan. Efforts to reach the McDougals in California had failed, and the bank had waived the requirement that the McDougals submit a financial disclosure form, noting in a memo that the loan was "guaranteed by Bill Clinton." But the bank set about getting the Clintons' form, as well as a financial statement for Whitewater itself. In a letter dated April 12, 1988, Wes Strange wrote Hillary, "I have also enclosed a renewal note, hoping that you could help me in getting all the signatures on this and returning it as soon as possible. In addition, we will be needing an updated financial statement on the personal, as well as the corporation."

After the previous year's struggle to get a financial disclosure form from the Clintons, it came as no surprise to Vernon Dewey that no updated statement was forthcoming. This year the bank appears to have simply given up. On July 13, Hillary signed and returned the renewal note. "I am enclosing the renewal note you sent for Bill's and my signature." There is no mention of the financial statement, and none appears to have been submitted.

Two days later, 1st Ozark agreed to waive requiring the Clintons' and Whitewater's financial disclosure forms, according to a document in 1st Ozark's files, "Request for Loan Documentation Waiver," dated July 15, 1988. Over the words "approved by" are the initials "WS," evidently referring to Wes Strange. According to the document, reasons for the waiver were that the escrow account was making the payments, and the value of the collateral was "sufficient." Still, waiving such a requirement was highly irregular, especially on a commercial loan, and Dewey felt it was imprudent to do so. For the first time, the bank now had no current financial disclosure forms for any of the borrowers. This was the only loan in the bank lacking such documentation. As Strange told Dewey, the troublesome loan was just something they'd have to live with until it was, they hoped, paid off.*

As these negotiations were underway, the Arkansas legislature was again considering the issue of countywide branch banking. Despite Twin City's success the previous year, the statute hadn't gone into effect because of Twin City rival First Commercial Bank's suit, which claimed the law was unconstitutional because it applied to only one county. But then a federal court ruling in Mississippi had authorized the Comptroller of the Currency in Washington to authorize branch banking despite restrictive state laws, prompting twenty-two Arkansas banks to seek approval for branches. With

---

* No financial disclosure statement for the 1988 loan renewal has surfaced, and, as noted in the text, the evidence suggests none was produced. David Kendall, the Clintons' lawyer, said that none was produced because the bank didn't ask for one. Hillary Clinton, in response to an RTC interrogatory, testified: "I cannot recall what information my husband and I provided to the banks, although I believe we would have provided them with whatever they requested in order to process the loan applications." Bill Clinton testified in precisely the same words, substituting "wife" for "husband."

But those assertions seem hard to reconcile with Strange's letter of April 12, 1988. Strange says that the bank did require the financial statement as a matter of policy and sought to obtain it. He says he has been instructed by his own lawyer and the independent counsel not to discuss this matter further. However, he did say, "If you're going to waive financial documents, especially on a troublesome loan, that's not standard banking. That's off the wall." He added, "As far as I know, all the documentation on the Clintons was complete. But I would have to check and to do that I would need authorization from the Clintons. Not David Kendall [the Clintons' lawyer], the Clintons." Told that Kendall confirmed that no financial disclosure statement was submitted in 1988, Strange responded, "I have a specific release from Bill and Hillary Clinton about what Kendall can and cannot do," adding that Kendall has not been permitted to see all the documents in the bank's files. Kendall also said no 1st Ozark financial disclosure form was required in 1987, and doesn't seem to have seen the document that later surfaced in 1st Ozark's files. If so, it seems startling—not to mention foolhardy—that the Clintons would be withholding any information from their own lawyer. If a 1988 disclosure form exists in the bank's files, despite the evident waiver of the requirement, any valuation of Whitewater would be of interest.

Curiously, just two months later, in September 1988, Bill Clinton submitted a personal financial statement to the bank of Cherry Valley in connection with an unrelated loan, in which he listed total assets of $152,000, including $120,000 in cash and marketable securities. There is nothing listed in the categories "real estate owned" and "real estate mortgages receivable," suggesting that he made no attempt to value Whitewater.

Margaret Davenport now handling the issue for Twin City, the
bank remained keenly interested in passage of a law that would
permit countywide branch banking throughout the state. Such a
bill was passed in a special session of the legislature held in July,
and was signed by Governor Clinton on July 15, the same day 1st
Ozark waived the Clintons' financial disclosure requirement.

Hillary had motives other than financial to take over the management of Whitewater and get it out of her and her husband's
lives. Even as she was negotiating with 1st Ozark and Security
Bank, she and her husband were focusing on far loftier ambitions:
a run for the presidency.

Since his reelection in 1982, Clinton had been reelected comfortably in 1984 (a rerun against Frank White) and in 1986, this
time for a four-year term. His approval ratings among Arkansas
voters were at historic highs. He began to develop themes that
could be adapted to a national stage, especially post–New Deal
notions like "opportunity" and "responsibility" that broke with liberal Democratic orthodoxy. The cornerstone was his successful effort to raise taxes for education and his stand against the powerful
teachers' union in favor of imposing competency standards for
teachers (a drive spearheaded by Hillary, who took a summer off
from the Rose firm to campaign for the reforms). He continued his
voracious networking at the national level by becoming chairman
of the National Governors Association in 1986. With Hillary and
staunch loyalist Betsey Wright keeping a firm grip on the administration in Little Rock, Clinton was able to give his national ambitions and imagination free rein.

Improbable as the likelihood of a young Arkansas governor
being elected president might seem, events were moving in Clinton's direction. In March 1987, Arkansas senator Dale Bumpers,
widely mentioned as a potential candidate, cleared the way for Clinton by announcing he wouldn't run. Clinton made an exploratory
foray into New Hampshire, demonstrating anew his formidable
warmth on the campaign trail, and came back inspired. Fund-
raising letters went out to a national audience. Clinton was eager.
He was growing bored with his tenure as Arkansas governor, and
there was no other obvious Democratic candidate.

As word of the possible national campaign spread through

the governor's circle in Little Rock, it triggered excitement and speculation, and not just among his policy advisors and political strategists. This was especially the case among a small group of state troopers who were as physically close to the governor as anyone, a group that included Roger Perry, Larry Patterson, and Danny Ferguson. Perry was a thirteen-year veteran of the police force, working as an undercover narcotics officer before joining the governor's detail. Patterson had been a trooper for twenty-two years, working for Clinton since 1986, and Ferguson, an eleven-year veteran, had joined the governor's detail a little over a year later. The three were well regarded by their colleagues. Perry was twice elected president of the Arkansas State Police Association, and Patterson was vice president three times.

Unlike many states, Arkansas assigns to its state troopers the tasks of bodyguard, chauffeur, receptionist, phone operator, and all-round gofer for the governor. Operating from a command post just outside the mansion itself, state troopers answered all incoming phone calls, took messages, greeted visitors, unlocked the public rooms in the house each morning, helped fix breakfast, drove the governor whenever he traveled by car, accompanied him on out-of-town trips. Slots on the governor's security detail, as the assignment was known, were coveted by veterans on the force, and troopers were carefully chosen by Buddy Young, the captain in charge of governor security, for loyalty and discretion in addition to police skills. They then had to be interviewed and approved by Bill and Hillary Clinton. Spending so much time together, the troopers assigned to the governor developed their own esprit de corps, carrying on from one governor to the next. They were bound together, too, by a powerful tradition of silence about events in the private lives of the governor and his family that they invariably witnessed.

Larry Patterson, in particular, had felt especially close to Clinton. He'd been serving Clinton in close quarters since 1986, each week working two sixteen-hour shifts at the mansion that started at 6:30 A.M., followed by an eight-hour stint. Soon after joining the governor, he accompanied Clinton to Washington for the signing of President Ronald Reagan's welfare reform bill, which Clinton had worked on. When Clinton and Patterson arrived at the entrance gate to the White House, they were told that only Clinton had been cleared for admittance. "I'm not going in without my trooper," Clinton had insisted. Once inside, Clinton introduced Patterson to Vice President George Bush. "Would you like to meet the president?" Clinton asked Patterson. He took him into the Rose Garden, where Patterson shook hands with Ronald Reagan. "This is my trooper," Clinton had said. Patterson would never forget that day. He'd never been so proud to be an Arkansas state trooper.

The intervening years, however, had inevitably shown aspects of Clinton that hadn't always inspired the troopers' admiration, and now the prospect of Bill Clinton as president of the United States triggered varying degrees of enthusiasm among them. Despite their close proximity to the governor, they were cut from a very different fabric. Though most had attended college, many didn't have four-year degrees and certainly hadn't attended elite Eastern colleges or professional schools. While they tended to be loyal Democrats, they were typically conservative Southern Democrats. While Patterson and Ferguson were divorced, the three troopers tended to live middle-class lives and put a premium on obeying the law. Hillary's independence, drive, and outspokenness were foreign to their experience. They never said anything, but they didn't like the forceful role she played in her husband's life and career. They were especially disapproving of her unladylike language and outbursts of temper. They would never tolerate this in their own homes.

The troopers were to varying degrees awed by the prospect of someone they actually knew running for, maybe even becoming, president. On the other hand, they held the presidency itself in tremendous esteem. They considered presidents to be national heroes, even if they didn't agree with their politics. They hadn't actually known any presidents, but some of them expressed doubts about whether Clinton had the mettle. While manning the governor's phone lines, all three had fielded numerous phone calls from Gennifer Flowers and other women. They never listened in, but they noticed that when Hillary was present, the governor instructed them to "take a message." When the first lady was absent, the calls seemed to go right through. Patterson often drove Clinton to Quapaw Towers, the apartment complex where Flowers lived. Clinton told him that he had to go there for meetings with Maurice Smith, the former aide who also had an apartment there. Patterson would wait in the car while Clinton was inside, often for extended periods. He doubted that Clinton was making such frequent visits to discuss political strategy. Smith was a notorious cigar smoker, yet Clinton often returned smelling of perfume.

While Patterson thought Clinton's personal life wasn't any of his business, he did think having to chauffeur him to such meetings while on duty was unprofessional. He complained to Young, his immediate superior, then to Tommy Goodwin, the director of state police. They told him, in effect, to do what Clinton wanted or get another job.

As rumors of Clinton's candidacy intensified, the three reminded each other of these and other incidents. Then, in May, the leading Democratic contender, Colorado senator Gary Hart, was photographed in a rendezvous with Donna Rice, triggering a media furor and effectively dooming Hart's candidacy. The troopers couldn't help but notice the parallels. One day, while Clinton was preparing to go jogging, Perry said, "Governor, you're gonna make Gary Hart look like a damned saint." Clinton laughed and said, "Yeah, I do, don't I?"

Clinton's political momentum continued unabated. In July he rented the ballroom at Little Rock's Excelsior Hotel to announce his bid for the presidency. But Perry's concern was being echoed by others. Just days before the scheduled announcement, Betsey Wright insisted on sitting down with Clinton. As she later recounted the scene to biographer David Maraniss, after going over a list of women he'd allegedly had affairs with, she told Clinton that he owed it to his wife and daughter not to run.*

The Excelsior ballroom went unused. Clinton decided not to run, phoning friends and supporters and then issuing a press statement. No doubt many factors contributed to his decision. "I need some family time; I need some personal time," his statement read. "The other, even more important reason for my decision is the certain impact this campaign would have on our daughter."

Still, Clinton held out the possibility that he would run for the presidency at some later date, and the troopers thought the governor would moderate his personal behavior in anticipation of the greater scrutiny he was likely to receive. Yet, if anything, they felt

---

*After publication of Maraniss's book, Wright issued a statement through her lawyer saying that the passage had been taken out of context.

that things were getting worse. Bill and Hillary were again having furious fights. Bill's behavior sometimes seemed erratic, with frequent nocturnal excursions. Sometimes the troopers had to drive him, other times he drove himself, leaving the troopers to monitor Hillary and worry about his security. One night, Bill came downstairs and asked Perry if he could borrow his car, a Chevrolet Corsica, so he wouldn't be recognized. Perry gave him the keys. Perry assumed Hillary was asleep. But later, his phone rang. "Roger, where's Bill?" Hillary asked.

"Oh, he couldn't sleep and he just went for a little drive," Perry said.

Hillary exploded: "That no good . . ." She slammed down the phone. Perry immediately called Clinton on a cellular phone. "God!" Clinton exclaimed repeatedly. About fifteen minutes later, Perry's car came screeching up to the mansion's kitchen door. Bill jumped out, leaving the door open. When Perry went to close it and retrieve his car, he could hear Hillary and Bill arguing in the kitchen. They were shouting. Perry left, trying not to overhear, uncomfortable about intruding on their privacy. About two hours later, he went into the kitchen. A cupboard door was broken off its hinges. Food, pots and pans, broken glass were scattered on the floor. Perry cleaned up the glass. Prison inmates working on the grounds and in maintenance cleaned up the rest.

Ferguson recounted other stories to his fellow troopers that fueled their reservations. As part of Clinton's security detail, Ferguson attended a Governor's Quality Management Conference sponsored by the Arkansas Industrial Development Commission in May 1991. Clinton was speaking at the conference and had taken a room at the conference center, the Excelsior Hotel in downtown Little Rock. While the governor was speaking, Ferguson struck up a conversation with one of the two receptionists, an attractive young woman in her twenties who was handing out name tags and had only recently been hired by the commission. Her own name tag identified her as Paula Corbin.

Governor Clinton is "good-looking," Corbin told Ferguson. She especially liked his hair, which she said was "sexy." Would he mention that to the governor?

Later, after the speech, Ferguson arranged to escort Corbin to Clinton's room. He accompanied her up in the elevator, indicated the governor's door, and returned to the main convention floor.*

Even Patterson, probably the most loyal of this group of troopers, became disenchanted during Clinton's 1990 gubernatorial re-election campaign. There had been much wavering on Clinton's part about whether he should run again in 1990 and commit to serving another four-year term, or concentrate instead on the 1992 presidential election. There were even reports that Hillary would run for governor in his stead. In the climate of uncertainty, he attracted a Democratic primary challenger, Thomas McRae, the highly regarded head of the Rockefeller Foundation in Little Rock, who compiled a withering assessment of Clinton's actual accomplishments as governor. But Clinton finally entered the race. McRae did surprisingly well—40 percent to Clinton's 53 percent in a six-person field. Then Clinton faced a vigorous and well-financed Republican challenger, Sheffield Nelson, the head of Arkla, the Arkansas-Louisiana Gas Co. Clinton was bereft of Betsey Wright's campaign management. As concerned as Perry about Clinton's behavior, dispirited by the fights between Bill and Hillary in the governor's mansion, she had taken a leave of absence in 1989, telling Clinton she was burned out.

As the primary campaign heated up, Clinton mentioned to Perry that he was worried Patterson and another trooper might "burn" him by leaking information about him. Speaking of Patterson, Clinton said, "I don't know if it's better to have him in pissing out or having him out pissing in." Perry shrugged off his concern. "You're still the governor and he still works for you. What are you worried about?" Perry replied.

But several weeks later, Clinton asked to speak to Patterson in private, and said he was concerned Patterson might be leaking information to the Republicans. "That's a fucking lie," Patterson indignantly replied. "Put me on the box. I'll take a polygraph test. If you think I am [leaking], then remove me from the detail."

*As will be seen, most aspects of Paula Corbin Jones's encounter with Clinton are in dispute. These facts are essentially Ferguson's version of events. But both Jones and Ferguson agree that Jones made small talk with Ferguson and that Ferguson escorted her in the elevator to Clinton's hotel room at the conference on May 8, 1991. Jones's comments are from Ferguson's sworn answer to Jones's complaint.

"Oh no, I won't do that," Clinton assured him. But Patterson was stunned by the suggestion of disloyalty.

During the campaign, Nelson went after Clinton with unusual zeal, giving rise to a bitter rivalry. In this atmosphere it's not surprising that rumors of Clinton's extramarital behavior reached an unprecedented intensity, fanned by Nelson's supporters. Nelson even went so far as to prepare a television ad attacking Clinton's moral standards, but then decided not to air it. In retaliation, the Clinton campaign enlisted Patterson and other troopers to investigate rumors that Nelson had fathered an illegitimate child, but the effort made little headway. Larry Nichols, a fired former state employee, held a press conference and named five women alleged to have had affairs with Clinton. No one took Nichols seriously, and the local press ignored him, but the incident was much talked about around the campaign.*

However titillating, none of these allegations made much of an impression on Arkansas voters. Clinton easily defeated Nelson in November. But the hard-fought race left Nelson eager for revenge. Patterson remained hurt and offended that his loyalty had been questioned. It was a tough time for him: he was drinking, and one night in December he downed several shots of whiskey, then slammed his state police car into a tree after running off the road. Perry was a passenger, suffered cracked vertebrae, and when he tried to collect on his insurance, he and Patterson claimed in unsworn statements they had only had one beer—the full extent of their drinking might have cost them their jobs on the force. In later testimony under oath, the real story emerged, and Perry didn't get the $100,000 he was claiming.

As Bill Clinton dreamed of a run for the presidency and his political star rose, that of his former mentor, Jim McDougal, continued its downward spiral. The medication prescribed for his manic depression seemed to be having no noticeable effect, and he was still subject to bouts of depression. His open-heart surgery had left him weakened, his eyesight impaired. The events of the past

---

* *Nichols later disavowed the allegations, saying he was trying to discredit Clinton. But one of the names on Nichols's list was Gennifer Flowers, which prompted a call from her to Clinton. It was the first of the calls of which she later produced tape recordings.*

year, especially, seemed a blur. After his departure from Madison Guaranty, the FHLBB had turned over the results of its investigation to the Department of Justice, and the U.S. attorney in Little Rock, Bush-appointee Charles Banks, launched a criminal investigation.

In October 1989, McDougal was indicted on eleven felony counts, including bank fraud, misapplication of bank funds, submitting false statements, and conspiracy. The indictment zeroed in on just two allegedly sham transactions, both related to McDougal's Castle Grande development, though not the parts Hillary Clinton and the Rose firm had worked on. Also indicted were two of Susan's brothers, David and James Henley, who'd gone to work selling manufactured homes for McDougal and whose names showed up as investors in the suspect deals. Susan, reached in California, told the *Arkansas Gazette* that she and Jim "are both such private persons. We practically have no one else. . . . Jim is a man of integrity. He would never break the law. He is the last person to have intentionally done something wrong." Both Susan and Jim, however, were dismayed by the reactions of people close to them, most of whom seemed to assume that the government wouldn't have indicted Jim unless he'd broken the law. Even former senator Fulbright expressed doubts to Susan, causing her to burst out, "There was nothing done wrong, Senator." And Jim's own mother, Lorene, with whom he'd always remained close, confided to Susan that "whatever Jim did, I'm sure it wasn't intentional."

McDougal said he couldn't afford a lawyer, so the court named Little Rock attorney Sam Heuer to represent him. Initially, Heuer indicated McDougal might mount an insanity defense, relying on his diagnosis as manic-depressive. But a court-ordered psychiatric exam found him fit to stand trial. Then, in February 1990, McDougal's former chief operating officer, John Latham, pleaded guilty to a felony of making false entries on the thrift's books, and agreed to cooperate with the government. He was sentenced to six months in a halfway house.

McDougal's trial, along with his co-defendants, David and James Henley, began in May. Susan and other members of the Henley family came to court every day, sitting just behind the defendants. The evidence was fully consistent with McDougal's cavalier approach to the banking business. In one instance, the purchaser of one of the tracts was a salesman for Madison, who had borrowed the entire $525,000 purchase price from Madison at McDougal's behest, and had earned a $50,000 real estate commission on the same sale. In the other, the Henleys and a developer friend of McDougal's had borrowed the entire $472,000 purchase price from Madison at McDougal's behest. Prosecutors alleged both deals were "shams" to create the appearance of sales, generate commissions for McDougal, and get the property off Madison's books.

But the Henleys, taking the stand in their own defense, proved to be strong witnesses. Jim, in particular, was a former Baptist minister and social worker who was now teaching elementary school after his brief foray into real estate development, and seemed convincing and sympathetic. He wept on the stand as he testified that he and his brother were the "last people" to knowingly get involved in an illegal scheme. "I did not conspire with anybody," he said. "I just accepted a proposal from Jim McDougal, and I was working very hard."

And McDougal's performance, in which he summoned all his oratorical skills from his years in politics and on the campaign trail, was a tour de force. He set the tone right at the outset, when prosecutor Ken Stoll asked what McDougal had been doing when regulators arrived at Madison. "I was working six or seven days a week, twelve hours a day," McDougal shot back. "I wasn't a lazy, overpaid government employee like you working four days a week and drawing $80,000 a year."

In cross-examination, Heuer emphasized that the deals in question hadn't made McDougal any money; indeed, McDougal was now all but impoverished, living in a guest cottage borrowed from his friends the Rileys. He hardly fit the profile of the high-rolling S&L operator. And McDougal emphasized repeatedly that, however questionable the documentation, the deals in question were real. He expected them to make money, and nothing was concealed. He was the big-picture person, leaving details to others. He didn't consider himself a banker so much as a visionary. Asked about the day-to-day operation of Madison Guaranty, he testified, "I stayed as far from it as I could. I'm not a paper man. I don't know how to do those things. . . . I wouldn't know how to fill a note out." Yet he didn't deny he was the boss. Referring to his humble origins in Bradford, he said, "Well, down at that grocery store when daddy walked in he is the boss. You know, he owned it."

The judge in the case dismissed the charges against David Henley even before sending the case to the jury. As he instructed the jurors, the case turned on intent: McDougal and James Henley had to believe they were committing fraud. McDougal had been especially convincing in that respect; he had fervently expressed his belief in his own innocence. The jury deliberated an afternoon before finding McDougal and Henley innocent on all counts. Just after the verdict was read, Susan called out, "Thank you, thank you," to the jurors, then burst into tears as she hugged Jim, her brothers, and other family members. McDougal told the *Gazette*, "This was a political show trial that would do Joe Stalin proud."

The result was all the more remarkable given the national climate of outrage over the nation's S&L crisis. Of the 247 S&L defendants indicted that year, Jim McDougal and the Henley brothers were the only ones who were acquitted.

The night of the verdict, McDougal got a call from the governor. Hillary was on the extension. After congratulating him on the outcome of the trial, Bill turned the conversation to Whitewater. Though he seemed embarrassed to bring the matter up—he stumbled over the words—he mentioned that he and Hillary had recently incurred about $3,000 in out-of-pocket costs. McDougal was incredulous. "What do you want me to do now?" McDougal asked. Clinton indicated he and Hillary felt the McDougals should reimburse them. "Talk to Sam Heuer," McDougal replied. "I'm too worn out."

Two days later, Clinton did talk to Heuer, but this time he said he and Hillary just wanted out of Whitewater. "Just get with Hillary," he told McDougal's lawyer. Heuer sent a letter to Hillary:

"I have talked to both Jim McDougal and Governor Clinton concerning [Whitewater Development Corp.]. . . . It is my understanding that all of the books have been delivered to Governor Clinton or his CPA concerning this corporation. . . . My suggestion would be to simply dissolve this corporation, and we would obtain a release of personal liability from the Bank in this regard. Let me know your thoughts. . . ."

But once again, Hillary kept them in the investment. She told Heuer she didn't know the financial condition of Whitewater, and would check and call him back. But she never did. And McDougal was too preoccupied to follow up on Bill's call by meeting with Hillary about Whitewater. Though he was initially buoyed by his acquittal, McDougal was exhausted by the ordeal of the investigation and trial, and decided to stay in Arkansas to sort through his life. He subsisted on a $591-a-month Social Security disability check. His luxury cars were a thing of the past; he drove a small Honda borrowed from the Rileys. He moved into a mobile home in Arkadelphia and adopted a stray cat. Then his eighty-year-old mother suffered a stroke and lost her eyesight, and he spent most of his time with her. Finally, in a humiliation he'd vowed he would never submit to, McDougal was forced to file for bankruptcy.

Shortly after Jim's conversations with the Clintons, Susan also received a phone call from the governor. With her, he adopted an entirely different tone than he had when Hillary was on the line with Jim. He seemed concerned, apologetic. "I wasn't that sensitive" to the fact that she and Jim were going through such hard times the last few years, he said. "I wasn't as caring, I didn't know how hard things had been." Susan was so flattered that Bill would make the call; it reminded her of the qualities she had most liked in him. "Yes, things have been hard," she said. "Jim couldn't function, and I didn't realize how serious his illness was, and we never talked about our problems."

"What can I do?" Bill asked. Nothing, Susan said, but then she thought of Jim's mother. "You know, you could call Lorene. She's sick, she's dying, and she really loves you. It would mean so much to her." Clinton said he would, adding, "You know, I think I might have a job for Jim."

Lorene McDougal was a devoted admirer of Clinton. As she put it, he'd "hug and kiss on me like I was his own mother." About a month after Susan's call from Clinton, Lorene called. Despite her illness, she seemed ecstatic. "Bill Clinton called me," Lorene reported. "He is just the nicest man." Overcome, she burst into tears. When she collected herself, she said, "He might give Jim a job." When Lorene told Jim about the call, she said Clinton told her, "I've got an important job for Jim." She was so relieved, she told Jim. "Your reputation will be restored."

Susan, too, thought that a political job was just what Jim needed to get back on his feet. She knew the prospect had already given him a hint of his old sparkle. But weeks, then months passed with no word from Clinton or anyone in his entourage. Finally Susan called Clinton aide Bruce Lindsey at the governor's office. "I understand from the governor that there might be a job for Jim," Susan said. Lindsey asked her about how Jim was feeling. How was his stamina and his mental health? Susan adopted her most upbeat tone. "He's back and he's great," she assured him. Lindsey said he'd talk to Clinton and get back to her, but she heard nothing further.

Jim was disappointed, more disappointed than he wanted to admit, but he figured he'd just forget about it and move on with his life. That proved impossible. Almost every day for the next year, until the day she died, Lorene McDougal asked her son, "Has Bill called you?"

On October 3, 1991, Bill Clinton, in dark suit and rep tie, and Hillary Rodham Clinton, in a bright red suit, appeared on the steps of the old State House in Little Rock, its stately pillars and a dozen American flags providing a suitably patriotic backdrop. As television crews recorded the moment, Clinton announced, "Today I am declaring my candidacy for president of the United States."

PART TWO

A Death in
the White House

SEVEN

THE *NEW YORK TIMES* BUREAU in Washington, D.C., occupies the seventh floor of the distinguished old Army-Navy Club building overlooking Farragut Square. Like many Washington bureaus of newspapers based in other cities, its control of the avalanche of news generated in the nation's capital makes it a power in its own right, one to rival not only the *Times*'s hierarchy in New York but the hometown *Washington Post*, the nearby bureau of the national *Wall Street Journal*, and other bureaus of major newspapers. Along with the *Post* and *Journal*, the *Times* is read by every major opinionmaker in Washington, from politicians to television news producers.

In late 1991, forty-seven-year-old investigative reporter Jeff Gerth got a phone call from the *Times*'s bureau chief, Howell Raines, summoning him to a meeting to discuss coverage of the intensifying presidential campaign. The New Hampshire primary was just months away, and the *Times* viewed as part of its mission the obligation to educate the public with in-depth coverage of the candidates. George Bush was a known commodity, but he had a surprising challenger in Pat Buchanan. And the Democrats, their ranks thinned by Bush's popularity after the Gulf War, included perennial candidates Jerry Brown and Jesse Jackson, but also lesser-known Paul Tsongas, Bill Clinton, Bob Kerrey, and Tom Harkin.

Gerth, an eleven-year veteran of the bureau and a former investigative reporter for the business section, had been lobbying for more coverage of financial aspects of the candidates, both their campaign finances and their personal financial dealings. He'd been troubled by what he deemed his own and his colleagues' failure to more aggressively probe the savings and loan crisis in the 1988 campaign. Gerth believed the savings and loan disaster was an event that had generated much of the voter alienation and cynicism so prevalent outside of Washington, and he felt the media had slipped badly in its coverage. Gerth himself had broken the story of President Bush's son Jeb's questionable dealings with a Florida thrift, but he felt the *Times* had downplayed the story, not even running it on the front page. He was determined the same thing wouldn't happen in the 1992 campaign.

To his editors, this kind of stubbornness made Gerth both an asset to the paper and a headache. Before joining the paper, Gerth had worked for the McGovern campaign, investigating some aspects of Watergate at the same time Hillary Rodham was working for John Doar and the House Judiciary Committee considering Nixon's impeachment. Then he had done some freelance journalism, including an expose of the La Costa resort's ties to organized crime that ran in *Penthouse*. He had also collaborated with the *Times*'s legendary investigative reporter Seymour Hersh, who broke the My Lai massacre story. It was Hersh who recommended that the *Times* hire him.

At the *Times*, Gerth plunged almost immediately into investigations of Jimmy Carter's former budget director, Bert Lance. Since then, he'd become one of the paper's most esteemed investigative reporters, a role he seemed to relish. Balding and professorial, he wore a battered topcoat with its collar turned up and a hat with its brim snapped down in all but the hottest weather. To some of his colleagues in the Washington bureau, he seemed secretive and mysterious. He never liked to tell anyone where he was going, where he'd been, or whom he was talking to—even his editors. He didn't socialize much with fellow reporters outside the office. He didn't like to rely on researchers, and rarely consulted them, preferring to spend hours at his desk poring over financial documents. Few colleagues knew that he'd been a star varsity golfer at Northwestern, or that he loved to play the piano. One of the highlights of his career was playing golf with Jack Nicklaus and then writing about it for the *Times*. Gerth often golfed with sources or played the piano for them in an effort to make them feel more comfortable.

Financial stories were his chief interest. He'd started on the

Times business staff and was still happiest when he had a meaty 10-K report in front of him. He'd attended a year of business school at Northwestern and entered a Ph.D. program in business at Columbia but then dropped out. Gerth prided himself on being strictly nonpartisan, and imposed even stricter ethical standards on himself than did the paper. He refused to give speeches or appear on talk shows. Since his wife worked on the Democratic staff of the Senate Foreign Relations Committee, Gerth emphasized that he would never report on her committee or on parts of the world that were subjects of her research.

Like many investigative reporters, writing was not Gerth's strong suit; he was an investigator first, a writer second. A colleague recalls an editor picking up a dense, lengthy opus by Gerth and moaning, "Oh my God, I can't look at this now." Some Gerth submissions left editors stunned, not even knowing where to begin. One of his editors was once overheard exclaiming, "He can't write worth shit." Even Gerth's staunchest supporters concede that as a prose stylist, he "would never be mistaken for Philip Roth," as Hersh puts it, but note that complicated tax and financial matters can confound even the most stylish writers. For that and other reasons, many of Gerth's stories, like a good deal of his S&L coverage, were buried deep in the paper and often hadn't gotten the attention Gerth felt they deserved.

By the time of the editorial meeting, *Times* reporters hadn't done much probing of Clinton, and only one major story had run. Robin Toner, a *Times* political reporter, had been to Arkansas, and when she returned to Washington, she reported that Little Rock was rife with stories about Clinton's "woman problem," as she put it. But the topic of sex made the *Times* editors squeamish. The paper had caused a furor when it investigated and then printed the name of the alleged rape victim in the William Kennedy Smith trial (doing so only after NBC News had revealed her identity); then it had been criticized for not printing the name of the Central Park jogger who was raped, beaten, and left for dead. The *Times* had covered the Gary Hart story after it was broken by the *Miami Herald*. Given the story's impact on the campaign, covering it was unavoidable, but the *Times* had done so reluctantly. As Joe Lelyveld, then the paper's managing editor, put it, "I as a reporter would not have wanted to stand in the bushes outside Gary Hart's house." As a result of these experiences, a policy had evolved: affairs between consenting adults should be private. The *Times* would not write about them no matter how much coverage they received elsewhere.

Clinton himself remained an enigma in Washington, an outsider, a governor from a small, obscure Southern state. Yet, within months of the announcement of his candidacy, he was widely viewed within the Washington media establishment as the likely Democratic nominee. Many reporters and editors liked Clinton, but more important, the media was hoping for a vigorous general election that would spawn good stories, and Clinton seemed the only challenger who could deliver. Paul Tsongas, though widely liked, had serious medical problems and lacked charisma; Nebraska senator Bob Kerrey lacked money; Harkin's New Deal rhetoric seemed anachronistic; Jerry Brown and Jesse Jackson were seen as fringe candidates. The last thing anyone wanted was another lopsided contest with no real suspense, like the McGovern-Nixon race, or even the Mondale-Reagan campaign.

At the meeting, Gerth pressed for a series of articles on the financial dimensions of the candidates, and the editors agreed. Howell Raines, in particular, had been struck by how little media scrutiny in Arkansas Clinton had received while governor, unlike former governors Jimmy Carter or Ronald Reagan. In contrast to papers in Southern states like Georgia, where Raines, a Southerner himself, had once been Atlanta bureau chief, the Little Rock press kept up a lively political commentary but had devoted few investigative resources to the Clintons' financial dealings. Given Clinton's rising stature, Raines assigned Gerth to delve into Clinton's past. Just after the holidays, in January 1992, Gerth set off for Little Rock. He avoided the visibility of the Capital Hotel, checking into the Holiday Inn.

Arkansas and its capital were familiar to Gerth from a 1978 investigation of the Stephens family empire, one of Gerth's first big stories after joining the *Times* in 1977. Despite Clinton's efforts at economic development, Little Rock had remained a sad testament to the failure of urban renewal and the decline of many inner cities. Despite a few modern towers—the TCBY building the tallest among them—the city's downtown shopping "mall" was pockmarked by abandoned storefronts, surrounded by empty parking lots. Virtually deserted at night, the scattered signs of life downtown after 5 P.M. were at the few hotels and restaurants, the slightly decrepit YMCA, where Clinton and other state officials exercised, and area churches, with dwindling, mostly minority congregations. By contrast, outlying neighborhoods and suburbs, like Pleasant Valley and the Heights, almost exclusively white, boasted large older homes, even some mansions, tree-lined streets, and access to modern shopping malls and schools.

The Stephens story reflected many of Gerth's abiding interests, including campaign finance, big business, conflicts of interest, and the public interest. Headlined "The Stephens Empire Faces a Challenge," the story focused on "whether Stephens companies have favored each other at the public's expense," and noted that one of the Stephens brothers, Jackson, had been a major fund-raiser for Jimmy Carter. Jack Stephens was an avid golfer, chairman of the Masters Tournament in Augusta, Georgia, and he and Gerth talked about playing a few rounds. Stephens even mentioned inviting Gerth to play the Masters course, a prospect that pained Gerth, since he felt he'd have to turn it down for ethical reasons. From that reporting experience, Gerth had gotten to know two other Little Rock sources fairly well: Bill Bowen, a former banker who was now Governor Clinton's chief of staff, and Sheffield Nelson, the former Arkla executive who'd run for governor against Clinton in 1990.

He arranged interviews with them, and collected names of other businesspeople in town he might talk to. One of the first calls he made was to Curt Bradbury, chief executive of Worthen Bank, the large Stephens-controlled bank in Little Rock. He and Bradbury chatted briefly, then Bradbury invited Gerth over to lunch in the bank's dining room. Bradbury didn't like Gerth's earlier story on Stephens—he was especially annoyed at a chart that labeled the Stephens holdings a "tangled web." He also got the sense that Gerth was suspicious of authority, that he didn't like anybody in a position of power, and that he saw his job as criticizing them. But it turned out Bradbury is an avid golfer, and he and Gerth hit it off.

It was a reminder to Gerth how friendly and accessible even top executives in Little Rock tended to be. Bradbury seemed to like Clinton, and over lunch he ranged from one anecdote to another, mostly casting Clinton in a positive light; few of these stories were of much interest to Gerth. But then Bradbury mentioned a call he'd

gotten from Clinton just before the 1990 elections. The governor
was in a "panic," Bradbury recalled, saying "I need $100,000." Clin-
ton had wondered if Bradbury could get the Stephenses to raise the
money. He thought maybe Warren Stephens would support him;
the younger Stephens was about the same age as Clinton and not
as conservative as his Republican father. He needed the money,
Clinton explained, to pay off a $100,000 personal loan he'd ob-
tained from the Bank of Perry County to pay for some emergency
television ads. The Stephenses did raise the money, Bradbury
added.

This intrigued Gerth. Apart from Jack's ties to Jimmy Carter,
he'd always considered Jack Stephens to be a staunch Republican.
Yet here he was raising money for Clinton. Gerth probably would
have done so in any event, but this revelation sent him to the
election records, where he got copies of Clinton's state and federal
financial disclosure documents. There was no mention of the
$100,000 loan. But on the governor's annual financial disclosure
form, required of all top Arkansas officials, Clinton listed one asset:
Whitewater Development Corp., with a post office box address in
Little Rock. It was Gerth's first encounter with the name Whitewater. It meant nothing to him, but he jotted it down. He wondered
what it was. But his attention was still focused on the loan from the
Bank of Perry County.

In preparation for his trip to Little Rock, Gerth had also done
a routine computer search of the media database on Nexus, looking
particularly for references to the Stephens empire and for names
that might be potential sources. The search had generated an obscure article in *The Daily Bond Buyer* about a Little Rock stockbroker and consultant to the public employee retirement system board
named Roy Drew. Drew had drawn the ire of Stephens interests
when he publicly criticized a proposed Stephens-backed industrial
development bond issue that Stephens wanted the retirement system to invest in. Just before Gerth's arrival in Little Rock, the
Arkansas Gazette ran a feature on Drew, "Stephens' Watchdog
Draws Flak," which reported that Drew had advised Sheffield Nelson on some bond deals during the 1990 campaign. Clearly, Drew
was someone not allied with either Governor Clinton or the Stephens interests, which made him a promising source. Indeed, Gerth
wasn't the only journalist from a national publication to discover

Drew; Jeffrey Birnbaum of the *Wall Street Journal* called Drew almost the same day. Drew agreed to see both reporters, first Birnbaum, then Gerth.

For reporters casting about for leads on Clinton, Drew was unusually well positioned in the relatively close-knit community of Little Rock business and politics. He had lived next door to Webb Hubbell, and the two often jogged together, though Drew soon outstripped Hubbell as he dropped from 230 to 165 pounds. A fellow University of Arkansas grad, Vince Foster was a co-investor with Drew in a Fayetteville hotel where they stayed on trips to see Razorback games. Drew's son, Ryan, was the same age as Chelsea Clinton, and at one of her birthday parties, held at a skating rink, he'd been thrilled that he got to skate with the governor. Drew's wife, a public school counselor, and Hillary sometimes corresponded about child care issues.

Drew had been working as a stockbroker at E.F. Hutton when Hillary called in the spring of 1983, wanting to open a joint brokerage account with Vince and Webb. Each would contribute $15,000, she said, for a total of $45,000. She'd be relying on Drew, she said, since she had never invested in stocks before. (She apparently overlooked the account she'd opened previously with William Smith.) Drew arranged a meeting with Hillary at the Rose firm, and Hillary mentioned how fit Drew was looking. He said he'd been running with an Olympic trainer. "I wish he'd work with Bill," Hillary said. "He goes running every day but he never seems to lose any weight." The three Rose partners opened an account with Drew called Midlife Investors. Until Drew quit the firm later that year, Hillary called nearly every trading day to check on the progress of Midlife's stocks.

Drew's relationship with the Clintons soured in 1987, in connection with the bond issue that had attracted Gerth's attention. The Stephenses and their political allies had been enraged by Drew's criticism of the bond issue, which he had described as a "damn flim-flam." Drew was fired from a consulting contract by one Stephens ally. When the retirement system submitted its annual budget to the state legislature, approval was blocked until a $10,000 item for "contracts for professional services"—which included Drew's salary—was deleted. As the state auditor told the *Gazette*, "I don't think I will hire him [Drew] again. . . . The legislature has the power to eliminate all of my budget." (A state representative on the budget committee confirmed to the *Gazette* that the legislature had held up approval to punish the auditor for criticizing the bond issue.) When Ryan invited Chelsea to his birthday party in November 1987, Chelsea's nanny called, saying Chelsea would not be attending.

Then, in April 1988, eight-year-old Ryan was killed in a car accident in front of the Drews' house. Despite an outpouring of sympathy from friends and neighbors, Drew never quite got over the loss of his son. Even though the governor was legendary for his sympathy for others in times of tragedy, the Drews heard nothing from either Bill or Hillary. (Drew says he didn't expect to.) Later that year, Drew wrote a blistering article in the *Arkansas Democrat* criticizing the Clinton administration, comparing Arkansas state government to a mushroom "kept in the dark by farmers and fed plenty of manure." In 1991, at the annual YMCA Thanksgiving race in which both Drew and Clinton were running, Drew felt Clinton avoided him, going so far as to close the car window as he passed the point where Drew was stretching in preparation for the race.

Since then Drew had managed money for a small group of wealthy clients. He had also emerged as something of a gadfly, monitoring the use of state finances and acting as a self-appointed "watchdog," as the *Gazette* had described him in its 1991 profile. It turned out that the same reporter who wrote Drew's profile, Joe Nabbefeld, had covered McDougal's bank fraud trial, and had mentioned McDougal's close ties to Clinton to Drew. The association had stuck in Drew's mind. When an interview with McDougal had appeared in the *Gazette* adjacent to an article about Drew, Drew clipped both articles out and stuck them in his files. The McDougal article was among the materials he gathered to pass on to Birnbaum and Gerth.

Drew met first with Birnbaum, at the Regis Grill in west Little Rock. They talked through lunch until 5 P.M. Drew inundated Birnbaum with materials on the state retirement system and its pension investments, the industrial development agency, the power of the Stephenses' interests. He gave Birnbaum the McDougal clip, and said he thought someone should look into McDougal's ties to Clinton. He mentioned that he had been in the same Arkansas ROTC unit that Clinton had been scheduled to join. There was something that didn't ring true, he said, about Clinton's explanations of his lack of military service. After leaving Birnbaum, Drew drove through west Little Rock and met Gerth at the Faded Rose, a popular bar and restaurant.

Drew went over much the same material with Gerth that he had with Birnbaum. Gerth wasn't interested in the draft stuff—his assignment was finances. He was especially interested in what Drew knew about any Stephens links; it was obvious that Drew had a strong antipathy to the Stephenses. Gerth didn't get the same sense about Drew's feelings toward Clinton. He was obviously willing to suggest potentially damaging leads, but he didn't express any personal dislike of Clinton. Drew later gave Gerth the McDougal clip, and though there was nothing of any great interest in it, Gerth thought he'd give McDougal a call. But McDougal's number wasn't listed in Arkadelphia, the town where the article said he was living in a mobile home. No one Gerth talked to in Little Rock had seen him recently, or knew where he was.

As he continued his work, Gerth scheduled an interview with Sheffield Nelson. With his wounds from the 1990 campaign still fresh, Nelson was eager to fuel any potentially negative article about Clinton, especially one in the national press. While discussing the 1990 loans, Gerth mentioned McDougal's name. McDougal was the operator of a failed thrift, Nelson said, and he pressed Gerth to look into the relationship. Later, on the phone, Nelson added that McDougal had held a fund-raiser for Clinton at the offices of Madison Guaranty. "This is like Keating," Nelson said, comparing McDougal to the notorious Charles Keating, the head of Lincoln Savings and Loan and a symbol of the nation's S&L crisis. Gerth thought Nelson's analogy was a stretch, but he was intrigued by yet another mention of McDougal. He told Nelson he'd been trying to contact him, but hadn't succeeded.

As he continued work on the loan story, Gerth had his first contacts with the Clinton campaign operation, headquartered in the handsome old *Arkansas Gazette* building (the paper had recently been sold to the rival *Democrat*, and the papers were merged in October 1991 into the *Arkansas Democrat-Gazette*). The Clinton campaign had moved into the newsroom, using the same desks and computers. Gerth made an appointment to see Dee Dee Myers, the campaign's press secretary.

He asked Myers for the Clintons' tax returns, mentioning that he understood they'd been made public in the 1990 campaign. But Myers, in Gerth's view, seemed evasive. She said she'd get back to him, then didn't. "I'm getting them; I'm working on it," she said in subsequent calls. Finally, on what was at least his fourth request, Myers said that since the tax returns related to an earlier campaign, the governor's press secretary would get them. Requests for the returns at the governor's mansion proved similarly fruitless. Gerth was exasperated. The returns had already been made public, so it should have been easy for Myers to get copies. One thing was clear: whatever Clinton's rhetoric about open government, the Clinton campaign was not making any real effort to be open and responsive to the press. In the end Gerth got the returns not from the Clinton campaign, but from an Associated Press reporter who had copies left over from the 1990 campaign.

Gerth also called David Ifshin, a Washington lawyer who was the campaign's general counsel. Ifshin, the former general counsel for the Mondale-Ferraro campaign, was one of the few campaign officials with previous experience in a national campaign. He happened to be with Bruce Lindsey when Gerth's first call came in, and Lindsey asked Ifshin what Gerth was like. "I've worked with Gerth and Babcock [Charles Babcock, an investigative reporter for the *Washington Post*]," Ifshin said. "They're tenacious. They love details. You don't fuck around. Get back to them and get it right."

Ifshin did respond to Gerth, acknowledging that the campaign should have disclosed the Bank of Perry County loans. The federal election commission disclosure forms were amended. At this point Gerth went ahead with his story. It ran under the headline "Wealthy Investment Family a Big Help to Clinton." The story noted that "No one is suggesting wrongdoing in the Stephens-Clinton connection. But it is a vivid example of the sorts of enduring political relationships that enable a small-state politician like Mr. Clinton to become a contender in the campaign for the nomination." The story also reported that "a review of Mr. Clinton's personal and political finances shows that he has accumulated little personal wealth. . . . Mrs. Clinton's career has produced most of the family's wealth. She is not required to disclose her income, and Mrs. Clinton would not answer questions on the subject." There was no mention of the real estate investment Gerth had noticed on the governor's financial disclosure form. The story ran on page 20 of the paper, and generated scant reaction.

About the time Gerth was finishing his story, McDougal happened to drop in on Sheffield Nelson. The two had never been friends. Their rivalry went way back, to when Nelson was a Faubus-backed candidate to head the Young Democrats, and McDougal had backed a reform candidate. McDougal had remained a staunch Democrat and didn't approve of Nelson's shift to the Republican party. But since then, Nelson had invested in McDougal's Campobello project. Now, McDougal was interested in finding a lawyer to represent his mother in a malpractice suit against Jim Guy Tucker, and for that he needed to consult a Republican lawyer. He didn't trust a Democrat to mount an effective case against such a prominent party member as Tucker. While in Nelson's office, the conversation inevitably turned to the presidential campaign. "That Bill Clinton is an SOB," McDougal remarked. "Really?" Nelson seemed surprised to hear McDougal say this; the two had always seemed friends. "There's a guy nosing around, a reporter for the *New York Times*," Nelson said. "I may suggest he see you."

"Send him on down," McDougal replied.

Gerth was back in Washington when he got a phone call from Nelson. Nelson said he'd been talking with McDougal and had mentioned Gerth's interest. "McDougal will talk to you," Nelson said and gave him McDougal's phone number. When Gerth called, McDougal agreed to meet Gerth at McDougal's favorite restaurant, the Western Sizzlin', a chain steak house just off the highway near Arkadelphia that McDougal usually referred to as "the Sizzlin'."

McDougal had always been wary of the press; his only interview, for the profile in the *Gazette*, had been months after his trial and acquittal. His remark to Nelson had been impulsive, but since then he'd given some thought to what he might say to Gerth. He recognized that an account of the Whitewater investment to which he had contributed so disproportionately would not help Clinton; on the contrary. Even now, he wouldn't have said anything had Clinton been the nominee; he was too loyal a Democrat to do anything that might help the Republicans. But this was still the primary stage.

More to the point, McDougal was still brooding over the promise to his mother; not, he insisted, because he hadn't gotten

any job offer, but because Clinton had, in McDougal's view, be-
haved "dishonorably." In McDougal's view, Clinton had been, at a
minimum, insincere, and at worst, duplicitous, taking advantage of
the affection of an eighty-year-old woman. McDougal had learned
in AA that he had to put the anger behind him, or it would consume
him. Maybe speaking to Gerth would be therapeutic.

McDougal may have fallen on hard times, but for the meeting
with Gerth he dressed impeccably in a dark suit, suspenders, white
shirt, and tie, much better than Gerth, in his usual worn topcoat.
When McDougal removed his hat, he was bald; he'd kept his head
shaved after his surgery. At the barnlike restaurant, Gerth and
McDougal worked their way past the large salad bar and through
the cafeteria-style line, McDougal helping himself liberally to the
Sizzlin's high-cholesterol menu. It was neither Gerth's nor McDougal's style to make much small talk, and at a table McDougal
plunged into his narrative.

He basically liked Bill Clinton, McDougal said, reminiscing
about the early days when both worked for Fulbright. But over the
years, he'd been doing favors for Clinton, and Clinton hadn't done
as much for him as he'd done for Clinton. "I've been bailing this
guy out since he was eighteen," he said.

What kind of favors? Gerth asked.

The first example McDougal gave was the jogging incident,
when Clinton pressured him to send work to Hillary and the Rose
firm, and he recalled with distaste how Clinton's sweat had stained
his new leather chair. "We put the Rose law firm on retainer, and
for eight months she [Hillary] didn't do a damn thing," McDougal
claimed. When the preferred stock issue arose, McDougal said he
had instructed John Latham to "get the Rose firm to do some work
for us."

It was clear to Gerth that however fond he claimed to be of Bill
Clinton, Hillary Clinton was another matter. McDougal seemed to
have developed an almost visceral dislike of the first lady, whom he
had once professed to admire. He asked McDougal why, and he
said he found Hillary to be "domineering." He continued, "When
I became the Democratic nominee for Congress in 1982, I scared
the hell out of the Republicans." At the state Democratic convention that year, McDougal claimed that his speech was so much
more dynamic than Clinton's that he "stole the convention. That

upset Hillary." He said things were never the same after that, and really hit bottom after his indictment. As soon as he got into trouble, he said, Bill and Hillary wouldn't have anything to do with him; they shunned him.

Then he got into Whitewater, making clear that he was inextricably linked with the asset listed on Clinton's financial disclosure form. McDougal explained the background of the land deal, and emphasized that over the years he'd contributed disproportionately to the investment. He seemed most upset about the handling of the Hillary house, claiming that the land had been transferred to Hillary at no cost to her, that he and Whitewater had made nearly all the payments on the loan to build the house, even though the loan was in Hillary's name, and that it was supposed to be a corporate asset. Yet Hillary had treated it as her own, buying the property out of bankruptcy court, immediately reselling it, and keeping the profit for herself. More than the money involved, it irked him that the Clintons, especially Hillary, had taken advantage of him. Incidentally, McDougal added, it wasn't as if Hillary desperately needed the money—she'd come to him in 1980 about some tax shelters, saying that Jim Blair had made her a lot of money trading cattle futures.

"I'm an easy mark," McDougal continued, saying that for years he didn't mind carrying the Clintons. "I didn't start getting irritated until the [Rose] retainer, the campaign deficit." He described the fund-raiser at Madison Guaranty in 1985, claiming Clinton had called him and asked him to "knock the deficit out" for him. "I was beginning to think I was being used," McDougal said.

He continued in this vein for about three hours. Gerth made another trip to Arkadelphia, this time visiting McDougal in his modest trailer home. Gerth had dug up the 1979 *Arkansas Democrat* article that first raised questions about the Whitewater development. He stayed in regular contact with McDougal by phone as he pieced elements of McDougal's rambling story into something that could be published in the *New York Times*.

From the first mention of McDougal, Gerth had been drawn to him because he was a failed S&L operator with financial ties to the governor. Now McDougal's account, if true, would link the biggest financial disaster of the 1980s to a candidate for president, as it had already been linked to George Bush through his son. This was undeniably newsworthy; this was the view of both Gerth and his editors. The story also promised elements of conflict of interest, since McDougal had run both a state-chartered S&L and a bank, both of them institutions regulated by the state presided over by Clinton. If McDougal had been doing all these favors for Clinton, what had Clinton been doing for him?

This, however, wasn't a theme that got much emphasis from McDougal. What McDougal kept complaining about wasn't the favors Clinton did him, but the opposite: the fact that Clinton had taken without giving in return. Still, McDougal had mentioned the stock issue, and he said he'd had a hand in getting Beverly Bassett named to her post. McDougal acknowledged that he had gotten approval from the state for the preferred stock issue, even though the financing had never gone forward. "How could I confirm this?" Gerth asked, and McDougal said that surely there were some records of the matter in the securities division in Little Rock, and that the Rose Law Firm would have billing records for the matter.

Back in Little Rock, Gerth went to the securities division of-fices and submitted a form request for documents in which he identified himself as a reporter for the *New York Times*. A low-level clerk handled his inquiry, and turned over the files on Madison Guaranty. Left alone with the documents, Gerth soon found the correspondence on the matter signed by Hillary, just as McDougal had predicted he would. He started making copies of virtually everything in the file, when a staff official appeared, asking him what he was doing. The official took Gerth's copies and the documents back into an office. When he returned, he said, "You can't have this," he said. "These are internal documents."

Gerth was a little nervous, not sure of his legal footing, but he was certain the correspondence wasn't "internal." "All this was sent to the Rose firm," he pointed out. "If they can get it, so can we." Gerth didn't believe it was a compelling argument, but it was the best he could come up with. But evidently it worked; a second official backed down, and Gerth hurried out with his copies. Now he not only had McDougal; he had the governor's wife representing an institution regulated by the state.

As he continued his reporting and was able to corroborate elements of McDougal's story, Gerth gained confidence in McDougal's accuracy. He kept going back to him, asking more questions and asking for any documents he had. McDougal told him that most of the Whitewater records had been turned over to the Clintons several years earlier, when Susan's brother Bill had dropped them off at the governor's mansion. But McDougal searched his files, and did come up with some original check stubs and records indicating that Whitewater was making payments on the Clintons' loan from Security Bank of Paragould. Gerth was excited to get his hands on such solid evidence. Then he checked the Clintons' tax returns, and discovered that they'd taken a deduction for the same payments that were actually being made by Whitewater. In addition to the other questions he was raising, Gerth now had evidence that the Clintons had filed inaccurate tax returns in 1980. But to Gerth, still obsessed with the S&L crisis, the most significant revelation was that Whitewater's account at Madison Guaranty was frequently overdrawn. Thus, it looked like payments to the Clintons had been made from an overdrawn account at a failed S&L.

After several weeks of work, the story, as Gerth saw it at this point, had a number of tantalizing elements:

- McDougal, the head of a failed S&L, had made payments for the Clintons in a hitherto unexamined joint real estate development;
- McDougal's S&L was regulated by the state, and thus Governor Clinton was in a position to return the favors;
- at the behest of the Governor, Hillary Clinton had been retained by McDougal to represent the S&L before a state agency;
- the state agency had given McDougal the ruling he wanted;
- the Clintons had improperly deducted interest payments on their tax returns.

Gerth concluded it was time to confront the Clintons. While he'd wanted to work for a while without the campaign staff following his every move, he was sure that by now word of his visit to the securities division had made its way to campaign headquarters.

While McDougal was still digging up his check stubs, Gerth had called Dee Dee Myers at campaign headquarters. His questions could hardly have come at a worse time. On February 4, just two weeks before the New Hampshire primary, the tabloid *Star* had landed on newsstands and supermarket checkout lines emblazoned: "My 12-Year Affair with Bill Clinton," PLUS "The Secret Love Tapes That Prove It!" While the *Star*'s credibility could be dismissed ("the *Star* says Martians walk on the earth and people have cows' heads," Clinton said), the ensuing media storm forced even the *New York Times* to deviate from its policy of not covering sexual affairs and acknowledge the story. The Clintons appeared on *60 Minutes*, where Bill denied having a twelve-year affair with Flowers. He acknowledged "problems" in the marriage, and argued he was being held to an unfair standard of perfection, especially compared to single or divorced candidates. He and Hillary stressed the stability of their marriage and her support for him. The situation was sufficiently dire that Betsey Wright was persuaded to join the campaign to prevent, in her words, further "bimbo eruptions."

Then, just twelve days before the New Hampshire primary, the *Wall Street Journal*'s Jeffrey Birnbaum broke the story of Clinton's inconsistent comments about the draft, the idea mentioned to him by Roy Drew. ABC followed up with a copy of an embarrassing letter Clinton had sent the ROTC colonel who'd accepted him into the program, enabling him to avoid the draft. The national media followed up the draft stories, which raised questions not just about Clinton's patriotism and willingness to serve in the armed forces, but his honesty and integrity.

Clinton was furious. "No one has ever been through what I've been through in this thing," he told staff members traveling with him in New Hampshire. "No one. Nobody's ever had this kind of personal investigation done on them, running for president, by the legitimate media. . . . I think that it is almost blood lust. I think it is an insatiable desire on the part of the press to build up and tear down. And they think that is their job, and not only that, their divine right."

Despite Clinton's outburst, and his lasting animosity toward the press, none of this seemed to exact a major toll. He finished a strong second in the New Hampshire primary to regional favorite son Paul Tsongas of Massachusetts, and, after Flowers, christened himself "the comeback kid." But within the campaign, there was talk that Clinton had suffered "two strikes," and that a third could be fatal.

Then Gerth called Myers. He outlined the subjects he wanted to discuss, and this time Myers just took down the information. His request didn't trigger any immediate consternation in the campaign; most people weren't even aware of the Gerth call and in any event were too absorbed in the Flowers and draft controversies. But both Bill and Hillary were informed.

Several days later, Gerth received a call from Harold Ickes, Clinton's New York campaign manager, whose father had been FDR's secretary of the interior. Ickes mentioned that he knew Sy Hersh, Gerth's former collaborator. Ickes had other ties to the *Times:* its executive editor had once been a client of his law firm. "I'm responding to your inquiry about McDougal and Whitewater," Ickes said. "It's been decided that you'll talk to Susan Thomases. She'll be acting as attorney for the Clintons." This immediately struck Gerth as odd; all his other inquiries had been handled through the campaign press office or, occasionally, the governor's press office. Nothing like this had happened on stories he'd done on the Bush campaign, or his work on previous presidential campaigns. What could be so important that the Clintons would hire a lawyer to handle his questions?

Susan Thomases was in her office at Willkie Farr on the forty-eighth floor of Citicorp Center in New York when she got a call from an obviously agitated Hillary Clinton. The brash, forty-seven-year-old Thomases had become one of Hillary's closest friends and confidantes. A reporter, Hillary said, not using Gerth's name, had stumbled onto a "stupid" investment she and Bill had made. The whole thing made her furious, she said, especially at her husband. He'd gotten them into it, McDougal was his friend. Then Bill had become governor, he didn't want to pay any attention to it, and she had to clean up the mess. It was a dumb investment, a flop.

And Hillary was practically beside herself about McDougal, the obvious source for this story. How dare he claim he'd been cheated by the Clintons? As far as she was concerned, he'd cheated them. She was scathing in her characterization of him. He wasn't credible, he was a "sick" person. How could anyone believe him?

Thomases didn't know what Hillary was talking about, even though the two had become so close she could all but read Hillary's mind. Thomases had first become friends with Bill Clinton, whom

she met during the summer of 1970 when both were in Washington, D.C., he on his way to Yale Law School and she a teacher at
Connecticut College. With their avid interest in politics and love
of conversation, the two hit it off instantly, and subsequently got
together when she visited friends at Yale. Theirs wasn't a romantic
relationship—Thomases had been dating Harold Ickes on an on-
and-off basis at the time. Thomases was more a confidante, in the
Betsey Wright vein. Clinton dated some of her friends and would
describe his romantic entanglements. Gradually, however, the name
of Yale classmate Hillary Rodham began surfacing with increasing
frequency—she was so smart, funny, articulate, beautiful. Thomases may have met Hillary at a Yale party, but she really made an
impression on her only when Thomases visited Clinton in Arkansas, stopping there whenever clients' business took her to Tennessee, Texas, or another nearby state. By this time Thomases herself
had gone to law school at Columbia, and she found that she and
Hillary had much in common, especially a passion for children's
issues and politics. Soon Hillary supplanted Bill as the more intimate friend and confidante. Thomases joined Hillary on the board
of the Children's Defense Fund, and, when Hillary became a Rose
partner, she advised her about segregating her billings from those
generated by work for the state.

Unexpected phone calls from Hillary were routine. Thomases,
too, liked to pick up the phone whenever the impulse struck, even
before July, when she officially joined the campaign. As the campaign was heating up, she was busy with her own law practice; she'd
become a partner at Willkie, Farr & Gallagher in New York, a
large, prominent firm that had surged during the mergers and acquisitions boom of the 1980s, acting as the firm's administrative
partner from 1982 to 1990. She'd recently gotten married, not to a
politically connected lawyer like Ickes, but to the handsome building contractor who renovated her apartment, and they'd just had a
child. Though she'd worked on Clinton's New York primary effort,
and had done fund-raising, she wanted time with her family in New
York. She hadn't gone to work full-time in the campaign. Part
of her wished she was in the thick of the campaign excitement,
but she was never out of touch, especially as informal advisor to
Hillary.

This call, however, was different. Even before Thomases could begin to sort out the story, Hillary retained Thomases as her lawyer. This would shroud their conversations in the attorney-client privilege, which meant Thomases couldn't disclose the substance of their talks without Hillary's permission, even if later asked to testify in court or Congress. "I don't want everyone digging into our personal records," Hillary said. It was clear that Hillary was upset that her privacy was being invaded; it touched a deeply rooted conviction that one's finances were nobody else's business, even if your husband was running for president. And the political implications were obvious, in the wake of the Flowers and draft controversies, with "Super Tuesday"—the day of most of the Southern primaries, including Florida and Texas—looming.

As Thomases tried to sort out the facts, it was clear that Hillary herself was vague about most of them. Whitewater was supposed to have been a second-home "paradise," she said, but it had failed. She didn't know how much she and Bill had contributed, let alone the McDougals. She was convinced the venture had lost money—a key fact that would surely help blunt any negative political implications —but she didn't know how much. She wasn't sure how the tax issues had been handled, though she again expressed her annoyance at Bill, who let the burden of tax returns fall entirely on her. From a political perspective, she was mostly worried about Lot 13—the Hillary house. The fact that she'd bought it out of bankruptcy court and then flipped it at a substantial profit might look bad if the transaction wasn't properly explained.

At first blush, Thomases wasn't unduly concerned. A long-ago real estate investment that lost money hardly seemed like fuel for scandal. Thomases didn't know Gerth, but her strategy was to explain what happened, show how innocuous it all was, and try to persuade Gerth that the information wasn't newsworthy—that "there was no there there," in a favorite phrase of Thomases', quoting Gertrude Stein's famous lament about Oakland, California. Thomases called Gerth to introduce herself and got the sense that Gerth believed Clinton had somehow abused his relationship with an Arkansas banker. Ninety percent of what he said she didn't understand and she felt that whenever she pressed him for facts, he'd respond in hypotheticals. "Talk to Jim Blair," she urged him. "He knows all these characters. He can get these people for you."

Meanwhile, she had to get the facts. She spoke again to Hillary.

According to Thomases' notes of a conversation dated February 21, 1992, Thomases asked Hillary if she'd ever talked directly with McDougal about Madison Guaranty, and specifically about the preferred stock offering. According to the notes, Hillary answered that she had "introduced" McDougal to Rick Massey, the associate who worked on the matter with her. Next Thomases spoke to Hubbell at the Rose firm. He evidently did some research on Hillary's involvement in Madison. Thomases' notes dated February 24 indicate that Hubbell told her that Massey had a "relationship" with John Latham and that Hillary had a "relationship" with McDougal. Nonetheless, Massey "will say," Hubbell told Thomases, that he "had alot to do with getting the client in." Hubbell went on to say that Hillary "did all the billing" and had "numerous" conferences with Latham, Massey, and McDougal. She even had one conversation with Bassett, the securities chief. The notes indicate that Hubbell based these comments, at least in part, on a review of the Rose firm's billing records.

This was hardly good news. It would be harmful, to say the least, if it were known that Hillary had not only worked for Madison on a matter pending before one of her husband's appointees, but had actually brought Madison into the firm as a client. More work had to be done if these issues were to be laid to rest.*

Thomases called James Hamilton, a Washington lawyer who was friendly with the Clintons and was working on the campaign, and said she needed some lawyers to go to Little Rock to investigate. They went, looked through some of the Clintons' records, found nothing of particular significance, and returned to more pressing matters. Webb Hubbell, at the Rose firm, gathered any materials there related to Whitewater and McDougal, and handed them over to the campaign; Vince Foster helped him. He knew

---

* Despite Hubbell's representation about what Massey "will say," Massey denied Hubbell's account, as described in chapter 4. The first lady testified in a later RTC interrogatory that "to the best of my recollection, the president of Madison Guaranty, John Latham, who was a friend of an associate at the Rose Law Firm, Richard Massey, became interested in having Madison Guaranty issue some kind of preferred stock to raise capital. Latham had spoken to Massey about doing the related legal work. . . . I believe Massey approached me about presenting this proposal to Jim McDougal because he was aware that I knew him. I agreed to go see McDougal. I visited him at his office on April 23, 1985. . . ." The Thomases notes suggest that Hubbell knew in 1992 that Hillary, not Massey, was responsible for bringing in Madison as a client.

what was turned over, including records relating to Hillary's work for Madison. (The computer print-out of those records is dated February 21, 1992, the day after Jeff Gerth went to the Arkansas Securities Department.) Loretta Lynch, a lawyer working for the campaign, also worked with Thomases. Lynch had been assigned to Whitewater a month earlier after Diane Blair got a call from Steve Smith, McDougal's co-investor in the Bank of Kingston. "Some Yankee reporter's sniffing around the Bank of Kingston," Smith had reported, and Blair asked Lynch to look into it.

Thomases flew to Little Rock to interview Yoly Redden, the Clintons' accountant. Hillary had now authorized Redden to speak only to Thomases, though the accountant had earlier talked to Lynch. But even after their interview, Thomases had to throw up her hands. Some records seemed to be missing, others were at the various banks. Lynch failed to provide the kind of support and advocacy Thomases was looking for. At one point, Lynch even volunteered that she thought Gerth's thesis might be true, at least hypothetically. "You're as bad as Jeff," Thomases had exclaimed. "Just find out the truth." Lynch felt she was just trying to stay ahead of the story, but her loyalty to the Clintons was increasingly questioned. Finally Thomases told the Clintons they needed an accountant; she didn't have the expertise or the time. James Lyons, a Denver lawyer, part of a nationwide network of lawyers helping the Clinton campaign, happened to be in Little Rock at the time, and he volunteered to do an investigation and prepare a report. The campaign asked him to answer definitively three questions: Were the Clintons passive investors in Whitewater? Did McDougal carry them to provide a favor to the governor? Did they lose money on the investment? In the meantime, Thomases tried to divert Gerth by suggesting he talk to Lyons. Lyons "has interesting information about Neil Bush's problems in Colorado," she said referring to President Bush's son's involvement in Silverado Banking, Savings and Loan. But Gerth ignored the suggestion.

On February 14, Gerth called Beverly Bassett, the former securities commissioner, now practicing law and living in Fayetteville with her new husband, Archie Schaffer, the head of public relations for Tyson Foods. Gerth quizzed her about her handling of Madison Guaranty, wondering why she hadn't acted more forcefully once the FHLBB concluded Madison was insolvent. Despite her regulatory experience, Bassett had had little experience with the press; still, she felt Gerth thought she'd done something improper. Almost immediately Bassett heard from Loretta Lynch, who seemed flustered. Lynch said she was about to call Gerth herself, and wanted to make sure she had her story straight. "Loretta, why does he care about me," Bassett pleaded. "Is this all? Is there something else here I don't know about?" Lynch was evasive. Finally she said, "There are other things," but she refused to say more. She said the campaign wanted as few people to know as possible in case the story didn't run.

"Did you know the Rose firm sued [Madison's] accountants for the FDIC?" Bassett asked. This was hardly the kind of information Lynch wanted floating around. "I'm aware of that," Lynch said tersely, "but that's not it." Bassett was mildly disgruntled that she wasn't being told more. Still, to protect herself, she wrote a thirteen-page memo that she sent to Gerth. It spelled out in laborious detail her appointment, her handling of the preferred stock issue, the treatment of Madison once it was found to be insolvent, and McDougal's removal—a step, Bassett emphasized, that she had supported. "I think all of us who had responsibility for savings and loans during the 1980s felt overwhelmed at times and lacking in the necessary power, authority or resources to act as effectively or as decisively as we might have under ordinary circumstances. While I never find it hard to defend the decision we made at the time or the actions we took, I often find them hard to explain," she concluded.

Lynch briefed Thomases on Gerth's contacts with Bassett, and Thomases thought the memo was an overreaction. Still, she could understand why Bassett was upset, and Gerth's insinuations angered both her and Hillary, when she informed her. In particular, Thomases and Hillary were offended at the notion that Bassett wasn't qualified for her job and might have been timid in dealing with McDougal because of his ties to Clinton. If Bassett weren't such a young and attractive woman, no one would be raising the issue. It was nothing but sexism, in their view.

By this time, Thomases had had several more phone conversations with Gerth, including one on February 25 and another on the twenty-eighth, emphasizing that she was trying to get accurate answers. "Give us time to search the records," she said, adding that the Lyons effort was underway, but she couldn't predict when it would be finished. Gerth asked for the Clintons' 1978 and 1979 tax returns. At Hillary's insistence, Thomases refused. Then she suggested he meet with her and Lynch in her office in New York. She said she'd do the best she could with the information she had, and would show Gerth actual records she'd collected. Thomases definitely felt that Gerth was developing into a problem for the campaign. She thought he was in love with his own theory, namely, that illicit favors had been exchanged between Clinton and a failed S&L executive. Anything she couldn't or wouldn't answer Gerth seemed to assume was nefarious. She wanted to try to force him to back up his allegations. She felt he was taking the word of one unstable person. She wasn't a press person, but wasn't there some rule that journalists needed multiple sources?

Gerth arrived at Thomases' law office on March 5. Thomases was warmly welcoming. "You're the most thorough reporter," she said. We understand "you're just trying to get to the bottom of something and find out what happened." Gerth was pleased by the compliment—thoroughness was, in fact, a quality he prized. "I'm not confident I can get all the checks," Thomases continued. "It isn't clear to either Loretta Lynch or myself that people in the Rose firm who hold all the documents have shown us everything." Gerth was intrigued and surprised by the suggestion the Rose firm was anything but cooperative. Who isn't showing you everything? Gerth asked. "Bill Kennedy," Thomases answered, referring to a close ally of Hillary, Vince, and Webb in the firm's litigation department. After emphasizing again that Lynch hadn't been able to see some records, and didn't know whether some documents even existed, Thomases seemed to shift tack entirely.

"We may demand an accounting," she said, "but right now is not the right time"—not during the campaign. "I'm not necessarily trying to resolve everything at this point." Gerth suddenly sensed that Thomases didn't want to disclose too much. She continued, "Nor is a newspaper the context in which we'd want to set it forth."

Still, Thomases was willing to share anything she had that might blunt Gerth's article or, better yet, persuade him to drop it altogether. She spent considerable time on the Hillary house transaction, and was effective. McDougal had told Gerth that he suspected the $30,000 the Clintons borrowed from Madison Bank and Trust in Kingston to finance the model home might have been diverted, and Gerth suspected it might have been used to make the down payment on the house the Clintons bought after Clinton lost the 1980 gubernatorial election. But Thomases was able to demonstrate that virtually all of that money went into the Whitewater project.

So how did the Clintons come up with the down payment for their house, Gerth wanted to know. "Investments and savings," Thomases replied, trying to brush aside the question. What investments? Thomases was vague. Gerth again asked for the 1978 and 1979 tax returns, pointing out that they might indicate the source of the down payment in the form of a capital gain, or interest payments. Thomases again refused.

In the spirit of cooperating to get to the bottom of things, Gerth had brought in the documents he'd gotten from McDougal, including copies of checks suggesting that he had contributed disproportionately. He showed them to Thomases and Lynch, who in turn tried to demonstrate that the contributions had been at least close to being even. Among other things, they showed Gerth a $20,000 check signed by Bill Clinton payable to Madison Bank and suggested that it represented reimbursement by the Clintons to Whitewater. Gerth examined the check, which on its face didn't indicate the purpose of the payment. "How do you know this is Whitewater related?" he asked. "Well, we're not sure, but we think it is," Thomases replied somewhat testily. She asked for another week to check.

On the other hand, Thomases conceded that the Clintons had made improper tax deductions related to Whitewater. That was "inadvertent," she said, and would be corrected, even though the error was now so old that the statute of limitations had run and the Clintons weren't required to do so. The amount at issue was only about $1,000.

The meeting lasted about three hours, and Gerth returned the next day to continue. By the time they were finished, Gerth and Thomases had distinctly different views of what had been accomplished. Thomases thought she'd demolished so many of the premises of the story that it would be derailed, if not by Gerth himself then by his editors. Indeed, Lynch called Bassett in Arkansas and told her that she could relax. The story wasn't going to run that week.

But Gerth felt that Thomases and Lynch had confirmed essential elements of the story, and that the campaign would not go any further to help him get at the truth. He finished his draft of the story and argued to his editors that there was no reason to further delay publication. Washington bureau chief Howell Raines agreed. He thought Gerth had already spent sufficient time with Thomases, who was stalling, slowing things down.

Since Gerth was in New York anyway to visit Thomases, he went over to the paper's headquarters on West 43rd Street. It was late on Friday, and he was aiming to get the piece on the front page of Sunday's edition. When he arrived, he was asked to meet with Joe Lelyveld, the paper's managing editor, and Max Frankel, its executive editor.

It was unusual, but not unheard of, for the paper's two top editors to converge on the editing of a piece like Gerth's. It wasn't that they considered the story so extraordinary, so hot, that it demanded top-level attention. But it was an investigative piece about the Democratic front-runner for president. They thought it mattered. In particular, Lelyveld felt there was something nagging about a reform-oriented candidate who was so reluctant to disclose information. He felt that the information Gerth had uncovered should be in the public domain.

But that didn't mean the story was ready to run. It was a complicated story with still-unanswered questions. Gerth had crammed all the themes into the first few paragraphs. It was hard to understand. The editors felt tone was particularly important—the story was as important for what it didn't say as what it did, and it shouldn't have a breathless tone that might suggest the Clintons were guilty of any wrongdoing that the story didn't demonstrate. There was no mention, for example, of the jogging incident, because Clinton denied it, or the fund-raiser at Madison Guaranty. Gerth hadn't followed up on McDougal's revelation of the cattle futures, so there was no mention of that. Thomases had dissuaded Gerth from saying anything about the source of the down payment on the Clintons' house.

Lelyveld and Frankel finally took the piece themselves, and rewrote the first six paragraphs or so. The question of the Clintons overstating their deductions—a point Gerth made in the top of the story—they relegated to an aside further down in the story. The magnitude of the error, in their view, didn't justify more attention, and it diverted attention from what they viewed as the main theme of the piece: the impropriety of a governor investing with the head of a state-regulated financial institution. By the time the editors left for the weekend, the story was cleared to run. It was earmarked for the front page of the Sunday edition, but not on the top half. Running "below the fold," meant that a story lacked blockbuster potential. That weekend there were still some calls from Gerth to Thomases and some minor changes. Gerth was furious over the editing, he confided in Thomases. He didn't even see some of the editing changes until the final deadline had passed and it was too late for him to object. He was so angry that he missed an auction that evening at his daughter's school.

On March 8, 1992, the story appeared. "Clintons Joined S&L Operator in an Ozark Real-Estate Venture," the headline read.

"WASHINGTON—Bill Clinton and his wife were business partners with the owner of a failing savings and loan association that was subject to state regulation early in his tenure as Governor of Arkansas, records show.

"The partnership, a real estate joint venture that was developing land in the Ozarks, involved the Clintons and James B. McDougal, a former Clinton aide turned developer. It started in 1978, and at times money from Mr. McDougal's savings and loan was used to subsidize it. The corporation continues to this day, but does not appear to be active."

The wording was cautious, and Gerth's report was careful to disclose that McDougal had been suffering from manic-depressive illness, adding that in his interviews he "appeared stable, careful and calm." But the major themes of the story were immediately established with such key phrases as "failing savings and loan," "subject to state regulation," "money from Mr. McDougal's savings and loan," and "subsidize." Several paragraphs later, the article is explicit, stating that the *Times*'s investigation "raises questions of whether a governor should be involved in a business deal with the owner of a business regulated by the state and whether, having done so, the governor's wife through her law firm should be receiving legal fees for work done for the business."

Still, no amount of rewriting by top editors could cure Gerth's story of its density and multiple threads. The possibility that Madison had received favorable treatment from Beverly Bassett, the securities commissioner, in a matter involving Hillary Clinton, was introduced in a paragraph that reads:

"After Federal regulators found that Mr. McDougal's savings institution, Madison Guaranty, was insolvent, meaning it faced possible closure by the state, Mr. Clinton appointed a new state securities commissioner, who had been a lawyer in a firm that represented the savings and loan. Mr. Clinton and the commissioner deny giving any preferential treatment. The new commissioner approved two novel proposals to help the savings and loan that were offered by Hillary Clinton, Governor Clinton's wife and a lawyer. She and her firm had been retained to represent the association."

Thomases' efforts had further confused an already complicated story, adding a layer of uncertainty and complexity to nearly every point the story made. In recounting the sale and repurchase of the Hillary house, Thomases is quoted as saying, "Hillary took the loan on behalf of the corporation." Then, the story continues,

"Ms. Thomases said Mrs. Clinton and the corporation regarded this as a corporate debt, though it was in Mrs. Clinton's name. . . . But Ms. Thomases said it was the corporation that took the loss on its books. . . . Ms. Thomases explained that the capital gain was small because, as part of that transaction, Mrs. Clinton had to pay off Whitewater's remaining $13,000 debt on the property, originally incurred by Mrs. Clinton."

Lynch had called Bassett the night before and warned her that, much to her shock, the story was going to run after all. Lynch added that she thought the story would be "devastating," especially since it was running right before Super Tuesday. When she read it, Bassett was floored. Now she understood. It was about Whitewater. She'd never known Clinton and McDougal were co-investors in anything. Neither Gerth nor Lynch had mentioned it to her. Yet the more she thought about it, the less concerned she was. "Archie," she said to her husband, "what's so bad about this?"

Early that morning, Thomases was at a Willkie Farr partners' retreat when she got a call from the campaign staff. Gerth's story was read to her in its entirety. Thomases was thrilled. She thought it was incomprehensible.

EIGHT

THAT MONDAY MORNING, David Ifshin, the Clinton campaign's general counsel, got on the phone with Mickey Kantor, the campaign chairman, who was leaving his home in Los Angeles to fly to Little Rock. Both Ifshin and Kantor felt blindsided by Gerth's story, which, the last they had heard, wasn't going to run. In contrast to Thomases' relief, they were concerned. It obviously didn't help to have Clinton linked to a failed S&L operator, especially in the wake of the Flowers and draft controversies. From his experience as general counsel to the Mondale-Ferraro campaign, Ifshin had developed a theme that he repeated like a mantra: "one news cycle." Get the facts, get them out, and get it over with in a single day. He was an advocate of full disclosure from a credible source. When allegations about Geraldine Ferraro's husband's business dealings had surfaced in the 1984 campaign, they'd hired a Big Eight accounting firm with no ties to the campaign to investigate and prepare a report on the Ferraro family finances. The issue had been largely defused.

Kantor readily agreed with the full-disclosure approach, and Ifshin recruited a group of four lawyers who were prepared to drop everything, go to Little Rock, and get to the bottom of Whitewater. Kantor called the next day asking where they were, and Ifshin assured him they'd be on the next plane.

But late that night, Ifshin got another call from Kantor. His voice sounded strained. Kantor said he didn't want Ifshin or any of the campaign's lawyers involved. Why not? Ifshin asked. "There's a conflict between the campaign and the candidates," Kantor said, meaning that because the personal interests of the Clintons might diverge from their political interests the campaign should keep out of it. "You've said many stupid things," Ifshin replied, "but none more stupid than this." Kantor didn't really elaborate—Ifshin had the sense someone else from the campaign was in the room with him—but he gave Ifshin the impression that the Clintons didn't want anyone delving too deeply into the matter, that the full story would be politically difficult and should not be disseminated. Kantor didn't say so, but full disclosure hadn't prevented Mondale and Ferraro from losing the election. "If you don't level with them," Ifshin argued, and Clinton is elected, "you'll wind up with a special prosecutor." But these and other comments only seemed to convince the Clintons and others on the campaign staff that Ifshin wasn't loyal. He was increasingly ignored, and eventually he resigned.

While it was made clear that Ifshin should stay out of Whitewater, it was confusing as to who was in charge of handling this new potential crisis. Thomases had been put on the matter by Hillary. Lyons was out doing his report. Kantor thought he was in charge. Campaign aides and lawyers pored over the fresh boxes of records retrieved from the Rose Law Firm by Vince Foster and Webb Hubbell.

Deputy campaign manager George Stephanopoulos and political consultant Paul Begala met with Bill and Hillary at the Warwick Hotel in Houston, where they were about to begin a campaign swing through Texas. They focused on the key points Clinton should emphasize: he'd lost money; he'd been at risk; McDougal wasn't an S&L operator when the investment began. Meanwhile, the campaign issued a Whitewater "fact sheet." It flatly denied that Hillary had solicited Madison Guaranty as a client and said she "did not intervene or attempt to influence in any matter concerning Madison Guaranty with the state securities commission or any other state regulator." The fact sheet added that another Rose partner, described as a friend of Madison's chief executive officer, brought in Madison as a client, evidently referring to Rick Massey.

Clinton himself didn't seem particularly upset. After Flowers and the draft, this seemed tame. He'd been so uninterested in making money, and so uninvolved in Whitewater, that he couldn't believe his financial dealings in Arkansas could become a serious scandal. He'd never even pushed for a pay increase as governor. He was, however, concerned about Hillary. Other allegations had focused only on him. Now, for the first time, Hillary's integrity was being questioned, especially her position as a lawyer representing clients before the state. Indeed, Hillary was much angrier about the Gerth story than her husband. She argued that Gerth was a pawn of the *Times's* Washington bureau chief, Howell Raines. She was convinced that Raines was out to get Clinton because he was jealous of a fellow Southerner his own age who was a serious contender for president. Hillary wanted to attack the *Times* as irresponsible and anti-Clinton.

That was the last thing Stephanopoulos wanted—war with the *New York Times*. He managed to talk her out of it, and later that day Clinton easily fielded a few questions from reporters who'd read Gerth's story, dismissing Whitewater as a "big money loser." "I know we lost over $25,000 in this deal," Clinton said at a press conference in Texas. "We never made a penny." But Clinton also denied elements of Gerth's story without, apparently, knowing the facts himself. He denied that McDougal had ever subsidized the venture. "Nothing could be further from the truth," he told the Associated Press. "We were jointly and severally liable for more than $200,000 of debt." Clinton also denied that he'd appointed Bassett to her post after Madison Guaranty was found to be insolvent by federal regulators, a point Gerth had made. Gerth, however, was referring to the regulators' findings in 1984; Clinton, apparently, to their 1986 report. Bassett was appointed in 1985. But the denials effectively blunted the story's impact.

Hillary wasn't so quick to put the matter aside. Musing to a *Newsweek* reporter on a plane in Florida the next day, she lamented what she saw as the decline of the press: the superficiality of reporting, the cynicism, the presumption of wrongdoing by candidates. She called the Gerth piece a "classic example. . . . They wanted to get Bill Clinton." She didn't understand how, after all she'd given up for a life of public service, the media could question her ethics. She continued, "What's really terrible is finding out that things your father told you are true. He used to tell me, 'Hillary, don't ever forget two things about the establishment: it hates change, and it will always protect its prerogatives.' "

The campaign staff braced for further media inquiries, but

there were surprisingly few. The television networks ran brief clips of Clinton responding to questions, but launched no inquiries of their own. The *Washington Post* focused principally on the issue of Hillary Clinton representing a client before a regulatory agency, noting that "the most recent allegations shift the spotlight to Hillary Clinton and the role she played as a lawyer in Little Rock, the state capital in which her husband was the dominant political figure for most of the last 14 years." Most major papers, including the *Los Angeles Times, Chicago Tribune,* and *Boston Globe,* reported Gerth's findings, but usually deep inside the papers and sometimes playing Clinton's denials at the top of the stories. A few newspapers around the country reprinted the *Times* story in its entirety.

The response from other candidates was more muted. The Republicans said nothing; President Bush was unlikely to call attention to anything that might highlight his own vulnerability on the S&L question. Instead, the Republicans were busy trying to impugn Clinton's patriotism, focusing on his student trip to Moscow, a move that backfired when they were accused of using the State Department for political ends. Among the Democrats, only Jerry Brown picked up on the issues raised by Gerth. Appearing at a televised debate in Detroit with other Democratic candidates, Brown said he thought Clinton had a "big electability problem." Clinton, he continued, "is funneling money to his wife's law firm . . . representing clients before the state of Arkansas. . . . It's not only corruption . . . it's the kind of conflict of interest that is incompatible with the kind of public servant that we expect as president." But Clinton was able to turn around Brown's attack by making it seem Brown was picking on Hillary. Showing a flash of anger, he retorted, "Let me tell you something, Jerry. I don't care what you say about me . . . but you ought to be ashamed of yourself for jumping on my wife. You're not worth being on the same platform with my wife . . . I never funneled any money to my wife's law firm—never!"

The next morning, Bill and Hillary, campaigning in Illinois, dropped in at the Busy Bee restaurant in Chicago. NBC reporter Andrea Mitchell, after getting Bill's approval to ask Hillary a question, plunged into the propriety of Hillary's representing Madison before a state agency. Hillary's famously acid wit immediately surfaced. "I suppose I could have stayed home and baked cookies, and had teas," she retorted. Off-camera, campaign strategist Paul Begala quickly intervened, urging Hillary to soften the comment. "I'm going to say what I feel," she insisted. "That's all there is to it." That flash of candor proved short-lived. As a result, enormous efforts were expended to reposition Hillary as more of a traditional wife and mother. She even participated in a "bake-off" with Barbara Bush, organized by *Family Circle* magazine. As a later campaign memo noted about Hillary, her "preoccupation with career and power only reinforces the political problem evident from the beginning."

On March 10, Clinton swept the Super Tuesday primaries in eight states including Texas, Florida, Tennessee, Mississippi, and Hawaii. The following week he easily triumphed in the big industrial states of Illinois and Michigan. Clinton's nomination seemed all but accomplished.

Jim and Diane Blair were almost as furious as Hillary over Gerth's article. Diane was working full-time with Betsey Wright, handling Arkansas aspects of the campaign. Jim had no official role, but was functioning as a freelance troubleshooter, spending weekends with his wife in Little Rock. He thought Gerth's article was slanted and full of unfair insinuations. Then Thomases called, suggesting he get involved in the fact-finding on Whitewater. He also spoke by phone with Hillary. His views fueled her own outrage. She felt misrepresented and mischaracterized; she was furious at the story's focus on her work at Rose for Madison. She'd barely been involved—Rick Massey had done everything. There was nothing "novel" about it, a word in Gerth's story that she found especially grating, in that it insinuated something was approved that shouldn't have been. She repeated her views on Howell Raines.

Blair said he'd get busy on damage control. He knew McDougal, and as an Arkansan, he might be more effective in dealing with people like Chris Wade and the small-town bankers. Blair also knew Sam Heuer, who'd represented McDougal in his bank fraud trial. Blair called Heuer to set up a meeting, and it was clear to him that Heuer's loyalties lay with his fellow Arkansans Clinton and Blair rather than an outsider like Gerth. Clinton had taught Heuer criminal law at the University of Arkansas, and Blair had referred some clients to Heuer. Indeed, after first agreeing to meet with Gerth prior to the story, Heuer had canceled the appointment.

Heuer told Blair he was very concerned. He'd been trying to keep McDougal out of trouble since his acquittal, and he felt McDougal was exposing himself to some risk by dallying with the likes of Gerth, as he put it. Blair expressed his own unhappiness with the story, how unfair it was, and said it all but accused McDougal of criminal activity. If McDougal had really made payments on behalf of the Clintons in return for favorable treatment, it amounted to bribery. Heuer had already faxed the *New York Times* threatening a libel suit, and Blair said he thought McDougal should sue, offering legal assistance. It went without saying that any publicity over such a suit would be just what the campaign wanted.

Heuer called McDougal and read him the riot act for talking to Gerth, mentioning Blair's point that the story implied McDougal had committed a crime. At Blair's urging, Heuer himself issued a statement to the press specifically denying any link between Whitewater and Hillary's representation of Madison, adding that Gerth's story was "not only false but probably actionable." In the statement, Heuer also said that Gerth had made no attempt to interview him—a claim that angered Gerth.*

Blair also spoke to McDougal's old friend and business partner R.D. Randolph, one of the donors at McDougal's Clinton fundraiser and a loyal Democrat, urging him to talk to McDougal. Randolph was indirect, knowing that McDougal never liked to be told what to do, but he reminded McDougal about the dangers of the press. "The press should be drowned, don't you think?" he said at one point. "I think you're right about that," McDougal replied.

McDougal seemed chastened. Though he was the major source, McDougal was already somewhat taken aback by Gerth's article. He was upset by the premise that Madison's money had subsidized the Clintons. As he thought he'd made clear to Gerth, it was his and Susan's money that subsidized them. He claimed he did not overdraw his accounts, or if he did, it was only until the next day, when funds were shifted to cover them. (Records show some overdrafts persisted from two days to two weeks.) He insisted he maintained a net positive balance in his accounts at Madison Guaranty. He was also upset over the implication that he'd gotten favorable treatment from Bassett in return for his favors to Clinton.

* *Gerth and Heuer continue to disagree about Gerth's efforts to interview Heuer.*

That was an insult. He, Jim McDougal, wouldn't even dignify an underling like Bassett with a phone call. If he wanted a favor, he'd ask Clinton directly. The problem was that Clinton had used him, never giving him anything in return—not even friendship in time of need. That's what he'd been trying to tell Gerth, but the reporter seemed to have missed the point.

So, when a reporter from the Associated Press reached McDougal for comment on Gerth's story, McDougal was testy and nervous about the call from Heuer. Perhaps he'd gone too far. He told the AP that "I've never done anything illegal, and as far as I know Bill Clinton has never done anything illegal or unethical." Asked whether money from Madison Guaranty was used to subsidize Whitewater, McDougal replied, "No, no, no. No funds from the savings and loan were ever used to subsidize the corporation."

On the other hand, McDougal was further annoyed by Clinton's and the campaign's responses, many of which, in his view, were false. He was especially angry about the denial that Clinton had ever steered business to his wife. Nor was he so annoyed with Gerth's story that he stopped talking to him. The two continued to speak on a regular basis, with McDougal complaining only about the reference to overdrafts and the notion that Madison subsidized the Clintons.

McDougal agreed to meet with Blair, and drove up to Little Rock the next day for a meeting at Heuer's office. Blair, accompanied by Loretta Lynch, was shocked by McDougal's appearance. He barely recognized him. Still, McDougal remained the raconteur Blair remembered. McDougal told him about the surgery to clear his blocked arteries. He mentioned that everybody on his mother's side of the family had been alcoholics, and everybody on his father's side had been manic-depressives. He was both, he said. Now he was taking both lithium and Prozac. Blair wondered how firmly planted McDougal was in reality.

How had McDougal gotten into this? Blair asked. McDougal told him that he'd gone to Sheffield Nelson about suing Jim Guy Tucker. The minute he heard Nelson's name Blair thought he knew where the trouble had begun. He told McDougal he should never have gone to someone like Nelson with politically charged information. But in any event, if what McDougal was saying now was true, Blair believed he had a libel suit against Gerth and the *New York*

Times. If he wanted help in finding a lawyer to sue them, Blair would be happy to help.

Blair was not there, however, simply to reassure McDougal or assist him with a libel suit. He hoped to persuade McDougal to talk to Jim Lyons, who was putting together his Whitewater report for the campaign. McDougal refused. "I don't want to waste my time being cross-examined by some lawyer who doesn't think half as fast as I do," McDougal retorted. Blair still considered him a potential threat to the campaign, and he also wanted him to be aware that there were risks to himself if he spoke out again. McDougal shouldn't be handing out information about the Clintons' investments, Blair said. McDougal had gone into business with them, and now he was giving away documents to the media, not giving them copies, and not telling the whole story. The press was making a big deal about what McDougal had put into the investment, but not, Blair said ominously, what McDougal had taken out.

What did he mean? McDougal asked. Blair said that from what he could tell, McDougal had taken out about $110,000 from the operation that he'd never reimbursed. He'd sold the remaining lots to Chris Wade for practically nothing, never consulting the Clintons. He had treated Whitewater like it was his, and his alone.

Now Blair had struck a raw nerve ending. McDougal was furious. How dare he suggest that he'd taken out of Whitewater more than he'd put in. "If you push me," McDougal retorted, "I'll be a hell of a lot more graphic than I have been."

"Well, the contributions look about even," Blair said of the Clintons' and McDougals' respective investments, further infuriating McDougal.

"I'll tell you a fucking thing," McDougal burst out. The Clintons, he said, had actually lost only $12,800 based on an accounting prepared by Charles James, the accountant who kept Whitewater's books. Then he launched into the story of Clinton's visit to McDougal's office that led to Hillary getting business from Madison Guaranty, adding that there was a witness to the event. "Is that the story you want me telling to the press?" McDougal asked, noting with pleasure the shocked look on Blair's face.

Blair dropped the matter, but shifting tack again, tried to impress upon McDougal the consequences of his speaking out. Didn't he realize the harm that this could do to Clinton? "I don't care if

Clinton is president," McDougal said dismissively. As Blair interpreted it, McDougal was expressing utter indifference. He wouldn't do anything to prevent Clinton being elected; he wouldn't exert himself to make it happen.

Blair and Lynch left the meeting feeling uneasy. McDougal was obviously excitable and unpredictable. He could not be counted on to support Clinton.

Next Blair headed for Flippin to meet with Chris Wade, the Whitewater realtor. Wade, too, was a solid Clinton supporter, and he'd been furious over the *Times* article. Gerth had spoken to Wade briefly, but after his article appeared and other reporters started tracking him down, Wade said he'd "thrash" Gerth if he ever came around, and vowed not to talk to him again. With other calls from reporters coming in, Wade called Clinton campaign headquarters and was handed over to Diane Blair. "I don't want to give anything out without Bill Clinton's okay," he said. Diane said he should talk to her husband. When Blair arrived, Wade got out all his records and walked Blair through them, pointing out that installment payments were still coming in, nearly all of them servicing the 1st Ozark loan. Much as Blair would have liked to get Whitewater out of the way by dissolving the company, he decided it was better to just leave things alone. But he shot off a letter to Sam Heuer, hoping to silence McDougal.

"Dear Sam:

"Sorry I missed your phone call on Sunday, but I believe I received the correct message."

Blair tried to deflect the touchy subject of whether McDougal had subsidized the Clintons: "It seems to me that the Clinton representatives more or less promised to release the work of an accountant who is attempting to reconstruct as to who put how much into, who took how much out of, and who lost how much in WWDC.

"I think you know that the Clintons simply regard WWDC and will characterize it as a bad business deal where money was lost."

Then Blair injected a threatening new element:

"Although the Statute of Limitations may not have run as to civil or criminal liability on the part of anyone who may have misused funds of WWDC (assuming such activity was concealed) there is no intent under the current state of developments to try to prosecute, sue or even point the finger at any such person, if any."

Finally, he wrote that "The McDougals have been through a lot of trauma. The Clintons are sure that the accusations made by the *New York Times* about Jim are not true. I regret that the McDougals gave away records we did not have copies of etc. without talking to you—obviously they were taken advantage of. I hope they will seek your counsel in advance in the future. I hope this clarifies the Clinton position.

"Sincerely, Jim Blair."

The letter made McDougal nearly apoplectic. The reference to the statute of limitations not having yet run, to criminal liability, and to "no intent under the current state of developments" to sue or prosecute was a thinly disguised threat that if McDougal further damaged Clinton in any remarks to the press, the Clintons would press charges against him. He told Heuer to respond with a letter to Blair, saying that if he had any evidence of wrongdoing by McDougal, he should turn it over immediately to the Pulaski County prosecutor. McDougal also picked up the phone and called Gerth, telling him about the meeting with Blair. He read him the text of the letter. He told Gerth that Blair looked "like I'd kicked him in the stomach" after he threatened to go public with the jogging incident. Still, McDougal admitted to Gerth that he was scared. He didn't want to be out front attacking Clinton. He even worried about his physical safety.

Blair, meanwhile, was continuing his effort to make sure no new questions would arise—especially anything having to do with the Clintons' dealings with 1st Ozark in Flippin. Blair met again with Chris Wade, who'd been erratic in his payments after assuming $35,000 of the mortgage when he bought the remaining Whitewater lots. In 1988 Wade had filed bankruptcy, and in November 1990 he'd asked Ron Proctor for a deferment in his payments until April 1991. Because Wade had been "very helpful with the managing of the collection" of the loan, as Proctor put it in an internal bank memo, he agreed. Wade's payments stopped.

Proctor was apparently referring to the fact that it was Wade who made sure the purchasers of Whitewater lots continued to make their monthly payments into the escrow account at 1st Ozark. Wade also paid his share of the monthly mortgage payment into the escrow account, even though the McDougals and Clintons remained liable for the full amount of the mortgage. Practically speaking, however, it was Wade who was keeping payments current, and there's no evidence that after the Clintons renegotiated the loan agreement in 1988 1st Ozark ever asked them for any payment when payments fell behind schedule.

Now, with Wade failing to make the payments, Blair, in effect, called Wade's mortgage loan, asking him to retire the obligation by paying the full amount of the principal and interest outstanding. Blair argued that the Clintons and McDougals had really paid off their part of the principal, even though they were still liable for the full amount of the mortgage, and that wasn't fair. Wade acknowledged to Blair that he still owed the balance of the part of the mortgage he'd assumed, and he was eager to do what he could to help the Clintons. But Wade didn't have any money, and his pending bankruptcy would ordinarily have precluded borrowing nearly $10,000, especially to retire existing debt. But the president of River Valley Bank, which was based in Fort Smith on Arkansas's Oklahoma border and didn't even have a branch in the Flippin area, was none other than Wade's old friend James Patterson—the former president of Citizens Bank in Flippin who had sold the Whitewater land in the first place. Patterson personally handled the matter, and River Valley lent Wade's Ozark Air Service the money. On May 12, 1992, Wade wrote a check on his Ozark Air account for $9,628. Blair had told Wade not to make the payment too quickly, so as not to attract attention. The troublesome Whitewater loan was formally retired.*

But not everyone in the campaign felt the issue could be buried through Blair's efforts. Lynch quit the campaign in June, in part because she thought Whitewater would continue to cause problems for the Clintons. As she later explained, "I did not want to remain responsible for keeping a lid on the issues that were on my plate, including Whitewater. I did not believe I could keep a lid on it."

In California, Susan McDougal hadn't even noticed the *Times* article about Whitewater, and, in their occasional phone calls, Jim never mentioned it to her, nor anything about the subsequent pres-

---

* *Given that he was then in bankruptcy proceedings, it's unclear why the Clintons and McDougals, as Wade's creditors, would have been allowed by the court to be paid by Wade's company ahead of other creditors. Patterson said he loaned Wade the money, even though he was outside of his bank's lending territory, because he knew Wade personally and thought he was a good credit risk, despite his bankruptcy. But the transaction seems irregular.*

sure he'd come under. He didn't want to burden her with anything else that might upset her. Susan was leading a peripatetic existence, staying with her brother Bill or with friends, trying to get back on her feet, trying to put her marriage behind her. Then Jim Henley called, the brother who'd been acquitted with McDougal. He was campaigning for Clinton in Texas, and he was furious that McDougal had talked to the *New York Times*. Susan came to her husband's defense. "This has nothing to do with you," she told her brother. "It's his choice" to talk to the press if he wants to, she argued.

Still, she was concerned. Then she heard that more reporters were calling Jim, even contacting their old friend Claudia Riley in Arkadelphia. Jim was referring all calls to Sam Heuer. Susan called Heuer to find out what was going on, and he briefed her, emphasizing how foolish McDougal had been. He also mentioned that he was in contact with the Clinton campaign; Susan knew Heuer was a big Clinton supporter. Indeed, it sounded to Susan like Heuer was more concerned about the Clintons than he was about Jim. She wondered if he was angling for a job in the event Clinton were elected. "Are you trying to get an appointment?" she asked, half-joking.

"No," he said, sounding defensive.

"Well, it's okay with me," she said. "Whatever you get out of it is fine with me, as long as Jim is your number one priority. I know Jim is difficult, and you've stuck by him."

Susan herself had been enthusiastically supporting Clinton, dropping his name with some regularity now that he was the Democratic front-runner. One evening, before Gerth's story, the phone had rung and it was Hillary. Susan could hardly believe it—in all their dealings, it was the first time she could remember Hillary calling her, rather than her husband. Susan was excited; she put behind her the ill-will that had developed between them. "I'm so proud of you!" Susan exclaimed. "You're running for president. You've made all of Arkansas proud." Hillary, too, seemed friendly, then mentioned, "I'm going to send you a power of attorney to sign."

"Oh, fine," Susan replied, trying to be agreeable. The power of attorney arrived, but Susan, her mind now on other things, didn't get around to signing it. Then she got another call.

"I have not gotten it back." It was Hillary again, this time her voice stern. Susan had left the letter with some friends. She called one, told her to sign her name for her, and drop it in the mail. She just wanted to get it out of the way.

The next day Susan heard from Jim, reporting that he, too, had gotten a call from Hillary demanding a power of attorney. "I don't think I will do that," Jim mused.

"I wish you'd called yesterday," Susan said. "I just sent mine back."

"You stupid, childish, naive fool!" Jim raged at her.

"Honey," she said, "these are people we know, they're our friends. Why are you so upset?"

"Don't you understand?" McDougal asked. He explained he wanted the Clintons out of Whitewater. It was just a shell, but he was planning to do some real estate development and he needed a vehicle. Whitewater, he said, had a track record; it had good credit; it had tax losses to shelter any future profits. He was broke, he had no friends, he needed something to do. He sounded desperate.

Susan felt sorry for him, realizing how much he needed this. She told him he could have whatever part of Whitewater she still owned. Then she mentioned that she hadn't actually signed the power of attorney herself; a friend had. Jim's spirits soared. "Call Hillary and void it," he said.

Susan called the governor's mansion in Little Rock and asked for Bill, leaving her name. Late the next evening, Hillary returned the call. Susan said she was rescinding her power of attorney, and said she didn't understand why Hillary and Bill didn't just sign over their interests in Whitewater to Jim. There was nothing left of any value.

Hillary was angry at the suggestion. "We own half of it, and we are not getting out of it," Hillary retorted. "It's incredible that partners would be asked to sign over their stock."

Now Susan was angry. "This was Jim McDougal's project, his idea, his money!" She couldn't believe Hillary was insisting on retaining half of an empty corporation. "Don't you understand that I don't want anything. It's all going to Jim. It's morally wrong for you not to give it to him." Susan felt herself near tears. "You're terrible people, after all he would and did do for you, that you wouldn't do this."

"I will not be blackmailed," Hillary responded. "You can't force us by making some threat."

Suddenly Susan felt frightened. She wasn't making any threat —she was just emotional and upset. Why was Hillary using the word "blackmail"? Was someone else there on Hillary's end of the line? Or worse, was the conversation being taped? Susan ended the conversation.

Shaken, she immediately called Jim. "For what it's worth, I did everything I could" to get the Clintons to turn over their interest in Whitewater, she said. "They should do it. But I believe they were taping the conversation or someone was listening in. She used the word 'blackmail.' "

Jim commiserated with Susan. This wasn't Little Rock anymore. Bill and Hillary were headed to the White House.*

On March 24, Jim Lyons had released his own report on Whitewater. Working with Loretta Lynch, another campaign lawyer, and an accounting firm in Denver whose head was a Republican, Lyons concluded that the Clintons were indeed passive investors in the venture, that McDougal didn't make any payments in order to extend any favors to the governor, and that the Clintons had lost $68,900 on the venture. The McDougals, he said, had a net loss of $92,200. The report stated flatly that "from the available records, it is clear that at all material times the McDougals or their agents exercised total control over the management and operation of the corporation and its investments." Lyons based his conclusions on some, but not all, of the Clintons' tax returns, the records in their possession, the available canceled checks, including the check for just over $20,000 that Thomases had shown Gerth. Bill Clinton himself told Lyons that it was a Whitewater payment. Lyons was pleased that the report was done in just over three weeks and that it had cost the campaign only $30,000. Lyons thought the report would end the matter.

And it seemed that it did. The report attracted routine press coverage in the news outlets that had bothered to mention Whitewater in the first place. Gerth handled it for the *Times*, emphasizing the one aspect that corroborated his earlier story. "Records Show Clintons Lost Less in Venture Than Partner," the

---

* The timing of these conversations is disputed by Hillary Clinton. David Kendall said that they must have occurred when Hillary sought a power of attorney in 1988. Susan McDougal insists that they occurred during the campaign.

headline read. Gerth further infuriated the campaign staff by reporting two days later that the Clintons had deleted a provision of
an Arkansas ethics law that would have required the governor to
publicly disclose actions that might affect their personal finances.
Then he did a piece on Clinton's tax policies in Arkansas. The
stories cemented the notion in the Clinton entourage that Gerth,
his bureau chief Raines, and the *Times* were pursuing an anti-
Clinton vendetta.

Thomases was also aware that Gerth was now at work on a
follow-up story, focusing on the jogging incident and the Madison
fund-raiser. The jogging incident was especially troublesome, because after meeting with McDougal, Blair had drafted a report to
the campaign that said McDougal claimed there was an eyewitness.
After their first conversation, Thomases had arranged for Gerth to
talk to Rick Massey, the Rose partner who was supposed to corroborate Hillary's version of how Madison had come to be a Rose
client, refuting McDougal's account. But when Gerth spoke to
Massey, the Rose partner was vague. Gerth felt the lawyer was
uncomfortable at the position he'd been put in. Gerth also spoke to
Webb Hubbell, who told him that any records relating to which
partner brought in Madison had disappeared. It all seemed suspicious to Gerth, who became even more convinced that McDougal's
recollections were essentially accurate.

At the campaign's suggestion, Gerth drafted some written
questions for the Clintons. In their answers, they flatly denied the
jogging incident, and that Bill had ever pressured McDougal to
send legal work to Hillary.

Gerth went ahead and wrote the story, but *Times* editors killed
it. Lelyveld didn't want it to look like the *Times* was "piling on"
Clinton. As for the jogging incident, the account essentially turned
on McDougal's word versus Clinton's. One source was a manic-
depressive failed S&L operator, the other was the Democratic
front-runner. Clinton deserved the benefit of the doubt. Gerth was
frustrated by his editors' lack of interest. They didn't encourage
him to make any more trips to Arkansas. They agreed there were
unanswered questions, but didn't see how they could be answered
without the Clintons' cooperation. They didn't want to devote any
more resources to the story.

And Gerth had now lost his most important source. Blair and

Heuer had succeeded in silencing McDougal. When Gerth called again, he didn't return the call. Gerth tried other numbers where he'd located McDougal in the past. No one knew where he was. McDougal had disappeared.

That looked like the end of Whitewater as far as Gerth was concerned. He turned his energies on the Republicans. His next stories were an investigation of the questionable business dealings of President Bush's brothers and sons, and a look at Republican fund-raisers' ties to failed S&Ls.

Gerth had no way of knowing, but his Whitewater story was read with unusual interest far from the power centers of New York and Washington. L. Jean Lewis, a thirty-eight-year-old investigator newly arrived in the Tulsa office of the Resolution Trust Corporation, the federal agency created to oversee the S&L catastrophe, was riveted by the reference to Madison Guaranty—one of the S&Ls under supervision of the Tulsa office when Lewis arrived. She had looked into it briefly, but put it aside when she saw how disorganized Madison's records were. But her suspicions had been aroused. Now, she focused on one section, deep in Gerth's story:

"It was during the period when Whitewater was making the Clintons' loan payments that Madison Guaranty was putting money into Whitewater. For example, Whitewater's check ledger shows that Whitewater's account at Madison was overdrawn in 1984, when the corporation was making payments on the Clintons' loan. Money was deposited to make up the shortage from Madison Marketing, an affiliate of the savings and loan that derived its revenues from the institution, records also show."

Lewis knew from experience that overdrafts covered by payments from affiliated institutions were a classic pattern in S&L fraud. She wasn't the only RTC official to notice the reference. In short order, she received two independent calls from RTC officials, one from her boss in the Tulsa office, the other from the regional investigations staff in Kansas. Both asked whether Whitewater had caused any losses at Madison Guaranty. Lewis was eager to find out the answer.

The nation's S&L crisis had been, in many ways, a godsend for Lewis. She loved investigative work. It had taken her out of her routine job of loan supervisor at Western Savings and Loan in

Dallas, a job for which she was too smart and energetic in any event, and into the more complex and demanding pursuit of financial fraud. When Western itself failed and was merged into Sun Belt Savings, Lewis had volunteered to help federal investigators assigned to the institution. She'd arrived at the S&L too late to be involved in any suspect transactions, and, with her almost photographic memory and mastery of financial detail, she proved to be a great help. Indeed, she clashed with the bank's new management when it tried to get her to spend less time investigating and more time issuing loans. As one friend and colleague put it, "The problem with Jean was that she wouldn't turn loose, especially when she had information that she knew would lead to tracking down criminal activity. She just couldn't stop."

In 1991 one of the federal investigators working at Sun Belt recommended Lewis for an opening in the Tulsa office of the RTC. Her boss at Sun Belt, Van Glover, was called by someone at the RTC, asking for a reference. "If you want a yes person," Glover told the person, "forget it." He said that sometimes Lewis had been more "blunt" than he wanted, but "she was honest." He added, "If you want someone to sink their teeth in deep and discover the facts and go with them as far as she could, then she's the one." Lewis got the job, left her husband in Dallas, moved to Tulsa, and then to Kansas City when the Tulsa office was consolidated there.

Lewis seemed to feel at home in the command structure of the RTC, dealing with FBI agents and federal prosecutors. The daughter of an army major general, Lewis had spent her childhood moving from base to base, and was comfortable in a male-dominated, hierarchical environment. She was churchgoing, a registered Republican, patriotic. She was no supporter of Bill Clinton, having recently written in a letter to a friend that her own stepson's "ability to lie surpasses that of our most astute politicians. (Gennifer who?? I never slept with that woman . . . quote the illustrious Governor Bill Clinton! Everybody in Arkansas knows he did, the lying bastard, and then put her on the state payroll!)" As she later described herself, "I was raised in a military environment that encouraged tenacity, courage, honesty and love of country. I was taught respect for our institutions and the rule of law. And I learned that under our Constitution, no one is above the law, no matter how powerful." Lewis was always neatly dressed, her hair permed, with large, distinctive glasses perched on her nose. She had a good sense of humor, telling stories in a soft drawl from her native Texas. She was also tenacious. She introduced Glover to his future wife, saying, "I know a fine Christian woman and I think you two would be very happy." Glover insisted that he could find dates on his own, but Lewis persisted. Finally he agreed to have dinner with the woman. To shut Lewis up, he invited her along. He married Lewis's friend six months later.

In April, Lewis and an investigator traveled to Little Rock, where they examined Madison's records, which were stored in a warehouse. Focusing on checking accounts at Madison Guaranty maintained by Whitewater and the McDougals, they painstakingly tried to reconstruct the flow of funds into and out of the accounts. As Gerth had before them, the two found a pattern of frequent overdrafts, usually covered by payments from another McDougal-controlled entity. From her investigative experience with failed S&Ls, the pattern seemed obvious to Lewis: McDougal was operating a check-kiting scheme, in which worthless checks were deposited into accounts intended to create the appearance of legitimate balances. Among other things, she noticed checks deposited into the Bill Clinton Political Committee account at the Bank of Cherry Valley.

The RTC itself has no prosecutorial authority, but instead turns over reports of suspicious activity in criminal referrals, usually directed to the U.S. attorney who presides over the location of the failed thrift. Lewis completed such a referral on Madison, describing in detail several instances where Whitewater wrote checks on insufficient funds that were covered by other McDougal-controlled entities and, in one instance, from the David Hale loan to Susan McDougal. She also noted that Whitewater's overdrafts didn't result in the usual service charges or fees for overdrawn checks except in two instances, and even then, the fees were later refunded. The criminal referral didn't allege any wrongdoing by Bill or Hillary Clinton, but as co-owners of Whitewater, it did mention them as beneficiaries of the scheme. "The overdrafts and 'loan' transactions, or alleged check 'swapping' and kiting," the referral read, "between the combined companies' accounts ensured that loan payments and other corporate obligations were met, thus clearly benefiting the principals of each entity." The referral was approved by Lewis's superiors and submitted on August 31 to the U.S. attorney in Little Rock, Charles Banks.

Lewis waited eagerly for a response. The next week, she called an FBI agent in Little Rock and left a message. "Am I becoming a pariah just because I want to know about these referrals or are you going to call me back by December?" In late September she called again, saying the referral could "alter history." But she heard nothing.

The RTC referral was hardly welcome news in Little Rock, where the U.S. attorney's office was still smarting from McDougal's acquittal and his public accusations that the case had been politically motivated because Banks was a Republican and McDougal a prominent Democrat. Banks met with an FBI agent in charge of investigating Madison and its staff. What was new in the referral was Clinton's alleged involvement, which made the whole thing even more politically charged. Banks may have been a Republican appointee, but he was an Arkansan first. He'd been a Democrat until 1982, when he switched parties to run for Congress. His father, A.A. Banks, was a county judge described in the press as a "power" in Democratic politics. Even as a Republican, Banks had to deal with a mostly Democratic business and legal establishment. Bill Clinton was the favorite son, the first time in history an Arkansas governor had a chance to become president.

Moreover, Banks had just been nominated by President Bush to the federal bench in Little Rock. But his Senate confirmation was being held up by Democratic senator Joe Biden, the Judiciary Committee Chairman. For Banks to launch a criminal investigation of Clinton—word of which would inevitably leak from Washington —little more than a month before the election was all but unthinkable. At the meeting, Banks said he thought Clinton's involvement with McDougal in any wrongdoing seemed "implausible," and, while conceding that further investigation might yield something, seemed set against prosecution.

Then, on October 6, the Little Rock FBI office got a call from headquarters in Washington, wondering what was going on with the Madison referral. This prompted a long teletype report, explaining the background of the case, including McDougal's earlier acquittal, his manic depression, and his allegations that he was a victim of a political prosecution. The teletype also focused on whether any case could be made against "witnesses" mentioned in the referral, specifically, the Clintons. "It is the opinion of the Little Rock F.B.I. and the U.S. Attorney that there is insufficient evidence to suggest that the Clintons had knowledge of the check kiting activity by McDougal . . . the RTC advises that there is not enough evidence at the present time to prove knowledge by the people named as witnesses," adding that Banks "was not inclined to authorize an investigation or render a positive prosecution opinion." The teletype concluded by saying that the U.S. attorney "intended to advise the Department of Justice of this matter due to its sensitive nature."

Banks himself called the Executive Office for U.S. Attorneys in Washington the same day, reporting to Donna Henneman, who worked in the office, about the Madison referral. Henneman was not a political appointee, and her job was primarily to act as a conduit between U.S. attorneys and top Justice Department officials. Banks's call in turn prompted what is known as an "Urgent Report" for the attorney general, the head of the criminal division, and the head of policy and communications. Marked "sensitive," the Urgent Report reached a very different conclusion than had the Little Rock FBI agent in his teletype: "it is the belief of the U.S. Attorney that further investigation is warranted."

At the Justice Department, Madison was referred to Robert Mueller, the assistant attorney general in the criminal division, who met with FBI officials. Mueller told them Madison should be treated like any other case, and the FBI should decide on an investigative course of action and carry it out. Still, the political implications, with the presidential election just a month away, were obvious. No thought was given to deferring the investigation until after the election. The FBI instructed its Little Rock agents, by teletype, to launch a "limited investigation" of the RTC's referral. There were to be no interviews conducted, no contact with witnesses, no grand jury proceeding, and the whole thing was to be wrapped up in one week. What such a limited investigation could be expected to uncover is hard to fathom, but even so, the prospect upset Banks. He fired off an angry letter to the head of the FBI in Little Rock:

"Neither I personally nor this office will participate in any phase of such an investigation regarding the above referral prior to

November 3, 1992. You may communicate this orally to officials of the FBI or you should feel free to make this part of your report.

"While I do not intend to denigrate the work of the RTC, I must opine that after such a lapse of time the insistence for urgency in this case appears to suggest an intentional or unintentional attempt to intervene into the political process of the upcoming presidential election. You and I know in investigations of this type, the first steps, such as issuance of grand jury subpoena for records, will lead to media and public inquiries of matters that are subject to absolute privacy. Even media questions about such an investigation in today's modern political climate all too often publicly purports to 'legitimize what can't be proven.'

"For me personally to participate in an investigation that I know will or could easily lead to the above scenario and to the possible denial of rights due to the targets, subjects, witnesses or defendants is inappropriate. I believe it amounts to prosecutorial misconduct. . . . I cannot be a party to such actions."

In such an atmosphere, the one-week FBI investigation predictably produced nothing new. The report emphasized McDougal's poverty and ill-health. Then it turned its sights on the RTC office in Kansas City, wondering why it seemed "obsessed" with Madison when two other Little Rock S&Ls had failed under suspicious circumstances, both involving far more money than Madison. The report went to Mueller along with a handwritten note from the head of the Little Rock FBI office: "I agree with the content— i.e., no investigation justified." John Keeney, the ranking career employee at the Justice Department, and the number two person in the criminal division, also sent the FBI report to Mueller with a note, "I don't see us as involved at this point."

At the same time Lewis's criminal referral was sent to Banks in Little Rock, copies were sent to the RTC's headquarters in Washington, where the mention of the Clintons led to high-level attention. Senior Vice President William Roelle showed a copy to the RTC's chief executive, Albert Casey, who noted the case was "high-profile" and would surely lead to intense press coverage given the approaching election.

About a week later, Casey received a call from C. Boyden Gray, White House counsel to President Bush. Somehow, the White House had found out about the Madison referral mentioning the

Clintons, and it was obviously a subject of tremendous political significance. Casey told Gray he'd call him back after talking to other agency officials. When he mentioned the call to Roelle, Roelle was alarmed. The RTC was established as an independent regulatory agency. Under no circumstances should the White House be privy to its investigative activities, especially when they involved the president's Democratic challenger. Roelle told Casey not to talk to Gray. When Casey returned the call, he told Gray that he couldn't discuss any such matter with him.*

Back in Kansas City, Lewis wondered what was happening to her Madison referral. In all her previous cases, she'd gotten a letter from the FBI acknowledging receipt of the referral. But this time she'd heard nothing. She made a note to herself to follow up. Though she did nothing for the time being, Lewis was hardly the type to let it drop.

During the summer of 1992, as Lewis had pursued her investigation, Whitewater had all but vanished from the campaign. Clinton was nominated in July at the Democratic National Convention in New York City, making a triumphal entrance into Madison Square Garden with Hillary and Chelsea. Only the *Washington Post* periodically questioned why the Clintons still refused to make public various records and all of their tax returns. In August, after a visit by Hillary Clinton with *Washington Post* editors and reporters, the paper ran a short story under the headline "Clintons Very 'Sensitive' to Conflicts of Interest; Candidate's Wife Won't Elaborate on Ozarks Deal." Asked about Whitewater, Hillary responded, "I think we've given you all we're going to give you, and I feel that's good advice I've received, and I'm going to stick with it." She then added, "We just feel we have gone the extra mile. Talk about accountability. We feel we have been more accountable than most people who have been in this position, and we feel very comfortable about it."

Still, Clinton's handlers made sure the candidate wouldn't be unprepared for any questions touching on the matter or on Hillary's

* *Gray says he doesn't recall the specific phone call to Casey, but says they may have spoken. He says he believes he learned about the RTC investigation involving Clinton over lunch with a political columnist. Gray adds that no one in the Bush campaign wanted to focus on anything involving S&Ls.*

work at the Rose firm. In preparation for the first televised presidential debate, they drafted some sample questions and answers:

"Q: You and Mrs. Clinton were involved in an investment with a man named James McDougal, who owned a savings-and-loan. Mrs. Clinton represented the S&L before the state banking commission. Is such an investment proper? Doesn't it at least raise the appearance of impropriety?

"A: No. One of the things I am proudest of is that even after 12 years as Governor, even my opponents have to admit we've had a scandal-free administration. I wish I could say the same about the last 12 years of Presidential Administrations. But about that investment: we lost money on the deal, so it wasn't smart from that standpoint. But you should understand that at the time we invested with Mr. McDougal he didn't own an S&L and I wasn't the Governor. By the time he did own an S&L and I was the Governor we were losing money hand over fist—and it would have been impossible to find a buyer for a failed real estate deal.

"Q: While you've been Governor, your wife has maintained a lucrative law practice with one of the biggest and most politically influential firms in Arkansas. While she does not do business for the state, her firm certainly represented clients before the state—a state government that you control. Isn't this at least the appearance of a conflict of interest? And if you win will Mrs. Clinton continue her law practice in Washington?

"A: Hillary has gone above and beyond the highest ethical standards in her law practice. She has refused to even collect her share of partnership profits derived from state business—a practice that has been praised by legal ethicists. I am proud that Hillary has done such a wonderful job of balancing career and family. As First Lady she has said she will not continue to practice law, but will instead seek to be a 'Voice for Children.' "

The nettlesome subjects never arose in the debates. Nor did any of Gerth's allegations dent Clinton's ability to turn disgust over the "greed decade" of the 1980s to his advantage. A campaign memo exhorted Clinton to "Look for an opportunity to pivot into a denunciation of the Decade of Greed. You know the riff—the worst legacy of the Reagan-Bush years is the greed, the get it while you can attitude; the to-hell-with-my-neighbor, quick buck mentality that created the S&L debacle, the looting of HUD, and the ransacking of our great companies." Clinton had inserted the theme in his nomination acceptance speech in August, saying, "I have news for the forces of greed and the defenders of the status quo: Your time has come and gone. It's time for a change in America." In a much-publicized speech at the Wharton School, Clinton had lambasted the greed decade, saying "together, we must bring an end to the something-for-nothing ethic of the 1980s." Hillary herself told the *Washington Post*, "the 1980s were about acquiring—acquiring wealth, power, privilege." No doubt that's one of the reasons Gerth's questions about the source of the down payment on their house—which, if answered, would have revealed Hillary's commodities profits—must have hit a raw nerve ending, and why the 1978 and 1979 tax returns remained undisclosed.

In any event, that fall the Clinton campaign was surging, running an average of ten percentage points ahead of Bush in tracking polls. The Democratic campaign was buoyed by its theme of "change," its appeal to the middle class, its emphasis on opportunity and responsibility rather than "special interests," its confidence in "activist" government. Bush, the victim of a flagging economy and his self-inflicted "Read My Lips" no-new-taxes pledge followed by a flip-flop, could never muster a compelling case for his own reelection. Ross Perot's campaign, emphasizing a politics of disaffection, while drawing impressive support, was never a serious challenge. On election day, Clinton won, but with a plurality of 43 percent to Bush's 37 and Perot's 19. The victory was more impressive in the electoral college, where Clinton rolled to a 370–168 majority, carrying every region but the Deep South.

That evening, Bill and Hillary Clinton again stepped onto the steps of the old State House in Little Rock, this time as the president-elect and first-lady-to-be of the United States.

After initially deciding that Whitewater Development Corp. should be left intact to collect the modest payments still being made by the lot purchasers, Blair changed his advice to the Clintons. Now that Clinton was the president-elect, he didn't want them entangled with the likes of the McDougals. Nor would Whitewater be included among Clinton's assets on any presidential disclosure forms.

The week before Christmas, Heuer called McDougal and

asked him to drive up to Little Rock. He said it was urgent. Heuer had gotten a call from Blair. The Clintons were willing to relinquish their interest in Whitewater, but it had to be done before the inauguration, now just a few weeks away. McDougal grumbled about the timing, but agreed. It was a foggy, rainy day, and he deliberately arrived over an hour late.

When he got to Heuer's office, Vince Foster was waiting for him. He had replaced Blair, whose plane had been fogged in. Foster had no official role in the campaign, but he was handling some personal legal matters for Bill and Hillary, and Blair had enlisted him for the "paperwork," as he put it, regarding Whitewater. Essentially, the agreement proposed by Foster called for McDougal to buy the Clintons' interest in Whitewater for $1,000 and release them from any further claims or liability. McDougal reviewed the papers, and was upset that the Clintons wanted to make him liable for the accuracy of various representations when they had all the records. The Clintons also wanted McDougal to prepare and file the overdue corporate tax returns, which McDougal was adamant they should do. "Vince, would you let your clients sign these?" McDougal asked. Foster replied, "Jim, I'm just the messenger."

So Heuer got Blair on the speaker phone to take over the negotiations. McDougal was contemptuous of Foster, whom he perceived as nothing but a lackey for Blair. At one point Foster was left alone in a conference room while McDougal and Heuer went to another office to call Blair. McDougal enjoyed the negotiations. He felt he won on virtually every contested point. The Clintons were desperate to get out of Whitewater before the inauguration, and the leverage had shifted to him. Blair agreed that the Clintons would prepare and file the tax returns within ninety days, a task that was assigned to Foster. Blair also agreed that the Clintons would return the Whitewater corporate records. Although the documents acknowledge receipt of the $1,000 purchase price, McDougal didn't even pay it. Blair did, in what he says was a "loan" to McDougal. But McDougal never reimbursed him.

McDougal and Foster, on behalf of the Clintons, signed the papers. It had been seven years from the time Susan had taken the stock transfer over to Hillary at the Rose firm, but McDougal was now the sole owner of Whitewater Development Corp.

NINE

Webb Hubbell's and Bill Clinton's tendency to leave their Christmas shopping until the last minute had led to a tradition of shopping together on Christmas Eve. But this year, just weeks before the inauguration, Hubbell was surprised when Clinton called and said he still wanted to go. He showed up with Chelsea and an entourage of Secret Service agents, and the group traipsed through stores in the Heights area and then to a nearby shopping mall. Hubbell had been doing some work for the transition team, looking into the ethical aspects of the ban on lobbying after government service, and he'd wondered whether it might lead to a job in the administration. He'd even made a pact with Vince Foster: he wouldn't go to Washington unless Vince did, and vice versa.

In the car, on the way home, Clinton asked, "So, are you coming with us?"

"Sure," Hubbell replied, gratified at the request even though he had no idea what job Clinton had in mind for him.

"Mack will call," Clinton said. McLarty was already designated as White House chief of staff. Hillary herself had seriously considered becoming her husband's chief of staff, but that was deemed too unorthodox. She was sufficiently close to McLarty, however, to assure her day-to-day influence over her husband's schedule.

Later that afternoon, Hubbell bumped into Hillary at the transition headquarters. "I'm glad you're coming," Hillary said, smiling. The two chatted, and Hubbell put in a plug for Foster, whom he'd been too busy to see lately. "Vince would make a great solicitor general," Hubbell said. "It's already been decided that he'll be deputy White House counsel," she replied. Foster had gotten his job offer that same day.

Later, Hubbell met Foster. "So you're going to Washington, too," he said. Foster was noncommittal. "Come on, Vince, don't be so secretive. I know you're going to be in the White House," Hubbell said. Foster smiled but also looked concerned. "Nobody's supposed to know."

"What am I supposed to be doing?" Hubbell asked. But Foster knew no more than he did. The two talked about the excitement of finding themselves thrust into the center of national policy making. Hubbell thought Foster was as eager as he was to be going. Though Foster had always eschewed politics, even his wife was encouraging. "I'm afraid if you don't do it you'll always be sorry," she told her husband.

A few days later, Clinton called Hubbell. He still had no specific job in mind, but he said Zoe Baird—his choice to be attorney general—was nearly overwhelmed with preparing to take over the department, and he wanted Hubbell to help out. Hubbell readily agreed.

Before he left, however, Hubbell had some papers he wanted to remove from his office at the Rose firm. That Saturday, he and his son went to the firm, took several cardboard file boxes, loaded them into the car and brought them back to their house. Much of it had been assembled during the campaign by Betsey Wright and Diane Blair. The materials included papers the campaign had gathered on Whitewater, such as the Rose firm files collected by Hubbell and Foster during the campaign. The papers were apparently destined for whoever would be designated as the Clintons' personal attorney. Hubbell left for Washington soon after, and soon found himself all but running the Justice Department. The papers stayed in Little Rock.

With Hillary in the White House and the top partners en route to Washington, the mood at the Rose firm was so euphoric that the firm announced it was opening a Washington office. It didn't bother either Hubbell or Foster that they weren't offered any of the top-tier, high-visibility jobs in the administration. Foster, especially, didn't want to be in the spotlight. They were delighted that the Rose triumvirate of Vince, Hillary, and Webb was being reconstituted. In a sense, all three of them would be operating in "deputy" positions, if the first lady could be considered the president's chief aide.

Over the Christmas and New Year's holidays, Bernard Nussbaum was trying to relax at his beachfront vacation home in Palmas del Mar, Puerto Rico. Even someone with his high energy and stamina needed a break from the twin rigors of the Clinton campaign and his high-powered practice at Wachtell, Lipton, Rosen & Katz, the prominent New York corporate firm where he was a partner. Nussbaum had to admit he was feeling a little disappointed. He'd been co-head of Clinton's transition team dealing with the Department of Justice, and he'd just overseen the completion of an extensive portrait of the department for the incoming president. He'd raised money and worked hard for Clinton's election after a long career as a liberal Democratic fund-raiser. At the height of the Gennifer Flowers controversy it seemed that he was the only partner at a major firm in New York City willing to publicly support and give money to Clinton. He wasn't pushing for anything, but he had thought there was at least the possibility that the transition work might lead to his being considered for the position of attorney general, fulfilling a lifelong dream shared by many lawyers. But he'd just heard on the radio that Zoe Baird had gotten the nomination. He knew he still might be appointed as U.S. attorney for the Southern District of New York, a job he'd once coveted, but at age fifty-five, he thought his moment had passed. He'd thrown his support for the job to Larry Pedowitz, one of his younger partners.

Then the phone rang, and Susan Thomases was on the line, calling from Little Rock. "Bernie," she said, "if you had a choice between deputy attorney general and counsel to the president, which would it be?"

Nussbaum laughed in surprise. He figured Baird would be picking her own deputy. As for counsel to the president, he thought James Hamilton, a Washington lawyer and a Southerner who was close to the Clintons and who'd been active in the campaign, was the likely choice. Counsel to the president was a job he hadn't even thought of, but he loved the idea. It might even be a job he would find more satisfying than attorney general.

"That's easy," he replied. "Counsel to the president."

"You have to get down here tomorrow morning," Thomases

said, even though Nussbaum was in Puerto Rico. "I want you to meet with Bill and Hillary."

The prospect of such high office was thrilling to Nussbaum, who was born on Manhattan's Lower East Side, the son of Polish immigrants. His grandfather operated a shoe repair store, and his father eked out a living as a labor organizer and political activist. The young Nussbaum was sent to Boys Brotherhood Republic, an organization founded by novelist and socialist Jack London, which teaches poor inner-city kids about civic responsibility and law. As editor of the *BBR Star* newspaper, Nussbaum wrote in 1949 of BBR's newly elected student officers that "Now that the election and the Inauguration are over the government should buckle down to hard work. . . . The elected representatives should not just lean back in their chairs and think, 'this is the life.' " In the scrappy world of BBR and Public School 15, Nussbaum had survived by his wits, not his physical stature. Former schoolmates say he was in constant arguments over schoolyard games and, though eloquent, lost most of them.

Despite going on to Columbia College (where he edited the *Columbia Spectator*) and Harvard Law School, Nussbaum never lost his street-wise, aggressive, and exuberant demeanor. He went on to a brilliant career as a federal prosecutor for the legendary Manhattan U.S. attorney Robert Morgenthau and then to a partnership at Wachtell Lipton. Though not the firm's managing partner, he often assigned lawyers to matters and they tended to gravitate to him for guidance. Young lawyers especially liked the way he shared credit for firm successes. Though active in Democratic politics, his main exposure to Washington had been during the highly charged Watergate era, when he served as associate counsel to the House Judiciary Committee.

Nussbaum didn't know Bill all that well, but he and Hillary had stayed in touch ever since they'd served on John Doar's staff. As senior associate special counsel, Nussbaum had been in charge of the investigation, and he thought Hillary was bright, aggressive, but young and naive. One night he and Hillary were the last lawyers in the office, and Nussbaum drove her home. "My boyfriend's coming down, and I'd like you to meet him," Hillary said.

"Who's that?" Nussbaum asked.

"He's someone I met at Yale. His name's Bill Clinton. He's from Arkansas. He's going into public service."

"Great," he said, almost absently.

"He's going into politics."

"That's good."

"Actually, he's going to run for Congress."

"When?" Nussbaum asked.

"This year."

"Really? Isn't that undertaking a lot? Shouldn't he have some experience?"

"You don't understand," Hillary said firmly. "He's going to be president of the United States."

Nussbaum was thirty-seven at the time, and he often felt like the young staff's father. He thought, "I really am working with kids who think their boyfriends are going to be president." To Hillary, he replied, "That's silly and ridiculous."

Hillary was furious. "You don't know what you're talking about! I know this guy. You don't. He is going to be president. You think it's silly. Well, someday you'll eat your words." She got out without saying good-bye, slammed the car door, and walked into her house.

The next day Nussbaum apologized. Later Hillary introduced him to Bill. He made scant impression. Then Nussbaum heard Hillary was moving to Arkansas. To a New Yorker like Nussbaum, this was crazy. She belonged in Chicago or New York.

As Clinton moved up the political ladder, Nussbaum always remembered his conversation with Hillary. When Clinton lost the 1980 election, he said to himself, "I was right." Then he was impressed with Bill's comeback, but still, it was Arkansas. He stayed in touch, and periodically sent money, which he was earning a lot of. Wachtell Lipton partners like Nussbaum are habitually ranked the highest-paid in the country, earning an average of about $1 million a year.

Then, in 1988, as jockeying for the Democratic presidential nomination was getting underway, Hillary had called Nussbaum at his office and said she wanted to get together for dinner. "Don't commit [to a presidential candidate] until we talk," she said, intimating that her then forty-one-year-old husband might be making the race. Nussbaum agreed.

The two had a three-hour dinner at a restaurant on 49th Street, near Nussbaum's Park Avenue office. It was their first long talk in fourteen years, and they talked about the progress in their lives and how they'd changed. Hillary dwelled on Chelsea, how important her daughter was in her life. Nussbaum knew Hillary to be difficult at times, and tough, but he found her more wonderful and warmer than he'd remembered. Toward the end of the meal, the presidential campaign came up, and Hillary said, "Don't commit for another week. Bill will make up his mind by then."

"Hillary," Nussbaum replied, "I know you told me he'd be president, and I acted badly. But isn't this a little early?"

"He's thinking about it," Hillary said. "Just don't commit." Nussbaum agreed. But then, a week later, Hillary called to say, "You're released from your commitment." Bill had decided against running.

Four years later, when Clinton announced his campaign, no one had contacted Nussbaum. He was pleased when he heard the news; no other prominent Democrat seemed willing to run against Bush, then the hero of the Gulf War. Then he got a call from Kenneth Brody, a partner at Goldman Sachs, urging him to join a small group of wealthy businessmen and lawyers that might form the nucleus of a Clinton fund-raising effort. They met at the office of wealthy New York investor Tommy Tisch, and when Nussbaum arrived, everyone seemed slightly befuddled. Who was Clinton? Nussbaum, the only one there who knew much about him, made the case: he had a shot at winning, he could bridge the gap between rich and poor, young and old; at forty-five, he was older than Kennedy had been.

Nussbaum was too busy defending the large New York law firm of Kaye, Scholer, Fierman, Hays & Handler in a suit by the RTC to get much involved in the campaign, but he proved an adept fund-raiser and stalwart supporter. He stayed in close touch with Thomases, and after the Flowers allegations surfaced, she and Hillary sought his advice and asked him to play a more active role. He flew to Little Rock to meet with Betsey Wright and Hillary. They discussed how to handle all the rumors swirling about Clinton, and whether there were any criminal penalties for spreading false stories. But by then Whitewater had faded, and wasn't even mentioned. The group was more concerned about rumors that Clinton had fathered a black baby. Nussbaum's involvement in the campaign ended up being minor. He occasionally gave Wright some advice over the phone and organized a Clinton tour and speech at the Jewish Museum, where Nussbaum is on the board, just before the New York primary. Nussbaum and his wife were part of a huge crowd that gathered in Little Rock on election night. When Clinton won, Nussbaum mentioned to Thomases, "If there's any position, I'd have no problem being considered, and I'd consider doing it."

After the call from Thomases, Nussbaum flew to New York, then to Nashville and Little Rock, arriving at eleven the next morning. He met with Thomases and Harold Ickes, who said he'd be meeting later with the president-elect, who was then tied up in a meeting with Mexican president Carlos Salinas de Gortari. But first they wanted to introduce him to the new deputy counsel to the president: Vince Foster. Nussbaum was surprised that the counsel's deputy had already been named; wouldn't the counsel ordinarily have a say in choosing his own deputy? Yet it was almost instantly apparent that the deputy was interviewing him for the top job. Nussbaum started to wonder if his appointment was as much a sure thing as he'd hoped.

His first impression of Foster did nothing to allay his concern. Foster was tall, reserved, Southern, WASPy—in sum, everything that Nussbaum was not. But as they began to talk, they quickly found common ground as lawyers. They moved in overlapping professional worlds, with the Rose firm occasionally acting as Arkansas counsel for the large corporations that turned to Wachtell Lipton for their high-profile mergers and acquisitions. They were both comfortable in the worlds of trials and appeals, of American Bar Association meetings, of judicial conferences. Nussbaum thought he was passing muster.

Next Nussbaum was ushered in to see Hillary in a living room in the governor's mansion. Ever since Thomases' phone call, Nussbaum had been organizing his thoughts about the job of counsel to the president. Nussbaum is an avid reader of history, and he'd dealt personally with John Dean, Nixon's White House counsel, during Watergate. To Hillary, Nussbaum emphasized that every recent president had gotten into trouble when a legal problem mushroomed into a political problem. With Nixon it had been Watergate, with Carter it was Bert Lance, Reagan and Bush had Iran-contra. Since Watergate, a legal problem had become a way to bring down a president. Anybody could be vulnerable, he emphasized. Lyndon Johnson, Kennedy, Eisenhower, FDR—none would have survived the public scrutiny of their personal, professional, and business lives that was now routine. Institutions had been created to investigate, dig up dirt, and a national media was standing by to disseminate the results. This was a profound shift in culture. The media had covered up FDR's health problems and relationships with other women. That was the culture of the time. It no longer existed.

Hillary listened attentively, nodding thoughtfully. When Bill stuck his head in, she motioned him into the living room. "Tell the president, tell Bill what you've just told me," she said. Nussbaum, warming to his theme, reiterated what he'd said, adding that the important thing was to do the right thing, without regard to immediate reactions. The nastiness of the press was to be expected and was nothing new, he pointed out. Truman had been reviled by the press (before being guided to reelection by Clark Clifford, his White House counsel). Lincoln looked like he was going to lose the 1864 election. But Truman and Lincoln did what they believed to be the right thing, and were vindicated by history. Nussbaum emphasized that counsel to the president should be a real lawyer— a passionate advocate for his client, the president.

Nussbaum thought it was a good sign that Hillary and Bill asked him to stay around. They invited him to dinner at the governor's mansion that night. "What do you think of Vince?" Clinton asked Nussbaum at one point.

"He seems like a good guy."

"He's a great guy," Clinton said. Nussbaum told him he thought he and Vince would get along fine together.

After dinner, Clinton loaned Nussbaum a leather motorcycle jacket so he wouldn't be the only one wearing a suit, and they went to a Little Rock mall to see a movie, *The Distinguished Gentleman*, in which Eddie Murphy, a con man, poses as a congressman. At about midnight the next night, the phone rang in Nussbaum's hotel room, and Clinton was on the line. "Bernie, I've been thinking," he said. "I'd like you to be my lawyer." Nussbaum was thrilled, especially the way Clinton put it: "I want you."

"I'd be honored and delighted," Nussbaum replied.

•

Even before they went to Washington, Foster and Nussbaum sat down together to plan the White House counsel's office. From the outset, Nussbaum felt comfortable with Foster's status and access to Bill and Hillary. Though he was counsel, and Foster was deputy, he thought of Vince as his law firm partner, a concept that Foster readily embraced. "We'll build a great little law firm," Foster said, obviously warming to the idea. It also quickly became clear that Foster thought of himself first and foremost as representing Hillary's interests. That was fine with Nussbaum, and it made for a convenient division of labor; Foster would function as Hillary's chief lawyer, and Nussbaum would be the president's.

Neither Nussbaum nor Foster required Senate confirmation, but given an investigative press and the sensitivity of their positions, they didn't want anything to surface that might prove embarrassing. Nussbaum raised the delicate issue by sitting down with Foster and proposing that each vet the other. "What's the worst they could say about us?" Nussbaum asked. He knew his answer—he was a rich mergers lawyer, a fat cat, a product of the 1980s, the very kind of person the Clinton campaign had excoriated. Foster looked uncomfortable, and came up with a very different answer. "There will be rumors of an affair with Hillary," he said. He added that during the campaign, there had even been a press inquiry along that line. He'd been so nervous about it that he'd had his home phone number changed and stayed away from his office for several days to avoid any press calls.

"Is it true?" Nussbaum asked.

"It's total nonsense," Foster replied.

Nussbaum and Foster arrived in Washington about a week before the inauguration, borrowing some offices at the law firm of Hogan & Hartson. Nussbaum moved into the quietly elegant Jefferson Hotel. But Foster indicated he couldn't afford such luxurious quarters, not with his Rose firm savings and the need to support his family in Little Rock. He moved in with his sister, Sheila Anthony, the wife of former congressman Beryl Anthony of Arkansas. Foster started looking for a house, but was shocked by the price of real estate in Washington. It was obvious he wouldn't be able to afford something nearly as nice as their home with pool in Little Rock, and even then, he'd be financially strapped.

The arrangement caused unusual strain in Foster's placid marriage. Lisa, his wife, had been understandably keen to make the move to Washington with her husband, envisioning a glamorous life of White House dinner parties and political galas. But Vince had decided that since their youngest son was still in high school, Lisa should remain behind in Little Rock until the end of the school year. The entire family came to Washington for the inauguration, but immediately after the ceremony, Foster left to take up his work at the White House, leaving his family to find their own way back to Sheila's house. Lisa resented it, but, as was typical in the marriage, said nothing to her husband, expressing her anger instead by refusing to attend the Inaugural Ball. As Lisa later told *New Yorker* writer Peter Boyer, "I was angry at Vince about 90 percent of the time. I wasn't angry at him for going [to Washington]. I was just angry at him for ignoring us and leaving us behind, and making me have to deal with everything, all the decisions, and he was getting up and getting all the so-called glory."

Glory seemed far from Foster's mind. When he and Nussbaum walked into the counsel's offices in the recently vacated White House, they were bare. They'd had a courteous meeting with Nussbaum's predecessor, C. Boyden Gray, but it was a shock coming in to the empty offices and realizing the "little law firm" would have to be built almost instantly from scratch, without so much as a few memos from their predecessors to guide them. To Nussbaum it was like arriving at Wachtell one day to discover that all the lawyers and files were gone forever, but all the clients had stayed, bombarding him with their problems. Nussbaum brought along a lawyer from Wachtell, Steven Neuwirth, and Foster later persuaded the Rose firm's managing partner, William Kennedy, to join them.

In the midst of all this, Foster was a steadying influence, a person others turned to for support and reassurance. He was a good listener, and almost never volunteered his own opinion on anything. He and Nussbaum got along very well, and Foster was painstakingly careful to include Nussbaum in all important meetings, so as not to suggest that his closer relationship to the president and first lady gave him greater status. But Nussbaum was probably a bit more enamored of Foster than Foster was of him; he confided that Nussbaum's impetuous style sometimes unnerved him. Foster became especially close to Maggie Williams, the first lady's chief of staff. The unmarried Williams liked to embarrass Foster by chiding him that she wished he were single, a comment guaranteed to make him blush. She sometimes said she wished he could be "cloned." In an administration that seemed to be sprouting leaks even before taking office, Foster's loyalty to the first family remained unshakable.

Still, however calming Foster's presence, his life in Arkansas hardly prepared him for the crises that started breaking around them. On January 14, the *New York Times* ran a front-page story that attorney general–designate Zoe Baird and her husband had hired illegal immigrants as a nanny and chauffeur and hadn't paid Social Security taxes on them until that month. Clinton had been aware of the situation, but had reassured Baird at the annual Renaissance Weekend—an annual New Year's Eve discussion of policy issues held on Hilton Head Island—that he didn't think it was a problem. But the revelation, indicating both a cavalier attitude toward the law and an upper-class lifestyle, was far more politically damaging than Clinton had anticipated.

Nussbaum hadn't been involved in clearing the Baird nomination; that had been handled by the transition team headed by Warren Christopher, who was Baird's godfather. Still, the day after the inauguration, the president called Nussbaum into the Oval Office for advice. "What do you think?" Clinton asked him. Nussbaum was decisive. "Fight," he said. "Don't walk away from a nominee." Nussbaum cited as an example Jimmy Carter's nomination of Theodore Sorensen to head the Central Intelligence Agency, a nomination that was withdrawn when Sorensen's antiwar views were criticized. In Nussbaum's view, Carter had been irremediably weakened. By contrast, he believed George Bush had been strengthened by his support for Texas senator John Tower to be secretary of defense, letting the Senate take the onus for rejecting him. Whether Baird should ever have been nominated in the first place was no longer the issue. "Once you go forward with a nomination, you go," Nussbaum argued, concerned that if Baird was abandoned, there would be a domino effect of attacks on other nominees. Nussbaum thought the Baird problem could be surmounted if she paid back taxes and complied going forward. Most people didn't understand the rules for domestic employees anyway.

But Nussbaum quickly encountered the powerful influence of George Stephanopoulos, the thirty-two-year-old communications director who functioned as one of Clinton's closest advisors. Stephanopoulos was adamant that Baird had to be dropped. The stories in the press, he argued, would otherwise go on and on. They had to cut their losses quickly, he argued. Nussbaum was concerned for reasons that went beyond Baird. It was a mistake, he thought, to be so concerned about the short-term reaction of the press. As Nussbaum had told Bill and Hillary during their meeting in Little Rock, what mattered was the judgment of history—not a daily newspaper or broadcast that would soon be forgotten.

In the midst of her confirmation hearings, with scant congressional support, Clinton withdrew Baird's nomination. He later said he shouldn't have rushed the appointment, and, on hearing of the illegal immigrants, he should have looked into the matter in greater depth.

The collapse of the Baird nomination meant two immediate things for Nussbaum and Foster: the vetting function was now in their hands, and it obviously carried enormous political risks. The Justice Department was rudderless. Hubbell was officially just a special assistant, but Nussbaum thought he should be nominated for a top position. He didn't like the idea that Hubbell might be seen as a presidential crony from Arkansas, acting like some Machiavellian figure in the Justice Department, outside the official chain of command. Perhaps Hubbell himself should be nominated as attorney general.

That notion was quickly dismissed. None of the four oldest cabinet posts—Treasury, Defense, State, and Justice—had ever been headed by a woman, and Hillary had insisted that Justice would be. So Nussbaum urged instead that Hubbell be given the number two job, associate attorney general, overseeing everything but the criminal division.

Curiously, Foster resisted the idea. He said he was concerned about the scrutiny, the "spotlight," as he put it, that would accompany the confirmation process. Indeed, Foster seemed very uncomfortable at the prospect. Nussbaum was surprised.

"Is there anything in his background or the Rose firm?" Nussbaum wondered.

"No," Foster replied. "But I'm afraid people will take shots at Webb to get at Hillary." Foster explained that he thought the focus would be on the Rose firm, and the Rose firm was a way to get at Hillary. Foster didn't elaborate, and Nussbaum assumed he meant simply that the Rose firm had represented many large corporate clients, probably in some matters that would be politically unpopular.

"If there's nothing there," Nussbaum said, "then he should be confirmed. Why not?" Foster didn't really have an answer, but he said again that he thought that "tearing down" Hubbell was a way to get at Hillary. The prospect seemed to leave him troubled.

Foster was already brooding about his relationship with Hillary, which was turning out to be much different from the close friendship they'd enjoyed at the Rose firm. The new dynamic had been made painfully clear to Foster in an incident that seemed trivial on the surface. Soon after arriving in Washington, Hillary had complained to Vince about the Secret Service agents that protected them at the White House. They were stationed inside the family living quarters on the second floor of the White House, within earshot of just about everything that happened. Four agents were positioned around the Oval Office. They were career officers, not political appointees, all holdovers from the Bush administration. Trained not to speak to the occupants of the White House so as not to be distracted from their primary duty, they came across as unfriendly, especially to people from Arkansas, who, when they said "good morning," expected a response. Hillary, in particular, had the sense that some of them didn't like her and Bill, preferring the more staid Bushes. The Clintons' close friend Harry Thomason had warned them to replace all the White House Secret Service agents, who might still be loyal to the Bushes. In Arkansas, the Clintons had been involved in choosing the troopers that guarded them, and loyalty was an important criterion. Hillary told Vince that she wanted their own people installed in the White House detail as well.

Foster discussed the first lady's concern with David Watkins, the Hope native who'd come to the White House as assistant to the president for management and administration, and communications director Mark Gearan. But Foster didn't see any immediate cause for concern. Foster agreed with a cautious approach. None of the agents was reassigned or replaced. Suddenly replacing the White House security detail could in itself have led to unfavorable press.

But then, on February 19, the *Chicago Sun-Times* reported that

Hillary, in a fierce argument with Bill, had smashed a lamp in the family living quarters. "Seems first lady Hillary Rodham Clinton has a temper to match her hubby's," wrote columnist Bill Zwecker, adding, "Just in case you care, Bill and Hillary sleep in separate bedrooms." The story spread like wildfire, embellished with the claim that Hillary had actually thrown the lamp at Bill in a raging argument. Hillary assumed the story came from the White House security detail, confirming her fears about their loyalty.*

Even after the story ran, Hillary was upset that no one from the Secret Service came forward to deny it. The story soon appeared in *Newsweek* (subsequently banned from an interview with the first lady), and Hillary and Bill vented some of their anger on Foster and Watkins for failing to act on her earlier concerns. They were "too naive and too nice, being from Arkansas," Hillary said. They should have acted more quickly and more forcefully.

Watkins accepted the reprimand, but Foster seemed stunned. In all their years together, years in which he had so often acted as Hillary's mentor and protector, she had never spoken to him like this. The encounter drove home the fact that he was now working for her—from that point on he almost invariably referred to Hillary, but not Bill, as "the client." He readily shouldered all the blame for the leaked incident involving the smashed lamp. His job was to protect the president and the first lady, and in this instance he had failed them. Foster faulted himself for not acting soon enough, and not acting more forcefully. Foster reported the first lady's concerns to Nussbaum. Watkins felt bad, too, but it was Foster who acted as though the whole thing was his fault. He dismissed the possibility that his advice—to avert a shake-up within the Secret Service staff that might have triggered even worse publicity—had been sound.

But to placate Hillary, Foster and Watkins felt some remedial steps had to be taken. They met with John McGaw, head of the president's private security division of the Secret Service, to convey the president and first lady's displeasure. McGaw thought they were overreacting. Silence didn't mean the agents were unfriendly. They were professional, strictly sworn to protect the first family's privacy.

---

* *Zwecker confirms that one of two sources for the item was someone "involved in White House security."*

Though the meeting was cordial, McGaw was later promoted to head the Bureau of Alcohol, Tobacco, and Firearms, in part because of the Clintons' displeasure over the lamp incident. Secret Service agents were reassigned. Henceforth they were excluded from the interior of the family living quarters. The size of the contingent was reduced.

Long accustomed to keeping his own counsel on personal matters, Foster had no one he could unburden himself to, even if he'd had the time. Telephone calls with his wife were especially vexing. Routine household problems, griping about the Country Club, the simmering resentment at being left behind—these were Lisa's concerns. She seemed to put them on a par with the weighty matters of state that were preoccupying Foster. As Lisa later described the period, "We had a lot of conversations over the phone that were sort of short, curt conversations, and we realized that we were both so tense about what we had to do that it was not easy for us to console each other."

Nussbaum had been eager to get off to a good start, but he and Foster never had a chance to catch their breath. In short order they were confronted with legal questions involving gays in the military, executive orders relaxing restrictions on abortion, efforts to keep secret the work of the health care task force. There were constant questions about the understaffed Justice Department. Clinton was being criticized for his failure to come up with a replacement for the Baird nomination, and Nussbaum was feeling the pressure.

In February Nussbaum called federal district court judge Kimba Wood, reaching her in Colorado. Wood was on a short list of candidates, all women. Nussbaum knew and respected Wood, a Reagan appointee to the bench best known for sentencing junk bond financier Michael Milken to a ten-year prison term. During their conversation, and without specifically referring to the "Zoe Baird problem," he asked if there were any similar situations in her background. She said there weren't.

Nussbaum arranged for Wood to meet Clinton in the White House. She brought all her tax records and financial papers, handing them over to Nussbaum's staff for vetting. Nussbaum wasn't especially concerned, since Wood had already undergone an FBI investigation to be named a federal judge. Gracious, soft-spoken, but firm, Wood seemed to make a favorable impression on the president. But Clinton hadn't yet made up his mind when someone on the White House staff, evidently eager to assure the press that Clinton was moving forward on the attorney general appointment, leaked that Wood would be named. Almost simultaneously, Nussbaum's staff told him there was a problem. Wood had hired an illegal alien as a nanny, but there was a big difference from Baird's situation. It wasn't unlawful when Wood did it; she'd paid Social Security taxes; and she'd begun the steps necessary for her nanny to obtain legal residency status.

Clinton was furious about the leak, raging at his staff the next day. Speculation within the White House centered on Stephanopoulos as the source of the leak, but the president faulted Nussbaum for sending him a candidate who hadn't been thoroughly cleared. Though Wood had done nothing wrong, Clinton and advisors like Stephanopoulos still thought there would be a "perception" problem, and were upset that Wood hadn't volunteered the situation to them. Nussbaum felt bad for Wood, but he didn't argue strenuously on her behalf. He would have had she been nominated—she hadn't really done anything wrong—but she wasn't the nominee, and thus he felt Clinton should feel free to choose another candidate.

After the meeting, Nussbaum told Wood the president hadn't made up his mind, and she could go home. But he didn't offer any encouragement. With the writing on the wall, the next day Wood issued a press release announcing her withdrawal from consideration. Clinton was enraged again. The news upstaged his signing of a family leave bill. It was darkly noted within the White House that Wood's husband, Michael Kramer, was a columnist for *Time* magazine and had attended the White House meetings with his wife. After angry conversations with Nussbaum and Stephanopoulos, Kramer had issued the preemptive press release.

Similar issues arose again later that spring over Lani Guinier, an old friend of the Clintons and their choice to head the civil rights division of the Justice Department. A Yale graduate, a law professor at the University of Pennsylvania, a black woman, she seemed ideal both for her expertise in the field and the symbolism of her appointment. Nussbaum had been alerted to some possibly controversial law review articles, and he had Walter Dellinger, one of his staff members and a former constitutional law professor, read them. Dellinger described them as academic ruminations that weren't "crazy or off-the-wall." Nussbaum backed her nomination. He felt strongly that no one should be judged solely on one or two passages she'd written in the past. And at least she had passion, badly needed in a division that had been nearly moribund in the Bush administration.

Then a contributor to the *Wall Street Journal* editorial page read Guinier's work, and had a far different reaction. Branding her a "Quota Queen," the article went on to say she "sets the standard of innovative radicalism."

The result was, if anything, worse than the Baird and Wood flaps. The domino effect Nussbaum feared was taking shape. Again, Nussbaum argued that the administration should forcefully back its nominee. Clinton had known and liked Guinier since they were students at Yale, and he and Hillary had vacationed on Martha's Vineyard with her and her husband. But Clinton was furious that he had not been told more about Guinier's writings before making the nomination. Then Guinier had the temerity to defend herself on national television, appearing on *Nightline*. Afterward, Clinton convened a meeting of his top advisors in the Oval Office. "Who really thinks we should stick with this?" he asked. Only Nussbaum raised his hand, and everyone glared at him. Clinton withdrew Guinier's nomination.

The succession of failures, Clinton's anger and unhappiness, the pressure of the work—all contributed to a beleaguered atmosphere in the counsel's wing of the White House. The botched nominations overshadowed the successes, like the long-awaited confirmation in March of an attorney general, Miami district attorney Janet Reno. Foster hadn't been directly responsible for the failed nominations, but he felt acute disappointment, even more keenly, it seemed, than Nussbaum. On the night the Baird nomination collapsed, Foster had suffered an acute anxiety attack. He didn't go to bed until 2:30 A.M., sweating profusely, saying he felt sick. He told his wife that "everyone was criticizing him," even at home. His mood was exacerbated by the pace of the work, requiring uninterrupted ten- to twelve-hour workdays, all conducted in a crisis atmosphere, with the press hovering just offstage.

•

Although Foster was now deputy White House counsel and not the Clintons' personal lawyer—Robert Barnett at the Williams & Connolly law firm had assumed that role—he continued to handle some personal matters for the Clintons that he'd been working on in Little Rock, including everything related to Whitewater. Technically, he probably should not have, since his job was to represent the president and first lady in their official capacities. Nussbaum was aware of the situation, but given that Foster was already handling these issues, and that the Clintons wanted him to continue, it seemed better not to question the arrangement. Nussbaum didn't really get involved.

As April 15 approached, Foster was confronted with the question of how to handle the Clintons' 1992 tax returns. This would have been uneventful were it not for the Clintons' "sale" of their interest in Whitewater to McDougal for $1,000 just before the year ended, since the sale of such an asset ordinarily results in either a capital gain or loss.

Preparation of the tax returns had been handed over to Yoly Redden in Little Rock, Hillary's accountant, who had traditionally handled the couple's tax returns—taxes being a subject that held even less interest for Bill Clinton than personal finance. The first week in April she sent a draft of the returns to Foster along with a letter saying that "we may be able to claim a $10,000 to $15,000 loss in the disposal of the Whitewater stock. The present return reflects no gain or loss on the disposal. I will let you know if a loss can be claimed. I realize that we need to take the most conservative approach possible and that was the position taken in the return."

Foster, however, was obviously troubled about the political implications. He asked a staff member to undertake a search to determine how the press had reacted in the past to the filing of presidential tax returns, especially to Bush's in 1989, his first year as president, and to those of Dan and Marilyn Quayle. Being of a different generation, Barbara Bush didn't have a career of her own, and thus her role in the family finances hadn't attracted any press scrutiny. But Marilyn Quayle, herself a lawyer, might provide some analogy for Hillary Clinton. Yet nothing controversial about Marilyn Quayle's taxes had surfaced. The staff also reviewed press treatment of the Clintons' taxes during the campaign, which had been perfunctory.

At one point, Foster complained to Thomases about how disorganized and incomplete the Whitewater tax materials were. Thomases told him not to handle it himself, but to get a good tax lawyer and rely on his advice, whatever it was. Instead, Foster consulted Barnett, the Clintons' personal lawyer at Williams & Connolly, writing that, "I guess the treatment of the Whitewater investment will be a very sensitive item . . . it seems that the opposition was contending that the Clintons' investment in Whitewater was such that they had an opportunity to realize half of the profits if the project was successful but were protected against losses if the project was unsuccessful. The President responded that they had lost at least $25,000.

"The return currently shows that disposition of the investment on Schedule D at a cost of $1,000 and a sales price of $1,000 and no gain or loss. It seems to me that this treatment bolsters the opponents' position. That is, they claim he was protected against loss—the President said he incurred a significant loss—the return shows no loss. . . .

"Thus, it appears that the $1,000 of proceeds on Schedule D is for cosmetic purposes. If that is the case, wouldn't the best course of action be to simply not report anything on the return. I am not aware of any provision in the tax law that requires one to claim all losses that have been incurred. . . ."

Meanwhile, in an April 12 letter, Redden reported that a $5,878.35 loss could be documented—far from the $25,000 Clinton had referred to during the campaign. But, she cautioned, "Because of the numerous problems with Whitewater records and the commingling of funds with other companies and individuals, I believe many explanations may have to be made if we claim a loss. I do not believe we should claim a gain, because the Clintons did suffer a loss, and that should be the implication in closing the transaction."

Foster appears to have agonized over the issue, making handwritten notes covering at least seven pages of a spiral notebook. The notes appear to reflect phone conversations with Redden, the accountants who worked on the Lyons campaign report on Whitewater, and James Lyons himself. Some of the notes seem to be questions and answers to himself, possibly in anticipation of various phone calls. And one note reads, "Get out of Whitewater."

Several of the notes reflect anxiety that the treatment of the sale could trigger an IRS audit, which would in turn lead to a probe of how much the Clintons and McDougals actually contributed to the investment. Because a gain or loss is calculated by subtracting the cost of property (or "basis") from its sales price, the cost must be documented. In discussing the possibility of taking a loss, Foster's notes read:

> "More importantly would result in an
> audit of proof of basis
> "Can of worms you shouldn't open."

That sentiment evidently proved dispositive. The approach finally adopted was the only one that guaranteed no investigation would be made of the actual cost to the Clintons of their Whitewater investment. Not only did they not claim a loss, they registered a gain, which was both factually incorrect and in conflict with their oft-stated claims of loss. The Clintons' 1992 Schedule D lists Whitewater Development Corp. and a sales price of $1,000. The line for "cost or other basis" is blank. The return reflects a gain of $1,000. Despite Foster's apprehensions, that aspect of the return generated no press.

In March, Leonard Strickman, dean of the University of Arkansas School of Law, had visited Foster in Washington, where they had dinner at the White House mess. To Strickman, the usually laconic Foster seemed as close to exuberant as he'd ever seen him. Soon after, Strickman called Foster to bestow a singular honor: he wanted him to be the speaker at the law school's commencement. Ever modest, and shy at the prospect of addressing such a large gathering, Foster protested, saying he wasn't worthy of the honor. "I don't know what to say at a commencement," Foster said. "I've never even been to a law school commencement, not even my own." But Strickman prevailed.

Foster returned to Fayetteville on May 7, the night before the speech. Strickman had dinner that night with Vince and Lisa, seizing the opportunity to suggest names of possible Supreme Court nominees. In contrast to how Strickman had found him in March, Foster seemed visibly under stress, and complained to Strickman of the pressure. At lunch the next day, Foster kept excusing himself to leave the table. At one point Lisa leaned over to say, "I've seen him go to court hundreds of times and I've never seen him this nervous."

Several Foster family members attended the speech, including Foster's elderly mother and his sister Sheila Anthony. They'd gathered in Arkansas to celebrate Mother's Day the next day. The ceremony was held at the Walton Art Center. Foster's speech was upstaged by a student protester who walked on stage and asked the audience to recite with him the Lord's Prayer. The traditional benediction had been banned that year after a Supreme Court ruling that found such prayers to be unconstitutional in high schools.

Foster did not deliver a groundbreaking speech by candidly describing life in the White House counsel's office, nor did he say anything controversial. Though he had written it himself, it revealed little of himself. This was very much like Foster: private, guarded, eager to make a good impression, unfailingly polite.

But while heavy on platitudes the speech seemed to acknowledge the anxieties the graduating law students might feel. He lectured them gently from the wise perspective of an experienced litigator, law firm partner, and now, public servant. Given the demanding, hectic life Foster was leading in Washington, some of his prescriptions, however well-intentioned and deeply felt, seem strangely disembodied from his own experience: Having left his family behind in Little Rock, he nonetheless urged his audience to "Balance wisely your professional life and your family life. . . . The office can wait. It will still be there when your children are gone." Though he hadn't taken a single weekend off since coming to Washington, he urged, "Take time out for yourself. Have some fun, go fishing, every once in a while take a walk in the woods by yourself. Learn to relax, watch more sunsets." And despite growing disillusionment with his own work, he quoted the first lady: "She said service means you get as well as you give. Your life is changed as you change the life of others. It is the way we find meaning in our lives."

There were also flashes of what seem to be deep feelings. "I cannot make this point too strongly. There is no victory, no advantage, no fee, no favor, which is worth even a blemish on your reputation for intellect and integrity. Nothing travels faster than an accusation that another lawyer's word is no good. . . . Dents to the reputation in the legal profession are irreparable."

Foster preached humility in the face of success, saying that "Along the way you will receive recognition for achievement, a complimentary newspaper article, an award, a plaque, and if the gods are with you, maybe even a commencement address. When you smile for the camera and bask in the applause and take your bow, pause and reflect and recognize who helped you get there. Your spouse, your law partner, your parents, your friends." But then, perhaps reflecting on his recent experiences, his message hinted at barely contained bitterness: "Because there will also be failures, and criticisms and bad press and lies, stormy days and cloudy days, and you will not survive them without the support of those same spouses, law partners and friends. So it is."

There was a prolonged ovation, and many students came up afterward to tell Foster how inspired they were.

Now, with the school year ending, it was time for Lisa and their son to join Foster in Washington. After the address, Foster returned immediately to work, and Lisa went back to oversee the packing. As she was going through a trunk that Vince had packed, she came across a silver handgun. She was surprised to see it there. In contrast to Vince's father, she knew her husband disliked guns. She'd been annoyed when Vince's father, in a handwritten note, bequeathed his collection of guns to him, and Vince had shared her disdain for the weapons. Still, she put the gun among the things they were taking to Washington.

Later, as she continued the packing by herself, Lisa felt overwhelmed by the prospect of leaving her life behind and moving to a strange city. She sat down on the living room floor and cried. She called Foster, still teary, complaining that she didn't know what to do. Foster was barely able to contain his frustration. Nearly overwhelmed himself, he could hardly believe that his wife was that helpless. He told her to look up a mover in the Yellow Pages.

That spring, Hubbell had been nominated to be associate attorney general, and confirmation hearings were scheduled. Foster continued to seem troubled by the prospect, worries that surely increased that spring. For Foster was aware of other potential problems that lurked within the Rose partnership having nothing to do with the firm's relatively benign work for corporate clients. Having taken on aspects of Whitewater on behalf of the Clintons, Foster knew that he and Hubbell had rounded up all the relevant documents and removed them from the Rose firm. He also knew of the Rose firm's work for Madison Guaranty and the still-unanswered questions stemming from Gerth's story. He knew that the Rose billing records revealed Hillary's work for Castle Grande.

There was also plenty of resentment of Hubbell at Rose, both for his role in the Giroir ouster, and for Hubbell's handling of firm finances while he was managing partner. There were already some rumors circulating in Little Rock that Hubbell had been linked to some mysterious overbilling—some Rose firm clients had received checks from the firm reimbursing them—and unreconciled expense reports. Indeed, on May 7, two Rose partners visited Hubbell in Washington and confronted him with about $25,000 in questionable expenses billed to clients. "Gee, I can't remember off the top of my head," Hubbell said when questioned about them. "But I'm sure there is an explanation, and I'll look into it and get back to you." The partners didn't speak to Foster on that trip, nor did they bring the matter to the attention of anyone involved in Hubbell's nomination to be associate attorney general. The Rose firm still believed it would help the firm to have former partners in high places, and didn't want to do anything that might embarrass Hubbell or the administration.

The next week, on May 12, another Rose partner, Amy Stewart, a close colleague from the Rose litigation department, visited Foster in his office and placed a call from there to Hubbell's office. The subject of the call hasn't been disclosed, but Stewart surely knew about the billing problems. As a former Rose partner and Hubbell's best friend, Foster almost certainly knew trouble might be brewing.

But Foster didn't mention any of this to Nussbaum. His anxiety was no doubt heightened by a series of editorials that ran in the *Wall Street Journal*. The first of these had been published in early March, when the paper had emblazoned an editorial with the headline "Who Is Webster Hubbell?" As the country's foremost exponent of conservative political doctrine, attacks from the *Wall Street Journal* editorial page—separated by a strict Chinese Wall from the paper's news pages—were to be expected. Veteran Washington Democrats read the paper's editorials with varying degrees of indignation and amusement, and though no one could afford to ignore them, they had long grown accustomed to brushing them aside. But in Little Rock, virtually all of Foster's and Hubbell's friends and colleagues read the *Journal*, and they didn't necessarily brush off the editorials as more concerned with ideology than fairness or accuracy, as liberal Washingtonians did. The *Journal's* views carried great weight there, and both Hubbell and Foster were stung by what they considered the mean-spiritedness of the *Journal's* attention.

Nothing in the Hubbell editorial touched directly on Foster's worries for Hubbell. But the editorial concluded, "We seem to have the spectacle of Hillary Clinton's former law partner fixing meetings between Justice officials and demand-waving pols . . ." and it described Hubbell as "a temporary appointee not subject to confirmation proceedings, apparently running the Justice Department as a partner of the First Lady." Nor did the *Journal* stop there. Over the next few weeks it ran a virtual series on Hubbell, concluding with "Who Is Webster Hubbell—IV." That editorial ran on May 12, the same day as Stewart's visit, a date sufficiently memorable that Foster made a note of the editorial in his appointment calendar.

Nonetheless, Hubbell's nomination as associate attorney general went ahead, and Foster's fears were unrealized. Indeed, attacks on Hubbell came not from conservatives, but from liberals. A minor flap broke out over Hubbell's membership in the once-all-white Little Rock Country Club. Though Hubbell claimed he'd tried to recruit blacks, and the club did have one black member, Hubbell announced the day of his confirmation hearing that he had resigned from the club. (Clinton had given up his honorary membership during the campaign.) That meant the rest of the Arkansas contingent—McLarty, Foster, Kennedy—also had to resign. It was of no great moment to Foster, but it was a blow to Lisa, for whom life in Little Rock deprived of the Country Club was all but unthinkable.

On Wednesday afternoon, May 12, the same day Amy Stewart from the Rose firm had visited, David Watkins called Foster. "Vince, I want to talk to you," he said. "Would you meet with

Catherine Cornelius, Harry Thomason, and me? Can we come up?" Foster reluctantly agreed, and when the group arrived, Watkins was struck by how harried Foster seemed. "I don't have much time," Foster warned. He had a haircut appointment at 4 P.M.

The group in Foster's office was part of the core of Arkansans who'd accompanied the Clintons to the White House, who usually had dinner together once a week. They never quite melded with the career staffers. Thomason and his wife, Linda Bloodworth-Thomason, were Clinton friends from way back; Thomason had met Clinton while Thomason was still a high school football coach in Arkansas. After doing some advertising production work, he and his wife had become wildly successful Hollywood producers, launching the hit sitcoms *Evening Shade* and *Designing Women*. Indeed, *Evening Shade* starred Burt Reynolds, who owned land near Flippin, and was set in Evening Shade, an actual town in Marion County, where Whitewater is located. Thomason credits Hillary Clinton with suggesting the name for the show. Clinton's half-brother, Roger, was playing guitar in a band that warmed up audiences for tapings of the Thomason TV shows.

Thomason, avuncular, bearded, disarmingly charming, had no formal job at the White House, but after successfully producing the inauguration, he'd been recently called back to help deal with the evident chaos and morale problems in the White House staff and to help stage press events. He had a temporary office in the East Wing and a pass enabling him to come and go freely. He'd known Watkins for years, going back to when Watkins was a prominent advertising executive in Little Rock and Thomason was a hungry young film producer looking to do TV commercials. Good-looking, trim, usually tan, Watkins was an avid golfer who had managed several of Clinton's gubernatorial campaigns and had held a top position in the presidential campaign. He'd hired Cornelius first as his secretary and then, when that didn't work out because Cornelius was chafing for something more substantial, he posted her to the White House travel office.

Cornelius, a third cousin to the president, had helped handle travel arrangements during the campaign and, from her post as Watkins's secretary, had already evidenced a keen interest in the travel office. She'd prepared several memos for Watkins, none of which he read carefully. She argued that the office was poorly run and "overly pro-press" and she proposed that she be named to head it. Watkins wasn't ready to go that far, but he told her to see if the 25 percent cut in administrative personnel promised by Clinton could be implemented at the travel office, and to write a report.

At the meeting in Foster's office, Cornelius was positively breathless. She'd stumbled on major corruption at the travel office, she said. She claimed money was being spent on motorboats, race horses, vacation homes, and trips to Europe. She'd been surreptitiously copying financial records and checks going out of the office, and she thought she could document a case. Billy Dale, who was in charge of the office and had worked there for thirty years, had been hostile to her since the day she arrived. "I was here when this president arrived, and I'll be here when he leaves," she quoted Dale as saying. Cornelius said she'd been isolated in a soundproof room where, she reported, she'd been receiving mysterious phone calls. "Do you live alone?" a caller asked; another said, "Are you scared?"

Thomason had heard independently of trouble in the travel office. He was part owner of a Cincinnati aviation consulting firm with Darnell Martens, and the firm had provided travel consulting services for the Clinton campaign. Martens had called the travel office about bidding on the air charter contract for the White House and, Martens reported, he'd been rudely rebuffed by Dale, who said "hell would freeze over" before Martens would be allowed into his operation. Thomason was furious, and had immediately called Watkins. "You've got some of the rudest people I've ever heard of working in that travel office," Thomason said.

That morning, Cornelius shared her mounting suspicions with Thomason. Thomason, in turn, discussed it with both the president and first lady. Thomason thought the travel office staffers, like the Secret Service personnel, should be Clinton loyalists. "We need to stay ahead of this," Hillary replied. The Clintons had asked Thomason to find ways of generating positive media coverage, and after the barrage of bad publicity, he and the first lady sensed an opportunity. Surely, if they discovered and rooted out corruption right inside the White House, something that had probably been going on for years, they could harvest some positive press. How could it be otherwise? Watkins picked up the phone to Foster, seeking guidance. They wanted to accelerate the process, so the positive press reports would appear as soon as possible.

Foster didn't express all that much enthusiasm. Cornelius was, after all, a twenty-five-year-old, new to Washington, dazzled by her proximity to power, full of a sense of her own importance. Foster said they shouldn't proceed until they knew the facts. He suggested Cornelius produce whatever records she had to back up her claim and that the group should reconvene later that afternoon. Meanwhile, he called Bill Kennedy, and asked him to join the meeting, then dropped into Nussbaum's office. "We're getting reports that the travel office may be operating in an improper fashion," Foster said, adding that he'd take care of it. Nussbaum nodded, not paying much attention.

Cornelius's records were inconclusive, though she thought they suggested possible wrongdoing. The discussion that afternoon quickly turned to getting to the bottom of the matter, which posed something of a problem, given that the White House maintains no investigative staff for its own employees. Was this a task for the Justice Department? The FBI? The General Accounting Office? An outside consultant? Kennedy said he was dealing with the FBI on some background checks for potential nominees, and he'd ask their guidance. Meanwhile, Watkins recommended hiring an outside consulting firm. A colleague knew someone at Peat Marwick, which was retained to conduct a "surprise" audit of the operation. When Foster briefed him, Nussbaum thought it was a good approach, as did McLarty, who'd already heard about the matter from Hillary.

The next day, Thursday, Foster had a late lunch and then met with the first lady about the health reform task force. This was Hillary's overriding priority. As her main resource in the counsel's office, she was relying on Foster for various matters, including some aspects of medical malpractice and defending her decision to conduct the preliminary work of the task force in secret. Hillary brought up the travel office, asking Foster, according to his later notes, "What's going on? Are you on top of it?" He said he'd asked Bill Kennedy to look into the matter. In his notes, which evidently describe Hillary's reaction, he wrote "general frustration," which appears to have made the usually unflappable Foster "mad at criticism" and "frustrated" that the White House had no auditors at its disposal. He responded that he "just heard about it yesterday." Later that same afternoon, Hillary had again inquired about the travel office. This time Foster told her an outside auditor would be going through the office. "Let's see what's there," his notes read.

The first lady's comments obviously made an impression on Foster, especially in light of his failure to act forcefully over the Secret Service matter. Watkins was attending his daughter's graduation in Tennessee that Friday when he spoke to Foster. "The first lady has been asking about" the travel office, Foster said. "I'd like you to report to her." Watkins immediately called Hillary. "There's nothing definitive yet," he said, "but it looks worse than we thought. The record keeping is terrible, there seem to be some discrepancies in the handling of petty cash." He told her he was out of town for his daughter's graduation, but would brief her again on Monday.

"Well, that's good," Hillary replied. Then she broached, for the first time, the possibility of using the results of the investigation to fire the travel office staff. "I think we should get our people in there. I've been advised . . . you have to have your own people in these places. We've been tardy in some areas," which Watkins took as an obvious reminder of the Secret Service leak.*

With the added impetus of the first lady's interest, the White House staff all but worked itself into a frenzy. Cornelius was incensed over her belief that the travel staff had leaked to the press that she was a cousin of the president (a *Time* magazine reporter had called asking about the relationship). That same day, Jeff Eller, a lawyer working in the White House press office and Cornelius's boyfriend, got involved, going directly to McLarty to press the argument that reforming the travel office could generate the kind of positive press coverage the administration desperately needed. Eller argued that the travel office staff should be fired and given only until the end of the day to remove their belongings, such a surgical approach being a way to minimize bad press. But McLarty decided to wait until Peat Marwick completed its review before taking any action.

Bill Kennedy, meanwhile, enlisted the FBI, mentioning that he needed to talk about "a very sensitive matter" involving theft or fraud, and that the matter was being "directed at the highest levels"

---

* *Hillary Clinton has repeatedly denied that she suggested the travel office personnel be replaced.*

in the White House. After a meeting at the White House on Thursday afternoon with Kennedy and Foster, the FBI indicated it felt there was insufficient evidence to launch a criminal investigation. Then Kennedy insisted the agents talk to Cornelius, and she reiterated her concerns and suspicions. Kennedy also told two FBI agents that if the FBI couldn't handle the matter, he'd find another agency, such as the IRS.* As a result, the FBI agreed to go ahead, assigning the matter to its Washington metropolitan field office. No one thought to mention any of this to Attorney General Janet Reno, who in her confirmation hearings had explicitly pledged not to use the investigative power of the FBI for political ends.

Peat Marwick completed its preliminary audit by Sunday night, concluding that there was evidence of mismanagement. Monday morning, while Watkins was working on the memo summarizing the report, McLarty dropped in. He told Watkins he'd had dinner with the president and first lady the night before, and that "this affair is certainly on the first lady's antenna." Even though the FBI investigation had just begun, Watkins told McLarty that the Peat Marwick report was conclusive: there were sufficient examples of mismanagement to justify terminating the entire staff. McLarty concurred. Watkins finished the memorandum to McLarty, which he copied to Hillary, reporting the Peat Marwick results and recommending that the travel office staff be "terminated" the next day, to be replaced by Catherine Cornelius. Charter air service would be handled by World Wide Travel, the Little Rock agency that had done most of the campaign's travel arrangements—and was a former client of Watkins's.

In anticipation of the favorable press they expected the action to generate, Watkins drafted some "talking points" for the press office. Remarkably, he highlighted almost every potential public relations problem: the fact that Cornelius was a cousin of the president's, that World Wide Travel was an Arkansas agency, that the entire staff was being fired without any notice. Yet none of this triggered any reservations on the part of McLarty, Foster, or Kennedy. Eager to emphasize the seriousness of the matter, Watkins

---

* Kennedy later denied threatening to go to the IRS, but both FBI agents, Tom Carl and Howard Apple, recalled the comment, and added that Kennedy seemed to have little understanding of how the federal government worked.

also mentioned in the talking points that the FBI was investigating possible criminal wrongdoing. Watkins was ignorant of FBI policy that all investigations are confidential unless disclosure is required by a compelling public interest, as in the wake of a major crime, such as the terrorist bombings of the World Trade Center and Oklahoma City federal building.

Watkins gave the talking points to press spokeswoman Dee Dee Myers, who was going to be handling the press release and briefing scheduled for later that day. He also sent copies to Foster and Kennedy, adding a handwritten note: "Vince—statement we prepared for Dee Dee Myers to use—Any comments you have please call before 9:30 a.m." Foster responded before the deadline. He and Kennedy came into Watkins's office, telling him to strike the reference to the FBI in the talking points, which he did. But when he walked over to Myers's office to give her the revised draft, she was somewhere else in the White House with the president. Instead, Watkins told Jeff Eller to make sure no one in the press office mentioned the FBI. But much to Watkins's dismay, when Myers returned, he learned that she'd been questioned by a reporter who already seemed to know what was in the talking points. She'd confirmed the information, including the FBI involvement, all before the talking points had been approved and before the press briefing. Watkins was furious. He thought it typical of the haphazard way the press office operated. Still, he figured the positive news of corruption uncovered would outweigh any concern over revealing an FBI investigation.

At 10:30 that Wednesday, Watkins walked into the travel office, where four or five of the employees were working. He began by saying that "this isn't easy," but "as you know, we've had a review team in from [Peat Marwick], and as part of the national productivity review, we're looking at offices in the White House." The result, he said, was a decision to take "drastic action." Watkins added that "we've found gross mismanagement in the operation" and "we feel it's time for a change, sooner rather than later."

The employees stared blankly, evidently stunned. "What does this mean?" one asked.

"In my experience, it's better to clean out your desk now. Don't hang around. We'll pay you for the next two weeks," during which, he said, they'd be placed on administrative leave. Watkins left, and the staff began quietly packing their belongings, vacating the premises by noon.

Calls to the press office started almost immediately, and the briefing was announced for 1 P.M., conducted by Dee Dee Myers. In response to questions, she said all seven of the employees were being held responsible by the White House for "gross mismanagement." Despite the earlier admonition about mentioning the FBI, she readily volunteered again that the matter was so serious that the bureau was investigating it. She brushed aside questions about Cornelius's relationship to the president—"she's a distant cousin" —and insisted that the firings were not an attempt to replace career bureaucrats with political loyalists. She confirmed the employees hadn't been given an opportunity to confront the charges, and, when asked if that was fair, replied that "All I know about it was I was told the people in charge of administering the White House found serious problems there and thought there was no alternative." Later in the briefing, she said "some" of the employees had been given an opportunity to respond (though they hadn't).

It was already a bad week for the administration in the media. Earlier, Clinton had had his hair cut on the runway at Los Angeles International Airport by Christophe of Beverly Hills, holding up air traffic, and that minor, if symbolic, incident had blown into a circus. The initial press coverage of the travel office shakeup, though hardly the positive news everyone involved had been expecting, was relatively uncritical. The next day, Thomason's involvement surfaced, and Stephanopoulos, after Myers's hapless performance, had to deny that Thomason was seeking business for a charter airline company in which he had an interest. As Christophe's friend, Thomason was already being pilloried for the haircut incident, so this new revelation involving him was especially tantalizing.

On May 22, the *Washington Post* obtained copies of the memo from Thomason urging travel business be granted to his consulting firm, and a copy of Cornelius's memo to Watkins urging that she be named to head the office. "Clinton's Friend's Memo Sought Business; President's Cousin Proposed Staffing Travel Office with Loyalists," the page one headline read, igniting a firestorm of negative coverage.

Nonetheless, and despite mounting criticism that the White

House was improperly using the FBI for its political purposes, Stephanopoulos convened a meeting in his office with Foster, Kennedy, Nussbaum, Watkins, and an FBI public relations official to urge the FBI to issue a stronger statement about its investigation. Nussbaum and the other lawyers hadn't known an FBI official would be there. They thought the meeting was going to be a discussion of how to "calm things down." But no one raised any objections. Foster said virtually nothing.

The FBI, in accordance with its policies, was preparing to issue a press statement that read: "We understand that the results of the audit of the White House Travel office will be referred to the FBI for our review." That, of course, was much more vague than the statements already made by Myers and Stephanopoulos. When Myers asked if the statement couldn't be more "consistent" with the facts, the FBI official, John Collingwood, agreed to add a sentence saying there was "sufficient information for the FBI to determine that additional criminal investigation is warranted." No one seems to have reflected on the fact the FBI was departing from its disclosure policies at the behest of the White House, and how that would look.

With that statement in hand, Stephanopoulos took to the press room to announce that World Wide Travel would not, after all, be handling White House travel. To the surprise of the travel office employees themselves, Stephanopoulos said they hadn't been fired at all, but had simply been placed on indefinite "administrative leave." He also released the text of the FBI statement. The president, meanwhile, ran for cover. Asked about the affair, he said, "The only thing I know is we made a decision to save the taxpayers and the press money. That's all I know."

The next day, the *Washington Post* blasted the administration in its lead editorial: "Now it turns out that three of President Clinton's principal aides, including the White House counsel, caused an FBI official to alter a press release to reflect the White House line in the increasingly smelly affair of the White House travel office." A *New York Times* editorial said that the affair made the White House look "inept, callous and self-serving." The matter had taken on sufficient trappings of scandal that it was now routinely dubbed "Travelgate." The White House appeared to be, in fact was, in chaos.

Foster was stunned. Eager to make up for his failure over the

Secret Service, he'd been swept up into the anticipation of good news for the president and first lady. Was that why he was so blind to the political implications of firing the entire staff and replacing them with a presidential relative? Why didn't he recognize the sensitivity of enlisting the FBI? Didn't he consider that the travel office employees should be given a chance to defend themselves before being fired? Why did the famously deliberative Foster allow action to be taken in such haste? Much more than in the Secret Service incident, the argument could be made that Foster did fail his clients. He, not Nussbaum, was in charge of the travel office matter. That realization must have been devastating to him, even though Nussbaum tried to reassure him by saying he'd done nothing explicitly improper.

When he next encountered Watkins, Foster appeared stricken. "My God," he said, "what have we done?" He seemed especially concerned that Hillary's involvement—her suggestion that the employees be fired, her eagerness to get "our people" in the jobs, her hunger for favorable press—might become public. They could only imagine what the press would make of Hillary's involvement. The whole issue of politicizing the FBI would be that much more potent if involvement could be extended from appointees like Foster and Watkins to the first lady. Foster pressed on Watkins the fact that they had to protect "the client," meaning Hillary. They agreed they wouldn't mention her involvement, and pledged to protect her.

Thomason was in Florida when the news broke. His first inkling of trouble came from a Republican friend in Washington. "Don't you understand the relationship between the White House press corps and the travel office?" the friend asked, incredulous. He said reporters and correspondents had grown accustomed to being pampered with first-class amenities; that they routinely evaded customs duties by bringing back merchandise on the planes; that the travel office would reimburse them for more than they spent, then bill the news organizations, which allowed the reporters to pocket the difference, citing several specific instances and various news personnel by name. He added that Ronald Reagan had tried to fire the same staff—only to back off when warned of the possible press reaction. This view—that the press had made an issue of the matter only because its perks were threatened—was quickly embraced by just about everyone in the White House.

Thomason flew back to Washington, and ran into Foster at

the White House. He looked terrible. "Before we came to Washington, I thought we were good guys," Foster mused to him, no humor evident in his voice. That evening Foster, Thomason, and their wives had dinner at the White House. "You can't believe the Washington press," Thomason told the Fosters, noting that he and Linda had been accused of "hightailing" it out of town when he'd had a previously scheduled trip to Florida. But Foster was nearly silent throughout the meal.

In contrast to Foster, Thomason and his wife took to the airwaves to vent their anger. At this point they hardly cared about the consequences—they were so fed up with Washington they were leaving for good, and, in any event, their friendship had become politically poisonous for the Clintons. As Linda Bloodworth-Thomason told *Good Morning America*, "This has been one of the most bizarre experiences in our lives. I wish everyone in the United States could have the experience of being the president's best friend. . . . From the first time that Bill Clinton became president, the first day really, the Inauguration Day, we have been characterized across the country in editorials as the president's sleazy immoral friends, and these are strange characterizations of us, we think." Thomason added that "I must say I'm disappointed to learn a lot of the ways Washington works."

A few days later, the White House announced that it would undertake an internal review under the direction of McLarty and John Podesta. No one from the White House counsel's office—which ordinarily would supply the personnel for such a venture—would be involved, given the obvious conflict of interest. John Podesta interviewed Watkins. Podesta had noticed that the first lady had been copied on Watkins's memo, and he wondered why. It was just routine, Watkins said.

"Is there anything you'd like to say" about Mrs. Clinton? Podesta asked.

"No," Watkins replied.

Later, Foster stopped by Watkins's office and asked him how his meeting with Podesta had gone. Watkins reported that Podesta had asked about Hillary.

"What did you say?" Foster asked.

"I fell on my sword."

CHAPTER

TEN

NOTHING STOPPED THE FLOW of bad press over Travelgate, a state of affairs that had the Clintons alternately incensed at the media and discouraged. There seemed to be constant meetings about how to stem the tide. Watkins, Foster, and Nussbaum weren't present at a meeting where Stephanopoulos persuaded McLarty that the bad coverage wouldn't stop until there was more of a mea culpa from the White House. To the dismay of Watkins and the lawyers, Stephanopoulos announced on May 25 that five of the seven discharged employees were being reinstated (they were actually given new jobs, and American Express was retained to run the travel operation). In Watkins's view, this was a total capitulation on the central issue in the affair, the wrongdoing and mismanagement of the travel office. In his view, it all but guaranteed that the conduct of the White House staff rather than that of the travel office employees would remain at the center of the affair.

Nor would that be the end of it. Stung by press criticism, the Justice Department, the FBI, the Treasury Department, and the IRS all announced their own investigations of the affair.

Stephanopoulos, backed by McLarty, demanded that Nussbaum issue a press statement acknowledging responsibility for the contact with the FBI. Nussbaum insisted that the statement begin by asserting that "The White House Counsel's office violated no policy, procedure or other requirement." But the release all but conceded that there should have been a policy, and a new one was announced:

"The Attorney General has expressed the desire that in the

future, even with regard to matters of internal White House security, to avoid any appearance of impropriety, the White House should inform the Office of the Attorney General, the Deputy Attorney General, or the Associate Attorney General before contacting the FBI. Since the White House shares the Attorney General's desire to avoid any such appearance of impropriety, it has assured the Attorney General that such contacts with the FBI in the future respecting matters of internal White House security will be made initially through the Justice Department, as she requested.

"There is nothing more important to this Administration than to preserve the integrity and the appearance of integrity of the Justice Department and the Federal Bureau of Investigation."

The statement did little to quell public criticism. In an editorial, "Myopia at the White House," the *Wall Street Journal* took aim squarely at the White House counsel's office, saying the new policy "only underscores the failure of Mr. Nussbaum's office to appreciate the seriousness of its dealings with the FBI."

Nussbaum was furious at having to issue the statement. He felt the attempt at damage control was yet another example of the short-term mind-set prevailing in the White House, with Stephanopoulos in particular its architect. It was one thing to admit error, but they'd done nothing wrong. Yet the whole approach was not to defend them. It was how to propitiate the media today, how to stop the story. What was important, as Nussbaum had so often said, was the judgment of history, not today's media spin. The White House's capitulation undermined any image of strength; it was demoralizing.

While Nussbaum was angry, Foster appeared depressed. It seemed that in a crisis the president would not stand behind them. The White House, the institution to which he had devoted himself, had let him down.

Still, there were more pressing matters, and Nussbaum told Foster they couldn't be sidetracked by the travel office. Justice Byron White had announced his retirement on March 19, giving the Clinton administration its first opportunity to appoint a Supreme Court justice. After the fiascoes of Robert Bork and Clarence Thomas, it had been Nussbaum's dream to restore some dignity to the process and to depoliticize it. He also had to contend with the need to get the FBI director, William Sessions, to resign and to find a replacement.

But Foster couldn't shake his preoccupation with the travel office. That Friday, before leaving for the Memorial Day weekend, Foster called Watkins. "Let's get together to talk," he said, adding, "Let's do this out of the office." He mentioned that his wife was out of town for the weekend, and Watkins suggested they get together the next day. But when Foster called again, Watkins had scheduled a golf game. They ended up talking on the phone Sunday morning. Foster seemed upset over Podesta's internal review, saying it wasn't "proper" and that "we shouldn't be beating ourselves up over this." Watkins agreed wholeheartedly. Foster again stressed the need to protect "the client."

That same weekend, Foster turned to his notebook. Under the headings "Attorney Client Privileged" and "In anticipation of Litigation," he began writing a detailed chronology of what had happened, injecting periodically questions or question marks where he couldn't remember or didn't know the answers.

When he returned to his office the next week, he was among the White House officials given a copy of the FBI report on the travel office. Although the report concluded that the FBI "reacted both correctly and responsibly to the contacts by the White House," it didn't purport to judge the propriety of the White House contacting the FBI in the first place. And from Foster's point of view, the FBI's version of what happened was both wrong and calculated to put the White House counsel's office in the worst possible light. Foster underlined several of the most offensive statements in the report, including a finding that Bill Kennedy had "commented the matter had to be handled immediately or he would refer the matter to another agency, specifically mentioning the Internal Revenue Service," and that the matter was "extremely sensitive and being directed at the 'highest level' at the White House." Moreover, the report said of Foster himself that he was "advised of the White House concern for the situation stating quick action was necessary."

The report appears to have triggered more entries in Foster's notebook, where dates indicate periodic entries through the first few weeks of June. In many cases he revised and repeated accounts of incidents he'd already addressed. By the end of the notes, these events seem to have turned into a near-obsession, with his thoughts becoming more rambling and disjointed. Even irrelevant minutiae appear to have received intense scrutiny.

At the same time, the White House strategy that had so upset Nussbaum and Foster was failing to stem the negative press coverage. The *Washington Post* reported that Kennedy had invoked the possibility of turning to the IRS, leading to more criticism that the White House was trying to politicize an investigative body. Then Congress weighed in. Senate minority leader Robert Dole and four Republican congressmen called for a congressional investigation. At a news conference, Dole said that "the only people looking into this are the ones who got the White House into the mess in the first place."

Among the most discredited of that group was Stephanopoulos, whose pronouncements were being openly derided by the White House press corps. Though his loyalty to Clinton was obvious, and he remained close to the president, McLarty and others insisted that he be replaced as press spokesman. On the Wednesday before Memorial Day, at the behest of the president and first lady, McLarty called David Gergen, a columnist for *U.S. News & World Report* and a veteran of three Republican administrations. McLarty told Gergen the president was looking for someone who knew Washington, was a "centrist" who would pull him back into the mainstream, and who knew the press. Gergen fit the bill. Though he'd worked for Republican presidents, he thought of himself as a moderate, and he'd actually voted for Clinton. He seemed to know everyone in Washington, including bureau chiefs and top editors at the major papers and at the networks. Gergen was intrigued at the prospect of trying to generate a more bipartisan spirit toward the White House, and he didn't think a failed presidency was in the country's interest.

Given a Saturday deadline for his decision—Gergen was surprised at the rush—he accepted a post as counselor to the president, in which he would assume many of Stephanopoulos's communications duties. But he insisted Stephanopoulos be told first. He didn't want to be seen as a party to his demotion. Still, Gergen sensed that Stephanopoulos and his allies resented him from the start, even though Stephanopoulos's closeness to the president seemed, if anything, enhanced by the change. Gergen was, after all, a Republican.

Gergen's arrival did nothing to dampen calls for public hearings into the travel office affair, and the prospect of questioning by hostile Republicans under the glare of publicity seemed to terrify

Foster. He started badgering Nussbaum about the prospect, saying he felt he needed to get a lawyer and recommending that Nussbaum get one, too. Nussbaum brushed Foster's suggestions aside. Later, Foster told Nussbaum he'd contacted James Hamilton, the fellow Davidson alumnus who'd been considered for Nussbaum's job. Foster's notebook jottings in some cases appear to be preparation for congressional cross-examination. His notes also suggest he was beginning to worry that he might even have violated some law.

Given his prominent role in the affair, it was remarkable that thus far Foster's name had not been mentioned in any of the press coverage. But then, in early June, with the travel office controversy in full swing, Foster had gotten a message that someone from the *Wall Street Journal* editorial page had called, asking for a photograph. Given the lengths he'd taken to avoid the press over rumors of an affair with Hillary, it isn't surprising that Foster didn't return the call. He told his secretary not to send a photo. His disdain for the press mirrored that of the first lady, and had only deepened since his arrival in Washington. He'd been especially appalled at the way the *Wall Street Journal* editorial page had hounded Hubbell. So the message must have inspired anxiety that the spotlight of public attention he so dreaded was approaching.

For the next couple of weeks he heard nothing further from the *Journal*, but any notion he could escape by simply ignoring the call was illusory. As the *Journal* later recounted, the editorial page was simply seeking file photos of Foster and Bill Kennedy in the event it needed them. Deborah Gorham, Foster's secretary, had returned the call, and responded high-handedly that "Mr. Foster sees no reason why he should supply the *Journal* with a photo," according to the *Journal*.

When further inquiries produced no results, the *Journal* filed a Freedom of Information Act request. Though the act requires a response in ten days, that request, too, went unanswered. Eventually someone at the White House did get back to Foster, saying they ought to send the *Journal* a photograph, and Foster reluctantly agreed.

But before it arrived, on June 17, the *Journal* unloaded with a sequel to its Webster Hubbell series: "Who Is Vincent Foster?" In place of the usual dot rendering was an outline of a man's head with a large question mark.

"In its first few months," the editorial began, "the Clinton

White House has proved itself to be careless about many things, from Presidential haircuts to appointing a government. But most disturbing is its carelessness about following the law."

After citing two other examples (including the secrecy of the health care task force, which, evidently unknown to the *Journal* at the time, was being defended by Foster), the editorial recounted its unsuccessful effort to obtain Foster's photo. "No doubt Mr. Foster and company consider us mischievous (at best)," the editorial observed. "Of course the Clinton administration has little reason to love us. . . . Even if we were as uniformly hostile as sometimes charged, there are larger points here. How an administration deals with critics is a basic test of its character and mores, and how scrupulously it follows the law is even more directly significant."

By its own admission, the editorial was somewhat whimsical, while dealing with more serious themes. Yet, significantly, it really wasn't about Vincent Foster. He was barely mentioned apart from the headline, and it doesn't even mention him in the withholding of his photograph. Yet Foster reacted as though he'd been hit with a broadside. Deborah Gorham thought it was the only time she actually saw Foster get angry. He was furious because he believed the *Journal* had misquoted Gorham, who had said only that Foster "preferred" not to send a photo.

Others made light of it. The morning the editorial appeared, Nussbaum said to Foster, "This is a real problem for the counsel to the president. You're going to upstage me." Yet Foster said nothing, not even cracking a smile, which surprised Nussbaum. The next day Foster bumped into Bruce Lindsey, who also dismissed the significance of the column. But Foster was still very upset, saying the editorial had wrongly accused him of playing "fast and loose" with the rules. "The damn thing is that I sent them a picture," Foster added. He told his brother-in-law, Beryl Anthony, that he'd spent a "lifetime" building his reputation, which was now being "tarnished." Most of the White House staff seemed amused by the item, and chided Foster for taking it so seriously. But he didn't share their humor. He said that he was convinced the *Journal* would hound him until he or someone from the Arkansas contingent was forced to resign in disgrace.

The *Journal* editorial page is nothing if not dogged, and a week later, photograph in hand, it began an editorial by saying, "Meet Vincent Foster." But that editorial was aimed at the secrecy of the health care task force, and mentioned Foster simply as the lawyer defending the approach. But it seemed only to confirm Foster's view that the *Journal* would hound him.

Perhaps Foster wouldn't have reacted so strongly if his conduct in the travel office affair didn't remain under scrutiny. As the Podesta inquiry continued, Foster and Nussbaum would hear periodic reports of what was being said and what steps were being considered. Foster's handwritten notes, labeled "Privileged/in anticipation of litigation," with the notation "Podesta meeting in my office," focus almost exclusively on the role of the first lady in the matter. While Foster acknowledged two meetings with Hillary to discuss the travel office, he concluded his notes by saying, "After discussing other issues we mutually exchanged views that HRC is perceived as being involved in decisions and events in which she has no participation."

Then one day Foster reported to Nussbaum that he'd heard Bill Kennedy was going to be formally reprimanded, and he was extremely upset. He uncharacteristically raised his voice, all but shouting that "This is my blame. Let me take it." Nussbaum was outraged. Foster and Kennedy "didn't do a damned thing wrong," he said, convinced that the White House was now about to unjustly sacrifice one of his staff for the same misguided, short-sighted reasons that had governed the entire affair. Nussbaum got on the phone and demanded to see McLarty. When he reached the chief of staff's office, he asked if he were going to reprimand Kennedy, and McLarty said he was. "Fine," Nussbaum said, raising his voice. "It's your decision. But you can't just reprimand him. You must also reprimand Foster, and you must reprimand me. Reprimand the counsel to the president and the deputy counsel to the president."

"You're probably right," McLarty testily agreed. Nussbaum was, in fact, serious about the reprimands. While still insistent that no one should be reprimanded, he didn't want his staff to be divided. They would accept their public humiliation together.

"Congratulations," Nussbaum told Foster when he returned to the office, feeling a perverse pleasure in the latest turn of events. "You're going to be reprimanded. I'm going to be, too." Foster looked grave, far less excited than Nussbaum at the prospect. "If Kennedy is, then we should be," he agreed.

On Friday morning, July 2, copies of the Podesta report were handed out within the White House. Nussbaum, Foster, and Watkins were all indignant over its tone and conclusions, which they believed to be harsh and unfair. Indeed, the report was a virtual catalogue of alleged misjudgment and bad management, though it stopped short of any charge of wrongdoing. To Foster's evident relief, it leveled no criticism at the first lady, barely mentioning her role, even though she had been a major impetus in the affair. It was her involvement that had given it its sense of urgency, and she, if anyone, had politicized the matter by wanting her "people" in the travel office.

Still, whatever good news could be extracted from the report was overshadowed. It singled out the counsel's office in its concluding overview: "The management problems in the handling of the Travel Office extended beyond the White House Office of Management and Administration. The Chief of Staff and the White House Counsel's Office had the opportunity to contain the momentum of the incident, but did not take adequate advantage of this opportunity."

David Watkins was summoned to McLarty's office about 10 A.M. "It's wrong; I don't concur," Watkins said immediately. "Well, here's what we're going to do," McLarty said. "We're going to reprimand you." Watkins was indignant. He'd been McLarty's Little League coach; he'd been the football team quarterback and the student body president ahead of McLarty. He could hardly believe McLarty was going to reprimand him.

"This is difficult," McLarty continued, but Watkins had been "the point man" and had to accept blame.

"What's a reprimand mean?" Watkins asked.

"I don't know," McLarty replied. "Not much. It will just go in your personnel file."

"Does this mean I can never get another government job?" Watkins asked, his voice laced with sarcasm.

"No."

"Don't you understand?" Watkins burst out. "I never want another government job." Then he asked who else was being reprimanded, and McLarty mentioned Catherine Cornelius, Jeff Eller, and Bill Kennedy. Then, he added, "Maybe Vince and Bernie. But probably not Bernie."

As soon as he returned to his office, Watkins called Foster to report that he was being reprimanded. "I'm going up" to McLarty's office, Foster replied.

For his part, Watkins later drafted an angry memo intended for McLarty, describing it as a "soul cleansing," carefully detailing what happened, an attempt "to be sure the record is straight."

Referring to press reports of the thrown lamp and possible leaks from the Secret Service, Watkins wrote, "As you recall, an issue developed between the Secret Service and the First Family in February and March requiring resolution and action . . . the First Lady in particular was extremely upset with the delayed action in that case.

"Likewise, in this case, the First Lady took interest in having the Travel Office situation resolved quickly. . . . Once this made it onto the First Lady's agenda, Vince Foster became involved, and he and Harry Thomason regularly informed me of her attention to the travel office situation—as well as her insistence that the situation be resolved immediately by replacing the Travel Office staff. . . .

"We both knew there would be hell to pay if, after our failure in the Secret Service situation earlier, we failed to take swift and decisive action in conformity with the First Lady's wishes . . .

"I think all this makes clear that the Travel Office incident was driven by pressures for action originating outside my Office. If I thought I could have resisted those pressures, undertaken more considered action, and remained in the White House, I certainly would have done so. But after the Secret Service incident, it was made clear that I must forcefully and immediately follow the direction of the First Family. I was convinced that failure to take immediate action in this case would have been directly contrary to the wishes of the First Lady, something that would not have been tolerated in light of the Secret Service incident earlier in the year."

Watkins, his immediate anger spent, never sent the memo, but gave a copy to his assistant, Patsy Thomasson.*

---

* In written replies to questions posed as part of the General Accounting Office's investigation of the travel office incident, associate White House counsel Neil Eggleston stated on April 4, 1994, that

"1. Mrs. Clinton does not know the origin of the decision to remove the White House Travel Office employees. She believes that the decision to terminate the employees would have been made by Mr. Watkins with the approval of Mr. McLarty.

"2. Mrs. Clinton was aware that Mr. Watkins was undertaking a review of the situation in the Travel Office, but she had no role in the decision to terminate the employees.

"3. Mrs. Clinton did not direct that any action be taken by anyone with regard to the Travel Office, other than expressing an interest in receiving information about the review."

Later that afternoon, Foster came into Nussbaum's office. "You're not being reprimanded and neither am I," Foster said.

"What?" Nussbaum was incredulous. "What do you mean?"

"I just talked to McLarty. They decided you were too important a figure as counsel to the president. It would be too significant a step to reprimand you or me."

Nussbaum was indignant, but Foster just shrugged. He seemed beaten-down, demoralized.

That evening, Kennedy and Watkins attended a dinner at the White House. While waiting to be seated, conversation turned to the travel office matter, and one of the guests, a stranger to Watkins and Kennedy, commented, "How terrible it must be for those poor travel people." With some effort, neither said anything.

Harsh though they may have seemed to participants, the report and the reprimands didn't lay the travel affair to rest. The *New York Times* dubbed them a "stealthy, evasive confession" and wondered "why was notice sent to Hillary Rodham Clinton and not her husband the President?" Though the Democratic-controlled Congress rejected Republican calls for hearings, the Republicans vowed to resurrect the matter if they gained control of the House or Senate. But most of the press, at least, its attention span already stretched, turned to other topics. The next night, the president phoned Watkins at home. "It's been a tough time," Clinton said. "But I want you to know that I'm behind you."

For his part, Foster met with the first lady for about an hour, his first conversation with her since the affair blew up. The door was closed, and when he emerged, Foster said nothing to Nussbaum. Nonetheless, Nussbaum was convinced that Hillary must have tried to reassure him. Foster seemed so stricken that Nussbaum couldn't imagine she would say anything else.*

At the Whitewater closing in December 1992, Foster had promised to complete the corporate tax returns and return the

---

* *Hillary Clinton testified that she didn't recall any conversations with Foster after mid-June. Asked by independent counsel Robert Fiske whether Foster had ever expressed to her any concern about "anything related to problems connected with the travel office situation," Hillary Clinton testified, "Not that I recall, no." This seems hard to reconcile with Foster's own notes indicating at least two conversations with the first lady about the travel office matter.*

Asked if anything at all seemed to be troubling him, Hillary answered, "No. I mean,

Whitewater records to McDougal within ninety days. Given the maelstrom Foster had been in since arriving in Washington, it wasn't surprising that that deadline had come and gone. Late in June, McDougal finally received copies of the returns from Yoly Redden, along with a letter asking him to review them carefully for any inaccuracies. But how could he do that without the records?

McDougal was annoyed that the records hadn't been sent, and he was growing suspicious. He was still brooding about the public statements the Clintons had made, and he was convinced that the records would vindicate him and show that they had been lying about the amount of their contributions to the venture. On June 21, McDougal finally called Foster at the White House.

"Does he know you?" the secretary asked. "What company are you with?"

"Vince has some records he's supposed to return, and I need to speak to him," McDougal explained. The secretary said Foster wasn't available but she'd give him the message.

Foster evidently did get the message. The same day, he called Jim Blair in Arkansas. "I don't want Jim McDougal calling me at the White House," Foster told Blair. Blair told Foster not to worry. "I'll take care of it," he said.

Foster had been working on the Whitewater returns. Correspondence indicates he was again in contact with Redden, and a June 23 letter from Redden to Blair indicates that copies of the completed Whitewater returns for the years 1990 to 1992 had been forwarded on June 18 to McDougal for filing.

But the Whitewater documents McDougal wanted were another matter. Sometime that month, Hubbell had the files he'd taken out of the Rose firm transferred from his home in Little Rock to his home in Washington. No one, least of all Hubbell, seems to have questioned the removal of documents that belonged to the Rose firm without so much as leaving copies behind. The first lady had asked that one of those files, containing material about Bill Clinton's natural father and whether Bill Clinton had an illegitimate

---

he like everybody would say things about, you know, how tough this was, and how different it was, and how stressful it was. And I would, you know, express the same feelings. I think we were all amazed at some of what we found when we got here. But he never confided in me. He never told me—I didn't know . . . that he took the Wall Street Journal *editorial seriously. If I had known that, I would have, you know, said something funny or dismissive in some way. But he never said that to me."*

half-brother, be removed and returned to her. Foster was at Hubbell's home the evening he looked for those files, and Foster helped Hubbell move some boxes in the basement to get to them. The boxes contained many of the Whitewater papers, including correspondence with 1st Ozark about the loan renewals and the Clintons' personal financial statements and loan applications.*

Despite McDougal's call to Foster, none of these materials were returned to him, even though he thought that had been promised him at the closing that Foster attended. Foster's call to Blair indicates he didn't want to deal with McDougal, preferring that Blair "take care of it." If he was worried about the potential of any of these documents to generate further controversy for the Clintons, he didn't mention it to Hubbell, or anyone else. Yet it is clear that Foster had access to as full a set of records of the Whitewater affair as anyone. Given what the materials contained—the evidence of McDougal's subsidies, the active role of Hillary, the questionable valuations on personal financial statements—he must have realized that in the hands of someone as unpredictable as McDougal, there was the potential for further great embarrassment, at the least.

During these weeks, Foster was acting as though anything could backfire and erupt into scandal. He seemed to be fearful that his phone calls might be tapped or recorded, telling Hubbell on various occasions that "I would like to talk to you, but I don't want to talk to you over the phone," or, "I'm not sure I can talk to you over the phone about this, but we will talk next time we get together in person."

In any event, Foster never returned McDougal's phone call asking for the Whitewater records. Nor did he send McDougal any records, either from his office or from the files in Hubbell's house.

The last week in June, Foster was planning a trip to Little Rock, where he was scheduled to receive the Arkansas Bar Associa-

---

* Copies of these materials later surfaced in the possession of the Clintons' personal lawyer, David Kendall, who replaced Robert Barnett in August 1993. The only two possible sources for them appear to be Foster's White House office files and the files kept in Hubbell's house, which were eventually turned over to Kendall. Presumably these materials came from the latter, since none of these papers were identified as being among the contents of Foster's White House files dealing with Whitewater, all of which were purportedly produced to Congress.

tion's 1993 Outstanding Lawyer of the Year award. (Had he not gone to Washington, Foster was in line to become president of the association.) As his commencement speech had indicated, the respect of his peers was enormously important to Foster, and he'd been looking forward to attending the ceremony. Instead, he had to cancel the trip and fly to Boston to interview the front-running candidate for the Supreme Court, Stephen Breyer. After the Zoe Baird and Kimba Wood disasters, the vetting process was crucial. Indeed, Foster was troubled about Breyer. The judge not only had a "Zoe Baird problem," having not paid Social Security taxes for his household help, but Foster felt he wasn't candid about the circumstances involving payment of the back taxes. Indeed, Foster told colleagues that he'd bolted up in bed one night with the realization that Breyer hadn't paid his back taxes when he claimed he had, but only after New York governor Mario Cuomo had taken himself out of the running. (Another federal judge, Ruth Bader Ginsburg, would be nominated instead, and Foster's reservations about Breyer were a factor.)

Despite the importance of the trip, Foster was mortified that he might leave the impression with his fellow Arkansas lawyers that he was too high and mighty for their ceremony; he found the time to write at least four letters explaining his absence and apologizing profusely.

Even though he had canceled his trip, Nussbaum noticed that Foster seemed to be working almost reluctantly. Nussbaum, by contrast, was fired up by the task of choosing both a Supreme Court Justice and a new director of the FBI. Yet after the travel office affair Foster didn't seem to approach either with much enthusiasm, and he showed almost no interest in the FBI.

As Washington's oppressive July heat settled in, Foster's physical appearance deteriorated. His weight had gone up as he'd responded to the pressures of the office by eating more junk food and exercising less, but now it dropped. His appetite vanished. He mentioned both to his wife and Hubbell that he was having trouble sleeping. He got a prescription for sleeping pills, but then refused to take them, saying he was afraid he'd become addicted.

Lisa coped as best she could. She'd finally completed the move to Washington, just as the travel office controversy peaked, and Vince greeted her with the news that he thought he should resign.

"You can't quit," she told him. "I just got here." After the boxes
arrived from Little Rock, Lisa mentioned the gun, saying she didn't
want any gun in the house in Washington and wanted Foster to get
rid of it. Indeed, possession of guns is illegal in the District for
anyone but police and military personnel. But Foster told her she
shouldn't mention the presence of any guns in front of their children. She reminded him on at least two other occasions to get rid
of the gun.

Now that Lisa had actually arrived in what she thought was
going to be the glamorous world of the nation's capital, she found
life with Vince verging on miserable. "He didn't want to go out. He
didn't want to do anything fun," she later recounted. "He wanted
me to stay home and cook. He never came home until nine or ten
o'clock at night, then went straight to bed, and he got up and left
at quarter to eight in the morning. By the time we got there, it was
basically awful."

New to Washington, plunged into the middle of the travel
office affair about which she knew virtually nothing, there was little
Lisa could do. "All I knew to do was to tell him I didn't think it was
that big a deal and that everything would be okay, and not to worry
about it so much, and to take care of himself, and to try to get more
rest," she said. Lisa called Foster's White House office frequently,
asking his secretary, "How's he doing?" Gorham always said,
"Fine," trying to maintain a professional distance, even though she,
too, thought Foster was suffering from strain.

Lisa also prayed for Foster every Sunday at Holy Trinity
Church in Georgetown. Foster himself, however, had never con-
verted to Catholicism and only rarely attended church with her. He
seemed bereft of spiritual solace. One day he asked his secretary
how she was doing. "Some days are fine," Gorham answered. "How
are you doing?"

Foster replied that he felt like he was trying to build a building
that other people kept knocking down. "You rebuild it and they
keep trying to knock it down," he said.

"Do you ever feel like you're in spiritual deficit?" Gorham
asked.

"Yes," Foster replied. "I know what you mean."

Gorham suggested he attend lunchtime services at St. John's
Episcopal Church, just across Lafayette Park from the White

House. He seemed to consider the suggestion, but apparently never took her advice.

On July 11, Foster was again complaining to his wife about the travel office, which he was convinced would lead to congressional hearings. He called James Lyons, who'd handled Whitewater during the campaign, for advice on Travelgate, asking him to come to Washington. Lyons agreed to meet with Foster the following Wednesday, July 21. But Foster again told Lisa that he intended to resign. Lisa told him she was tired of hearing about it, and suggested he write down what was bothering him. He should take the offensive, she said, and defend himself.

Foster went upstairs. Taking a pen and a piece of yellow legal paper, he wrote:

"I made mistakes from ignorance, inexperience and overwork.

"I did not knowingly violate any law or standard of conduct.

"No one in the White House, to my knowledge, violated any law or standard of conduct, including any action in the travel office. There was no intent to benefit any individual or specific group.

"The FBI lied in their report to the AG.

"The press is covering up the illegal benefits they received from the travel staff.

"The GOP has lied and misrepresented its knowledge and role and covered up a prior investigation.

"The Ushers Office plotted to have excessive costs incurred, taking advantage of Kaki and HRC.*

"The public will never believe the innocence of the Clintons and their loyal staff.

"The WSJ editors lie without consequence.

"I was not meant for the job or the spotlight of public life in Washington. Here ruining people is considered sport."

After the exercise, Foster's mood seemed to brighten. He said to Lisa, "I haven't resigned yet. I've just written my opening argument."

The following Wednesday, Susan Thomases was in the White House, as had become her weekly custom, and dropped by to see

---

* The reference apparently refers to redecoration of the White House by the ushers office and Kaki Hockersmith, the Clintons' decorator from Little Rock.

Nussbaum. She was worried about Foster. As someone who saw him less, the change in his appearance and demeanor was more noticeable. "How is he?" Thomases asked about Foster. "Has he relaxed?"

Nussbaum was feeling good about progress on Ruth Ginsburg for the Supreme Court and Louis Freeh for the FBI. "We're feeling good," he said. "This is coming together."

Thomases wondered if the "we" really included Foster. "Help take the weight off his shoulders," she said. "You've been focusing on Ginsburg, and Vince is carrying the load."

"I'm going to get Vince the help he needs," Nussbaum said, acknowledging that they were all overworked. "Let's get through this first. It will be calmer."

Earlier, Foster had turned to Thomases to express frustration over the travel office report, and, like many in the White House, she had become something of a confidante. Now she tried to reassure Foster, but he said he needed to talk to her "off the campus," somewhere they wouldn't be seen. Thomases suggested 2020 "O" Street, a private rooming house where she herself sometimes stayed in Washington.

When Foster arrived that evening, Thomases thought he looked a little better. He looked around the house and seemed amused by its garish Victorian decor. He mentioned that he and Lisa were going to get away for the weekend. But then he began to unburden himself.

He mentioned how overworked he was and how he lacked the time and the support staff he was used to in Little Rock. If he didn't get more help, he said, he was afraid he'd "let the president and Hillary down." Predictably, he brought up the travel office affair, adding that he didn't trust David Watkins, who he feared might fabricate or embellish the facts to cover himself—possibly at the expense of the first lady. And he indicated he was homesick, not just for Little Rock, but for the quieter, predictable life he had there.

But then the conversation took a curious turn. One thing he had not missed about his life in Little Rock was Lisa, his wife. The marriage had not been what he'd hoped for, and it hadn't been for years. He had to make all the decisions in the family. She was completely dependent on him, and this had become a burden. He found he couldn't confide in her. Lisa's recent arrival in Washington had brought this to the fore, just when Foster himself needed someone to lean on.

Thomases didn't know what to say. Foster seemed calm, dignified—but infinitely sad.

The next night Foster complained to Lisa that his heart had been pounding, and on Friday he had his blood pressure checked at the White House. Two readings were taken, and both were normal. After Foster told her the results, Lisa suggested he call their family physician in Little Rock.

The same day, Foster called his sister Sheila Anthony, and told her he was depressed. His voice, she thought, sounded tight and strained. She herself had suffered from depression, and she offered to help. She gave him the names of three psychiatrists he might contact, and offered to call any of them on his behalf. Foster said she should wait; he wanted to think about talking to a psychiatrist over the weekend. He said he hadn't yet obtained his White House security clearance (one of many administrative procedures far behind schedule in the Clinton White House) and he was afraid that if he had to answer that he was under the care of a psychiatrist, it would be denied. Still, Foster did call one of the psychiatrists mentioned by his sister, once at 12:41 P.M. and again at 1:24, each time taking the precaution of charging the calls to his home phone. The psychiatrist wasn't in; apparently Foster reached the answering machine but left no message.

That afternoon, Foster and Lisa drove to the Eastern Shore of Maryland for dinner. Foster seemed in an even darker mood than earlier in the week, and was again talking about resigning. "Do you feel trapped?" Lisa asked him. Tears welled up in his eyes, and he began to cry. Though he wanted to quit immediately, Lisa urged him to finish the year, then stay in Washington until their son could graduate from high school.

It turned out the Hubbells were also on the Eastern Shore that weekend, staying with Michael and Harolyn Cardozo, friends of the Hubbells. They invited Vince and Lisa to join them for dinner Saturday and to return for the day on Sunday. Tennis pro Nick Bollettieri, a friend of the Cardozos, was also visiting, and Lisa was excited at the prospect of taking a tennis lesson with him. Lisa also got to play with Pam Shriver, the tennis star, but Foster didn't come to watch the match. That evening and the next day, Hubbell and

Foster had several extended conversations. They'd mutually agreed not to discuss work during the weekend, but Foster commented he needed to get away more often, and said he missed the summer month he used to take off from his practice at the Rose firm to spend with his family in Luddington, Michigan, a lakefront former Methodist camp resort popular with a close-knit group of Little Rock families. Otherwise the weekend was relaxing and uneventful. Despite his aversion to golf, Foster gamely hit some golf balls with Hubbell and Cardozo; he went boating; he ate fresh crab for the first time.

On Monday morning, the *Wall Street Journal* editorial page sent Foster into another tailspin. An editorial criticizing the imminent ouster of William Sessions as head of the FBI began, "So the gang that pulled the great travel office caper is now hell-bent on firing the head of the FBI." After criticizing the roles of Hubbell and Bill Kennedy, the editorial continued, "Mr. Hubbell and Mr. Kennedy are alumni of Little Rock's Rose Law Firm, as are Mrs. Clinton and Deputy White House Counsel Vincent Foster, both of whom were also involved in the travel-office affair." That was the sole mention of Foster, surely one that would have failed to register with the vast majority of readers. Yet it was the first time that the *Journal* mentioned Foster as being directly involved in the travel office matter, as well as the first lady. Given Foster's views of the *Journal*, it must have seemed a warning shot of more to come.

Outwardly Foster seemed calm, and made no comment about the *Journal* item. He mentioned to Hubbell, who dropped by, and his sister, on the phone, that he'd enjoyed the weekend and was hoping to take the next weekend off as well. Gorham, his secretary, noticed that he didn't seem very busy, which was surprising. The previous week he'd spent a lot of time writing thank-you notes and catching up on correspondence, much of which she typed. On Monday, he seemed to be spending an inordinate amount of time going through his drawers, looking through files, and spending time alone in his office with the door closed.

Though he made no further effort to contact any of the psychiatrists suggested by his sister, at some point during the morning Foster took Lisa's suggestion and called the Foster family physician in Little Rock, Larry Watkins. Foster told him he was battling depression, and Watkins called in a prescription to a Washington pharmacy for an antidepressant, which was delivered to the Fosters' home.

That afternoon, Marsh Scott dropped in to see Foster. Scott was part of the Arkansas contingent that had come to Washington, where she was in charge of the president's correspondence. She was one of the attractive young women once hired by McDougal for the Fulbright campaign. She'd been friendly with Foster for more than twenty-five years, but they became especially close once they arrived in Washington. Scott came by to see him almost every day, and she was a fixture in the Tuesday evening Arkansas dinners.

During the last week or so, Foster had seemed tired and depressed, mentioning to her that he wanted "out" and that he felt "eternally tired." But now he smiled and seemed happy to see her, which she attributed to his being away for the weekend. She spent about a half hour with him. The last thing he said to her was, "The staff cuts are killing us."

When President Clinton saw the latest *Journal* editorial that day, he knew Foster would be upset. He asked about Foster when talking to Hubbell, who mentioned their weekend together. "Vince has been down about the travel office," Hubbell said, "but we had a great weekend. He's doing better." Still, Clinton knew the counsel's office had been under high stress, and he realized he hadn't seen Foster for a while. That evening at 7:45 he called to invite Foster to a White House screening of *In the Line of Fire*, starring Clint Eastwood as a Secret Service agent who fails to protect the president. Fellow Arkansans Hubbell and Bruce Lindsey were going to be there, and he thought Foster would enjoy it. Clinton expected to reach Foster at his office, but he was already at home, and said he didn't think he should leave Lisa and return to the White House. Clinton mentioned the weekend, Foster said they'd had a good time, and then Clinton asked if they could meet on Wednesday, so the president could get his advice on some organizational issues. "Yes, I've got some time on Wednesday," Foster said. "I'll see you then."

Lisa was relieved that her husband was staying home for her home-cooked dinner of scallops. In any event, he'd seen enough stressful movies, having recently watched *A Few Good Men*, starring Tom Cruise and Jack Nicholson. In the movie, lieutenant colonel Matthew Markinson conspires to cover up the circumstances of the death of a young soldier. As an investigation progresses, the colonel is called to testify at upcoming hearings against his commander, an old friend. Torn by guilt over his role in the soldier's death and over the prospect of incriminating his commanding officer, Markinson puts a revolver into his mouth and pulls the trigger.

Nussbaum was feeling elated. Tuesday morning Foster and he had watched in the Rose Garden as federal district court judge Louis Freeh was nominated as the new director of the FBI. The choice was being hailed by Democrats and Republicans alike. Freeh had been a Republican appointee to the bench, backed by New York senator Alfonse D'Amato, he was a former FBI agent, and—significantly—he was not a personal friend of Bill Clinton. It had taken strenuous argument from Nussbaum to persuade Clinton not to name his old friend and fellow Rhodes Scholar Richard Stearns to the post, and then it had taken strenuous effort to get Freeh to accept the job and move to Washington. In one deft stroke, the controversy over Sessions and the so-called politicization of the FBI was being banished.

As soon as Nussbaum got back to his office, he switched on the television to watch the confirmation hearings for Ruth Ginsburg. As she deftly fielded softball questions from the Judiciary panel, he saw another success in the making. His dream of restoring the integrity of the Supreme Court nominating process was being realized.

As Nussbaum watched with mounting satisfaction, Foster walked in, looking as though he had something on his mind.

"What's up?" Nussbaum asked.

Foster said he'd heard the TV.

"How are you?" Nussbaum said, one eye still on the television. Foster mumbled something. "Look," Nussbaum continued. "Ruth Ginsburg is testifying. She's doing well. We've just hit two home runs for the president: Ruth Ginsburg and Louis Freeh."

Foster mumbled, but didn't say anything audible. In fact, he'd had nothing to do with the Freeh nomination. Nussbaum turned off the TV and headed out for lunch. "I'll see you later," he said to Foster.

"Okay," he replied.

Just after noon, Foster asked the executive assistant in the office, Linda Tripp, to get him lunch from the cafeteria, ordering a hamburger from that day's menu. Tripp added a handful of M&M's to the tray. Foster seemed in a hurry, asking Tripp what had taken so long when the food arrived. She noticed he took the onions off the sandwich, and ate while reading that day's paper. When he finished, he left the office, mentioning to Tripp that "There are lots of M&M's left in there. I'll be back." He had his suit jacket slung over his shoulder, but wasn't carrying his briefcase. It was about 1 P.M.

When Nussbaum returned from lunch, he was eager to relive the two successful nominations. Foster was the equivalent of his law partner, and he was the only person he felt he could really savor his good feelings with. "Where's Vince?" Nussbaum asked Gorham, who'd been out herself when Foster left. "He's not here," she said. Late in the afternoon, Nussbaum asked again. There'd been no word. Nussbaum paged him, but there was no answer. Nussbaum was disappointed, but figured Foster must have gone home. They'd had a good day, and he deserved some rest.

But at about 5 P.M., Lisa Foster called the office, asking for Vince. He's "unavailable," Gorham told her, though she told other callers that afternoon—Maggie Williams, Bill Kennedy, James Lyons—that he was "out of the office."

Lisa didn't give Vince's unavailability much thought. They were going out that night, a "date," as she thought of it, that she'd proposed the night before. Maybe he was on his way home.

Foster had taken one of the antidepressants the night before, and that morning he'd seemed stiff and uncomfortable. Lisa noticed that he didn't kiss her good-bye, and was tempted to say something, but didn't. She'd gone on to a tennis game with David Watkins's wife, a charity meeting, and then lunch with Donna McLarty at the Four Seasons Hotel—they discussed what a nasty town Washington was—and had gotten home around 3:30 P.M.

By 7 P.M. there was still no sign of Vince, so Lisa called his office again. He wasn't there, but she learned that the president was about to appear on *Larry King Live*. She figured her husband must have gone to watch the show with people from the White House. She and her daughter, Laura, went upstairs and turned on the TV.

The doorbell rang, and Laura went to answer it. Some Greenpeace volunteers were asking for a contribution.

The Clinton interview ended, and the doorbell rang again. Laura ran downstairs. Lisa heard the door open, and there were some muffled voices.

"Mother," Laura yelled. Then, screaming, "Mother!"

PART THREE

SHROUDING THE TRUTH

ELEVEN

BERNIE NUSSBAUM and his wife, Toby, were at dinner at Galileo's restaurant, celebrating the Freeh nomination, with the actress Estelle Parsons and her husband, New York lawyer Peter Zimroth, when his beeper went off at about 9 P.M. Usually he got beeped only if the president himself needed him. "Well, the White House is calling me again," he said to his guests, excusing himself to go to the phone. He was in such high spirits he didn't mind the interruption; indeed, he felt it made him seem even more important.

When he reached the White House, Mark Gearan came on the line.

"What's up?" Nussbaum asked.

"Bernie, Vince Foster just killed himself."

"What?"

"Come back here right away."

Nussbaum, his mind a blur, walked back to his table.

"I have to go back," he said. "Vince just killed himself." There was stunned silence, and Nussbaum repeated the message, almost as if to convince himself. "Vince killed himself."

The group hastily left and found a cab, dropping Nussbaum off at the White House. He'd forgotten his ID, but the guard recognized him and let him enter. When he got inside, staff members, some crying, were gathering in the corridor on the ground floor. Gearan told Nussbaum the president was upstairs, appearing on a live broadcast of Larry King, and would be told as soon as the interview ended. Nussbaum was still in the corridor when Clinton joined the group. He had heard the news. He said nothing to

Nussbaum, but the two briefly put their arms around each other. The president was on his way to the Foster home, and Nussbaum decided to stay behind, in deference to those who had known the family for many years. Instead, he thought he'd go up to his and Vince's offices, one floor above the Oval Office. He wanted to call people on his staff and tell them personally, and he wondered if Foster might have left a note in his office.

As he approached the offices, he noticed that Foster's door was ajar and the light on inside. He walked in. Patsy Thomasson, Watkins's deputy, was sitting at Foster's desk. Maggie Williams was sitting on the sofa, crying. She'd seen the light on in Foster's office and wandered in, half hoping she'd find him there at work. "What's going on?" Nussbaum asked.

"We just got here," Thomasson said. "I'm looking to see if Vince left a note." Both Watkins and McLarty had called Thomasson, asking her to look in Foster's office for a note. She opened a desk drawer and looked in.

Nussbaum came around the desk and looked, too. They quickly opened the top desk drawers, found nothing, then looked around the room. They glanced at Foster's leather briefcase, standing on the floor against one wall, but didn't look inside. They thought that if he'd left a suicide note, he wouldn't have hidden it. It would probably be in an envelope, somewhere in plain view. They didn't look in any of the file cabinets. After a few minutes they gave up. Nussbaum kept repeating his last conversation with Foster, how he'd exulted that they'd just hit two home runs for the president. Finally Williams got up from the sofa, and the three walked out. As they left, they turned out the light in Foster's office and closed his door.

Nussbaum busied himself with calls to his staff, breaking the news and trying to console them. He stayed for about another hour, continued after he got home, then, drained and exhausted, went to bed.

Dee Dee Myers, Mark Gearan, and some others also stayed behind at the White House, trying to absorb the shock, comfort each other, and anticipate public reaction. As they were about to leave, Myers finally said something she'd been feeling all evening. "I have this strong feeling," she said, "that weird things are going to start happening."

Nussbaum was awakened the next morning by a phone call from Lisa Foster.

"It's terrible," Nussbaum said.

"Yes, it's terrible." Lisa sounded like she hadn't slept, but was calm. "I want to ask you . . . did you fire Vince yesterday?"

"What?" Nussbaum was startled. He'd never have fired Vince, and in any event, he couldn't, not with Foster's close relationship to the Clintons.

"Did you dismiss him?"

"Lisa," Nussbaum answered, "I didn't fire Vince. I would never fire Vince. I love Vince. I thought he was great."

"I was just trying to figure out why he did it," she said. "I just wanted to know."

Nussbaum was struck that Foster's wife had no insight into what had happened, and seemed to be grasping at long-shot theories. "Stay strong," he counseled.

When he arrived at the White House, Nussbaum met briefly with his stunned staff. Afterward, he met with two of his colleagues, Steve Neuwirth and Cliff Sloan. They said they'd been discussing the matter, and thought that Foster's office ought to be sealed. "But this isn't a crime scene," Nussbaum said. Nussbaum's secretary had gone into Foster's office that morning to straighten up his desk, and Nussbaum had told her not to go back in. But he hadn't thought sealing it would be necessary. His staff lawyers agreed that there wasn't any evidence of a crime, but argued that it would still be best, given that an investigation was in progress. They thought people would want to do a thorough search, and sealing the office would minimize later questions. Both Neuwirth and Sloan were worried that Nussbaum wasn't sufficiently sensitive to appearances.

This was the first time the idea of sealing was mentioned to Nussbaum. Cheryl Braun had apparently told Watkins the night of Foster's death that the office should be sealed, but in the rush to notify the Foster family, Watkins didn't get the message to Nussbaum. Though concerned about how sealing the office might be interpreted, Nussbaum agreed, and called the Secret Service to guard the office, which didn't have a lock. From that time, sometime after 10 A.M., an agent was posted at the office door, and that evening a lock was installed.

At about 11 A.M., Nussbaum and Bill Kennedy went to David

Watkins's office for a briefing by the Park Police. George Stephanopoulos was there, along with Webb Hubbell and David Gergen.
Given the sensitivity of the investigation, the Park Police had assigned Peter Markland and Charles Hume to head the investigation, though Rolla and Braun, the officers on the scene, remained
involved. The two officers described the discovery of the body and
results of the initial medical examination. While it looked like a
suicide, they explained that any death had to be thoroughly investigated, and that they'd need the White House's cooperation. Nussbaum readily agreed, saying he'd arrange interviews with anyone
they wanted to speak to. The police said they wanted to search
Foster's office to look for a suicide or extortion note.

     Hubbell, however, questioned whether Nussbaum's office
should be handling the investigation. After the travel office affair,
he said, perhaps it should step aside and have someone independent
coordinate the investigation.

     "Really?" Nussbaum asked. He seemed surprised at the sug-
gestions. "Do you really think so? Well, I'll talk to you about that."
But in his own mind he brushed aside the suggestion; he was a
strong believer that government officials should do their duty, not
duck it at every whiff of an appearance of conflict of interest.

     At the meeting, it dawned on Nussbaum that Foster's death
was likely to trigger numerous investigations. The night before, all
he'd thought about was that it was a tragedy and a suicide. Until
that morning it had never crossed his mind that Foster's office
should be treated like a crime scene. Nussbaum thought he'd better
find someone to coordinate the searches of Foster's office. He
wasn't even certain that the Park Police were the people with jurisdiction. Mindful of the policies regarding contact with law enforcement officials stemming from the travel office affair, he said he
wanted to check with Janet Reno at the Justice Department and get
them to oversee the investigation.

     About an hour later, twelve o'clock or so, the president showed
up at Nussbaum's office, and he called in his staff. Clinton spoke
about what a wonderful person Foster had been, and how lucky
they'd been to work with him. Nussbaum had a sudden inspiration,
and went into Foster's office to get a photograph he knew Foster
kept there. It was a picture of Miss Mary's kindergarten class in
Hope. Clinton and Foster are standing next to each other (McLarty

was absent the day of the picture). Nussbaum brought the picture back to his office and showed it to the president, which triggered some emotional reminiscences of their boyhood in Hope. Tears came to the president's eyes.

Then, at about 1:30 P.M., the president, Nussbaum, and the counsel's office joined the rest of the White House staff in a large room in the Old Executive Office Building, one of the rare occasions when the entire White House staff convened. There were several reasons for the meeting, the most important being to acknowledge grief and pay their respects to a much-loved colleague. But there were several other, more pragmatic goals: to restore morale and get people working again, to stop speculation about what might have caused Foster's death, and most of all, to forestall any leaks to the press. In particular, there was high anxiety that any talk about Foster being depressed might be connected to the travel office affair. That could result in a public relations nightmare.

McLarty, after breaking down and weeping briefly outside the room, spoke first, in his usual soft-spoken, understated manner:

"Today is not only appropriate in terms of our coming together as a White House to express our sympathy, but also, frankly, for us to take an appropriate step in working through our feelings individually. Because it is essential that we continue to move forward in this period, in this very important period in the life of our country. We will all feel the loss and express the loss in our own personal way, as it should be.

"There always is conversation and discussion about the loss of anyone whose friendship and relationship we value, and there may be particular interest in this situation. I think all of us certainly understand the appropriateness of that situation, and that no one can say with any certainty what causes the loss of a life under these circumstances, and in most cases under any circumstances. And this matter needs to be handled, as I know all of you will handle it, with the utmost appropriateness and dignity and respect for a special individual and friend."

Nussbaum spoke briefly, more personally and directly about what Foster's loss meant to him. "We were going to create in the White House a little law firm—a little bit of his law firm, a little bit of my law firm, but we would be equal partners. And that's what we were on our way to doing. . . . We'd have trust in each other, we'd be supportive of each other and we'd work together, and we would laugh together, and we would play together, and we would always keep in mind our mission, which is to protect the interest of our client, our wonderful client, the president of the United States and the other people in the White House."

Finally President Clinton came to the microphone. Speaking of Foster, he reminded his staff that "When I started my career in Arkansas politics, he was there to help me. When I decided to run for attorney general, he was the first lawyer in Little Rock I talked to about supporting me. When the Rose Law Firm hired Hillary after I moved to Little Rock, Vince Foster and Webb Hubbell became her closest friends."

Then he reiterated points raised by McLarty, making them more forcefully. "I want you to think about the following: in the first place, one can never know why this happened. Even if you had a whole set of objective reasons, that wouldn't be why it happened, because you could get a different, bigger, more burdensome set of objective reasons that are on someone else even in this room. So what happened was a mystery about something inside of him."

Clinton concluded by emphasizing the need for discretion. "And the last thing I want to say is that Vince Foster spent a lifetime knowing when not to put himself first. And maybe he did that too much. But he had an extraordinary sense of propriety and loyalty, and I hope that when we remember him and this, we'll be a little more anxious to talk to each other and a little less anxious to talk outside of our family. We'll be a little more concerned about how we can help one another look good and achieve one another's goals, rather than how we might pursue our own objectives at the expense of someone else here. Those are the kinds of things that he would never have done."

Despite the president's admonitions, trying to stem talk and conjecture about a suicide in the White House was futile, human nature being what it is. The audience filed out quietly, but most work in the White House all but came to a halt.

Susan Thomases arrived just as the meeting was breaking up, and met with the president later that afternoon. He said he still could hardly believe it, that he was taken totally by surprise. Thomases said she had had an inkling, then told him in detail of her meeting with Foster the previous week. Clinton said that if he'd known, he would have dragged Foster over for the movie and would have tried to cheer him up.

Even though virtually everyone in the White House, from the president on down, had by now heard some accounts of Foster's depression, the official line remained that Foster's death was unfathomable. Foster himself had been such a private person that it seemed unseemly to mention anything so personal, and everyone in the White House was eager to spare the Foster family any embarrassment. McLarty briefed the press that afternoon, emphasizing that, "Try as we might, all of our reason, all of our rationality, all of our logic, can never answer the questions raised by such a death." Meanwhile, Lisa and other members of the Foster family retained James Hamilton, the Clinton campaign lawyer who'd handled some early Whitewater inquiries, as the family lawyer. Aside from the Arkansas contingent, people in the White House didn't know Lisa all that well, and there was concern she might be a "loose cannon." But Hamilton, too, did all he could to cut off inquiries, emphasizing that Foster had been a victim of a disease, depression, that had struck him at random. He rebuffed press efforts to speak to Lisa, emphasizing the family's interest in privacy. (No one appears to have raised any questions about the propriety of a Clinton campaign lawyer representing the Foster family.)

When Nussbaum returned to his office, the Park Police officers were waiting. "What are you doing here?" Nussbaum asked, as if he'd forgotten the entire earlier meeting. They reminded him that they wanted to search Foster's office, and that he'd promised to check with the attorney general. But Nussbaum was already hearing concerns about the search from McLarty and others in the White House. He didn't feel ready to let them go ahead, and later he suggested they return the next day at 10 A.M. Meanwhile, they could schedule interviews with people in the office, but he wanted lawyers present. The police officers were furious, both at their thoughtless treatment, and the way the investigation was being handled. It was becoming clear to them that the entire investigation would now be tightly controlled by the White House.

When Nussbaum had first talked to McLarty about letting the Park Police conduct their investigation, he'd said he was inclined to let them in to do their search. But McLarty had had reservations, and now concerns started pouring in to Nussbaum. Bill Burton,

McLarty's chief assistant, who was also a lawyer, argued that allowing a search would set a bad precedent. Jack Quinn, chief of staff to Vice President Al Gore, asked his opinion by McLarty, agreed.

Nussbaum pondered the options. He could give the investigators free rein, which meant the White House wouldn't be criticized for hiding anything. But that looked increasingly untenable. There might be privileged materials that he, as counsel to the president, had an obligation to keep in confidence. There were various privileges that might later be asserted, and he couldn't waive them. He knew there was sensitive information on potential Supreme Court nominees, other nominations, the health care task force. And there was concern about Foster's privacy. The man had committed suicide, so why dredge up anything that might be private or embarrassing to the family?

The second option was to do the search himself, as Burton and Quinn wanted. That would preserve confidentiality, but it would surely create suspicions. Nussbaum knew that law enforcement people would be strongly opposed to being shut out.

There was a possible compromise. Nussbaum would conduct the search himself, with law enforcement people present. He'd look at the materials first, then describe them. If the police were interested, they could ask to see it, and he'd decide whether they could. Nussbaum began advocating this approach to callers weighing in.

Later that afternoon, McLarty summoned Nussbaum into his office, where they met with Burton and Quinn. "Is that the right way to proceed," they asked, "to let people into a lawyer's office, a high executive branch official? Why are you doing what you're doing?" It was clear from the tone of their questions that they strongly disagreed with Nussbaum's compromise. The two aides emphasized that there might be confidential materials, even secrets involving national security, that should not be seen by anyone outside the White House. They urged Nussbaum to make the search himself, deciding what might be relevant and should be disclosed, and what should remain confidential. He should make a detailed inventory, decide what was privileged, and only then provide access to law enforcement officials. "We should tell the law enforcement people that they cannot go into Foster's office," Quinn argued strenuously.

"Jack, that would mean, that will take days, maybe weeks to do it. There's hundreds of pages of documents, thousands of pages of documents in that office potentially. That means people won't go in for weeks to his office, they won't have any clue for weeks. They're looking for a suicide note, or an extortion note, and that's their job, that's law enforcement.

"This is a high-visibility investigation, and for me to tell law enforcement that this is like some major antitrust case, go home, we will do a log, that's not realistic. They'll be frustrated. They'll be angry. They may be suspicious. . . . It's crazy for us to keep them out and create all these negative feelings and potential suspicion, when all we've got to do is just walk in and we'll look through the office."

Yet Quinn remained opposed to Nussbaum's approach.

Nussbaum never heard directly from the president or the first lady, but he assumed McLarty had discussed the issue with them and that they, too, were concerned about their privileges and any precedent that might be set. Hillary had been a practicing lawyer; she knew the importance of the attorney-client privilege, and had often asserted her rights to privacy. Confidentiality would not be a privilege she would discard lightly.

Mindful of the policy generated by the travel office fiasco of contacting only top Justice Department officials, Nussbaum had called Philip Heymann, deputy attorney general in charge of the criminal division, that morning for his views on how to proceed with a search of Foster's office. Nussbaum and Heymann had known each other for years, and both had been involved in the Watergate investigation, where Heymann had worked as a lawyer on the special prosecutor's staff. He'd been assistant attorney general in the Carter administration, heading the criminal division, when the Bert Lance affair broke open. Heymann had been named to the high-ranking Justice post in part because of Nussbaum's recommendation. He was on leave from his teaching post at Harvard Law School.

While Heymann recognized that the White House had legitimate concerns about executive privilege, his experience had convinced him that, politically, it was essential to preserve the credibility of law enforcement, especially when a high government official is involved. He pressed on Nussbaum the notion that the

White House counsel should not be the only one deciding what papers were relevant or privileged when it was a lawyer in that very office who was the subject of the investigation. He proposed that two Justice Department lawyers be there as Nussbaum conducted the search, looking at the documents with him and making an independent determination if they could be turned over to investigators. It was Heymann's understanding that Nussbaum agreed, and Heymann arranged to send two Justice Department lawyers, Roger Adams and David Margolis, to the White House. They waited all day there, but Nussbaum told them to come back the next day at 10 A.M.

There was a flurry of phone calls the next morning. Thomases spoke to Hillary in Little Rock from 7:57 to 8 A.M., then had Nussbaum paged a minute later, leaving a phone number at the Washington hotel where she was staying. When he reached her, she asked, "What are you doing and why are you doing it that way?" and when he explained his approach, she said, "It sounds fine to me." Still, when he later discussed his plan for the office search with Neuwirth, he indicated that both Thomases and the first lady were "concerned about anyone having unfettered access" to Foster's office.*

By then, Nussbaum had pretty much decided on option three, which was to conduct the search himself in the presence of Justice Department lawyers, FBI agents, and the Park Police officers. A meeting convened at 8 A.M., including Nussbaum, Sloan, Neuwirth, McLarty, Burton, Quinn, and Bruce Lindsey. Quinn remained strongly opposed to giving law enforcement any access. But Nussbaum said it was his decision as counsel to the president. If the president didn't agree, he should overrule him.

By 10 A.M. the Park Police were again in the West Wing, waiting for the search to begin. They'd been joined by Margolis and Adams, Secret Service and FBI agents. Also present was a law partner of James Hamilton. There were eleven people in all. Nussbaum described to them how the search would be conducted. To the consternation of Adams and Margolis, he announced that he would be the only person present allowed to look at the docu-

---

* In testimony, Nussbaum said he didn't recall making such a comment. Thomases denied the first lady expressed any concerns about Foster's files.

ments before making a determination. They protested, but he cut them off.

The Justice Department lawyers immediately called Heymann, who was angry and got on the phone to Nussbaum. "This is a bad mistake," he said. "This is not the right way to do it. And I don't think I'm going to let Margolis and Adams stay there if you're going to do it that way, because they would have no useful function, and I don't want this to happen." Nussbaum said he'd consult with some other people and call Heymann back.

Instead, without talking again to Heymann, Nussbaum assembled the participants and proceeded with the search on his terms. At about 1 P.M., he took them into Foster's office; the Justice Department lawyers sat on chairs and watched. Nussbaum began by removing files from the desk, then moved to the file cabinets in a credenza. He would pick up a file, describe it, then put it in one of three piles: materials that any of the agents and police officers would be allowed to examine; materials that were personal Foster papers to be turned over to Hamilton; and everything else, including materials that belonged to the "client," the Clintons, destined for their personal lawyers at Williams & Connolly. The last category of files he returned to their drawers.

"Ethics rules," Nussbaum announced, placing it in the first pile. "Tax returns for the president and first family," he continued, placing that in category three. They dumped the contents of his trash can on top of the desk, and looked through the refuse. A notebook containing Foster's handwriting seemed to be some kind of diary, or chronology of events beginning with Clinton's election; Nussbaum put that with the Hamilton materials.

Finally Nussbaum opened Foster's briefcase, standing where he and Thomasson had left it two nights before. There were several files inside, which Nussbaum removed. Among the materials was a bound notebook containing Foster's handwritten notes on the travel office affair, marked "personal and confidential." He nonetheless placed the notebook in the pile of materials destined for the Clintons' lawyer. Nussbaum didn't glance back into the briefcase to see if anything had slipped through, or if something might have been underneath the files.

When they were finished, after about two and a half hours, law enforcement personnel left. Nussbaum called Maggie Williams, the first lady's chief of staff, and asked her to remove the Clintons' personal papers. He said he was sure they'd want to send them on to their personal lawyers at Williams & Connolly, but in the meantime Williams suggested she could simply move them to the family quarters in the White House. She did so, having an intern carry them in a cardboard box and place them in a closet. Among the materials were files on "Whitewater Development"; the Clintons' income taxes, including materials on how to treat the sale of the Clintons' interest in Whitewater; the Clintons' blind trust; "HRC: Personal and Confidential"; "HRC: Financial"; and a file labeled "Clinton financial statements."

Nussbaum thought the exercise had gone smoothly. The only incident occurred when one of his staff lawyers, Cliff Sloan, accused an FBI agent of trying to "peek" at a confidential document. The agent was indignant, saying he'd only stood up to stretch his muscles. As far as Nussbaum could tell, law enforcement personnel would be allowed to see whatever they wanted, after lawyers had reviewed it for possible privileges. Nussbaum reported to Thomases that the search had gone "very well."

When he heard the search had gone ahead without him, Heymann was furious. When he returned to his apartment, he called Nussbaum, who was at home in his apartment in the Watergate. Heymann didn't know if it was clumsiness or paranoia, but excluding lawyers from the administration's own Justice Department looked suspicious. Heymann accused Nussbaum of misusing the Justice Department by creating the illusion they were involved in the process when in fact they were just bystanders.

"How could you have misused me this way?" Heymann demanded. "How could you have done this to me?"

"Well, we're sorry," Nussbaum said. "We just did it."

"Bernie, are you hiding something?" Heymann asked, pained at having to ask his old friend such a question. "Is there some horrible secret here that you're hiding?"

"No, there's nothing like that," Nussbaum replied.

That Friday, everyone was flying to Little Rock for Foster's funeral, where Nussbaum was going to be one of the pallbearers. Nussbaum was eager to clear out Foster's office and get on with things, and he asked Neuwirth to make an inventory of the remaining files for distribution to other lawyers in the office, and to collect remaining personal objects, such as pictures and decorations, for return to Lisa. At lunch that Friday in Little Rock, the first lady told Webb Hubbell that she was upset about a phone call alleging that Foster's death was part of a wider conspiracy. Hubbell told her to refer any inquiries like that to him, and he'd handle it.

Back in Washington the next Monday, about midafternoon, Nussbaum was paged and told to return to his office. When he arrived, he saw Neuwirth sitting at his conference table, fiddling with some scraps of yellow paper. "What are you doing?" Nussbaum asked.

"I just found these, and I'm putting them together," Neuwirth said.

Nussbaum hurried over to the table. Neuwirth had almost finished putting together the jigsaw of paper scraps, twenty-eight in all, which had been torn with ragged edges. Nussbaum recognized Foster's handwriting. "I made mistakes from ignorance, inexperience and overwork . . ." it began. As he read it, Nussbaum wasn't sure it was a suicide note. But it was something close to it, evidently reflecting what was recently on Foster's mind.

He asked Neuwirth where he'd found the pieces of paper, and Neuwirth said he'd picked up the briefcase to pack it in a cardboard box that was being sent to Hamilton. As he turned the briefcase upside down, he noticed some scraps of paper floating out of it. He looked at some of the pieces and noticed there was handwriting on them. He had scooped the remaining pieces from the bottom and brought them to Nussbaum's table.

Had Nussbaum found the scraps earlier, he would certainly have turned them over to law enforcement officers, and he knew immediately that they would have to be produced now. But he didn't feel he could just pick up the phone and call the Justice Department. He'd just seen Lisa at Foster's funeral, and he didn't want her to hear about the note on the news. He felt he should show her the note first, and show it to the president and first lady as well.

The president was in Chicago that day, but Hillary was in her office next door to the counsel wing. Nussbaum walked in, and said, "Come with me. I found something that you should take a look at." He led her into his office and pointed to the note. She sat down, glanced at the note, and seemed to struggle briefly with her emotions. Then she said, "I can't deal with this thing. Bernie, you deal with it." She turned and left the office.

Nussbaum also went to see McLarty, but he was in Chicago with Clinton, and instead he spoke to Burton. The president would be in the Oval Office the next morning, Burton said. Nussbaum told him about the note, and Burton came back to Nussbaum's office to look at it. "We have to turn it over," Nussbaum said.

"Well, let's research the issues," Burton said. "Is there any basis for withholding it? Privacy?"

"Fine, we'll do the research," Nussbaum said. Nussbaum called McLarty in Chicago and read him the note, and they agreed to meet the next morning to decide how to handle it.

Nussbaum knew what the result of the research would be. They'd have to turn it over, and there'd be a storm of publicity. Law enforcement would be embarrassed over questions about why they hadn't found the note when they searched the office. Nussbaum knew he'd be criticized. Perhaps worst of all, the note inconveniently contradicted the public relations spin everyone had been putting on Foster's death. Plainly Foster was upset, if not depressed, and the travel office affair was prominent among his concerns.

Before he left that night Nussbaum took the scraps and put them in an envelope in his desk. The president was busy the next morning. Nussbaum called Jim Hamilton and said he had something he thought Lisa should see. Hamilton said she would be in Washington by 3 P.M. That afternoon, Lisa came into the office. Nussbaum spread out the pieces; he thought she should see the actual note. She seemed calm and composed, and she identified the writing as her late husband's. After reading it she paused, and then said, "I don't think this is a suicide note. I think he did this a couple of weeks ago." She explained how she'd urged Foster to go on the offensive, and write down what was bothering him. She confirmed that she knew some of these things had been on his mind, and that he'd seemed depressed. She said she had no objection to the note being given to the Justice Department

Even though he still hadn't spoken to the president, Nussbaum next called Janet Reno, and asked the attorney general to come over to the White House with Heymann at about 7 P.M. "We want to talk to you about something," he explained, and it was obvious that it was something important. She agreed.

At about five, the president summoned Nussbaum, and he took a copy of Foster's note for the president to read. "Do you want to see the note?"

"No," Clinton said, "I know all about it," evidently from McLarty. "Do what you think is right."

"I've called the attorney general," Nussbaum said.

"Fine, do whatever," Clinton said, indicating he didn't want to discuss it.

"I'm going to turn it over," Nussbaum emphasized.

"Fine," Clinton said again. He seemed depressed, detached. Nussbaum started to describe how Neuwirth had found it, but the president seemed uninterested.

When Reno and Heymann arrived, they met in McLarty's office with McLarty, Nussbaum, and Neuwirth. Nussbaum explained what had happened, and offered her the scraps of paper. The attorney general seemed startled. "I don't think I'm the person you should hand it to," she said. "You should give it to the people doing the investigation."

Nussbaum said he'd called her because she was the head of the Justice Department, the appropriate point of contact under the new travel office–inspired guidelines. "Give it to the law enforcement people investigating the case," she said. "Give it to the Park Police." To Nussbaum's astonishment, Reno refused to take the note.

"If that's what you believe, which is logical, I'd be glad to do it," he said.

"Why did you wait twenty-four hours?" she asked.

Nussbaum said he wanted to show it to Lisa and the president.

Heymann immediately got on the phone to the Park Police, who sent an officer over for the note. Nussbaum had to concede that Reno's reaction was the right one—it shouldn't appear that the attorney general was interfering in the investigation; if she needed to see the note, it should reach her through regular channels. After the travel office affair it would hardly seem necessary to repeat the point, but the investigation of Foster's death should proceed strictly through established channels.

After the meeting, Heymann called communications director Gearan, saying that Reno wanted to know why the note hadn't been found during the previous week's search. Still smarting over the exclusion of the Justice Department lawyers, Heymann added that in his view the White House had exerted "much too much control from the beginning." Heymann continued that "all hell would break loose" if the White House rather than law enforcement announced the existence of the note.

Though the note was now out of the hands of the White House—thirty hours after its discovery—the White House strategists decided that any damage could be minimized by not publicly revealing its contents. The law enforcement officials, too, asked that they be allowed to investigate aspects of the note before disclosing its existence. So no mention of it was made. On July 27, in response to a *Newsweek* story reporting that the president had spoken to Foster on the phone the night before his death, Dee Dee Myers reiterated that, while the president may have known Foster was having a "rough time . . . there was absolutely no reason to think Vince was despondent; nobody believed that." Separately Mark Gearan told reporters that Foster "never said anything to indicate that anything was out of the ordinary to his colleagues."

Then, just a day later, CBS Radio broke the news that a note had been found, prompting an avalanche of new questions. When was the note found? Why hadn't it surfaced in the earlier search of Foster's office? Why the delay in notifying law enforcement of its existence? And, of course, What did the note say? The White House continued to fuel speculation by deflecting the questions, refusing to disclose the text of the note. The day after the CBS report, Gearan conceded only that the note went to Foster's "state of mind" and wasn't "inconsistent" with the conclusion that he committed suicide. Others denied that it was a suicide note, characterizing Foster's writings as "a written argument with himself." Nussbaum received numerous calls from reporters, but, with only a few exceptions, heeded instructions not to say anything, even though he thought much of the speculation could be curbed with a few explanations.

The refusal to disclose the contents of the note only fueled interest in the media, such as far-fetched speculation that Foster had been murdered by drug-dealing military officers. As Margaret Carlson wrote in *Time*, "The secrecy surrounding the note and the delay in turning it over to authorities—from Monday afternoon until Tuesday evening—set off a frenzy of speculation that would rival anything John Grisham could make up."

Given its series of editorials, and rumors of the contents of the note, the *Wall Street Journal* came in for a round of harsh criticism from Clinton loyalists, such as Sidney Blumenthal, writing in *The New Yorker* that the *Wall Street Journal* was what made Washington such a tough place. The paper's editorial page conceded that "we certainly did raise pointed questions in our commentary on the practices of the administration's Rose Law Firm partners," and defended itself. "There is no way to cover national government on the assumption that a high official and steeled litigator secretly suffers from depression, and may commit suicide if criticized." The *Journal* also noted that the thirty-hour delay, and the changes in stories about whether Foster was depressed, was leading to "the wildest speculation."

Skepticism of the White House was further encouraged by comments from Park Police investigators, who, still annoyed by their treatment by the White House, commented that they felt White House officials were hindering their investigation. Everyone they talked to had their own lawyer, as well as a lawyer from the White House counsel's office, turning the interviews into group scenes. The testimony seemed rehearsed. Hamilton, representing the Foster family, seemed particularly difficult. Rolla, the Park Police detective who'd examined the Fort Marcy Park site of Foster's death, went to Hamilton's office to examine the personal papers that had been removed from Foster's office, but Hamilton objected to Rolla's looking at the notebook Foster had kept, claiming it was "personal."

"We don't want to embarrass anybody," Rolla replied, "but it's potential evidence, and if there's something here we need we are going to take it." Hamilton reluctantly handed over the notebook. There were about a dozen pages with handwriting on them, undated. As Rolla later described his review of Foster's writing, "The time frame of the diary—the writings concerned a party at the governor's mansion, the time frame seemed to be post-election with Mr. Clinton, post-election and pre-inauguration. There was nothing seamy in the diary or—I don't know why he made a fuss about us looking at it. There was obviously some friendship, a close friendship between him and Mrs. Clinton. Again, there's nothing seamy. They talked about parties, going here, going there, talked about him mentioning that—speaking of Mrs. Clinton. Hillary wanting to get to Washington, she is not just going to sit back. She is—something about the health care reform, she is going to take command. These are not the exact words. These are my impressions, from my memory. But she was going to be involved in this presidency."

There was nonetheless no public disclosure that such a "diary" even existed.

Hundreds of tips had poured into Park Police headquarters, more than the force could investigate. Most of them seemed like far-fetched theories or crank calls. One of the more bizarre that the police nonetheless took seriously was an anonymous call from Little Rock claiming that Foster had been having an affair with the son of a local banker who was HIV-positive. Because of the location of Foster's body at Fort Marcy Park, and its reputation as a gay meeting place, the police had an HIV test performed on Foster's body. It was negative, and that "lead" was discarded.

The Park Police had trouble understanding the apparent evasiveness of so many of Foster's colleagues and family members, but much of it no doubt stemmed from embarrassment and a sense of propriety deeply rooted in the upper-middle-class culture of Little Rock. Foster's life was a testament to the importance of appearances, even to the point where appearance may have been more important than reality. Suicide, a mortal sin for the devoutly Catholic Lisa, was an all but unspeakable affliction for a family that had always portrayed itself as loving and untroubled. Even depression could be acknowledged only if it had no rational cause, as though it were a virus. Still, despite the reluctance of Foster's family and friends, a picture of Foster's depression did gradually emerge in the interviews. His sister Sheila Anthony, after initially denying Foster's depression, was more forthcoming, describing their last conversations and her offer to contact a psychiatrist. Lisa, too, was candid about her concerns, though she denied there had been any domestic problems in their entire twenty-five-year relationship. These impressions were buttressed by the contents of the note.

Finally, on August 10, two and a half weeks after its discovery, the text of the note was released publicly at a press conference to announce the results of the official investigation into Foster's death. Deputy Attorney General Heymann began by announcing that "I have directed that the full text of the note that was found be made public now. At the very strong urging of the family of Vince Foster, we are not making available photocopies of the note itself." Then he turned the meeting over to Robert Langston, chief of the Park Police.

"Good afternoon, ladies and gentlemen," he began. "The United States Park Police has completed its inquiry into the death of Vincent Foster and, as you are aware, that occurred on the twentieth of July at Fort Marcy National Park. . . . The condition of the scene, the medical examiner's findings, and the information gathered clearly indicate that Mr. Foster committed suicide. Without an eyewitness, the conclusion of suicide is deducted after a review of the injury, the presence of the weapon, the existence of some indicators of a reason, and the elimination of murder. Our investigation has found no evidence of foul play. The information gathered from associates, relatives, and friends provides us with enough evidence to conclude that Mr. Foster's—that Mr. Foster was anxious about his work and he was distressed to the degree that he took his own life."

TWELVE

A FEW WEEKS after Foster's death, Citizens United communications director David Bossie was in his office in suburban Fairfax, Virginia, when he got a phone call from one of his best sources, the "Judge." The Judge was Jim Johnson, who'd challenged Fulbright in the same 1968 election in which the young Clinton and McDougal had forged their friendship. Now a retired Arkansas Supreme Court justice, Johnson had been an important source for *Slick Willie: Why America Cannot Trust Bill Clinton*, by Floyd Brown, Bossie's boss at Citizens United. The book had come out just in time for the election, but lacked the "silver bullet," as Brown and Bossie put it, to derail the Clinton campaign. In the book's acknowledgments, Brown described Bossie as his "bloodhound," and also mentioned Johnson, who had introduced Bossie and Brown to Clinton detractors all over Arkansas.

Bossie and Johnson made a symbiotic pair. Bossie, twenty-seven, had become the chief investigator for Brown, thirty-two, a conservative political activist who founded Citizens United in 1988 as a reaction to opponents of Supreme Court nominee Robert Bork. With an annual budget of nearly $3 million, and contributions unfettered by election law limits, the organization had turned its sights almost exclusively on the president, especially after Gennifer Flowers went public with her accounts of an affair with Clinton. Brown attacked Clinton regularly on his daily syndicated radio show, *Talk Back to Washington*, and in his *ClintonWatch: Proving Character Does Count in a President* monthly newsletter. Bossie, of medium-build, usually animated, had been national youth coordinator for Bob Dole's ill-fated 1988 campaign, and had now turned his indefatigable energy against Clinton, routinely working sixteen-hour days.

Brown and Bossie had become a formidable two-man team. "The truth is a sword to be used in the battle for justice," Brown's grandfather, a logger and member of the anarchist-socialist Industrial Workers of the World, had taught him, and he'd instilled the maxim in Bossie. Brown's politics had moved to the opposite end of the political spectrum, but he'd inherited his grandfather's zeal. Six foot six, 240 pounds, a former basketball center, Brown had been national vice chairman of the conservative Young Americans for Freedom while a student at the University of Washington. He'd been Midwest director for the 1988 Dole campaign, which took him to Arkansas. But he was best known in political circles as the creator of the "Willie Horton" ad during the 1988 presidential campaign. The ad showed the mug shot of Horton, a black convict who had raped a woman while furloughed under a program approved by Massachusetts governor Michael Dukakis. The ad indelibly stamped Dukakis as a soft-on-crime liberal, even though it was eventually disowned by the Bush campaign. The controversy generated what Brown estimates as $2 million in free media exposure for the ad, leading Brown to boast at the time that "When we're through, people are going to think that Willie Horton is Michael Dukakis's nephew."

The Judge, as Bossie usually called him, was now living in Conway, Arkansas, about a half hour's drive from Little Rock. Johnson was a crusty country lawyer, a Democrat-turned-Republican, and an opponent of Clinton going back to 1966, when the nineteen-year-old Clinton supported Johnson's opponent in the Democratic gubernatorial primary. Johnson had been the youngest person elected to the Arkansas State Senate, and his politics had veered steadily to the right. In 1964 he was the only statewide elected Democratic official in the country to openly endorse Republican presidential nominee Barry Goldwater, and in 1968 he organized support for Alabama governor George Wallace's third-party presidential campaign. (Arkansas was one of four states carried by Wallace that year.)

Over the years, Johnson's scorn for Clinton had grown more virulent. His views were evident in a 1993 speech he gave at the

Conservative Political Action conference in Washington. Speaking in his strong Southern drawl, the Judge told the crowd that a friend had given him the following advice about what to say about Clinton: "He said I guess the first thing you ought to do on behalf of the decent people of Arkansas is apologize to the world for our having fostered [sic] upon them a president of the United States who is a queer-mongering, whore-hopping adulterer; a baby-killing, draft-dodging, dope-tolerating, lying, two-faced, treasonist activist."

Johnson's son, Mark, an aide to former Ways and Means Committee chairman Wilbur Mills, had gotten to know Brown after Brown hired Mark's wife to help run the Dole campaign in Arkansas, and Bossie had gotten to know Mark and his father while in Arkansas looking for material to use against Clinton during the campaign. He and the Judge had stayed in regular contact.

"I've got a friend in trouble," the Judge drawled. He explained that David Hale, who ran a small business lending operation in Little Rock, and was also a lawyer and municipal judge, had been "pressured" by Bill Clinton to make a loan to a business partner of Clinton's. Johnson was a friend of Hale's father, who'd been a farmer active in Democratic politics. Now Hale was under investigation, and prosecutors were ignoring information Hale had about Clinton, the Judge asserted. Hale was "scared," Johnson said, and had come to see Johnson for advice.

David Hale had indisputably fallen on hard times since granting the $300,000 loan to Susan McDougal in 1986—the loan that Susan had found so easy to come by when she needed the money to buy the International Paper land. Others, too, all supposedly "disadvantaged" borrowers, were defaulting or needing to borrow even more. Hale decided to solve his liquidity crisis with a $6 million offering of preferred stock (much the same route considered but then abandoned by Madison), and in October 1992 he had approached the Small Business Administration about increasing Capital Management's capital base, a move that would allow him to borrow $45 million more from the SBA.

To buttress the appearance of Capital Management's financial solidity, Hale met with Wayne Foren, the SBA administrator in Washington overseeing Capital Management, and told him that he had received $13.8 million in noncash assets as a "donation."

But Foren had trouble figuring out the actual value of most of Hale's assets, so he sent an SBA investigator from San Francisco to

Little Rock to go over Hale's operation. At this point, February 1993, Hale called Foren and said he'd changed his mind and would scrap the preferred stock offering, asking him to "turn back the clock" and just forget that he'd ever applied. But by now the issue of the value of Hale's assets was at the forefront of Foren's concerns, and he was growing skeptical. "David, why on earth would these people have donated their assets to you?" Foren asked.

"Because I have influence in Arkansas, influence with the president, and influence with the governor [Tucker]," Hale replied. Citing a company that had approached him before moving its operations to Arkansas, he added, "They're willing to pay a fee for my influence."

"David, you're scaring me to death," Foren replied. "You should be scared to death. You are a sitting judge. And either these assets are not worth anything or it looks like people are trying to bribe you."

But Hale brushed aside Foren's concerns. "Oh, Wayne, you just don't understand how we do business in Arkansas."

Foren was appalled. He found Hale's claims of influence plausible; he knew Governor Jim Guy Tucker, Clinton's successor in Arkansas, had borrowed large sums. No doubt Hale thought of these payments as some sort of consulting fee. After additional inquiries failed to provide satisfactory explanations, on May 5 Foren turned the Hale matter over to the SBA's inspector general. That same day, an SBA administrator mentioned Hale's claims to McLarty in the White House. Foren, meanwhile, told Hale of his decision, and Hale again begged him to ignore his request for additional capital and call off the investigation. The inspector general, in turn, referred the case to the FBI. On July 20, the day of Foster's death, the FBI obtained a search warrant and the next day raided Hale's offices, seizing his records.

Hale hired a lawyer, Randy Coleman, who got in touch with the new U.S. attorney in Little Rock, Paula Casey, a former legislative assistant to Arkansas senator Dale Bumpers. Even though Coleman hinted broadly that Hale had information implicating the "political elite" of Arkansas—and would be willing to enter into an undercover operation to gather additional evidence—Casey and her assistant on the case said they wouldn't consider reducing charges to anything less than a single felony.

In an effort to shore up his story and gain some leverage with the U.S. attorney, Hale drove down to Arkadelphia to meet with McDougal at his mobile home. Secretly tape-recording the conversation, Hale tried to get McDougal to corroborate his story. But McDougal begged off, saying he remembered almost nothing from those months of 1986, not long before he blacked out and had to be taken to the hospital. McDougal promptly called his lawyer, Sam Heuer, telling him that Hale was quizzing him, and Heuer dutifully reported this to Jim Blair.

In frustration over his own efforts to find corroboration and the failure to strike a plea bargain with the U.S. attorney, Hale had turned to Johnson for advice, and was now visiting the retired judge on an almost daily basis. When Johnson called Bossie, he said he'd urged Hale to tell him his story. "I'll call him this afternoon," Bossie said, even though he was already busy on two other Clinton projects: research into Clinton-appointed Surgeon General Joycelyn Elders and Webster Hubbell. But Johnson must have already called Hale, for even before Bossie could place the call, the phone rang again and it was Hale on the line.

Hale explained that he ran a lending operation called Capital Management Services, which loaned money to disadvantaged entrepreneurs and in return received matching funds from the Small Business Administration. He was now under investigation, and facing a likely indictment, for fraudulently misrepresenting the kinds of loans he was making to the SBA in order to get the matching funds. Instead of legitimate small businesses, many of the loans had actually gone to what Hale, quoting McDougal, described as his Democratic "political family" in Arkansas—Jim Guy Tucker, now Clinton's successor as governor, and the McDougals. The McDougals were business partners with Clinton, he alleged, and the U.S. attorney handling his case, a Clinton appointee, was ignoring his allegations that Clinton had pressured him to make loans to Clinton's friends. He was being "set up as the fall guy," Hale claimed.

Bossie knew Tucker, of course, but he had only a dim memory of the McDougals, probably from Gerth's story the previous March. He searched for descriptions of Whitewater in Brown's book, *Slick Willie*, and found only a brief reference. What did he mean by "pressure"? Bossie wondered.

Hale said that in October 1985—he couldn't remember the precise date—Jim Guy Tucker, then in private practice, and Jim

McDougal had come to him seeking a loan, mentioning real estate deals that Governor Clinton was also involved in, they claimed. Two months later, Hale bumped into Clinton coming out of the State Capitol, and Clinton, in passing, said he hoped Hale would make the loan to McDougal to "help Jim and me out." Hale obliged, issuing loans of $260,000 to a real estate partnership that included Tucker, $100,000 for McDougal's Campobello venture, and $50,000 to Steve Smith. "I didn't ask any questions," Hale said.

Then, in February 1986, Hale said he met with McDougal and Clinton one evening at the Castle Grande development outside Little Rock. McDougal had moved his headquarters—a double-wide mobile home furnished with three desks—there after the FHLBB auditors moved into Madison Guaranty. This time McDougal and Clinton wanted a loan of $150,000, and Clinton offered to put up land in the Ozarks as collateral, Hale said. Hale pointed out that SBA regulations didn't permit raw land as collateral, so they decided instead to make the loan to another Susan McDougal concern, Master Marketing (as distinguished from Madison Marketing), which had the added benefit of keeping Clinton's and McDougal's names off the loan. Later, the amount of the loan was increased to $300,000.

In return, Hale claimed, McDougal arranged for Madison Guaranty to finance the purchase of a Hale property for $825,000, vastly more than the property was actually worth. With those "profits" in hand, Hale was able to extract an additional $1 million in additional funding from the SBA.

Bossie stayed on the phone with Hale for over two hours, taking notes, asking questions that might later help him corroborate the story. He was almost immediately intrigued. This was a story he could sink his teeth into, something that went directly to the ethical and financial probity of the president. The Gennifer Flowers story had proven to be a big disappointment. While it had generated a fair amount of media heat, it had proven negligible in the campaign. Looking back, Bossie felt that Clinton had cleverly deflected the whole issue by denying the Flowers affair and attacking her credibility and reputation, though he had all but conceded marital infidelity. He had successfully invoked a right to privacy and showed that he had Hillary's support. Clinton had remained outspoken on ethics and finance, tagging Republicans with the "greed" decade. This story, Bossie thought, would be perfect for *ClintonWatch.*

As soon as he hung up the phone, Bossie hurried into Brown's office to brief him on Hale's allegations. But Bossie was disappointed by what seemed Brown's lack of enthusiasm. Preoccupied with his syndicated radio show, Brown didn't seem all that interested. Bossie agreed he'd finish up some other projects he was doing for Brown first, but vowed he'd investigate Hale's allegations at the first opportunity.

Besides arranging the call with Bossie, Johnson urged Hale to get in touch with Little Rock lawyer Cliff Jackson. As a Fulbright Scholar, Jackson had been at Oxford at the same time as Clinton, the two had played together on a basketball team, and both harbored political ambitions. Though Jackson was a Republican and supporter of Richard Nixon, he and Clinton both worried about the draft, and when Clinton actually got his notice, he conferred with Jackson, who was about to return to Arkansas. Jackson helped Clinton get admitted to the ROTC program at the University of Arkansas, where Clinton enrolled in law school. But Clinton had returned to Oxford, and had later written a long, impassioned letter to the ROTC commander withdrawing from the unit and asking to be reclassified 1A. He was then subject to the lottery but drew a high number.

This was the story first mentioned by Roy Drew, the Little Rock stockbroker who'd fallen out with Clinton, to both Jeff Gerth and Jeff Birnbaum, and Birnbaum had gone on to break the story in the *Wall Street Journal.* Judge Johnson had been instrumental in gaining a copy of the letter Clinton wrote to the ROTC commander, Colonel Eugene Holmes, and in getting Holmes to come forward publicly with his account. Though Cliff Jackson was actively opposing Clinton in the election, raising money for ads castigating Clinton's record as governor, he'd largely forgotten his interaction with Clinton over the draft, other than a vague feeling that he'd been used when he learned that Clinton had backed out of the Arkansas ROTC unit and applied to Yale Law School instead. He pretty much accepted Clinton's public response, which was that a crisis of conscience born of principled opposition to the war had motivated his change of heart.

Jackson didn't respond to a few press calls seeking more information about Clinton and the draft. But one evening, looking for some papers at his house, he found a trunk of old letters from his college years. In one was a copy of a letter he'd written to a girl-friend, describing in detail the steps he'd taken to help Clinton avoid the draft after he received his draft notice—a letter that revealed Clinton had already been drafted before his crisis of con-science. Jackson agonized through a sleepless night, but then de-cided to release copies of the letter to the press. To Jackson, it was a concrete example of a Clinton pattern: "exploitation followed by deception," as he put it.

Since then, Jackson had become something of a lightning rod for anyone with allegations involving Clinton, such as Judge John-son or David Hale. Many of them were baseless, and most of them Jackson ignored. Though he had strong convictions that Clinton shouldn't be president, he didn't want to devote his life to investi-gating him. Jackson wasn't involved with any of the other anti-Clinton forces, like Jerry Falwell, whom he actively disliked. But then, in mid-1993, he got a call from an old and trusted friend, Lynn Davis. Davis said he was calling on behalf of a group of state troopers, including Roger Perry, Larry Patterson, Danny Ferguson, and Ronnie Anderson. Anderson, who had been a state trooper for thirteen years and had joined the governor's detail in 1990, had quickly come to share the others' concerns. The troopers wanted to talk to Jackson about their experiences while working on then-governor Clinton's security detail. The information they had, Davis said, was explosive.

About a month into the Clinton presidency, Perry had called Patterson. The flap over gays in the military was at its height and the administration had already acted to ease restrictions on abor-tions. "Can you believe this?" Perry said in dismay. It wasn't that Perry himself felt so strongly about either issue, but at a time when he thought matters like Bosnia and the economy merited the president's attention, he saw these as Hillary's agenda. Even Perry's mother, a strong Clinton supporter, had expressed bewilderment at Clinton's liberal policies. Perry had explained that Clinton was too weak to stand up to Hillary. "He's smart, book-wise," Perry had told her, "but he's not a good, moral, decent man."

To varying degrees, Patterson, Ferguson, and Anderson shared these views, though each had their own reasons for being upset.

Patterson, for example, was especially troubled by the way he thought he and other supporters had been used by the Clintons. He'd never gotten over being accused of disloyalty. The four had talked throughout the campaign about taking some of their information to the press, but always held off, given that Clinton was still technically their boss. They felt they owed him a duty of loyalty while he was governor, and they feared for their jobs. Still, it had annoyed them that they were constantly pressured to keep quiet. The head of the governor's security detail, their boss, Buddy Young, had called Patterson four times during the campaign, especially after the Gennifer Flowers story surfaced. "If you know what's good for you, you'll keep your mouth shut," Young had said. The troopers thought it was obvious that Young was angling for a better job in the Clinton administration, and after the election, he got one: he was named regional head of FEMA, the Federal Emergency Management Agency, in Denton, Texas, a job paying $92,300 a year.

From time to time, Perry and the other troopers mentioned their concerns to Lynn Davis, former director of state police and a federal marshal, who was something of a legend to Arkansas state troopers. A former FBI agent and a lawyer, Davis was credited with cleaning up gambling in Hot Springs. In 1968, Arkansas governor Winthrop Rockefeller persuaded Davis to run on the Republican ticket for secretary of state, and a young Cliff Jackson was his campaign coordinator. They'd remained friends ever since. During the spring, the four troopers visited Davis, and said they'd searched their consciences and reached a decision. "We have a responsibility" to speak out, Patterson said.

Still, the troopers were nervous. They were sure there would be retaliation. They might lose their jobs. There might be lawsuits and legal expenses. They wondered if there might be money or a book deal. They wanted to get their story out, but they didn't know where to turn. None had had any dealings with the national media. So Davis called Jackson. He not only knew and trusted Jackson, but Jackson had gone out on a limb over the draft issue. He'd stood up to the Clinton campaign. He knew how to deal with the media.

Their first meeting was at Shorty Small's restaurant, the next at a McDonald's. Davis was so nervous that he didn't want to talk on the phone, or meet at Jackson's office, out of fear that Jackson's phone was tapped. Davis was convinced he was being followed. He was worried about retaliation, and wasn't sure the troopers would go through with any disclosure. But he thought Jackson should hear their stories. Jackson agreed, saying he'd sit down and talk to them and see if he agreed with Davis's conclusions that they were telling the truth.

They all got together the first week in August. All four troopers participated, their recollections pouring out seemingly at random. Jackson found them credible, and internally consistent. And he knew the information was potent. None of the troopers were yet willing to speak on the record, but they agreed to test the waters by speaking on background to a reporter recommended by Jackson. Before making any contacts, Jackson had the troopers sign an agreement. Describing the troopers generically as "bodyguards," it provided that the troopers:

"—will adhere to the course now embarked upon until the objective of full disclosure is attained;

"—will not accept any 'hush money,' jobs, or other inducements from President Clinton, his supporters or any one else, to cease and desist in their present effort to bring their unique information and perspective to the attention of the American people;

"—will not be intimidated from the present course of action by threat or coercion of any kind;

"—will promptly report to Jackson and to each other any approach or contact, direct or indirect, seeking to deter them from full disclosure;

"—will make every effort to record, photograph or otherwise secure hard evidence of any such approach or contact."

The agreement further provided that:

"Jackson will negotiate and arrange subject to the approval of bodyguards the initial timing, manner and terms in which their story is brought to the attention of the American people provided

—Jackson is expressly instructed not to contact or engage in any negotiations whatsoever with any tabloid

—Jackson is expressly instructed not to inform, contact or in any manner deal with the Republican party or the Perot organization or anyone connected with these two groups."

Jackson further agreed that he would act as the troopers' lawyer "to secure compensation for bodyguards for all . . . damages suffered by them" and to use his "best efforts to secure alternate, acceptable employment opportunities outside the state of Arkansas."

There were four signature lines on the document, but only

Perry and Patterson signed it. Jackson deemed the agreement to be so important that he kept it under his pillow and took it with him when he went on a hiking vacation in Colorado.

Jackson and Davis agreed that, if at all possible, they wanted the story to appear in the mainstream media, to maximize the troopers' credibility and the impact of the disclosures. On August 9, Jackson called Bill Rempel at the *Los Angeles Times*, the reporter who'd written the story of Jackson's allegations about Clinton and the draft. Rempel had spent months in Arkansas during the campaign, and Jackson had grown to like and trust him. He knew Rempel had been trying to talk to troopers during the campaign, going so far as to file a Freedom of Information Act request for their personnel records. So he was almost sure that Rempel would be interested. Rempel was intrigued, and agreed to meet Jackson and the troopers on August 14. Only two top editors at the *Times* were told the real purpose of his trip.

As insurance, Jackson also wanted someone from the conservative press working on the story. Jackson had waited for months before the *L.A. Times* had finally run the story of his draft allegations, and he knew there was a possibility that the country's major newspapers would be too squeamish to publish the troopers' allegations about a sitting president. But Jackson was at a loss; despite his visibility as a Clinton opponent, he had no contacts in the right-wing press.

A wealthy, conservative benefactor who had encouraged Jackson after the draft stories was strongly supportive, going so far as to offer financial assistance should the troopers get into trouble. And he urged Jackson to contact David Brock at the *American Spectator* magazine. Brock, too, agreed to come to Little Rock to meet the troopers, though Jackson informed him he'd also contacted the *L.A. Times* and that Rempel would have the first interview and the first opportunity to publish a story. Neither publication, Jackson emphasized to both reporters, would be able to publish anything without the troopers' and Jackson's consent.

The meetings went as scheduled, with Rempel meeting Jackson and the troopers at the Lake Hamilton resort outside Hot Springs and Brock at a Holiday Inn at the Little Rock airport. Each reporter spent hours debriefing the four troopers. Within days, Perry got a call from his former boss, Buddy Young, now in Texas as Clinton's regional FEMA director. Young later said he'd gotten a call from Clinton, asking about rumors the troopers were going to go public with their stories and write a book, and suggesting he call the troopers.

"I hear you're thinking of coming forward," Young began.

"We're thinking about it," Perry acknowledged.

"I represent the president of the United States," Young said. "If you and whoever do that, your reputations will be destroyed, and you will be destroyed."

Perry didn't have any bone to pick with Young, but the comment angered him. "Buddy, if you called to threaten me, what you've done is piss me off."

Young then adopted a different tone, saying he knew Perry had met with an *L.A. Times* reporter in Hot Springs. "Why would anyone want to do that when it would ruin a man's life, writing about shit that's insignificant?" he asked. Perry assured him that no decision had yet been made to go forward.

Young spoke also to Anderson and Ferguson. The two troopers moonlighted for National Safety Consultants, a Little Rock company owned by Young that teaches safety habits to long-haul truckers. From their conversation, it was clear to Young that Ferguson was already wavering about speaking out, telling Young that he "wanted out" of the group. Later, Young called Ferguson's wife, Sheila, and asked her if she'd like a job in the White House.

Anderson told Perry that he, too, wanted out because Young told him he'd lose his job "if he participated in any kind of publicity." Young briefed Clinton on his calls, saying he'd talked to "those boys" and that Perry was "apparently writing, giving information out or something."*

---

* *In a later interview with the* Los Angeles Times *reporters, which they tape-recorded, Young acknowledged making these calls to the troopers at the request of Clinton. "He heard several rumors about this and about that," Young said, according to the transcript of the interview. "Like they were going to get $100,000 for a book. So I primarily called Roger Perry to find out what was going on." But Young disputed the troopers' recollections of the conversations, denying that he was trying to threaten them or that he said he "represented" the president. Of Perry, he said, "I told him to think about it. And I never told him not to do anything. I merely inquired as to what he was doing." He said of his subsequent conversation with Clinton, "I told him that I'd talked to those boys about it and that Roger was apparently writing, giving information out or something, but I didn't know what."*

About a month later, in early October, Ferguson and Perry got together for a golf game. On the course, Ferguson told Perry he'd gotten three phone calls from the president. Clinton had been concerned about rumors about the troopers' plans, and asked Ferguson to keep him informed. At the same time, Clinton asked if Ferguson might be interested in a federal job, either as a U.S. marshal or FEMA regional director like Buddy Young. Perry, too, could have a federal job, the president had said. Ferguson said that he told the president that he wasn't interested in either job—he and his family wanted to stay in Little Rock—and assured him that he wouldn't be involved in anything that might hurt the president. Ferguson told Perry that he then suggested the president call Perry directly. "I can't do that," Clinton had replied.

A later recounting by Ferguson of these conversations with Clinton was recorded. Ferguson narrated the encounter as follows:

The president "asked me, he said, 'Dan, would you like to have a job? Would you like to come to D.C.?'

"I said, 'No sir, I don't have enough time to.'

"He said, 'Well, there is going to be a regional job open up, just like Buddy's.'

"He didn't specify a city. He said, 'Or there is a U.S. marshal's job open.'

"I said, 'I'm not interested in any of that because I don't have enough time in the state police. And the kids are here. I don't want to move or anything like that.' "

Perry never heard directly from Clinton. Ferguson didn't say that Perry's silence would be a condition for getting a federal job. Still, the implication seemed obvious. Perry would have to think it over. He had dreamed of someday being a U.S. marshal.

In the midst of working with the troopers, Jackson spoke to Hale, and invited him to visit him at his boathouse. Hale outlined his predicament, and Jackson was concerned that Hale had already gone to Brown and Bossie. As he'd advised the troopers, Jackson agreed that Hale should get his story out, but by speaking to the mainstream press, not political operatives whose allegiances could undermine Hale's credibility. Jackson agreed to make some calls to reporters on Hale's behalf, but he was wary about dealing with someone who seemed about to be indicted for fraud. He didn't take on Hale's cause as he had the troopers'. Still, Hale heeded Jackson's advice, and he and his lawyer, Coleman, decided to make contact with reporters at major papers like the *Washington Post* and the *L.A. Times.*

In a further attempt to gain leverage, Coleman had called Bill Kennedy in the White House counsel's office, whom he knew from Little Rock, in mid-August. "We have an investigation down here that is of interest to our mutual clients," Coleman said, going on to describe Hale's predicament and the Clintons' alleged involvement. "If Heidi Fleiss is the madam to the stars, David Hale is the back-door lender to the political elite of Arkansas," Coleman said, referring to the Hollywood madam then much in the news. Kennedy didn't really respond, but a few days later he called back and wanted to know whether Hale would be alleging any "face-to-face" meetings with Clinton. Coleman said he would be. "They are not stopping at us, I can guarantee you that," Coleman said of the FBI. He urged Kennedy to meet with him in Washington. Kennedy reported the conversations to Nussbaum, but they decided to ignore Coleman and Hale, and didn't mention the calls to anyone else in the White House. A week later Kennedy did ask Webb Hubbell about Hale, but the last thing they wanted was the perception that the White House might be interfering in a federal investigation.

Exasperated by the pace of negotiations with the U.S. attorney's office, Coleman wrote Paula Casey a letter on September 15, complaining that "I cannot help but sense the reluctance in the U.S. Attorney's office to enter into plea negotiations in this case. I cannot help but believe that this reluctance is borne [sic] out of the potential political sensitivity and fallout regarding the information which Mr. Hale could provide to your office, but at the same time it is information which would be of substantial assistance in investigating the banking and borrowing practices of some individuals in the elite political circles of the State of Arkansas, past and present. I can certainly understand the reluctance of anyone locally to engage in these matters, political realities being what they are.

"Would it not be appropriate at this point for your office to consider terminating participation in this investigation and to bring in an independent prosecutorial staff . . . ?"

The next day, Casey responded in writing, saying, "My recollection of our meeting of September 7 is that I told you that I would not consider granting immunity to your client nor would I consider filing only misdemeanor charges. You made it clear to me that one felony would be as disastrous to your client as multiple felonies. Therefore, our plea negotiations are at an impasse." She added that if Hale pleaded guilty to felony charges, she would bring any cooperation by Hale to the court's attention as part of sentencing—a routine prosecutorial gesture, and one that gave Hale little incentive to cooperate.

In any event, Coleman's efforts were to no avail. On September 23, Hale was indicted on conspiracy and three counts of making false statements to the SBA. Only the *Arkansas Democrat-Gazette* made note of the event, mentioning for the first time in print that Hale's defense might involve allegations involving other prominent officials—Jim Guy Tucker and Bill Clinton among them.

Foster's death had galvanized the Washington bureau of the *New York Times*, which was in hot competition with the *Washington Post* over the Foster story, but it had had little impact on Gerth. This was a major political story, with an army of political reporters from every imaginable media outlet battling for the same crumbs of new information. Gerth hated pack journalism. He liked to be out in front of a story, break new ground, then get out of the way and on to the next project. Still, it brought Gerth's attention back to Arkansas. He received an anonymous phone call alleging that Foster's death was related to Whitewater. Then he got an anonymous letter about Clinton's finances. Neither seemed credible, and Gerth went on vacation. Then, in mid-September, Gerth got a call from Coleman, who remembered Gerth's original Whitewater story. "I've got a client," the Arkansas lawyer began, "with a story that links Clinton and McDougal."

Since the election, Gerth had had little reason to be in touch with McDougal, but he was still interested, since he'd never reached the bottom of the Whitewater story. Coleman summarized what Hale had to say, mentioning the meetings with Clinton at the Capitol and at Castle Grande. Would Hale make his allegations on the record? Gerth wondered, and Coleman was noncommittal. Still, Gerth was intrigued, and said he'd like to come down to Little Rock to hear Hale's story.

Gerth met Hale and Coleman at Coleman's office in the

TCBY tower in downtown Little Rock. Hale did most of the talking in what stretched into a five-hour interview. Gerth was impressed by Hale. He knew he wasn't a "saint" or "choirboy," as Hale himself put it. Hale readily conceded that Capital Management's lending bore little relation to SBA requirements, and Gerth knew Hale was likely to be indicted and was trying to gain leverage with the U.S. attorney by implicating others. Indeed, Coleman showed him copies of the correspondence with Paula Casey. Still, Hale's story was exceedingly detailed, it was internally consistent, and it drew on facts that would have been hard for Hale to know unless something like what he described had occurred.

But given the nature of the allegations and the fact that Clinton was now the president, Gerth called his editors in Washington and asked that another *Times* reporter, Stephen Engelberg, join him to assess Hale's credibility independently and to help him corroborate the story. At first Hale resisted the idea of speaking on the record, but Gerth said that would surely kill the story. "You can't make an accusation against the president and have it be anonymous," Gerth warned. "We won't publish it, and I wouldn't put my name on it." Reluctantly, Hale agreed, and he had two more three-hour interviews, one with Gerth, the other with Engelberg.

While he was in Little Rock, Gerth also drove down to see McDougal, apparently the only eyewitness to the alleged meeting with Clinton other than Clinton himself. Gerth hadn't been in touch since McDougal had vanished the previous year, but he'd succeeded in reaching him in Arkadelphia. This time they met at the truck stop across the highway from the Western Sizzlin'. McDougal told Gerth the same thing he'd told Hale—his memory was a blank for that period. But he did comment on Foster's recent death, mentioning that Foster had shown up for the Whitewater closing in December 1992—the first time McDougal had linked Foster's name to the land deal. He mentioned that he'd been trying to get the Whitewater tax returns from Foster, that Foster was the "point person," and that he'd been pressing to get all the Whitewater records from Foster just before he died. McDougal wouldn't go so far as to say he thought Whitewater had caused Foster's death, but he was convinced it was a factor.

At about the same time, McDougal also met with a *Washington Post* reporter pursuing the Hale allegations at the Shoney's restaurant near Arkadelphia. His memory was clearer, and he seemed eager to exculpate Clinton from Hale's allegations. "Bill Clinton and I never discussed any loan with David Hale anytime," he told *Post* reporter Howard Schneider. He said he'd "take a lie detector test on national television absolving the president of this ridiculous accusation." The *Post* didn't run any story. Then McDougal again disappeared, retreating to Galveston, Texas, without leaving an address or phone number. He had become convinced that reporters were passing on information to Paula Casey, the Little Rock U.S. attorney, and even suspected Gerth of secretly recording their conversations. (Gerth denies that.)

Gerth's and Engelberg's efforts to find corroboration for Hale's story yielded little. Gerth tried to interview Paula Casey, who, appropriately, declined comment. Both reporters were nonetheless convinced that Hale's story was newsworthy; he was speaking on the record, he was prepared to repeat the story to law enforcement authorities. While they lacked independent confirmation, they'd found no one to contradict anything Hale had to say. They returned to Washington, and after conferring with their editors, called the White House. "We've got a story with serious allegations involving the president," Gerth told David Gergen. After learning it involved business dealings in Arkansas, and had at least peripheral connections to Whitewater, Gergen arranged a meeting with Bruce Lindsey.

Lindsey had virtually no comment about Hale's allegations, saying he'd have to look into the matter before responding. But the conversation soon veered into Whitewater. This was Gerth's first conversation with a White House official on the matter, and unanswered questions still nagged at him. Now that he knew McDougal had been trying unsuccessfully to get Whitewater documents from the Clintons, he was even more curious to know what they might contain. "Why don't you make public all the Whitewater documents?" Gerth asked.

Lindsey seemed to ponder the request. Then he asked, "What if you got access and then you found something else? Would you feel you had to write about it?"

"Yes," Gerth answered, somewhat surprised by Lindsey's naïveté, "of course I would." That ended the discussion.

Immediately after the meeting, Lindsey called Jim Blair in

Arkansas. Because of his continuing contacts with McDougal's lawyer, Heuer, who seemed remarkably willing to share information with Blair, Blair was able to brief Lindsey on Hale's status. He told Lindsey about McDougal's meeting with Hale. Blair also reported that Heuer had spoken to the U.S. attorney's office trying to find out whether Hale was likely to be indicted. A few weeks later, Jim Guy Tucker was in Washington for a Governors Association meeting, and he met with Clinton himself for about a half hour. Whether they discussed either Hale or the dissident troopers isn't known; the ostensible subject of the meeting was health care and highway financing.

Gerth had the distinct impression that Lindsey wouldn't be cooperative and, indeed, Mark Gearan got back to him with a statement from the president saying the president had "no recollection" of any such meetings with Hale. No Whitewater documents were offered. But the exchange with Lindsey stuck in Gerth's mind. Gerth figured there must be something in the documents the White House didn't want him to see.

Gerth and Engelberg went ahead and drafted a story, making sure they stated Hale's allegations with appropriate qualifications, noting that Hale was facing indictment and had an incentive to implicate others. The story was sent to New York. Gerth was in Boston for the funeral of his father-in-law when Engelberg called with the news that the *Times*'s executive editor, Max Frankel, had killed the story. The explanation was simple: an about-to-be-indicted person lacking corroboration was making a charge of possibly criminal behavior against a sitting president. The *Times* wouldn't run it.

Gerth was disappointed, but not overly surprised. He called Coleman and Hale and told them the outcome, thanking them for their help. He kept all of his Hale notes and other information he and Engelberg had gathered in Arkansas. He had the distinct feeling the Hale story wasn't over.

That summer, shortly after Foster's death, Richard Iorio, a former FBI agent and bank president, now director of investigations for the RTC in Kansas City, stopped by the office of Jean Lewis, the indefatigable Madison investigator. With Iorio's encouragement, Lewis was now spending most of her time on the Madison

Guaranty case, even though it was one of the smaller S&L disasters under her jurisdiction. Indeed, the FBI had asked her to spend more time on two other S&Ls, which she all but ignored. Though Lewis had quickly developed a reputation as one of the office's most dedicated and tireless investigators, Iorio mentioned that he'd received a complaint from the professional liability section, the civil counterpart to Lewis's criminal unit, that she was having too much contact with the U.S. attorney's office and the FBI office in Little Rock. There had been a specific complaint that Lewis was talking to the U.S. attorney about Madison.

Lewis was startled. In her experience, cooperating with prosecutors and investigators working on criminal referrals was routine. Iorio left her with the impression that she was being warned not to press the criminal referral involving Madison—and the Clintons.

The timing also struck her as suspicious. Only a few weeks earlier, Julie Yanda, the head of the professional liability section in Kansas City, had been briefed on Lewis's latest findings regarding Madison, which pointed to additional criminal referrals. Lewis had put the Madison file aside in late 1992, but as she'd made a note to herself to do, she hadn't let the matter drop. She had told Iorio at the time that she felt the case warranted further investigation. Then, in May, still not having heard anything about the status of her earlier criminal referral on Madison, she called the executive office of U.S. attorneys at the Justice Department in Washington. Lewis was told that the Madison case had been submitted as an "urgent report" to then–Attorney General William Barr, but no one seemed to know what had happened to it after that. In any event, it was no longer an active file at the executive office, nor had it been sent back to Little Rock.

The apparent disappearance of the referral only furthered Lewis's determination that Madison be thoroughly investigated. She pressed Iorio on the matter, and he agreed that the investigation should be reopened. He placed Lewis in charge of an investigative team that returned to Little Rock and began a more thorough review of Madison's records.

As the renewed investigation continued that summer, Lewis had indeed contacted the acting U.S. attorney in Little Rock (the Republican Charles Banks had resigned, part of a nationwide replacement of Republican appointees by the Clinton administration) as well as the FBI office in Little Rock. In early July, after numerous calls to the Justice Department, she finally learned from the department that her original referral had been returned to the U.S. attorney's office in Little Rock for a decision, the Justice Department having rejected Banks's contention that his office had a conflict of interest. There, she was told that the office intended to "let it sit" until Clinton's nominee for U.S. attorney, Paula Casey, was approved.

But Lewis had no intention of letting the matter drop. She and her team had by now gathered enough material for not one but multiple criminal referrals. As she later described her findings, Lewis had evidence of "insider abuse, self-dealing, money laundering, embezzlement, diversion of loan proceeds, payments of excessive commissions, misappropriation of funds, land flips, inflated appraisals, falsification of loan records and board minutes, chronic overdraft status of various subsidiaries, wire fraud, and illegal campaign contributions" at Madison.

She had specifically zeroed in on McDougal's 1985 fund-raiser at Madison, tracing, for example, the alleged $3,000 contribution of former Senator Fulbright to a cashier's check payable to the "Bill Clinton Campaign Fund" to a check in the same amount from Flowerwood Farms, one of the McDougals' real estate operations.

By early September, Lewis had drafted nine separate criminal referrals, alleging bank fraud, conspiracy, false statements, false documents, wire fraud, aiding and abetting, and misuse of position. But given the fate of her earlier referral, she called the executive office for U.S. attorneys in Washington, and told Donna Henneman she was worried "the same situation could befall the next referrals to be submitted," as Lewis later put it in an e-mail message summarizing the conversation. "She [Henneman] assured me that she and her supervisor . . . would stay closely in touch with the situation, due [to] its potentially political ramifications, some of which I explained for her edification. She asked me to stay in touch as to the responses that I get from the U.S. Attorney's office, and assured me that, if necessary, the 'higher-ups' at Justice would make sure something got done with these referrals, including the first one, which 'should have been handled by now, one way or the other.' "

Perhaps a single criminal referral could be buried in the bureaucracy of the Justice Department. Now she'd see what would happen to nine.

William Roelle, the RTC senior vice president who'd initially briefed RTC head Albert Casey on the 1992 Madison referral, got a phone call that September from the Kansas City office vice president. He told Roelle that the Madison referral had been resurrected, this time in the nine separate referrals. The RTC official read directly from a summary of the referrals, adding that the office planned to file them on Friday, October 1, just over a week away. The political ramifications were obvious, even more so now that Clinton was president. "Don't turn right. Don't turn left. Don't go up. Don't go down. Walk a straight line," Roelle said. "No matter what you do on this, somebody is going to raise hell about it. Just make sure that they get processed normally."

Roelle, as a civil servant, had stayed on after the election, but Casey had resigned. Now, nine months into the administration, there was still no replacement for him as RTC chairman. Approval of Clinton's initial choice, a Republican, had been stalled by congressional Democrats. That left Deputy Secretary of the Treasury Roger Altman as acting head of the RTC, a post he'd initially accepted expecting the job to last only a matter of weeks.

Responsibility for the vast cleanup operation of the S&L disaster, not to mention the numerous related investigations, was hardly something Altman had sought when he joined Treasury Secretary Lloyd Bentsen as his deputy. Indeed, he'd spent comparatively little time on the RTC, largely limited to twice-weekly staff meetings intended to alert him to issues that might become public and therefore have political ramifications. Altman had been too busy spearheading the administration's efforts to get its economic plan approved and gain congressional approval of the North American Free Trade Agreement, two of the Clinton administration's notable successes. As Bob Woodward notes in *The Agenda*, Altman "became a hero to . . . the Clintons and seemed a rising star in the Administration." Indeed, Altman was already widely recognized within and outside the administration as the probable successor to Bentsen as treasury secretary (Bentsen was expected to retire soon). Still boyishly good-looking at age forty-seven, Altman had returned to Washington after having served as assistant secretary of the treasury in the Carter administration and a lucrative stint as an investment banker in New York with the Blackstone Group.

When Bentsen asked Altman to take temporary responsibility for the RTC, neither gave much thought to the fact that, in its investigative function, the RTC acts as a quasi-independent agency, like the FBI. In any event, Altman retained Roelle and other Bush appointees, so the agency hardly had a partisan cast.

After hearing from the RTC official in Kansas City, Roelle immediately called Altman to warn him that the Madison case had resurfaced. As Roelle later explained, "Mr. Altman had told us when he first took over that he did not want to read things like this in the paper. He did not want to find out after the fact in the paper." Roelle had mentioned the matter to Altman once before, in March, when he had alerted him to the existence of the earlier referral. Altman didn't remember the earlier exchange, but he had apparently spoken to Nussbaum in the White House counsel's office. He also faxed Nussbaum some Whitewater materials: Jeff Gerth's original New York Times stories and an article about Ellen Kulka, the RTC's general counsel, in which one person described her as an "extremist" in pursuing alleged S&L malefactors.

Altman was preoccupied with other matters that Friday, September 24, and after listening for about five minutes, told Roelle to take the matter to Jean Hanson, the Treasury Department's general counsel. The following Monday, Roelle briefed Hanson in detail, reporting that nine criminal referrals "were on their way from the RTC in Kansas City to Washington," where they would be forwarded to the Justice Department. The president and first lady would be cited as "potential witnesses," but he cautioned that in the previous year's Madison referral, "the language that related to President and Mrs. Clinton could be read to indicate that if further work were done, their involvement might be something more than as simply potential witnesses."

Roelle went on to emphasize the need for confidentiality. He urged Hanson "not to tell anybody," that "it was only for Mr. Altman's knowledge," and that "these things had their own way of going and they had their own life to lead, and it wasn't something that somebody should discuss or have any activity about." On numerous occasions, Roelle, Hanson, and Altman had bemoaned the problem of leaks to the press from within the RTC, with Roelle going so far as to describe the agency as a "sieve." Now, he cautioned her that one reason she should speak only to Altman and do nothing was that anything they did was likely to be leaked once the referrals arrived at the Justice Department.

But much of Roelle's admonition apparently didn't register with Hanson. Tired and overworked, having never handled an RTC criminal referral, she heard only that the referrals were in imminent danger of being leaked. When she briefed Altman that same day on the conversation with Roelle, this seems to have been foremost in her mind. She took away the distinct impression that Altman told her to contact Nussbaum so the White House would be prepared for inquiries from the press about the referrals. The conversation made little impression on Altman. Though he was familiar with the articles he'd faxed Nussbaum the previous March, he'd never given Madison, McDougal, or the Whitewater affair much thought. He couldn't believe the matter bore much political risk for the president. While they hadn't been close friends, he'd known Clinton for many years, and he didn't think the president had a financial bone in his body. He doubted he could balance his checkbook. He had no interest in money. So none of the allegations seemed plausible to him.*

Two days after briefing Altman, Hanson was at the White House to discuss the impending release of the Treasury report on the Waco/Branch Davidian disaster, and stayed after the meeting to talk to Nussbaum. She briefed him on the Madison referrals, adding that the Clintons were "potential witnesses" though not suspects, or targets. She emphasized that "undoubtedly this type of thing will leak to the press," and Nussbaum and the White House should prepare themselves for press inquiries. Nussbaum thought the referral would just be one more "hassle" with the press, though nothing terribly serious, and he asked one of his lawyers, Cliff Sloan, to alert Bruce Lindsey, who was continuing to handle questions about Whitewater and other Arkansas dealings.

Like Nussbaum, Lindsey didn't seem unduly concerned. Nor did anyone at the White House express any reservation about being

---

*Altman later testified that he had no recollection of suggesting that Hanson contact Nussbaum, recalling that he said "the matter should be dealt with in an identical fashion relative to any other case." Yet it seems unlikely that Hanson would have contacted the White House without such a directive.

privy to a supposedly confidential criminal investigation that might involve the Clintons, as long as they didn't do anything to interfere with the investigation. White House officials were sufficiently sensitive to the issue that they had Nussbaum's staff look into the question of whether communications between the RTC staff and the White House were unlawful, and found no specific prohibition. Still, they were mindful of Nussbaum's travel office–inspired memos intended, as Nussbaum later put it, "to make sure that people don't either willfully or inadvertently start seeking to influence or direct the outcome of criminal investigations. That's why those memos were written."

Nonetheless, Lewis, in Kansas City, was getting the impression that someone "higher up" was interfering with the referrals. On September 29 she wrote another e-mail to Iorio, noting that she'd arranged for the Justice Department to receive copies of the referrals directly from Kansas City and that "they have made the decision to get the Deputy Attorney General's office involved in this situation." But the next day, right after copies of the new referrals were given to RTC officials in Washington and Kansas City, Julie Yanda, the head of the professional liability section, said she wanted a "legal review" of the referrals before they were submitted, a step that was unprecedented in Lewis's experience, thereby delaying the referrals. (Yanda insisted they were routine.) Lewis went over Yanda's head by complaining to RTC regional inspector general Dan Sherry; the legal review was subsequently completed, and the referrals finally sent to Washington on October 8.

But Lewis's formal involvement in the Madison referrals was abruptly ended. The professional liability section removed her from responsibility for any subpoena compliance, assuming that function itself. Lewis was also ordered to stop communicating with the U.S. attorney's office in Little Rock. As Lewis put it in another e-mail message, "The Powers That Be have decided that I'm better off out of the line of fire (and I ain't arguing)."

By the fall of 1993, the existence of the referrals had indeed leaked, as Roelle and Hanson had predicted. During the first week in October, Gerth had gotten a call from someone he knew, tipping him to the existence of new referrals. Gerth had gotten a "whiff" of the earlier referral, as he put it, while doing his reporting in Little

Rock the previous winter, but nothing substantial enough to include in any of his Whitewater stories. Spurred by the latest tip, Gerth found a new source who had very detailed information, including the fact that at least one of the referrals involved the 1985 Madison fund-raiser. But the source was unwilling to go on the record, preferring to remain anonymous. Gerth again enlisted Steve Engelberg, and the two began trying to corroborate the information. Among the people Gerth called was Beverly Bassett, now married to Tyson Foods's public relations head, Archie Schaffer. Still reeling from her last encounter with Gerth when he was working on his first Whitewater story, she called her husband. "He's back on me," she said. "He's after me again." Archie suggested she at least find out what he was working on, so she returned Gerth's call.

"What's the deal now?" she asked. Gerth mentioned the RTC referrals, and asked if she had represented McDougal or Madison Guaranty while in private practice.

"No, I did not," she said testily (her firm had, and Gerth later found one memo written by Bassett).

"I'm not bringing this up," Gerth said, "the RTC is."

"Do you have the criminal referral?"

Gerth read a sentence mentioning her, and it sounded like a direct quote.

"I cannot believe this," she said. A reporter seemed to have a copy of the referral even before she knew of its existence. "Well, you can't upset me any more than you already have," she said. "I'm beyond it." She and Gerth had several more conversations, but she knew nothing about the events of greatest interest to Gerth, such as the fund-raiser.

It took little time for news of such inquiries to reach the White House. Denver lawyer Jim Lyons, who'd prepared the earlier Whitewater report, promptly reported a call from Gerth, as well as from *Washington Post* reporter Mike Isikoff, to Bruce Lindsey. He warned Lindsey that both reporters were asking questions about criminal RTC referrals involving Madison that mentioned the Clintons.

That same day, Lindsey mentioned the call from Lyons to President Clinton, who responded indistinctly, with a "hmm . . ." and nothing further.

But the reporters' efforts were stirring up a flurry of e-mails,

phone calls, and meetings within the RTC and the Treasury Department. Eager to scoop the *Times* after it had beaten the *Post*
with the original Whitewater story, *Post* reporter Sue Schmidt was
pursuing the story even more aggressively than Gerth. Isikoff had
also interviewed Hale after someone anonymously faxed him a copy
of an *Arkansas Democrat-Gazette* story mentioning Hale. Like the
Times, the *Post* had doubts about Hale's reliability, and no story
appeared. But Schmidt, encouraged by Isikoff, decided to look
again into the RTC angle, a subject she'd begun researching the
previous March. She flew to Kansas City, which prompted an e-mail
message from Lewis to her supervisor, Iorio: "The following is a
recap of what transpired when Washington Post report[er] Sue
Schmidt showed up at my front door.

"She arrived around 7:15. I allowed her to step inside my door,
I listened to what she had to say, and then I escorted her out the
door at approximately 7:30. When I showed her out the door, my
parting comment was, 'When you contacted me last Thursday, I
told you that I had no comment, and made every effort to be
polite in doing so. What you have done this evening is the most
unprecedented breach of professional courtesy that I've ever witnessed, so I will say this one more time, and one more time only.
Do not contact me again at my office, or at my home. I have no
comment on your investigation and will not answer any of your
questions. Do not waste any more of my time or yours.' "

Still, Lewis continued, she was concerned that Schmidt might
have a copy of the previous year's referral and that "she intends to
pursue the story." Among the reporter's questions were:

"—if I was frustrated that my 'work product was stymied and
road blocked at certain federal levels';

"—if the late 'Vince Foster was tied to any of this';

"—if I was aware that Jeff Gerth of the New York Times was
reopening his investigation of the Whitewater story he wrote last
year. She then added that he would probably be the next reporter
to appear on my doorstep. I thanked her for the heads up."

A copy of Lewis's e-mail worked its way up to Stephen Katsanos, head of public affairs for the RTC, who mentioned the inquiry in an *Early Bird*, an RTC publication intended as an alert to
possible press inquiries. When treasury counsel Hanson got the
Early Bird, she called Sloan in Nussbaum's office, who in turn

alerted Lindsey. Lindsey seemed perturbed over the *Early Bird,* saying it seemed a "strange" publication, a "leak sheet" and a waste of taxpayers' money.

Then, on October 11, Gerth called Jack DeVore, assistant secretary of the treasury for public affairs, who'd worked with Bentsen on Capitol Hill. Gerth liked and respected DeVore, whom he'd talked to periodically. Gerth had done an investigative piece on Bentsen that ran on the front page of the *Times* just as the Clinton administration was taking office, and DeVore had handled Gerth's questions. Though the piece was hard-hitting, Gerth thought DeVore had been professional, accurate, trustworthy, and mature. There hadn't been any whining about the results—in marked contrast, Gerth thought, to the Clintons' reactions to his original Whitewater story. Perhaps most important, a veteran like DeVore had the stature that Gerth felt was important in handling a story as potentially explosive as this one.

Gerth knew that DeVore was planning to leave the administration fairly soon, so when he reached him, he said, "Jack, I'm going to throw a hot one at you during your final days in office." He briefed DeVore on what he knew, focusing on the 1985 fund-raiser. He also asked whether it was usual procedure to send referrals directly to Washington, and mentioned that other reporters, especially Sue Schmidt, were pursuing the story. This was the first DeVore had heard of the referrals, and he told Gerth he was surprised there was such an investigation, but he'd look into it and get back to him.

Other press calls, from Schmidt and other reporters, began to pour in. It was clear the press effort was reaching a crescendo, and after a flurry of phone calls, Treasury and White House officials gathered in Nussbaum's office on October 14. No one from the RTC itself was there. DeVore began the meeting by describing his conversation with Gerth. He said he'd confirmed that the referrals had been sent, and they'd already been forwarded to the U.S. attorney in Little Rock. His instinct had been simply to confirm the existence of the referrals; he wanted to get back to Gerth and make sure he didn't print an incorrect story, and mentioned that his understanding was that it wasn't unusual for the RTC to confirm the existence of a criminal referral. DeVore seemed concerned that if he didn't respond to Gerth, Gerth would write a story saying the referrals had been sent to the Little Rock U.S. attorney's office only after the *New York Times* started asking questions.

DeVore was surprised that Lindsey already seemed to know about Gerth's questions. Evidently referring to the Hale piece that never ran, Lindsey said that the *New York Times* had been looking into more Whitewater-related stories, but had concluded there was nothing there. But then Hale had been mentioned in the *Arkansas Democrat-Gazette* (the same story faxed to Isikoff), which, Lindsey said, just went to show that even when there wasn't a story, if something was confirmed it would crop up somewhere. Moreover, with shadows of the travel office affair fresh in his mind, Nussbaum, too, was opposed. The White House had been excoriated for confirming the existence of an FBI probe, so why should they respond to Gerth's questions?

Lindsey argued that DeVore should say, off the record, only that whatever had been sent by the RTC to Washington had been forwarded to Little Rock, while refusing to discuss just what had been sent. After the meeting, Lindsey did some research into the fund-raiser Gerth was asking about, and typed up a memo that was circulated to Maggie Williams in the first lady's office, Bill Kennedy, and Mark Gearan. (Lindsey later said the copies had been sent by mistake.) Hanson looked into the question of direct referrals to Washington, and was assured that the procedure was used for major cases.

Despite admonitions, DeVore got back to Gerth on October 14. Convinced that the existence of the referrals would find its way into print anyway, he felt he had an obligation to correct Gerth's impression that the referrals had been "bottled up" in Washington. He confirmed the existence of the referrals related to Madison and emphasized to Gerth they'd been forwarded to Little Rock before their first conversation on the subject. "Can't you tell me more?" Gerth asked, a little disappointed. "I asked you a lot of specific questions." It was good to know the referrals existed, which helped buttress the reliability of his source, but the fact there were new referrals on Madison wasn't news. It was the content of those referrals, specifically, the mentions of the president and first lady, that would be news. On that subject, DeVore was silent, even though Gerth sensed he knew more and wanted to talk about it. "I'm not going to go into it," DeVore said.

Gerth felt frustrated. Though he was tantalizingly close, he didn't have a story, and he knew he continued to face competition from Schmidt. Indeed, Schmidt's persistence prompted another phone call to the White House from the RTC. As Katsanos, the RTC communications official, later described the situation in a memo, he was instructed by a Treasury official that Treasury "wanted a 'heads-up' on reporters' queries concerning the Rose Law Firm and Hillary Clinton, but suggested they not be identified in the *Early Bird*. She [the Treasury official] also instructed me to call Lisa Caputo at the White House [press secretary to the first lady] to discuss Sue Schmidt's interest in Hillary Clinton. She gave me Caputo's number and said it would be good for me to keep her informed."

As instructed, Katsanos did call Caputo, telling her that Schmidt was trying to verify that Hillary Clinton had participated in a meeting with RTC lawyers regarding Madison. Caputo said she was surprised that Schmidt hadn't called her directly.

Then, on October 27, the odyssey of Lewis's original criminal referral on Madison finally came to end. Paula Casey decided not to launch an investigation. She wrote Lewis: "As you know, this referral was reviewed by the Criminal Division of the U.S. Department of Justice at the request of the previous U.S. Attorney for the Eastern District of Arkansas. The matter was concluded before I began working in this office, and I was unaware that you had not been told. . . . I reviewed the referral, and I concur with the opinion of the Department attorneys that there is insufficient information in the referral to sustain many of the allegations made by the investigators or to warrant the initiation of a criminal investigation."

While it was true that her predecessors had not recommended prosecution, with the agreement of Justice Department officials in Washington, there was enough in the letter to further inflame Lewis. She knew from her own inquiries that Casey was not simply rubber-stamping someone else's decision—the referral had been returned to Casey's office for her decision.

In the event, neither the conversations and meetings between White House and Treasury officials nor Casey's decision to drop the first referral could stem the press momentum fueled by the fact that someone had leaked apparently accurate information about the latest set of referrals. On the front page of the *Washington Post* on

October 31, Schmidt broke the story: "U.S. Is Asked to Probe Failed S&L." Attributing the information to "government sources familiar with the probe," she reported that "The Resolution Trust Corp. has asked federal prosecutors in Little Rock to open a criminal investigation into whether a failed Arkansas savings and loan used depositors' funds during the mid-80s to benefit local politicians, including a reelection campaign of then-governor Bill Clinton." Deep in the story, Whitewater was brought squarely back into the news for the first time since Foster's death: "The RTC went to extraordinary lengths to trace real estate transactions involving Whitewater Development Corp., a land company Bill and Hillary Clinton jointly owned with McDougal and his former wife, Susan McDougal, according to government sources." The story then revisited much of the information from Gerth's original story.

Because it was as interesting for the questions that weren't answered as it was for those that were, Schmidt's story was a classic example of the kind of investigative piece that sets the stage for day after day of new revelations, as more sources come forward and more reporters jump on the story. The *Wall Street Journal* had the story on Monday. With competitive pressure mounting, Gerth finally weighed in on Tuesday, using some of his information from Hale and adding new details about the 1985 fund-raiser. Because the paper had been scooped, Gerth suffered the embarrassment of having the story run on page 20.

The *Washington Post*, finally having scored against the *Times*, streaked ahead with front-page stories on Tuesday, Wednesday, and Thursday, a seemingly relentless sequence of further embarrassing revelations for the Clintons. In "Clintons' Former Real Estate Firm Probed," which ran on the *Post*'s front page the same day as Gerth's piece, Isikoff first connected Hale to Whitewater, reporting that some of the $300,000 loan to Susan McDougal was used to buy the International Paper land for Whitewater. The story was also the first to mention that Foster had worked on Whitewater matters. Successive days brought *Post* readers "Regulators Say They Were Unaware of Clinton Law Firm's S&L Ties" and "Gov. Tucker's Finances Become Probe Focus."

Despite all the internal phone calls and meetings ostensibly intended to prepare for news stories, the White House seemed taken by surprise by the sudden resurrection of Whitewater. Confronted by reporters at an otherwise routine photo session, the president said, "We did nothing improper, and I have nothing to say about it—old story."

The weekend before Schmidt's story appeared in the *Post*, Lindsey had told the paper that he was aware of the referrals only through press inquiries. After the story appeared, Jeff Eller, who'd been a key strategist in the travel office affair, issued a statement saying that the White House knew nothing about the criminal referrals before they were publicly disclosed. "The first we heard about the investigation into political contributions was from press calls," he told the *Wall Street Journal*. The *Post* reporters were disbelieving. More than any other comments, these convinced them that the White House was hiding something. As a result, the *Post* began considering it a front-page story, and the investigative team—Isikoff, Schmidt, Charles Babcock, and Howard Schneider—intensified its efforts. Soon after the first burst of stories, the *Post* reporters sent Bruce Lindsey a compendium of about twenty written questions dealing with Whitewater, Madison, and related issues. There was no response.

David Bossie was ecstatic over the sudden media explosion. It confirmed his own instinct that this was a story—unlike Gennifer Flowers—that would attract the interest of the mainstream media, and now he was poised to take advantage of it.

Since their first phone calls, Bossie had stayed in touch periodically with Hale and Coleman, and he knew they were dealing with reporters from the *New York Times*. Bossie hadn't spoken with Gerth, but when he learned from Coleman that the earlier story Gerth was working on had been killed, he figured the story needed a boost. By then he'd finished the other work he was doing for Floyd Brown, and had persuaded him to pursue the Hale allegations. Bossie told Hale and his lawyer that he'd like to come down to Arkansas himself and meet them.

About the same time, an NBC producer in Washington, Ira Silverman, gave Bossie a call. Bossie made a point of being in regular contact with a network of reporters and congressional aides, and he'd been mentioning Hale's name to several of them, saying he had some intriguing information on Clinton. "I hear you've got some stuff on this guy," Silverman said, referring to Hale.

Bossie liked Silverman. They'd gotten to know each other during Hubbell's confirmation hearings, when Bossie had been trying to interest news organizations in his allegations of insider trading and other questionable financial transactions by Hubbell. NBC had never done a story, but Bossie had given Silverman plenty of material, and he'd been especially impressed that Silverman came out to the Montgomery County firehouse where Bossie lives, working as a volunteer fireman on weekends and nights. (He has no other residence, and sleeps at the firehouse virtually every night.) Silverman was only vaguely aware of Bossie's connections to Brown and Citizens United. What impressed him was that Bossie's information was accurate, and he'd already gone to such lengths to gather original materials, thereby saving Silverman untold hours of legwork in a competitive environment where timing can be everything.

Silverman, a twenty-eight-year veteran of NBC News, was one of the network's most experienced producers, often assigned to complicated investigative subjects. He'd done specials on the S&L crisis and the Bank of Commerce and Credit International scandal involving Clark Clifford. But over the years, he'd seen network news evolve steadily toward celebrity journalism. It was getting harder and harder to get his kind of story on the air. Whitewater, thus far, had been dismissed by NBC producers in New York, with just a hint of condescension, as a "print story." Vincent Foster's death had begun to change that. Correspondent Andrea Mitchell had learned that Jim Lyons, author of the earlier Whitewater report, had tried to call Foster the day of his death. Then the *Post* had put the Hale story on its front page. At some indefinable point, enough print stories reach a critical mass where the networks can't ignore them. The day after the *Post* story, NBC bureau chief Tim Russert called Silverman, sounding urgent, meaning he wanted to be first with an on-camera interview. Silverman said he'd try to get Hale.

He called a Senate aide whom he'd worked with on the Hubbell story, who referred him to Bossie. Bossie was elated at Silverman's interest. Brown had a maxim that a story wasn't a story until it had been on network television news. There may have been a day when the country's news agenda was set by the big newspapers, when a story on the front page of the *New York Times* or the

Washington Post would all but guarantee that it would be on that night's TV broadcasts. But Bossie and Brown had concluded that was usually no longer the case. Now, a story on the evening network news broadcasts was almost certain to appear on the front pages of the country's newspapers. Not only did Bossie fill Silverman in at length on Hale's allegations, but he invited Silverman to join him on his forthcoming trip to Arkansas. He said he'd introduce the producer to Hale. Silverman said he'd check with his bosses, then called back to accept. Silverman and Bossie had seats next to each other on the flight to Little Rock.

The two spent about a week together in Arkansas. In addition to meeting and talking with Hale, Silverman rented a helicopter, and he, Bossie, and an NBC camera crew made several passes over the Whitewater terrain. Bossie, acting as navigator, was using binoculars to try to locate the Hillary house. Flying at tree level, they managed to get lost and twice had to land the helicopter in someone's front yard to ask directions. Still, they ended the day with ample footage of the remote, rugged tract.

When Silverman and Bossie arrived together at Coleman's office, Hale seemed tired and worn down from his unsuccessful effort to plea-bargain. That was the story Hale and Coleman most wanted to tell—how their efforts were being rebuffed because of political influence. It took more coaxing to get Hale to share on camera his account of the meetings with Clinton, but ultimately he did. That afternoon, with Bossie in the conference room to give him support, Hale was taped as he answered Silverman's questions. In the crucial segment, he repeated his allegations involving Clinton for what would be a national audience:

"He just simply asked me if I was going to be able to help he [sic] and Jim out," Hale said, "and that was . . ."

"Governor Clinton?" Silverman injected.

"Yes, sir. Yes, sir."

"And what did he mean by—what did you take it that he meant by helping him out—helping McDougal out?"

"That I was going to be able to make the loan to them as requested by Jim McDougal." Hale continued, "Yes, sir. There was a—a—a scheme to assist some very prominent people here in Arkansas who had connections with that S&L. They had some problems there, and they asked for my help. And I did help them in that matter."

Silverman filled three videocassettes with the interview. Hale had performed just as Bossie had hoped.

With Hale suddenly in the spotlight of national publicity, the once reluctant Brown was now eager to get Hale on his radio show and into *ClintonWatch*. That Friday, November 5, with Brown doing the interviewing from his studio in Fairfax, and Bossie with Hale at Coleman's office, Hale made his radio debut on Brown's *Talk Back to Washington*. "I'm just a little bitty guy in a great big pond," Hale told Brown's listeners. In the next issue, the Hale story led *ClintonWatch*. "Clinton Fingered in Loan Cover-Up," the headline read. "Arkansas judge refuses to be the fall-guy for the president and his greedy friends." In addition to the newsletter, with 15,000 subscribers, many of whom had returned the coupon included with each copy of *Slick Willie*, Bossie had the story faxed to thousands of reporters and opinionmakers.

The following Thursday, November 11, Bossie, now back from Arkansas, Brown, and their staff gathered in front of the TV set in the Citizens United conference room for the *NBC Nightly News*. Alerted by Silverman that the segment would air, the staff watched as the helicopter footage of Whitewater that Bossie had helped obtain appeared for the first time on network television. Correspondent Andrea Mitchell narrated: "This beautiful riverfront land in the Ozarks was supposed to be a gold mine for the Clintons and their partners when they bought it in the booming 1980s. . . ." Then Hale came on camera. "This man, a former local judge under indictment on an unrelated case, has told NBC News that Clinton asked him in 1985 to make a loan to the McDougals, who were in financial trouble," Mitchell said, as excerpts from the Hale taping attended by Bossie proceeded to air. Then the segment concluded with a connection that not even Bossie had made:

"Before his death in July, former White House lawyer Vince Foster also got involved, helping the Clintons sell their share of the land company. He also discovered a tax mess; the partnership had not filed federal or state returns for three years. Now questions are being raised about a possible link between the growing Arkansas investigations and Foster's death. NBC News has learned that Lyons talked to Foster a few days before he died. He also called Foster the day Foster died. But the White House said Lyons didn't get through. That same day, in Little Rock, a judge signed a search warrant for the FBI to raid David Hale's offices. White House officials insist that Foster could not have been tipped off about the impending raid, and they correctly point out that the Clintons are not the targets of any of these investigations.

"Andrea Mitchell, NBC News, at the White House."

Brown, Bossie, and the rest of the staff celebrated. It was their first success on a national news broadcast, a success even beyond their fondest expectations. Whitewater and Vincent Foster's death had now merged.

THIRTEEN

AFTER MEETING AND INTERVIEWING the troopers in August, Bill Rempel had enlisted another investigative reporter in the *Los Angeles Times*'s Washington bureau, Douglas Frantz, to help corroborate the troopers' allegations. The mission was still top secret, even within the *Times*. Though the paper's editor, Shelby Coffey, was kept apprised of developments, the paper's highly respected Washington bureau chief, Jack Nelson, was deliberately kept in the dark by the reporters and Los Angeles national editors, even though the story arguably fell within his jurisdiction. When Frantz left to join Rempel in Little Rock in mid-October, he was instructed by the paper's Los Angeles editors to tell Nelson and others in the bureau that he was working on a Whitewater project. There had been concerns in Los Angeles about possible leaks to the White House, and a sense that the bureau was too close to the Clintons. Rempel and Frantz appreciated the need for secrecy, but were still uneasy about the deception within their own paper.

The pair of reporters made one of the most experienced teams on the paper. Rempel had been at the paper for twenty-three years, covering the Iran-Contra and BCCI affairs, and was the first reporter the *L.A. Times* sent to Arkansas for the campaign. Frantz had been at the paper seven years, recently leading the *Times*'s coverage of weapons smuggling to Iraq. He'd also written several books, most recently a biography of Clark Clifford.

Their rival on the story, David Brock, was a study in contrast, as much a symbol of a new, openly ideological journalism as Rempel and Frantz were of traditional journalism. From his days as an

unabashedly conservative student journalist at the University of
California at Berkeley, the thirty-one-year-old Brock's career had
been nurtured by the conservative movement, first as a reporter at
the openly partisan *Washington Times* and then at the even more
conservative *American Spectator,* a magazine whose circulation and
impact had burgeoned with the backing of radio talk show host
Rush Limbaugh and had received major funding from conservative
philanthropist Richard Mellon Scaife. Unlike most mainstream
journalists, Brock had no reluctance about accepting funding from
the conservative Allen Bradley Foundation.

Articulate, usually charming, and often devastatingly effective,
Brock had achieved celebrity status with the publication of *The Real
Anita Hill,* a scathing polemic that portrayed the accuser of Supreme Court Justice Clarence Thomas as "a bit nutty and a bit
slutty," as Brock himself put it. More than just about any other
partisan journalist, Brock had managed to inflame other reporters,
not so much because of his conservative ideology, but because of
what they deemed his unfairness.*

Even so, the troopers' stories had given Brock pause. The
whole question of a politician's sex life wasn't really something
Brock wanted to get into. But Clinton had involved state employees, and in Brock's view, he'd displayed a lack of discretion and poor
judgment that had a bearing on his fitness for public office. Brock
went back and reviewed the transcript of Clinton's interview about
Gennifer Flowers on *60 Minutes.* Clinton had flatly denied having
a twelve-year affair with Flowers, and implied that all such behavior
lay in his past. But if the troopers' accounts could be corroborated,
both those claims were, at best, highly misleading.

For both Brock and the *Los Angeles Times* reporters, any lingering misgivings were resolved when Cliff Jackson called to report
that the troopers had come under pressure from Young, and that
Clinton himself had called Ferguson offering him a federal job.
This elevated the story to a different plane: the president's call was
not only corroboration (why else would the president of the United

---

* *To cite just one example, he cast doubt on the credibility of one of Supreme Court Justice
Clarence Thomas's accusers by saying she refused to submit to an FBI interview and that
the statement she made was unsworn. She was interviewed by two FBI agents and the
statement was sworn and notarized according to* Strange Justice *by Jill Abramson and
Jane Mayer.*

States call a state trooper about an unsubstantiated rumor?), but it raised questions about whether the president was trying to suppress the story. The *L.A. Times* had developed a standard during the campaign. As Rempel put it, "If a woman calls and says she had sex with the governor, it's not a story. If he offered her a job, it is."

Rempel and Frantz rented a suite at the Excelsior Hotel in Little Rock, so sources could come and go without passing through the highly visible lobby of the Capital Hotel, where most journalists stayed. They used the suite's living room for face-to-face interviews, so they wouldn't be spotted calling on their sources. They spent hours and hours with Perry and Patterson. They were the only troopers still talking, though neither had yet given permission to use their material. The reporters tried to check every allegation that had surfaced, without doing anything too public. In many cases that proved impossible, though they found nothing to contradict the troopers' accounts, either. And other efforts yielded significant evidence. The reporters later made a Freedom of Information Act request for Governor Clinton's cellular phone records, and found numerous calls to the phone number of a woman the troopers said they heard Clinton speaking to. In one such instance, there was a ninety-four-minute call in the middle of the night from a hotel room where Clinton was registered. The cost of these calls came to about $44; the reporters discovered a check from Clinton in roughly the same amount reimbursing the cost of the calls.

After they flew to Los Angeles to meet with top editors, Rempel and Frantz received permission to take the reporting to the next step: confronting the women mentioned by the troopers. In the case of the recipient of the phone calls, they drove by her house, then called from a nearby phone. She wouldn't talk to them or let them stop by. Then they called her again. She said she didn't even know Bill Clinton. "You mean the man who used to be governor?" she asked. She again refused to see them. When they pressed her about the phone records, she said she couldn't talk because she was about to leave for Dallas. She promised to call them back, but didn't. The next day, they again reached her at home. This time she seemed more collected. She now acknowledged that she knew Clinton, but denied having any "improper" relationship with him. She refused to meet them or speak any further.

Rempel and Frantz also flew to Texas in an attempt to meet

with Buddy Young, the troopers' former boss who'd been promoted by Clinton to the FEMA post. They called him on a cellular phone from a car parked outside his house. Young said he wasn't feeling well and didn't want to talk; they could try again the next day. They reached him then, and mentioned some of the potentially embarrassing information they'd gathered about him. They intimated that there might be legal problems with a presidential appointee drawing income from an outside business like his trucking safety company (now owned in his wife's name). Young seemed nervous and agreed to answer questions about the trooper situation. The reporters again taped the conversation, in which Young confirmed that he had called three of the four troopers after talking to Clinton and reported on the conversations to the president. He attempted to put the information in context:

"Roger [Perry] has a way of twisting things around," he said. "I told Roger to let his conscience be his guide and to do whatever he thought he had to do. I never told him he was ruining his own reputation. I said he very possibly might come out the loser in this."

Referring to the troopers' work, Young continued, "When they're with a man day and night, they know everything about him, his personal life and everything else. They're in an entrusted position, seeing and hearing what's nobody else's business. If a man's going to run his head off every time he goes over there, he's got no business being over there." Still, Young insisted that Perry and the other troopers had nothing of interest to say.

"I think whatever they're telling you is bullshit and hearsay. . . . In the ten years I was there, I saw nothing on Bill Clinton's behalf that the public is interested in. And I don't think anybody else did either. I can't imagine what you all are trying to do. You know, Roger Perry was a good friend of mine. I helped him once when he was in lots of trouble himself. And now for him to turn around and say these damn things to try to burn me is ridiculous. . . . I don't understand this whole business unless it's money. Are you paying him?"

"No," the reporters answered.

"Then it's got to be revenge or jealousy." Young seemed befuddled.

Even though Ferguson had dropped out of the agreement with the other troopers, the reporters called him again and persuaded him to meet with them on condition that his name wouldn't appear in their story. With his wife present, Ferguson went over his earlier statements, told of his encounters with Young and Clinton, and discussed his decision to back out. The reporters taped his comments.

"When you all started talking to Buddy [Young], that's when the bells started ringing," Ferguson told them. He said he'd already come under pressure to contradict whatever Perry and Patterson had to say, but he assured Rempel and Frantz that, if asked, he wouldn't deny what he'd already told them as long as they kept his name out of the paper. "If another newspaper comes to me and asks if this is true," Ferguson said, "I'm not going to lie but I'm not going to confirm it. Like I told Roger, if they get on him too heavy, me and [my wife] Sheila discussed this, if they hurt him in any way, we'll come forward and we'll go on the record. We're not going to let them hurt Roger. It is stuff that we want to keep back for our security." Clinton "knows what I've got," he added.

The pieces of the story were falling into place by early December. By Thanksgiving, Perry and Patterson had given the green light. No federal job offer for Perry had materialized, and despite Ferguson's tantalizing suggestion, he'd seen no reason to stop meeting with the reporters. But Perry said he still wanted to talk to Governor Jim Guy Tucker. He met with him one morning at the governor's mansion. Perry had worked the night shift that day, which ended at 6:30 A.M., and he waited two hours before the governor, still in his bathrobe, summoned him. Tucker asked Perry to sit down.

"Are you and Larry going through with this article?" Tucker asked.

"Well . . ."

"Have you talked with anyone other than the *American Spectator*?" Tucker continued, obviously familiar with his contacts with Brock.

"Yes," Perry replied.

"These people are not your friends."

"I don't know that, Governor."

"You are not attacking the president, Bill Clinton," Tucker said. "You are attacking the presidency." He paused, letting the point sink in. Perry said nothing. "Roger, you will not survive this.

Your reputation will be destroyed. You can never work in law enforcement again." Tucker spoke softly, almost paternally. There was
no hostility.

"Governor, a lot has happened," Perry said. "Things have gone
too far to turn back, even if I wanted to." He added, "The more
I'm threatened, the more determined I become."

Tucker seemed saddened. "You have made your mind up," he
said, turning and leaving the room without shaking Perry's hand.

The next day Perry was summoned to Tommy Goodwin's office. Goodwin had replaced Young as the head of the governor's
detail.

"You can't work in governor's security," Goodwin stated. "I
have three slots available." They were all entry-level positions.

"Do you have anything in Little Rock?" Perry asked. Goodwin
said he might have a narcotics slot.

"Is this a disciplinary transfer?" Perry asked.

"Oh no, not at all," Goodwin replied.

"Could you put that in writing?"

"You don't need that," Goodwin responded.

At the White House, spirits had been improving since the low
point of Foster's death. After the flurry of Whitewater stories in
early November, there had been a period of relative calm in the
media. In early December, a *Washington Post* poll put President
Clinton's approval rating at a much-improved 58 percent, the highest since the first months of his presidency. The nation's economy
was thriving, with unemployment at a new low of 6.4 percent.
Hopes were high for Hillary Clinton's ambitious plan to reform the
nation's health care system, and the president was pressing a popular crime-fighting initiative.

The first week in December, David Gergen got a call from
Robert Kaiser, managing editor at the *Post*. Gergen and Kaiser were
old friends; Gergen had been a year ahead of Kaiser at Yale, and
Kaiser had worked for Gergen when Gergen was managing editor
of the *Yale Daily News*. "Listen, David," Kaiser began. "We know
each other. We need to talk in a serious way." He explained that the
Post had submitted a series of written questions about Whitewater
to Bruce Lindsey, and said they'd heard nothing, not even an ac-
knowledgment. "We're taking this very seriously," Kaiser said. "Is
there anything that can be done?"

This was the first Gergen had heard of the questions. "I don't have a clue," he said, promising he'd get back to Kaiser.

Gergen called McLarty, and then met with him and Lindsey. After receiving the written questions from the *Washington Post*, Lindsey had taken them to Nussbaum, and they and several others were discussing how best to respond. But they hadn't reached any decision. Gergen looked over the *Post*'s questions. They didn't strike him as all that penetrating or exhaustive. "We have to take this seriously," Gergen said.

But McLarty and Lindsey seemed uncomfortable. "Well," Lindsey said, "if we give them this they'll just want more."

"We can't just sit here and stiff them," Gergen argued. "You're just inviting a tough response. My strong recommendation is see what they want and then see what should be in the public domain and release it," he said. The last thing Gergen wanted was the *Post* in a full-court press over Whitewater. He'd lived through Watergate as part of the Nixon White House, and he knew that if the *Post* takes up a cause . . . He didn't want to think about it. Gergen also made the case to Maggie Williams, Hillary's top aide, but she seemed equally uncertain. Hillary's instinct was to withhold, but she might be persuaded. Finally McLarty told Gergen to go ahead and deal directly with the *Post*, since he knew the top editors there.

Gergen took that as authority to reach an agreement with the *Post*. He got back to Kaiser, proposing that they have a meeting and "come to an understanding." Gergen, Lindsey, and Gearan went to the *Post* headquarters on December 6, where they met with executive editor Len Downie, Jr., and several other editors and reporters, including Sue Schmidt. Lindsey said the White House didn't want to release any more records because it would only raise more questions, much the same objection he'd raised with Gerth. But Downie made the case for answering the questions, which Gergen found persuasive. He couldn't see how any of the answers would be damaging. He promised Downie that the *Post* would have an answer within a week.

After the meeting, Gergen, Gearan, and Lindsey met with McLarty. Gergen and Gearan both recommended that most of the documents and financial records the *Post* wanted be turned over to the paper, then made available publicly. "That seems fair, but we need the president's blessing," McLarty said. By the end of the week, Gergen had still heard nothing. "Mack, we're on the line.

We haven't replied. My relationship with Downie is involved. Let's agree and decide," Gergen argued. McLarty checked his calendar, and suggested they meet in the residence Friday evening. "You can make your case then," he said.

That evening, before Gergen's arrival, McLarty, Lindsey, and Nussbaum were already discussing the issue with the president and first lady, and Hillary's views had hardened. "I don't want them poring over our personal lives," she had said in an earlier discussion with Nussbaum. Nussbaum had never seen any of the Whitewater documents—he hadn't looked closely at anything in Foster's files— and he accepted Bill and Hillary's word that there was nothing to fear. Still, he agreed that "You're entitled to your privacy. If you turn them over . . . they'll pore over them. Every document will be a new story. It will go on and on." Why turn over personal documents? Where would it end? Wouldn't this just encourage scandal-mongering, which is what they thought the *Post* and the rest of the media was indulging in? With the president's approval rating on the rise, and the latest Whitewater stories behind them, there didn't seem to be any reason to give a hostile media new fodder.

This and other discussions had also provided a perfect opportunity to vent the resentment that had persisted toward Gergen. The president and first lady were upset that Gergen had all but told the *Post* they'd get the documents before getting their consent. To some, this demonstrated what Gergen's detractors had been saying all along: he wasn't really loyal to Bill and Hillary, he was out for himself, he was more interested in being a "media darling." Even though Gergen had been brought into the White House precisely because he did have ties to the media, almost anything he now said about the press was deemed suspect.

When Gergen arrived that Friday evening, he was told to wait outside. Finally McLarty came out and told Gergen there was no need to meet with the Clintons. "They don't need to hear you," McLarty said. "The lawyers made an argument which they find compelling not to release these." What argument did the lawyers make? Gergen asked. "They said the files are incomplete. They will only raise new questions and a wild-goose chase."

Gergen was upset. "Mack, this is wrong. The president needs to hear this argument. It's a mistake to jam the *Post*." McLarty wearily agreed, penciling in Gergen to meet with the president the next morning, after his regular Saturday morning radio broadcast. Gergen had to call Downie at the *Post*, since the self-imposed week's deadline was expiring. "We're close" to turning over the documents, Gergen told Downie, "but we're not quite ready. Can I have a few days?" Downie agreed.

The next morning, Gergen met with Clinton after the broadcast, pressing the case for disclosure. The president agreed that Gergen had made some good points and said he'd reconsider. He promised to get back to him. Gergen again called Downie, saying he needed another week. That afternoon, McLarty called Gergen. "I'm sorry, there will be no re-argument." The decision to refuse the *Post*'s request, he said, was final.

That evening, Lindsey wrote a three-sentence letter that was hand-delivered to Downie: "As you know, in March, 1992, the Clinton Campaign released a report by an independent accounting firm which established that the Clintons lost at least $68,900 on Whitewater Development Corporation. They received no gain of any kind on their investment. The Clintons were not involved in the management or operation of the company, nor did they keep its records. We see no need to supplement the March, 1992 CPA report or to provide further documentation."

On Monday, Downie called Gergen. His tone was calm and professional. "I just want to tell you," he said, "that this is a serious mistake. We're not going to drop this. We will go full-bore on this investigation."

The second week in December, Rempel and Frantz told their editors in Los Angeles they were ready to write the story. Coffey agonized for three days before agreeing that the two reporters could fly to Washington. The editors, in confronting the personal life of the president, felt that whatever they did would set an important journalistic precedent.

The reporters rented a suite at the Embassy Suites Hotel and wrote the story. A draft was finished on December 15, and the next day Rempel and Frantz called Gergen.

News that the *L.A. Times* was doing the story came as no surprise to the White House. Since the president's calls to Ferguson and Young, Lindsey had been monitoring the troopers' progress. Besides reports from Young, Lindsey had heard directly from

Brock. Betsey Wright had been enlisted in the damage control effort. She questioned Brock extensively about his sources and tried to find out what was going to be in his story. Gergen had been talking about Rempel and Frantz's story with *L.A. Times* editor Shelby Coffey, a friend from their days together at *U.S. News & World Report*, and Coffey had assured him the paper "wouldn't go off half-cocked." Lindsey had convened an ad hoc group to discuss the trooper problem, which included Stephanopoulos, Gergen, Gearan, Nussbaum, and the first lady. It was especially awkward discussing the troopers' allegations in front of Hillary, but she didn't seem to flinch.

Just about everybody in the group was indignant that the troopers' allegations were even being raised. No sitting president had ever been subjected to such a probe of his personal life before taking office. Still, the developing stories didn't seem all that threatening. Lindsey still couldn't believe the troopers would actually go through with a story. If so, the *Spectator*'s story could be dismissed as a partisan attack. A consensus developed that the president and the White House should ignore any specific allegations, and treat the whole sordid thing as something that had been raised and dismissed during the campaign. After Gennifer Flowers, it seemed safe to assume that the electorate wasn't all that concerned about a man's personal life before he was elected president.

Rempel and Frantz told Gergen they were about to fax him a series of questions they hoped would form the basis for an interview with the president, saying they didn't want to blindside him. Gergen had learned from Coffey that the *Times* had obtained signed affidavits from the troopers, and he asked for copies. The reporters declined, believing the affidavits were like notes, raw material for the story that shouldn't be disclosed. After Gergen read their fax, they spoke again, and this time Gergen, already under pressure from the *Washington Post*, was furious. "How can I take questions like this to the president of the United States?" he asked in exasperation. But the reporters were firm, and Gergen told them he'd get back to them. Gergen himself knew little about what had gone on in Arkansas, so he checked with Betsey Wright about the troopers' allegations. She shrugged them off as old news, but Gergen was startled when she said that, as far as she could tell, the troopers were telling the truth.

Rempel and Frantz finally gave a copy of their draft to their bureau chief, Jack Nelson, along with a memo describing their reporting. "This is a hell of a story," Nelson said, but he didn't seem all that thrilled. Indeed, the next day, Nelson came up with the idea that they should further corroborate the story by getting the troopers to take a lie detector test. The reporters were indignant. They said it was "voodoo, not reporting." It was insulting even to ask the troopers, not to mention time-consuming and costly. But Coffey agreed with Nelson, and said the story would not run without test results. It turned out that Perry and Patterson didn't seem to mind, and readily agreed to take a polygraph. The reporters set about finding an operator outside Arkansas, where they felt anyone would be biased either for or against Clinton, and wound up paying someone in Atlanta $2,500 to be on call. Meanwhile, the deputy bureau chief came up with a long list of questions, some highly technical, such as whether a particular make of camera mentioned by the troopers had the capacity to capture images at the distance mentioned. (It did.) The reporters felt like Dorothy in *The Wizard of Oz*. Frantz was so angered by all the obstacles that were being interposed by his own editors that he ran a red light and was ticketed.

Meanwhile, Cliff Jackson was beside himself. With each new development, it looked less and less likely that the *L.A. Times* would actually publish the story. The troopers had risked everything. Then Brock met Jackson and the troopers at the Legacy Hotel and gave them a copy of his piece. They were shocked. It was explicit, and detailed, with a focus on sex. They had realized that some recounting of what the troopers had witnessed would be necessary, but that had never been their emphasis. Their concern was what they believed was a misuse of tax funds and Clinton's misleading the American public by denying the Gennifer Flowers affair. But Brock's article was graphic. They were concerned that it would be dismissed as a partisan screed.

The content of the article didn't violate the letter of their agreement—Brock had retained full editorial control—but it certainly violated the spirit of it, and the assurances Brock had given them during the course of the interviews that it wouldn't be lurid. But when they complained both to Brock and his publisher, Ron Burr, Brock responded that they couldn't tell him how to write the story. All he wanted to know was whether it was accurate, and they conceded it was, however distasteful.

The nature of the *Spectator* story made it all the more imperative, in Jackson's view, that the *L.A. Times* publish first. Then, late that week, Betsey Wright got a copy of the *Spectator* story. She had a copy hand-delivered to the hotel where Rempel and Frantz were working. It was slipped under their door on Friday morning. Then she flew to Little Rock, driving to Ferguson's house and meeting separately with his wife in an effort to get him to repudiate publicly what she saw as the most damaging element of the *Spectator* story: Clinton's alleged job offer.

Rempel and Frantz were furious; the White House still hadn't responded, and the troopers hadn't yet taken the lie detector test. They could see the White House strategy all too clearly: stall, and if the story couldn't be killed, make sure the *Times* was scooped by the right-wing, easily discredited *Spectator*. But when their complaints reached Coffey, he said, "We'll go when we're ready. We will not be rushed by the *Spectator*." Indeed, he further ordered that the troopers' affidavits be produced for Gergen, and said he wanted the White House to have time to respond. With that, he left for a skiing vacation in Snowmass, Colorado.

In Little Rock, Jackson was undergoing what he considered the worst week of his life. He despaired about the *L.A. Times*. Then CNN and ABC called: both networks had copies of the *Spectator* article. CNN correspondent Matt Saal flew to Little Rock Friday night. Jackson met him at his hotel at midnight, begging him to hold off. "These reporters have gone to the wall to do this story, and they don't deserve to be scooped," Jackson argued. He finally reached an agreement giving Saal all the access to the troopers he wanted the next day in return for a promise they wouldn't run the footage before the *L.A. Times* story broke. He made the same agreement with ABC. But obviously the story was leaking, and time was running out. On Sunday morning Jackson called Rempel and Frantz. He said he'd done everything he could, but he couldn't hold out for them any longer. He called Brock to authorize him to go ahead with publicity for his story.

That afternoon, about 3:30, Frantz was hosting a Christmas party for his children when he got a call from Mark Gearan at the White House. Rempel and he should come in at 6:30 P.M., Gearan said, and they'd get their questions answered. That wasn't so bad, the reporters figured. If they could wrap everything up by 8:30, the piece could run in Monday's paper, at least tying the *Spectator*. When they arrived at the appointed time, they were seated in the lobby area of the West Wing, near a Christmas tree decorated with Razorback ornaments. Gergen came out to say hello, and asked them to be patient; they'd be right with them. They waited an hour. Then they were ushered into a room where Lindsey, Nussbaum, one of his assistants, Dee Dee Myers, and Gergen were waiting. The reporters handed over the promised affidavits, and the White House people questioned them at length about their methods and sourcing. The reporters described at length the corroboration they'd obtained. Lindsey said they wanted to look over the affidavits, then they'd get back to them. Rempel and Frantz went back to the lobby to wait, expecting the next step would be a meeting with the president. At one point Gergen came out. He said it was so embarrassing to be discussing this with the first lady.

As the White House aides examined the affidavits, Lindsey immediately spotted what he claimed were several demonstrable errors. Obviously, they felt, people like the troopers had no credibility, but the reporters seemed to think they had enough "sources." The White House would be wasting its time trying to demonstrate the troopers had lied. For everything they knocked down, the paper would just run with something else. The situation reminded Nussbaum of a recent encounter with a reporter, who, when told he had a story all wrong, responded, "But Bernie, this story's too good to check." It had been a joke, but within the increasingly cynical White House it rang true.

There was never any chance that Rempel and Frantz would be allowed to meet with Clinton. The strategy to ignore the allegations was firmly in place, and nothing the reporters had raised had led anyone to challenge it.

An hour later, the reporters were summoned again. This time only Lindsey and Nussbaum, now in his shirtsleeves, remained. They handed the reporters a single written statement, the same response that they'd given the AP that afternoon when it had called with questions, having also gotten a copy of the *Spectator* story. "These allegations are ridiculous," the statement read. "Similar charges were made, investigated, and responded to during the campaign. There is nothing that dignifies a further response."

Rempel and Frantz were stunned and disappointed. "That's all we're going to say," Lindsey insisted. The reporters pressed for a few more answers, and Lindsey did deny that Clinton offered anyone a job in return for silence. He conceded that calls had been made to Ferguson—"there was nothing inappropriate or improper about any of those conversations," he said. He insisted that "any suggestion that the president offered anyone a job in return for silence is a lie. . . . My understanding is that the president did not offer [Ferguson] a job." Then Lindsey said, "It's time for you to leave."

As they were walking out, Lindsey seemed unable to contain himself. He said Rempel and Frantz were "irresponsible," "full of big allegations with little response." Angered, Frantz shot back, "Why would the president call a woman in the middle of the night?" Suddenly Lindsey grabbed the reporters and hurried them to the exit. "I think we've just been thrown out of the White House," Rempel said to Frantz.

It was almost midnight. They rushed back to the bureau and called Los Angeles, where two national editors were waiting. "Let's go," they said. There was still time to get the piece in Monday's paper. The editors there said they'd have to call Coffey in Snowmass—the first the reporters knew he was on vacation. The reporters waited anxiously, then national editor Mike Miller called them. "Shelby doesn't want to go with it tonight," he said. "We want to look at it on Monday, go over it one more time."

Both Rempel and Frantz were furious, but it was Frantz who spoke out. "Mike, do what you want. But I'm not working at this paper. I won't work at a place that treats its reporters like this." But Miller persuaded him to stay at least until the story was over.

Even as Rempel and Frantz were leaving the White House, the *American Spectator* issued a press release touting Brock's eleven-thousand-word article in its January issue. It was the magazine's cover story, emblazoned with the headline "His Cheatin' Heart" and a cartoon drawing of Clinton, his clothes disheveled, carrying his shoes through the night. CNN began running the story, using the exclusive footage of the troopers it had gotten through Jackson.

Most of the media plunged into intense debate about whether, and how, to deal with the story. The *Wall Street Journal*, after vigorous discussion, ignored the story. Consistent with the policy on sex that it had applied to Gennifer Flowers, the *New York Times* made a brief mention deep inside the paper. "The *New York Times* is not a supermarket tabloid," bureau chief R. W. Apple told the newsletter *Political Hotline*. But others reached different conclusions, both to satisfy public curiosity and out of a sense that the troopers had raised more serious questions and had more credibility than Flowers did. ABC and NBC, but not CBS, aired the story Monday night. ABC's anchor Peter Jennings said, "We struggled all day with this," but "character and judgment are always an issue." Tuesday morning, the *Washington Post* ran a story on its front page, focusing on Clinton's calls to Ferguson. The tabloids and talk shows predictably went wild, with Brock appearing on Rush Limbaugh's radio show and on CNN's *Crossfire*.

Finally, on Tuesday morning, the *L.A. Times* ran Rempel and Frantz's piece, even though the once essential lie detector test had never been performed. Its editorial agonizing was evident. The story opened on the front page, but at the bottom right-hand corner, not the coveted lead space on the upper right side of the page or the "Column One" space usually reserved for long features and investigative pieces. The headline gave little indication of the story's content: "Troopers Say Clinton Sought Silence on Personal Affairs," followed in boldface type by "The White House calls their allegations 'ridiculous.' " Even before any details, in several paragraphs inserted by editors, the paper reported that "Allegations about the personal lives of Presidents are not new," and proceeded to exhume reports that Thomas Jefferson had "an intimate relationship with one of his slaves."

At the White House, the president remained silent, leaving an avalanche of questions to Dee Dee Myers and Lindsey. The daily press briefings were canceled on both Monday and Tuesday. All three major networks had Christmas week interviews scheduled that day with the first lady. All canceled after being told they could only ask questions about Christmas at the White House—"about the crafts and the ornaments and what kind of entertainment the Clintons were having," as spokeswoman Lisa Caputo put it. But in a previously scheduled interview with the Associated Press, Hillary lashed out, coming to the defense of her husband. "I find it not an accident that every time he is on the verge of fulfilling his commitment to the American people and they respond . . . out comes yet a new round of these outrageous, terrible stories that people plant for political and financial reasons. . . . For me, it's pretty sad that we're still subjected to these kinds of attacks for political and financial gain from people, and that it is sad that—especially here in the Christmas season—people for their own purposes would be attacking my family. . . . I think sometimes everybody forgets that, even if public figures don't have any protection from these kinds of attacks, you still have feelings."

Still, under pressure from persistent questions, Lindsey was forced to issue more detailed denials and explanations for the calls from the president to the troopers. He told the *Washington Post* that after "receiving information" that the troopers were being offered money for their stories, "President Clinton expressed disbelief and asked why they would do something like this. The trooper with whom he [the president] spoke said that at least one trooper, Perry, was unhappy because he had written to the president asking for a federal position and had received no response. The president had subsequent conversations with other troopers who were also concerned about this matter."

Lindsey was also busy orchestrating damage control. ABC producer Chris Vlasto had arranged an on-camera interview with Buddy Young, with a camera crew in Young's office in Denton, Texas, while Vlasto asked questions over the phone from Little Rock. The interview was proceeding uneventfully, with Young insisting that the troopers couldn't be believed, when Vlasto heard a phone ring in Young's office. "Hold on a second, I've got another phone call," Young said, putting Vlasto on hold. Vlasto waited about forty-five seconds, then Young got back on the line.

"Who was that?" Vlasto asked.

"CNN wants to talk to me," Young answered.

"I'm glad you're talking to me and not them," Vlasto said, half-seriously.

The cameraman sent the footage by Federal Express to Vlasto. When he began editing it the next morning, he noticed that the tape had recorded the phone call Young received while Vlasto was on hold. Vlasto listened in amazement.

"Buddy?"

"Bruce. Yeah," Young said, as Vlasto heard Bruce Lindsey's voice—not CNN. Vlasto turned to a colleague. "My God, we've got the White House on here." The tape continued:

"What do you know?" Lindsey asked.

"I am on the phone right now in the middle of an interview."

"With who?"

"ABC." Young turned to the cameraman. "Is that right?"

"Okay," Lindsey continued. "We need you to do CNN at some point. Will you call me? Will you have them page me after you get off?"

"Have . . ."

"Call the White House and ask them to page me while you hold or have me call you right back."

"Okay . . ."

"Thanks."

Vlasto was amazed that a top aide to the president was apparently orchestrating Young's TV appearances. ABC News executives hadn't been sure they would even run the story, but when they realized how involved the White House was in controlling the story, they decided to air the segment.

Wright's efforts in Little Rock also helped the White House contain the story. Though she never succeeded in getting Ferguson to issue an affidavit, she persuaded Ferguson's lawyer, Robert Batton, to issue a sworn statement on Ferguson's behalf. "President Clinton never offered or indicated a willingness to offer any trooper a job in exchange for silence or help in shaping their stories." The statement seemed carefully crafted to enable Ferguson both to honor his pledge to do nothing to repudiate his promises to Perry and the *L.A. Times* reporters, and to help the president out of an awkward spot. For the statement didn't deny that the president had offered jobs, only that jobs had been offered "in exchange" for silence. In Ferguson's earlier recountings of the conversation, both to Perry and to the *Times* reporters, such an exchange had never been explicit. It was simply an implication, however obvious.

But the statement was tremendously effective at blunting the impact of the stories. ABC News led with it as a "denial." And once Ferguson was reported as denying a critical element of the stories, the credibility of all the allegations came into question. Only then did Clinton respond to the stories, denying that he abused his office by offering jobs for silence, and saying, "I don't have anything to add to what's been said. I think what I should do is keep working, doing the best I can at my job." Inside the White House, Nussbaum and others among the group that had dealt with the trooper situation were pleased and relieved.

Inevitably, the troopers themselves came under attack, as reports surfaced of Perry's and Patterson's efforts to collect on an insurance policy by giving false testimony about the car accident in 1990. "I did not tell the truth," Patterson confessed to the *New York Times.* "I was in fear of my job. That happened in 1990. I have not lied about anything in this. I have told the truth. Bill Clinton knows it." At a press conference, Perry said, "I'm scared to death. Larry is scared to death. I've never felt so alone in all my life."

Having devoted months to getting the troopers' story out, Cliff Jackson felt dismayed now that his goal had been achieved, genuinely pained by the tone of the *Spectator* story and the tabloid-style reactions by much of the press. Hillary, in her comments to the Associated Press, had singled out Jackson as "obsessed" with the president; others in the White House described him as "right-wing," engaged in a "personal vendetta." The charges stung. He wrote a lengthy letter to the president. At once high-minded, presumptuous, and apologetic, the letter is a window into Jackson's state of mind. After saying he had acted in what he believed to be the best interest of both Clinton and the country, he continued:

"My hope—dare I say expectation—is that you will genuinely change. I know you are capable of change. We all are. If you change and assert moral leadership, America will follow you, and I believe that you will then have the potential to be one of the most effective presidents this country has known.

"Lest I be misinterpreted, let me make clear that when I say change, I am not talking about any sexual peccadilloes. They are the symptom, not the disease. I am not judging you. I am not condemning you. I am not casting stones.

"It is much more fundamental than mere sex. I am talking about your fundamental nature—seemingly in-bred and long polished—and your casual willingness to deceive, to exploit and to manipulate in order to attain personal and political power. I am talking about your willingness to compromise principle until there is no longer any principle left to compromise. I am talking about your expectation that others around you practice these same traits to cover up for you.

"Without trust and integrity, there can be no covenant, new or otherwise, between the government and the governed. There can be only a perpetuation of the current pandemic distrust and cynicism which even now eats like a cancer at the very fabric of our society.

"I know, Bill, that you know what I'm talking about. You said something similar to me years ago. You understand when I speak in terms of a rebirth, a renaissance of the American spirit leading to a renewal of old, traditional, American values.

"You know that I believe in these values not because they are old but because they are timeless; not because they are traditional but because they are true; not because they are American but because they are universal. Moreover, these values are not the exclusive domain of either the Republican or Democratic parties, nor of either the political left or political right. Universal values are ideologically neutral. . . ."

Jackson concluded with these paragraphs:

"I trust you will hear what I am saying and respond in the spirit in which I say it. I feel for your pain and that of your family. Forgive my role as an attorney for the troopers (a role which I did not seek and undertook only with great trepidation when the truth of their allegations became apparent) in inflicting such public pain on you and yours.

"Let us hope and pray, however, that good and truth will ultimately triumph . . . that you will lead this country into a bright new era of change, and that a renaissance of the spirit, beginning with and led by you, will sweep across our people and propel a reinvigorated America into the 21st century.

"Your friend (still),

"Cliff Jackson."

There was no reply.

"Troopergate," as it was quickly dubbed, was eclipsed even before it had exhausted the national media's attention span. The Monday the trooper story broke, the *Washington Times* and the *New York Times* both reported that Whitewater files had been removed from Vince Foster's office the day after his death. The *Washington Post* had reported the previous week that a Park Police investigator had seen "paperwork" mentioning McDougal among the materials removed from Foster's office and turned over to the Foster family's lawyer, James Hamilton. With the latest disclosures, the *New York Times* editorial page called for a congressional investigation; "The Arkansas savings and loan mess, and the Clintons' relationship to it," the lead editorial read, "is not as the White House keeps saying an 'old' story that has no relevance to Mr. Clinton or his present job."

Indeed, the White House had become progressively upset with the *Times* since Howell Raines, the former Washington bureau chief who oversaw Gerth, had taken over the editorial page after the election. His predecessor, Jack Rosenthal, had been reliably supportive of Clinton; now, beginning with the travel office pieces, the page was often sharply critical of the president. Dark intimations continued to emanate from the White House staff that Raines, roughly the same age as Clinton and a Southerner, suffered from some deep-seated resentment of the fact that Clinton was president rather than himself, intimations that Raines heard repeatedly and brushed aside. The Clintons were sufficiently concerned that McLarty had come to visit Raines, saying he was "surprised" at some of Raines's editorials. Raines explained that it was simply that much of his career as a journalist had focused on issues of clean government, full disclosure, and the notion that in a democracy information belongs to the people, not the government. These principles he was determined to apply to Democrats and Republicans alike.

As the calls from the press rolled in, Myers and Gearan called Nussbaum, asking what had happened during the search of Foster's office. Nussbaum was indignant at the notion that some files were "missing." "There's nothing missing," he insisted. "We did send files over to Williams & Connolly," the Clintons' personal law firm, he said, but he didn't know what files there were, or whether there was a Whitewater file. "There might have been," he said. He hadn't been paying any attention to Whitewater at the time of Foster's death.

Since then, however, the Whitewater files had been much on the minds of White House officials. After the story had reappeared the first week in November, and after Hale's allegations surfaced, it was belatedly recognized that the Clintons needed a lawyer outside the White House counsel's office to handle Whitewater. Robert Barnett, their usual lawyer at Williams & Connolly, stepped aside because his wife was assigned to cover the White House for CBS, and the Clintons chose David Kendall, one of Barnett's partners, to replace him. On November 5, the Friday after the series of front-page *Post* stories, Kendall had met with Nussbaum; Lindsey; Bill Kennedy; Denver lawyer Jim Lyons, author of the Whitewater campaign report; and Steve Engstrom, a Little Rock lawyer retained by the Clintons as local counsel for everything from Whitewater to the trooper allegations. Kennedy kept notes of the meeting, which begin:

"1. Gather the facts
"2. Try to find out what's going on in investigation
"3. Respond to requests that are made
"4. Strategy for dealing with the media—one person."

Though the notes are cryptic, written in abbreviations and a kind of shorthand, and don't identify the speaker, they suggest that the White House counsel's office was becoming deeply involved in Whitewater-related issues. One notation reads: "Vacuum Rose Law files WWDC Docs—subpoena" followed by an under-scored entry: "*Documents—never know go out Quietly (?)"

The next week Hubbell had had lunch with Kendall to add his perspective, and he handed over three files of Whitewater materials he'd removed from the Rose firm (the files dealt with Hillary's work for Madison Guaranty regarding the preferred stock issue). Kendall, recognizing the files as the Rose firm's property, returned them to the firm. Hubbell also mentioned the documents in his basement that he and Foster had gone over the month before Foster's death. Kendall had a Williams & Connolly van pick those up. (They remain in Kendall's possession.)

So at this point, all the documents the administration had in its possession had purportedly been turned over to Kendall. Nussbaum emphasized that nothing had disappeared or been destroyed. But that distinction was being lost on the media. After talking to Nussbaum, Myers and Gearan spoke to Kendall, who confirmed that there were, indeed, Whitewater files removed from Foster's office. So Myers asked Nussbaum to draft a statement, which he cleared with Lindsey. It said simply that no files were missing, that Whitewater files and other materials belonging to the Clintons had been turned over to their lawyers at Williams & Connolly. The statement was released, and Nussbaum thought that would be the end of it.

Instead, there was a media explosion, much of it focusing on the White House's failure until now to mention the removed files, which gave everything an air of mystery. Peter Jennings led the *ABC World News Tonight* with the pronouncement that "Last night, the White House said that some documents were removed from Mr. Foster's office before investigators had a chance to look at them." Virtually every major newspaper carried the story on its front page. The mystery of what was in the papers naturally stoked curiosity. Editorial pages clamored for public release of the files. Nussbaum was horrified by the reaction. He sensed that all the media that had hesitated over the trooper story were playing the latest Whitewater story with a vengeance.

Amidst the uproar, Nussbaum, his assistant Joel Klein, and Kendall discussed whether to go ahead and turn the documents over. But then they learned the Justice Department was about to subpoena them anyway. At Heymann's direction, the department had begun an investigation of Foster's death after Foster's note was revealed accusing the FBI of lying. It was also examining the RTC's criminal referrals. Now the White House thought the investigations gave it an out: the Clintons could turn the documents over to Justice, demonstrating they had nothing to hide, but invoke their right to privacy and refuse to make them public. Both Hillary and Bill Clinton remained strongly opposed to making anything public. As the first lady put it in one meeting, "We're cooperating fully, we're not claiming any privileges, it's enough. We're the president." So the White House announced on Christmas Eve that the president had instructed his lawyer David Kendall to make the Whitewater documents available to the Justice Department in response to a subpoena, but not Congress or the public. "Most people would grant that any president maintains the right to have his personal documents private," a White House official said.

The Clintons spent Christmas Day in the White House, then left for Arkansas. It had surely been the worst week of the Clinton presidency.

The holidays brought no respite from Whitewater. The president's preoccupation with the affair was evident at that year's Renaissance Weekend, which, since Clinton's election, had burgeoned into the preeminent networking occasion for the baby boom elite.

Eugene Ludwig, an Oxford and Yale Law School friend whom Clinton had named comptroller of the currency, a post under the treasury secretary that regulates the nation's banks, was attending a seminar on international affairs when Clinton sat down in the seat next to him. Clinton wanted to know if it would be "permissible" for Ludwig to advise him on the burgeoning Whitewater affair, saying he'd lost money on the deal and hadn't done anything wrong. The conversation was brief, and Clinton soon left, but Ludwig followed up by trying to get some more information about Whitewater, and sought advice from the White House counsel's office. After a flurry of phone calls, Joel Klein, Nussbaum's deputy, who was also attending the weekend, spoke to Ludwig and told him he shouldn't have any more discussion with the president about Madison or Whitewater. Clinton was cautioned in similar terms, and agreed not to mention the subject again.

That same weekend, Representative Jim Leach of Iowa, the ranking Republican on the House Banking Committee, wrote an op-ed piece in the *Washington Post*. After briefly reviewing the known facts about Whitewater and Madison, Leach wrote, "The dilemma we now confront is how society pursues and what society does about possible wrongdoing committed by a president prior to his taking office. . . . The dilemma of the Justice Department is self-evident. The attorney general is the chief law enforcement officer of the United States and the chief legal advisor to the president. She cannot credibly fulfill her obligations to the president and at the same time direct her department in a forthcoming investigation embarrassing to him. Accordingly, the case for designating a special counsel has seldom been more compelling." The appeal from Leach was especially effective, because Leach had a long-standing reputation as moderate, even-keeled, even nonpartisan. As Tom Harkin, Iowa's Democratic senator and a strong supporter of Clinton, put it, "When Jim Leach does something like this, it has a serious tone, and it can't be dismissed lightly. . . . I just don't understand why the White House just doesn't say, 'Okay, fine.' "

The congressional drumbeat had begun the previous week, in the immediate aftermath of news of the removal of the files. Senator Alfonse D'Amato of New York, the ranking Republican on the Banking Committee, and Senate Minority Leader Bob Dole had called for hearings. In a letter to Attorney General Reno, Leach had first broached the possibility of a special counsel, but Reno had resisted. The statute authorizing appointment of an independent counsel—the legislation growing out of the appointment of a special prosecutor in the Watergate scandal—had expired and hadn't yet been renewed, in part due to Republican ire over the protracted investigation of both Presidents Reagan and Bush by Lawrence Walsh, the independent counsel for the Iran-contra scandal. Reno had argued that if she appointed a special prosecutor, it would be little better than using the career Justice Department officials already investigating the case. "Anyone she appoints, the prosecutor is under her supervision and influence," said department spokesman Carl Stern.

While technically correct, the argument ignored historical precedent: the special prosecutor had become such a visible fixture in law enforcement that any interference from an attorney general would trigger an uproar. Still, it enabled Reno to sidestep the politically charged subject. When Nussbaum returned from his annual holiday trip to Puerto Rico, he was dismayed by all the talk about a special prosecutor. Having lived through Watergate, he was determined to prevent anything similar from afflicting the Clinton presidency. As he told Joel Klein, "I'll tell you, I will vehemently oppose any independent counsel. The Clintons have done nothing wrong. The independent counsel is an evil institution. It is designed to find things."

The White House was so consumed by the latest developments that Clinton decided to convene a cabinet-level strategy meeting for dealing with Whitewater. Despite the earlier warnings about contacts with the Treasury, Secretary Bentsen was invited, but recognizing the possible conflict with his role as overseer of the RTC, he declined to attend. The invitation, however, had triggered a conversation with his deputy, Roger Altman, who summarized it in a diary he was keeping.

"—LMB [Bentsen] called me in yesterday to discuss it [Whitewater]; as usual, his judgment is superb; the situation requires a 'cut your losses' strategy, tells me he did that during the 'Breakfast Club' imbroglio [the story that Gerth had earlier written involving Bentsen's meetings with lobbyists]; talked about Nixon's incredible failure to cut his losses; about the press getting 'too invested' in a situation and deciding itself to bring someone down.

"—he had been asked to come to W.H. [White House] to speak to President about Whitewater . . . but Christine Varney [a Treasury aide] rushed over to urge him not to do it . . . he took that advice."

But Bentsen did meet with Stephanopoulos in early January to discuss "the press frenzy that was taking place over Whitewater," as Bentsen later testified. He told Stephanopoulos point-blank that, while he knew nothing about the facts of Whitewater, "it was important that they open up to the press any of the facts and to get the subject behind them." Altman's diary entry for January 4 notes that Bentsen told the White House it had to "lance the boil" on Whitewater. (Stephanopoulos later said he had no recollection of any such meeting with Bentsen or having received that advice.)

Elsewhere in the White House, the mood was captured by Altman's entries during the first two weeks in January:

"Sadly, the Whitewater affair is exploding into a press frenzy. It's mostly a testimony to the press mania and crazed world of Washington. . . .

"This Whitewater situation is one big mess. Administration perceived as stonewalling; 'there must be something to hide.' Big issue is independent prosecutor. Lots of speculation that HRC [the first lady] is the one who handled this in Arkansas. . . . W.H. seems engulfed in this and [is] mishandling it, for the President's lawyer to persuade DOJ [Department of Justice] to issue a subpoena for the documents, so they won't be subject to FOIA [Freedom of Information Act requests], looks very weak. . . .

"On Whitewater, Maggie [Williams], told me that HRC was 'paralyzed' by it. If we don't solve this 'within the next two days,' you don't have to worry about her schedule on health care."

Concern in the White House that Whitewater was derailing the president's legislative agenda was such that McLarty created a "Whitewater Response Team," as he later called it, "basically to deal with the plethora of issues that would come up, primarily on a press basis, regarding matters relating to Madison and Whitewater." He added that "It was publicly discussed that these types of personal allegations . . . could be distracting from a productive legislative agenda . . . that was one reason the White House response team was formed—to deal with these types of matters." Heading the team was Harold Ickes, the New York lawyer who'd recently joined the White House as deputy chief of staff. On the team were Nussbaum, Lindsey, Williams, Stephanopoulos, Gearan, Lisa Caputo, and Neil Eggleston, another lawyer in Nussbaum's office. John Podesta, staff secretary, later was added. Conspicuously absent was David Gergen.

Even the death of Clinton's mother, Virginia, on January 6, brought no reprieve. As the president flew to Arkansas for his mother's funeral, Republicans renewed their calls for hearings and an appointment of a special prosecutor. Gergen went on the *Today* show, asking "as the president goes home to bury his mother, to have the political opposition on the warpath, hammering away, rais[es] all sorts of questions about what has happened in this town. Where is the decency? There is a cannibalism loose in our society in which public figures, such as the Clintons, could try to come to this town to do something good for the country and then they get hammered away."

On January 10, Clinton left for a state visit to Russia, the Baltic states, and Ukraine, his first since becoming president. His aides hoped fervently that his diplomacy in such an important, volatile part of the world would sweep Whitewater off the front pages and news broadcasts. But with the *Washington Post*, its vow to Gergen still fresh, setting the pace, the story continued unabated. The day after the president's departure, the *Post*'s lead editorial blasted the administration, referring to "a gaggle of spinners and legal advisors whose only success thus far is to have managed by word and deed to make it appear as if the Clintons have something to hide." The editorial concluded that "The need for the current probe to be turned over to someone independent of the administration is overwhelming." Even Democrats began echoing the call for an independent investigation, not, they said, because they believed the president had done anything wrong, but because the facts needed to be aired.

At a news conference with Ukraine president Leonid Kravchuk on the evening of January 11, reporters pelted the president with questions about Whitewater and about the recent Democratic calls for an independent investigation. "I have nothing to say about that on this trip," he replied, furious that Whitewater had followed him to Europe. Earlier that day, when an NBC News reporter, in an interview, had asked Clinton about Whitewater, Clinton had stood up and turned off the reporter's microphone. "You had your two questions," he said. "I'm sorry you're not interested in the trip." CBS anchor Dan Rather, in Moscow, intoned that "a cloud has followed Mr. Clinton this entire trip."

At the White House, the Whitewater Response Team hurriedly convened in the Oval Office, along with Hillary and the Clintons' lawyer, David Kendall. The issue of an independent counsel, or special prosecutor, had dominated meetings and conversations around the White House all week. Thus far, Nussbaum's opposition—strongly echoed by the first lady—had prevailed, but an opposing camp, eager to propitiate the media in Nussbaum's view, had emerged, led by Stephanopoulos. As the political and media cries escalated, this group grew more insistent. Finally, after the press conference in Ukraine, Clinton told them he wanted the issue resolved.

Ickes served as a moderator. Stephanopoulos agreed to make the argument for the appointment of an independent counsel, Nussbaum would argue against it. Even at this juncture, no one involved in the decision actually knew what the Whitewater documents contained except Kendall and the Clintons. With the possible exception of Lindsey, no one else really knew what had happened in Whitewater; they simply accepted, without question, the Clintons' assertions that they had done nothing wrong.

The president got on the speakerphone; it was evening in Washington, about 2 A.M. in Europe. The evening broadcasts had all showed the president rebuffing Whitewater questions. Stephanopoulos began, warning that "they'll keep hounding us" unless an independent counsel took over the investigation. He'd prepared a study of all the prior special prosecutors and independent counsels, demonstrating that many of the investigations hadn't resulted in any indictments. He particularly emphasized the investigation of President Carter and his brother, Billy, over their involvement in a peanut warehouse. The independent counsel, Paul Curran, had concluded the investigation in six months. No one had been charged. "You've done nothing wrong," Stephanopoulos emphasized to the president. "This will all be over in six months. Health care is coming up. Let's get this behind us."

Nussbaum's arguments took a broader perspective, emphasizing the potential damage to the institution of the presidency.

Whether the institution of an independent counsel is good or bad, he said, it is wrong to unleash such an investigation when there has been no credible evidence of wrongdoing. A media outcry, a lot of "smoke," as he put it, should not be the threshold, or it would become the standard for future presidents and future investigations.

More important, however, Nussbaum argued that Clinton had to better understand the nature of the institution of an independent counsel or special prosecutor. "I lived this in Watergate," he reminded them. The institution of the independent counsel "is evil," he said. "Not because of the people, but no matter how saintly they are, there is enormous pressure to come up with something. It's designed to ferret things out. It's dangerous. It has a dynamic. You must understand this." Nussbaum said that the Carter investigation gave him little reassurance. It had only tangentially involved the president. The only other one that did—Iran-contra—had dragged on for seven years.

"You did nothing wrong in Whitewater that I know of," Nussbaum continued. "What this does, the frustration of finding nothing in Whitewater will make them investigate every one of your friends. Mr. President, I don't know what happened in Arkansas in the last twenty years, but I can't believe some of your friends did nothing wrong. Somebody did something wrong. They will broaden [the investigation] to areas we haven't even contemplated."

At this point, Nussbaum was getting emotional. Others started interrupting him. "But this is about Whitewater," someone called out. "No," Nussbaum replied. "This will be a roving searchlight." He looked around the room, stopping for some reason at Lindsey. "Mr. President, one year from now Bruce Lindsey will be under investigation. They will chase you, your family and friends, through your presidency and beyond."

"Look," Stephanopoulos interrupted. "Bernie is getting hysterical. Janet Reno is a good person. She'll appoint a fair person." Then, when legislation extending the independent counsel law was passed, as was expected, the court would simply reappoint that person, Stephanopoulos said.

Nussbaum could feel himself becoming even more agitated. "I'm not sure the court will appoint the same person," he said.

"That's crazy," someone said, as conversation broke out in the room. Nussbaum had to retreat, "Okay, it's fifty-fifty they'll reappoint the same counsel. But it's not automatic. And, no matter who it is, the dynamic is there, and it's terrible."

Finally Clinton himself interrupted, practically screaming at Nussbaum over the speaker phone. "So what do you suggest I do to stop this thing? I'm in Russia and they ask me about Whitewater. I cannot take this. You're telling me all these dangers, so what can you do? We can't get health care hearings, we can't pass a bill . . ."

"Mr. President, I'll tell you," Nussbaum replied. "If you feel we can't function, this is not the answer." Suddenly Nussbaum realized that Gergen had been right—they should have turned over all the documents when the *Post* asked for them. "If it's that serious, we should release every document we have. Demand congressional hearings within thirty days. You and the first lady should offer to go down and testify. Congress is not an independent counsel. It's not twenty-five prosecutors and a hundred FBI agents. Give the papers to the press and to Congress and ask for a hearing on Whitewater!"

A hubbub broke out. "What?" Clinton shouted. "That is crazy. Do you know what the publicity would be?"

"I'd rather deal with publicity than an independent counsel," Nussbaum continued, even though others were muttering. "It will only momentarily calm this down. You'll have congressional hearings in any event."

Nussbaum had lost virtually everyone at this point. Hillary rose to calm the group. "Mr. President," she said, "let me summarize what George and Bernie have been saying." After briefly doing so, she said, "You've heard everything." Everyone waited expectantly for a decision, but from the president there was silence. "I'll sleep on it," he finally said. Hillary turned to the group. "Everyone please leave the room except David Kendall and me."

As they filed out, Lindsey turned to Nussbaum. "Why did you mention me?" he asked.

"I just meant they'll chase his friends," Nussbaum said. "You're his best friend." Lindsey shrugged and moved on.

Nussbaum went back to his office and closed the door. He was as upset as he'd been since Foster's death. The president's words, "I cannot take this," reverberated. He couldn't help but wonder how Foster would have reacted if he were alive. Surely Foster would have backed him on the special counsel. Then again, he might have folded under the stress. The travel office affair seemed tame compared to this.

The next day, Stephanopoulos announced that the president had decided to ask for the appointment of a special counsel. "In view of the gravity of the president's responsibilities and the need for a speedy and credible resolution here, the president requests that this investigation be conducted as expeditiously as possible," Stephanopoulos told reporters.

Nussbaum couldn't get past the gravity of the decision. Whatever had happened so far, the investigation of Whitewater and related issues had remained under the overall direction of the executive branch and the president. Now it was out of the Clintons' control. They didn't seem to realize what they'd given up.

That morning, Hillary came into Nussbaum's office. "Bernie, I don't want you to be upset. You made your point, you made it well, you impressed the president. You were great." As they talked, it was obvious to Nussbaum that he'd not only lost the argument. He'd probably lost a lot of credibility as well. Nussbaum knew what others in the White House would say: he was hysterical, naive, a tough litigator with no political sense. He'd already heard these things.

"He just believes he has no choice," the first lady continued, trying to explain the president's decision. "If he's going to get on with his agenda, he has to appoint the special counsel."

Nussbaum shook his head. "I just think this is a tragic error," he said.

FOURTEEN

EVER SINCE FLIPPIN, Arkansas, was founded in the late-nineteenth century, a highlight of the year has been the annual Turkey Trot just before Thanksgiving. Originally, wild turkeys had been dropped from the courthouse roof as local citizens scrambled to catch one for their Thanksgiving dinner, but since World War II the turkeys had been dropped from a low-flying plane. Accompanied by the crowning of Miss Drumstick—in those years when there are enough teenage girls to serve as contestants—the Turkey Trot was something of a homecoming, where Flippin natives could count on meeting just about everyone in the county. It was the town's main claim to fame, as people put it—at least until 1994, when the national press descended.

The media calls had started in November, but it was only in January, after the revelations of the files removed from Foster's office and the calls for the special counsel, that the town found itself inundated by representatives of the media. The media activity was so intense that news organizations sent reporters who had no idea what the story would be—they were simply under orders to send something back. The *New York Times* alone had sent three reporters to Flippin—Michael Kelly and Engelberg, now followed by Gerth. They and other reporters settled in at the Red Raven Inn, a large Victorian house with seven guest rooms, and other area motels and guest houses. Usually occupied only intermittently by small-mouth-bass fishermen headed for the White River, the Red Raven was now fully booked, two reporters per room. They made the trek between the inn and the local courthouse, returning with armloads of documents. One evening Gerth entertained everyone with a medley of Gershwin tunes on the piano.

Business boomed at the nearby Front Porch restaurant, where crews from as far away as Europe, China, and Japan, along with their translators, dined on the all-you-can-eat $4.95 Bar-B-Q buffet. Local entrepreneurs cashed in by offering guided tours of the hard-to-find Whitewater property for $50.

One morning Chris Wade walked into his modest real estate office and found reporters from CBS, CNN, *Time*, a St. Louis paper, and a Japanese network waiting for him. "Take a number," he told them, adding, "This isn't where the story is. This is just a bunch of land." But with all the media attention, he dreamed up a scheme to capitalize on the remaining lots he owned. He took one of the least desirable of the undeveloped Whitewater lots and began selling "dirt deeds"—ownership of one cubic foot—for $19.95. Little Rock radio station 103.7 K-ROCK launched a contest in which listeners could win the dirt deeds, complete with the signatures of Jim and Susan McDougal. Wade got over fifty requests for interviews and was suddenly featured on radio call-in shows and articles. McDougal himself appeared on *Larry King Live* and plugged the deeds, leading to hundreds of sales. Some deed buyers drove cross-country to Flippin to have Wade take their picture digging up their foot of dirt at the Whitewater property.

At the courthouse, county clerk Mary Jo Layton and her three assistants were swamped with reporters' requests, but they welcomed the diversion from looking up marriage records, which usually took up most of their time. All the real estate records, dating to 1887, when a fire had destroyed the old courthouse, were kept in a vault; a computer had only been recently introduced to coordinate driver's licenses with voter registrations. When she realized how much interest there was in Whitewater, Layton brought a rock from the Whitewater property, painted "Whitewater" on its side, and used it as a paperweight in the office. She thought she might sell a few, but found no takers.

Despite the media attention, Layton was at a loss to figure out what was so interesting in the Whitewater records, which she'd looked over many times herself. Finally she asked a reporter, "What are you all thinking you're going to find?"

"Well," the reporter replied, "if that Madison Bank up in

Huntsville, if they were defrauding people and the government, then that's important."

"Oh well, whatever." Layton shrugged.

Flippin's population was solidly pro-Clinton, proud of a native son who owned land nearby. Layton, like many residents, had actually met Clinton, and she liked him. Still, local residents welcomed the media folk with open arms; they were slow to connect them with stories that were not only damaging to the president, but conveyed a distinctly negative impression of Flippin and Arkansas. The Red Raven's owner, Cam Semelsberger, was delighted by all the excitement. Cam's husband loved discussing national issues with the visiting Washington press corps. He was keenly interested in the proposed health care legislation, and had obtained copies of the competing plans, including the first lady's massive reform proposal. After a lively debate between Semelsberger and the local pharmacist, *Times* reporter Michael Kelly joked that people in Washington rarely talked about big policy issues. "We only talk about gossip," he told Semelsberger.

At the even more remote Whitewater development itself, John and Marilyn Lauramoore lived in the modest modular home now known nationwide as the Hillary house. He built log homes for a living, and she sewed sails at a nearby sailboat factory. They'd moved to Whitewater to get away from the "stress" of Atlanta, and they liked the quiet, remote location. Still, they were initially flattered by reporters wanting to take pictures of them in front of their home. But more and more reporters and TV crews started appearing on the doorstep, often demanding answers to questions having to do with Whitewater's financing. The Lauramoores knew nothing about it, but they felt the reporters acted like they were hiding something. Worse, at least one helicopter a day was making a low pass over their house, whipping up a fierce wind and droning like something out of war movies like *Apocalypse Now*. (It was on the Lauramoores' lawn that Bossie and Silverman had been forced to land their helicopter.) Tourists, complete strangers, started pulling into their driveway. The Lauramoores finally strung up a six-by-ten-foot canvas banner on which they painted the message "Go home, idiots!"

For reporters unwilling or unable to make the trek to Flippin, Brown and Bossie's office at Citizens United was the next best thing. Having already done all the legwork in Flippin himself, Bossie maintained a virtual library of original documents and other Whitewater materials, which he'd begun collecting the previous September. To save reporters time, he'd organized the materials into bound volumes by topic, each several inches thick: "WW Related Documents"; "Bill and Hillary Rodham Clinton Tax Returns"; "Lawsuits Involving Jim McDougal"; "Business Documents Associated with WW." Bossie also wrote "The Conspiracy of Silence," a twelve-page summary of Whitewater including 158 footnotes to other reference materials, and "WW/Madison," providing a basic chronology and guide to characters in the story. When reporters arrived to pick up copies of the documents, Bossie would often have lunch with them at Bravo's, a nearby Italian restaurant, using the occasion to debrief them about the stories they planned and offering to be of further help. He distributed hundreds of copies of his collected documents and had contact with nearly every reporter working on the story, keeping them up to date with his *WW* fax bulletins—three thousand copies a day at his peak.

While Brown and Bossie made no pretense of being objective about Clinton, they recognized that their influence would vanish if their information proved unreliable. It had taken months, years in some cases, to earn the trust of reporters in the mainstream media, so Bossie was scrupulously careful about accuracy. This was a lesson he'd learned from watching the Clinton administration itself. Virtually every reporter he dealt with had started out either friendly or at least neutral toward the Clintons, and skeptical, even hostile, toward him. But over time, they confided in Bossie, they had all had experiences where they felt that someone in the administration had lied to them. Bossie recognized that as reporters' trust in the Clintons declined, their trust in him increased.

Nor were Citizens United's efforts directed only at the media. Bossie was equally willing to funnel information to Congress. He had always deemed Representative Leach to be too liberal to be of much use, but after the Iowa congressman spoke out on Whitewater and led the calls for a special counsel, Bossie developed a close relationship with Leach's press secretary, Joe Pinder. He began providing Pinder with copies of newly unearthed documents even before members of the press, which allowed Leach to break news and keep the pressure on the Democratic majority on the

Banking Committee. At the same time, an announcement by Leach all but guaranteed press coverage. Pinder would also pass on tips to Bossie that the committee didn't have the resources to pursue. Bossie would do the investigation, then report back to Pinder. Bossie often felt that it was Citizens United that was partly funding the congressional investigation of Whitewater.

The widely respected Leach proved the perfect cover for disseminating Citizens United's research. Still, public recognition that Bossie was working with Leach might have so damaged the congressman's bipartisan credibility that the relationship between Bossie and Pinder was shrouded in secrecy; it isn't clear that Leach himself knew the source of all the information Pinder generated. Pinder charged calls from the office to his home phone credit card; he borrowed other fax machines. Bossie would hand over documents at obscure restaurants, like the L&M restaurant in Pentagon City. When someone else answered their phone calls, they always used only their first names and never left messages or phone numbers.

While Leach was usually the preferred congressional outlet for their research, Brown and Bossie didn't want to be taken for granted, and would sometimes leak choice items to senators Lauch Faircloth (R.-N.C.) and Alfonse D'Amato (R.-N.Y.), whose Senate Banking Committee was also calling for Whitewater investigations. CU's information wasn't only aimed at the Clintons. When Arkansas senator David Pryor, a staunch Clinton ally, tried to defend the president on the Senate floor—going so far as to describe Citizens United as a "poison factory"—Bossie hit back with faxes to 2,500 media outlets alleging that Pryor had once intervened to secure a state job for Patsy Thomasson, now a figure of controversy for having been in Foster's office the night he died. The counterattack served not only as retaliation for Pryor, but as a warning to any legislator who might be thinking of coming to the Clintons' defense.

But it was with the national media that CU continued to find its greatest success, taking credit for originating or providing significant research for stories in *Money*, *U.S. News & World Report*, *Newsweek*, and *Time*. In January, Brown and Bossie were invited to meet with the editorial page staff of the *Wall Street Journal*; they flew to New York and spent six hours at the paper's headquarters.

But NBC producer Ira Silverman remained Bossie's favorite

outlet. The two had traveled to Little Rock together two more times after their first trip the previous September. Bossie helped Silverman get footage of the troopers. But by then, Chris Vlasto of ABC News had tracked down McDougal in Arkadelphia, and McDougal had agreed not to grant any other TV interviews until ABC News and *Nightline* aired segments on him.

With McDougal now a captive of ABC, Silverman felt intense pressure to get its own exclusive footage of one or more key players. Every time a fresh story ran in the *Washington Post* or *New York Times*, which was virtually every day, he'd get the same phone call from his bureau chief or news executives in New York: "What can we do to advance this story?"

One person came to mind: Beverly Bassett. Since the Whitewater story's resurrection, the former securities commissioner had been deluged with calls from the media, but after her experience with Gerth she wanted no part of it. She'd turned down countless requests, which meant no one had any good footage of her. Silverman managed to get her into a conversation on the phone. She'd honeymooned on the island of Maui, where Silverman had also vacationed, and the two discussed their trips. As the friendly conversation shifted back to Whitewater, Silverman was struck by what seemed a crack in Bassett's support for the Clintons. She said that while she'd had calls from Bruce Lindsey to tell her how much the president appreciated what she was going through, she hadn't heard a word from Hillary or anyone on her staff, which was upsetting. She and other people in Arkansas "were being dragged through hell," she said. Hillary was not being supportive. The first lady was "always thinking of herself," Bassett said. She could take a lot of pressure off the president and people in Arkansas if she'd just come forward about her involvement in Madison. After this outburst, Silverman got correspondent Lisa Myers to join him on the call. Bassett said she'd discuss with her husband the possibility of going on camera.

That was enough encouragement for Silverman. He had several angles he wanted to pursue in Little Rock—the Rose firm, the Madison fund-raiser—and Bossie was already gathering information on the Arkansas Development Finance Authority. Once again, Bossie accompanied Silverman on the trip, and the two checked into the Capital Hotel.

When they arrived, Silverman spoke to Bassett's husband, Archie Schaffer, who said they'd get back to him. He didn't call back, nor did Bassett. Silverman told Lisa Myers that they were now avoiding him, and he was giving up on getting an interview. But late one evening, at about 10:30, he got a call from Myers at the bureau, insisting that he get Bassett on camera. "Get her on the sidewalk, get her on the way to work. It will be less politically problematic for her." Myers thought the confrontational tactic might get Bassett to talk, as it often did with other interview subjects. It might be easier for Bassett vis-a-vis the Clintons, since it wouldn't look like she was volunteering anything. Silverman agreed. He knew Bassett would be arriving at her office the next morning, and he decided to take Bossie along. He didn't want any other producer to get Bossie, whom he deemed one of his valuable assets.

As Bassett pulled up in her car, the NBC team was waiting. Four cameramen approached as Silverman knocked on Bassett's car window. "It's Ira. Roll the window down," Silverman said.

"Ira, this is absurd," Bassett said. "You ought to be ashamed of yourself." Bassett drove around the block, followed by the camera crew. Afterward, afraid to return to her own office, she drove to her brother and father's law office, followed by Silverman, Bossie, and the crew.

"You've got to do this," Silverman said as she tried to get to the office door.

"I can't believe you're doing this," she said. Then she noticed Bossie in the background taking notes. "Who's he?" she asked.

"Roll the cameras," Silverman ordered. Bassett was determined to ruin the footage. She threw her arm around Silverman's shoulders, pulling him into the picture. "This won't look good on camera," she said.

The cameras were turned off, and finally she said Silverman could come in for some coffee. He had the microphone on as she repeatedly refused to be interviewed. Silverman said the crew wouldn't leave, and the footage would show her running like a criminal. Was that what she wanted? "You can stay till midnight," she said, and called her husband for help. "I feel real bad about what's going on," she told him. She added she was worried about someone she didn't recognize taking notes.

When Schaffer arrived, he asked Silverman what was going on and who the guy in the car was. "A friend," Silverman replied, but wouldn't say more. Bassett called Vlasto at ABC, who'd also been trying to interview her on camera. She was in tears as she described being ambushed by Silverman. "All you guys are out there trying to get me," she sobbed. "I can't take it anymore." Schaffer got on the line, asking if Vlasto knew who was working with Silverman. He didn't, so Schaffer decided to get a photo.

Schaffer went to the car and confronted Bossie. He wouldn't give him his name or a card. Schaffer took out his instant camera and took a picture, then faxed the photos around. Betsey Wright got back to him saying she thought it was David Bossie, from Citizens United. They had a local reporter check to see if Bossie was registered at the Capital—he was. So Schaffer called the local ABC affiliate, asking that they send out a crew to do a story on how NBC News was trying to "ambush Beverly." Before they arrived, Silverman, Bossie, and the cameramen vanished. Furious, Schaffer called Tim Russert in Washington to complain.

This was the first that Russert had heard that Bossie had accompanied Silverman to an interview, and he was concerned. Russert told Schaffer that Bossie was "absolutely not" working for NBC News.

Still desperate for usable footage, Silverman trailed McDougal as Vlasto took him to the Little Rock airport for a flight to New York. As they walked to the plane, an NBC camera crew filmed McDougal as Vlasto called to Silverman, "That was a shitty thing for you to do to Beverly." The footage of Bassett never aired, but the McDougal tape did, with a glimpse of the ABC producer at his side.

When Silverman got back to Washington, Russert called him into his office. Russert and Silverman were close, and Russert thought he had done wonderful work. He hadn't had any problem with Silverman reaching out to Bossie for information; he'd accept information from just about anybody. But Silverman should not have taken Bossie with him to an interview, and should not have led anyone to believe he was part of the NBC team. He told Silverman his conduct had been "inappropriate." It was Bossie's last trip to Little Rock with Silverman.

As part of their arrangement, Vlasto had agreed that ABC would pay for McDougal to fly to New York, where they put him up for five days at the luxurious Nikko Essex House hotel overlooking Central Park. (All the major networks bar payments to news sources, but transportation and lodging aren't deemed payments, however lavish or unnecessary.) McDougal ran up a huge minibar bill (not in liquor, but in peanuts and snacks). ABC did draw the line when McDougal said he wanted the network to buy him a new suit. Instead it borrowed a suit from the costume department of *All My Children*.

With McDougal as the centerpiece, ABC devoted eighteen minutes of its twenty-two-minute *World News Tonight* news hole to Whitewater on February 10. Anchor Peter Jennings introduced the segment by saying, "We are going to attempt something ambitious this evening, which is to try to explain in one fell swoop the Whitewater jam that Bill and Hillary Clinton seem unable to get themselves out of." ABC followed the broadcast with more coverage on *Nightline*. Besides an overview, ABC was able to cast doubt on the Lyons report claim that the Clintons had invested and lost $68,000 in Whitewater. McDougal said flatly that the $20,744 check that Gerth had first questioned had "nothing at all to do with Whitewater."

The ABC appearances with Jennings and Ted Koppel—his first on network television—turned McDougal into a minor celebrity. He followed up on ABC with appearances on *Good Morning America* and *This Week with David Brinkley*. Freed from his exclusivity arrangement with ABC, he granted interviews with nearly everyone else who called, appearing on *Larry King Live* and in broadcasts in Europe and Japan. Back in Arkadelphia, he was the center of attention at the Sizzlin', where everyone recognized him and congratulated him on his new fame. In March, McDougal even entered the Democratic congressional primary, saying, "It's time to come out again and give these Republicans a fight," and adding that he wouldn't have to advertise very much because of his name recognition. (He lost.) At the end of the year, McDougal called Vlasto and thanked him for putting him on television. It had made it "the best year of my life," McDougal said.

In Little Rock that January, the *American Spectator* article, much copied and quietly circulated, was probably the most read article in town. When Debbie Ballentine, a secretary at an engineering firm, finally got a chance to read a copy at work, she gasped. She immediately called her best friend, Paula Corbin Jones, the young woman who'd met with Clinton at the conference at the Excelsior Hotel. Jones and her husband, Steve, and their new baby, Madison, had since moved to California, where Steve worked for Northwest Airlines and Paula hoped to launch a modeling or acting career, but that January they were visiting Paula's family in Arkansas. "You're not going to believe what is in this magazine," Ballentine told Jones. Then she read a passage from Brock's story:

"Clinton asked him to approach the woman, whom the trooper remembered only as Paula, tell her how attractive the governor thought she was, and take her to a room in the hotel where Clinton would be waiting. . . . On this particular evening, after her encounter with Clinton, which lasted no more than an hour as the trooper stood by in the hall, the trooper said Paula told him she was available to be Clinton's regular girlfriend if he so desired."

Jones was beside herself. If Ballentine had figured out that she was "Paula," everyone else would soon know. She was angry and embarrassed. She was now a married woman with a child. She had not had sex with Clinton, which the article implied, and she had certainly never offered to be his "regular girlfriend." She'd been dating Steve at the time. Her mother, who still lived in Arkansas, was a fundamentalist Christian who banned television and makeup and had made Paula and her sisters wear long dresses with long sleeves to school. Jones wanted to call the editor of the *Spectator* immediately and demand a correction and apology. "Wait a minute," Ballentine said. "You can't just call them up like that. I've got an attorney and I'll call him."

Ballentine called Daniel Traylor, a local attorney she'd gotten to know while working as a secretary at a company where Traylor was then in-house counsel. "Have you seen the article in the *American Spectator?*" she asked. He had; a copy had been faxed to him by a friend in Buffalo. He'd read it, but given it little thought. "My girlfriend is mentioned in this article," Ballentine said, and she's "hopping mad." Traylor agreed to talk to Jones, and later that day she called and told him her version of what happened with the governor in the Excelsior Hotel. She said another friend, Pam Blackard, could corroborate elements of the story, and after interviewing Blackard as well, Traylor concluded that Jones had credibility. Still, he warned her that if she was hoping for money out of this, "you've got the wrong motivation because there may be no money and even so, it's not worth the grief." Jones insisted that what she really wanted was to clear her name so her husband wouldn't think she was "fooling around" during their engagement. She wanted apologies from Clinton, the troopers, and the *Spectator.*

On the other hand, when Paula asked for advice from her sister Charlotte, it seemed clear that Paula was also dazzled by the possibility of publicity, fame, and, at least indirectly, the money that she thought would flow from that. Charlotte wanted some time to ponder Paula's options, and she decided going public would be a mistake. Among other concerns, she thought it would kill their mother. But Paula never called Charlotte back to get her advice, which hurt Charlotte's feelings. Jones went ahead and retained Traylor on a contingency basis, in which he'd get half of any damages or settlement payments. Jones was unemployed in California, and couldn't afford any fees.

A general practitioner who tended to handle divorces, real estate contracts, and wills, Traylor had little idea how to handle a libel claim or how to approach the White House. He called a friend to report that he had another "bimbo eruption" on his hands, and the friend put him in touch with George Cook, a Little Rock insurance agent who'd been a strong supporter of Clinton's. He thought Cook could act as an intermediary with the White House. The next day Cook and Traylor met, and Traylor repeated Jones's story, complete with her version of what had happened in the hotel room. "Ask the White House what they want to do on this," Traylor told Cook. Traylor didn't say so explicitly, but he thought a payment of about $1,000 to cover his fees and an apology would clear things up.

Why Traylor would approach the White House so quickly— or even at all—is hard to reconcile with his and Jones's insistence that all they wanted was to clear Jones's name. Their grievances were with the *Spectator,* the author of the story, and Ferguson, not Clinton, who obviously wasn't a source. Cook later made an affidavit for Clinton, in which he claimed that Traylor "said [Jones] had a claim against President Clinton and, if she did not get money for it, she would embarrass him publicly" and that "it would help if President Clinton would get Paula a job out in California." Cook took that to mean a job with the Clintons' producer-friends the Thomasons, which would further Jones's acting ambitions. He added that Traylor said he "needed the client and needed the money."*

Whatever Jones's and Traylor's motives, Cook called Traylor back the following Monday. "We can't do anything for you," he reported. "We can't do anything with you." Cook added that the troopers' allegations hadn't dented the president's popularity as reflected in poll numbers. "People don't care about Clinton's extramarital affairs," he said.

Traylor was surprised and angered by the rejection. Even though he was "a yellow-dog Democrat" and a Clinton supporter, he told Cook he'd turn the case over to a "competent lawyer." Cook asked if Cliff Jackson was involved in the case, and Traylor said no.

But then Traylor did call Jackson, since Jackson represented the troopers, and told him his client had a claim and was thinking of suing them. Jackson told Traylor he was wasting his time; he didn't represent Ferguson, who was the trooper who had mentioned Paula. "I was there and heard him [Ferguson] say it, and Brock got it right, but you don't have a claim against the *Spectator*, Brock, or my clients. If you're going after anyone, it should be Ferguson," Jackson argued. Traylor asked Jackson to meet with him and Jones so he could hear her story.

Jackson met with Jones and Ballentine soon after, and came away believing Jones's story. Since he'd been instrumental in getting the *Spectator* story published, he felt personally responsible for Jones's name having been mentioned, and he felt a responsibility to help her set the record straight. Soon the ostensible adversaries were all but plotting strategy together. Traylor was impressed with Jackson's contacts and experience with the media, and Jackson was intrigued by another incident that raised questions about Clinton's character. After Traylor expressed his frustration at getting the White House's attention, Jackson suggested he and Jones appear with him at the upcoming Conservative Political Action Conference (CPAC), where the troopers were scheduled to make a public appearance and Jackson was going to speak. Jackson warned Traylor that the appearance risked associating Jones with him, a well-known

---

* *Traylor says Cook's affidavit "mischaracterizes" their conversation.*

anti-Clinton partisan, at a conference generally dismissed as right-wing. But representatives of all the national media would be there, offering Jones an unrivaled opportunity to attract their attention.

Jones herself was upset at the rejection by the White House, and, having gone so far as to hire Traylor, she was now more determined than ever to press her claim. She and her husband agreed to accompany Traylor and Jackson, though it wasn't certain until the last minute that she would actually appear. Even then, she refused to make public any of the details of the encounter she claimed to have had with Clinton in the hotel room, agreeing to say only that Clinton asked her to engage in a "sexual encounter."

The CPAC conference was an orgy of Clinton-bashing. As Roger Perry drew spontaneous applause and David Brock was besieged by autograph seekers, vendors sold "Impeach Hillary" T-shirts and doctored photographs of the first lady in various states of undress. About a hundred reporters attended Jackson and Traylor's press conference, where Traylor insisted details were being omitted "out of deference to the first family" and said the suddenly shy Jones wouldn't answer the inevitable questions about just what had happened. Jones did say she was speaking out to clear her name after the *Spectator* article. As for Clinton, she said that he had asked her to perform "a type of sex" and added, "It's wrong that a woman can be harassed by a figure that high. It's humiliating what he did to me."

Jones was unhappy with the tittering in the audience. Worse, press coverage was minimal. Mike Isikoff, of the *Washington Post*, called to say the paper wasn't running a story on the press conference, but he was interested in doing a longer piece. Jones gave him her exclusive cooperation, but was disappointed when she learned the story was being delayed indefinitely by *Post* editors.

But what Jones found most upsetting, she later claimed, was the White House reaction. Dee Dee Myers said of Jones's account that "It's just not true." The White House issued a statement saying that the incident with Jones "never occurred," that the president had never met Jones. Stephanopoulos described her press conference as a "cheap political fund-raising trick."

Feeling ignored and rejected, Jones began to fall in with anyone who seemed sympathetic—and promised media exposure. When producers for right-wing televangelist Jerry Falwell told her that they were working with the troopers and Cliff Jackson, she agreed to be filmed, then signed a release. Only then did she think to tell Traylor, who was dismayed by the news. He and Jackson wanted nothing to do with Falwell, and the claim they'd been working together was false. Still, Falwell put the footage to use in a half-hour video, *The Clinton Chronicles*, and there was nothing they could do about it. She also agreed to be interviewed by conservative media critic Reed Irvine, founder of Accuracy in Media, on his CNBC cable show, *The Other Side of the Story*. Then she joined Pat Robertson on his *700 Club* show on the Christian Broadcasting Network. These appearances, too, had a partisan slant that did little to bolster Jones's credibility. Traylor concluded it had all been a big mistake, and ordered Jones to make no further public appearances.

That was hardly the end of the matter. As Jones later put it, "Only after Mr. Clinton and his staff denied that these events had ever happened, and called me 'pathetic,' and in effect a liar, did I decide to seek legal relief. . . ." Traylor eventually turned to outside counsel in Fairfax, Virginia, Gilbert K. Davis and Joseph Cammarata, who approached him on the recommendation of a mutual friend. A history buff and a Republican, but not a conservative activist, Davis ran a small firm and was something of a legal gadfly. He organized a Paula Jones Legal Defense Fund, which received modest contributions from conservative organizations such as the Legal Affairs Council. But most of the money—$25,000—came from the $50,000 Jones earned in a No Excuses jeans promotion. (The other $25,000 went to a women's shelter in Virginia.)

President Clinton—despite the earlier vows from Cook that the White House "can't do anything with you" and "can't do anything for you"—hired prominent Washington lawyer Robert Bennett to negotiate with Jones's lawyers, instantly lending her claim more credibility than anything Jones herself had said. Despite the White House denials and statement claiming the president had never met Jones, negotiations got to the point where Clinton agreed to read personally a statement that apologized but didn't concede Jones's version of events. But no agreement was reached, and Jones's lawyers vowed to file suit against the president.

The Christmas week revelation that Whitewater files had been removed from Vince Foster's office had not only linked Whitewater to Foster's suicide. To many, especially the conspiracy-minded, it raised the question of whether Foster's death was a suicide at all— or whether he was murdered because he knew too much. Perhaps the question could have been dismissed as idle speculation, confined to the fringe of extremist newsletters and talk shows. But then, on January 27, the *New York Post* brought speculation about Foster's death into the mainstream. Trumpeting the results of a *"New York Post* Investigation" by Christopher Ruddy, the tabloid's headline read "Doubts Raised Over Foster's 'Suicide.' "

The *New York Post* hardly wielded the clout of the major national newspapers or even conservative outlets like the *Wall Street Journal* editorial page or the *Washington Times*. It was often sensational and irreverent, unabashedly tabloid in its orientation. Since being taken over for the second time by conservative media magnate Rupert Murdoch in 1993 after a debilitating strike, the paper had fired striking reporters and replaced some of them with openly conservative and ideological writers, and had maintained a strong conservative slant on its editorial page under the leadership of Eric Breindel. Still, it was widely circulated in New York, the nation's media capital, and was read by news executives at all the major networks and newspapers.

At Murdoch's behest, Breindel had sought investigative reporters with a conservative bent, and Ruddy's work in a conservative Long Island newspaper, *The Guardian*, had caught his eye. The son of a New York policeman who attended the London School of Economics and taught school in the Bronx before becoming a journalist, Ruddy had gained widespread attention for an article he wrote attacking a highly acclaimed PBS documentary, *Liberators*, which told the story of how an all-black U.S. tank battalion liberated Jewish inmates of the concentration camps Buchenwald and Dachau. Ruddy reported that the battalion was actually engaged in combat sixty miles away when the camps were liberated. Debunking the notion that blacks liberated Jews brought Ruddy immediate acclaim from some conservatives who saw the documentary as a liberal attempt to paper over divisions between the two groups. Ruddy revealed his own view in his story, stating at the outset that "Many believe that if something appears in the major media, it must then be essentially true. For these individuals, let me present an egregious case of media manipulation, one that is an out-and-out lie, produced and broadcast largely at taxpayer expense, and cheered by sugary columnists from coast to coast." In another article, Ruddy had attacked the New York school system's proposed "Rainbow Curriculum," intended to foster tolerance for minorities, including homosexuals. This, too, showed an anti–liberal establishment, investigative bent that Breindel found appealing.

Once hired, Ruddy cut quite a swath in the *Post*'s newsroom. Portly, balding, with a pencil-thin mustache, Ruddy was always impeccably dressed in suit and tie, looking more like a Wall Street banker than his casually dressed colleagues. He was charming, poised, and a devout Catholic. He was given carte blanche to pursue investigative stories, to travel, to entertain sources, at a time when the *Post* was understaffed and other reporters felt constantly strapped. But the investment seemed to pay off when Ruddy contacted the Fairfax County fire department office of public affairs and obtained permission to interview the emergency workers who had been summoned to Fort Marcy Park the evening of Foster's death—a group almost entirely overlooked in the initial press coverage of Foster's death.

Ruddy had gotten interested in the story after talking to Reed Irvine, who had also admired Ruddy's *Liberators* story. Irvine had suggested stories to Ruddy before, and this time he mentioned that he'd heard at a cocktail party from someone with law enforcement connections that the investigation of Foster's death had been botched. Ruddy located George Gonzalez, a paramedic who was one of two emergency medical personnel who viewed the body after it was discovered by the Park Police.

Ruddy interviewed Gonzalez, as Ruddy later described it, "late on a January night six months after Foster's death." Gonzalez described his arrival at the park, his route toward the site of the old fort, accompanied by two other emergency workers, and the discovery of the body, lying on its back, as if it were "ready for the coffin." Gonzalez's description was essentially the same as those given by the Park Police officers and others at the scene, but many of Gonzalez's observations hadn't been made public, largely because, in and of themselves, they seemed insignificant. Yet to Ruddy, they "raised new questions about the 'suicide' of the White House deputy counsel."

His article continued, "The questions involve the position of

Foster's body; the fact that the gun was still in Foster's hand and had no blood on it; the small amount of blood on and near the body; and the swiftness with which the death was declared a suicide." And he quoted Gonzalez saying that the death scene was "strange" and "peculiar."

Ruddy took Gonzalez's observations to various "experts," and then quoted them to the effect that "there should be pools of blood"; "I've never seen someone shoot themselves in the mouth and still hold the gun perfectly at his side"; "Normally when a person commits suicide, the gun doesn't end up in their hand"; "It's hard to explain how he shot himself."

Gonzalez's observations were accurate, and the questions raised by Ruddy seemed legitimate. Yet Ruddy omitted the answers to those questions—all of which were readily available—choosing instead to leave the impression that something sinister had occurred. Obviously, Foster's apparent suicide was strange and peculiar, but not because of the factors Ruddy seized upon. The lack of visible blood was readily explained by the course of the bullet, which exited the back of Foster's head, and the position of the body. When Foster's body was rolled over there was a substantial pool of blood on the ground where his head had been and the back of his shirt was bloodstained. Since his body was on a downward slope, blood had also descended in his body, rather than flowing from the wound. The gun remained in Foster's hand because the thumb used to pull the trigger had become trapped between the trigger and the trigger guard. When the Park Police removed the gun from the body, they had to pry Foster's thumb loose by half-cocking the trigger. Because Foster appears to have been sitting down when he fired the shot into his mouth, and because his thumb was caught in the gun, he would naturally have fallen backward with his hands at his side.

Yet the *Post* story, its insinuations made credible to some by the White House's initial evasiveness and the removal of Foster's files, was uncritically picked up and recycled in much of the national media, from the *Wall Street Journal* editorial page to the major television networks. Gonzalez was so deluged with media inquiries that he scheduled a news conference, subsequently canceled by Fairfax County officials. That led to a new round of stories reporting that Gonzalez had been "silenced."

Ruddy vaulted to instant celebrity, with camera crews pouring into the *New York Post* newsroom to interview him, and a flood of speaking invitations. He quickly followed his initial story with another "exclusive," "More Questions About Foster's 'Suicide,' " asking, "Who was the man in the white utility van?" one of "many nagging questions that remain unanswered in the official account of the 'suicide' of deputy White House counsel Vincent Foster." While questioning the identity of the man in the van who discovered the body, it also revisited the issues raised in his first story, again quoting only those "experts" who found the evidence "strange."

Even if all of Ruddy's conclusions were tenuous, there was probably no way so sensational a story—the possible murder of a high government official, or at least a cover-up of the circumstances of a suicide—could be contained. Yet the story gained currency because on at least one point Ruddy's conclusion seemed unassailable. However understandable, the Park Police's conclusion that Foster's death was a suicide was hasty. In the wake of Ruddy's reporting, the *Washington Post* felt compelled to reexamine the circumstances of Foster's death, and it discovered that the Park Police hadn't even asked firearms experts to conduct forensic tests until two days after their official ruling that Foster committed suicide. While the firearms tests by the Bureau of Alcohol, Tobacco, and Firearms were consistent with the ruling, the timing left them suspect. That triggered another wave of follow-up stories, and lent credibility to Ruddy's original story.

For conspiracy buffs, the possible murder of Foster was the most exciting story since the assassination of Kennedy. Tailor-made for call-in shows, the wildest speculation was aired, was repeated, and gained credibility. "Vince Foster" and "Whitewater Scandal" home pages were established on the Internet. A London newspaper claimed to have unearthed travel records showing Foster made secret trips to Geneva, Switzerland, and elsewhere, which "raises the question: was Foster a U.S. agent at a time when he was ostensibly in private practice as a Little Rock lawyer?"

Perhaps the most persistent of these theorists was Sherman Skolnick, the Chicago-based publisher of *Conspiracy Nation*, an Internet newsletter, and host of a public access cable show, who maintains a twenty-four-hour hotline with recorded updates of his latest discoveries. Skolnick insisted that Foster was not only murdered, but that the unassuming deputy White House counsel was positioned at the center of an international conspiracy financed by Tyson Foods and Wal-Mart that linked Israeli spy Jonathan Pollard, George Bush, former defense secretary Caspar Weinberger, weapons sales to Iran, and the "October surprise." Foster was murdered, Skolnick claimed, because he was about to go public with his information.

Speculation even spilled over into the financial markets, periodically roiling the stock and bond markets. When a memo to clients prepared by a respected financial consulting firm, Johnson Smeck International, reported that aides to Democratic senator Daniel Moynihan were saying that Foster's body had been moved to the site in Fort Marcy Park from an apartment in Virginia maintained by the administration, thirty-year Treasury bonds plunged over one and a half points and the Dow Jones industrial average dropped over twenty points. Dee Dee Myers had to issue a statement, calling the report "ridiculous. There is not a shred of evidence to suggest that this is true. It is a complete fabrication." The report itself cautioned that this was just one among "millions" of rumors, none of which had panned out, and staffers in Moynihan's office hastily denied the report, but that didn't stop it from gaining widespread currency. Rush Limbaugh trumpeted the report on his radio show, even embellishing it with the claim that the mysterious apartment was owned by none other than Hillary Rodham Clinton. When David Smeck, the author of the report, returned to his office from lunch with a Japanese government official, his staff was being deluged with press calls, and a group of reporters and two network camera crews had shown up on the premises.

Ruddy, too, weighed in with his latest findings, "Foster's Secret Hideaway Apartment Revealed." Ruddy quoted an unnamed "White House source": "It was like a clubhouse, a place to kick back, have a drink, hide out." Ruddy seemed more and more obsessed with the story, insisting to his editors that he would work on nothing else.

Weeks later, the story gained new fuel when the mysterious "confidential witness" in the white van, the first person to see Foster's body, called G. Gordon Liddy, the notorious leader of the Watergate "plumbers," and now the host of a popular nationally syndicated right-wing, conspiracy-minded talk show, *Radio Free DC*. The witness, concerned by what he said were inaccurate reports and what he viewed as a government conspiracy to cover up the truth, said he considered contacting either Rush Limbaugh or Liddy, but decided on Liddy as someone who "wouldn't give me up." Liddy met the witness, interviewed him, and later turned his notes over to the FBI, who also interviewed the witness.

There were few new details—the witness, a construction worker who routinely passed the park on his way home, said he was stuck in traffic and had gone into that remote section of the park to urinate. But he did say he didn't see any gun in the body's hand. Indeed, he insisted that he'd stood about three feet from the body and had seen the palms of both hands, facing upward, empty. Photographs taken by the Park Police when they discovered the body show that the hand holding the gun was partly concealed by Foster's leg, and foliage also obscured the right hand. The Park Police officer who first discovered the body hadn't seen the gun either, nor had the paramedics until they reached the corpse. But to Liddy, this was evidence a gun had been planted on the corpse and that the hand holding the gun—perhaps even the entire body—had been moved. The information surfaced on Liddy's talk show on March 25.

"All right, let's now go back to the telephones. And up first, from Peru, Indiana, is Bart. Bart, you're on Radio Free DC. . . ."

"Um. I had a question regarding a talk show I heard the other day. . . . There was a woman who claimed to, she was investigating mysterious deaths around the Clintons and the Whitewater ordeal and one of them she mentioned was the head of security for his campaign. But the number she listed, she said there could be as many as twenty-nine deaths that came under mysterious circumstances. Besides the, Mr. Clinton's head of security for his campaign, are there any other men from Little Rock . . . ?"

"Well, yeah, I never heard the figure twenty-nine before, certainly, but we do know that there was that fellow who was killed and then there was a man who was investigating Clinton's infidelities, you know, all the way back into the 1980s and he was, died by gunshot. I think about ten bullets took him out. . . . There is, of course, Vincent Foster. You know, they keep making out that it's a suicide. Maybe it was. But, for example, I have received information which would lead me to believe that it was not, or at least that the body was moved. I'm working to verify what I have received as best I can. I am, I promised the person who gave me the information not to reveal that person's identity, and I will not, but I will reveal, with that person's permission, all the information given me. It's the man in the van, in the mysterious van that disappeared, the man who actually found the body. This individual claims to be that person, he gave me a lot of information as recently as last night. I was in Fort Marcy Park using maps this person gave me in his own hand, uh, to verify whether he knew what he was talking about or not. And as best I can tell, at least from the maps and things like that, he sure did."

"Wow. . . ."

"I will not give up this person's identity because this person told me flatly, 'I don't want to end up like that body I found on the ground.' "

"I don't blame him."

FIFTEEN

ROBERT B. FISKE, JR., was in his corner office at the midtown Manhattan law firm of Davis, Polk & Wardwell when he received a call on January 13 from JoAnn Harris, head of the Justice Department's criminal division, who'd worked for him as an assistant U.S. attorney in the Southern District of New York. It was just a day after Clinton had issued his call for a special counsel to investigate Whitewater, and that morning, Nina Totenberg had reported on National Public Radio that Fiske was one of two people being considered by the Justice Department for the job. "Are you available?" Harris asked.

The possibility of being named special counsel was appealing to Fiske. One of New York's most sought-after litigators, especially for criminal matters, Fiske, sixty-three, also had a strong commitment to public service. He'd been named U.S. attorney in New York by Gerald Ford and continued in the post under Jimmy Carter. He'd recently defended Goldman Sachs partner Robert Freeman, a figure in the Ivan Boesky scandal who pleaded guilty to insider trading, and was among the lawyers representing Clark Clifford in the BCCI scandal. Attorney General Janet Reno had said publicly that she wanted someone "ruggedly independent," and Fiske fit the bill. A Republican in the moderate, Rockefeller mold, he had alienated zealous conservatives when, as head of the judicial screening panel for the American Bar Association, he had opposed some Reagan nominees with stronger ideological than legal credentials. Investigating the Whitewater affair would obviously be disruptive. He'd probably have to move to Arkansas, leaving his firm and family. The investigation could take years, as Lawrence Walsh had demonstrated in the Iran-contra affair. But he told Harris that, yes, he could be available.

The next week Fiske flew to Washington to meet with Reno, Philip Heymann, and others at the Justice Department. Since the independent counsel statute had lapsed, they were operating in uncharted terrain, but tried to work out an arrangement modeled on the prior law. Fiske was particularly concerned that he have the independence and jurisdiction to pursue the case wherever it might lead. Reno's staff had drafted a proposed charter, and she gave it to Fiske, saying that he should make any additions he wanted, within reason.

The charter they agreed on had four key provisions. The first authorized an independent counsel to investigate "whether any individuals or entities have committed a violation of federal criminal or civil law relating in any way to President William Jefferson Clinton's or Mrs. Hillary Rodham Clinton's relationships" with Madison Guaranty, Whitewater Development Corp., or Capital Management Services. The second was much broader, granting the authority to investigate "other allegations or evidence of violation of any federal criminal or civil law by any person or entity developed during the independent counsel's investigation . . . connected to or arising out of that investigation." That meant the independent counsel could gain leverage over any potential witnesses by investigating them for unrelated crimes. This was the kind of provision that had given Nussbaum such concern. It all but ensured that anyone close to the Clintons would come under scrutiny. The last two provisions specifically extended the independent counsel's jurisdiction to include obstruction of justice and conspiracy.

When Fiske met with Reno later that day, she thanked him for his willingness to take on such a highly charged task, and emphasized what an important service he would be rendering. "Are you satisfied that you have all the authority you need to do this right?" she asked. Fiske replied that he had all the authority the attorney general herself would have had. "Do you have the jurisdiction, the independence you feel you need?" He said he did.

Fiske accepted, and said he wanted to announce it at a press conference the next morning. An overnight storm cut power to the Justice Department building. The press conference was moved to the Willard Hotel. Reno introduced Fiske as "the epitome of what a prosecutor should be" and said she would have no further oversight of the investigation. "I expect him to report to the American people, and I do not expect to monitor him," she said. One of the first questions from reporters was whether Fiske would investigate the death of Foster. He said he would, to determine whether Whitewater played any role.

After briefing lawyers and staff at Davis, Polk and notifying clients over the weekend, Fiske set about assembling a staff and organizing offices in Little Rock. He flew to Washington on Monday, where he met with officials investigating the nine RTC referrals—now handed over to Fiske—and arrived in Little Rock on Tuesday. He took office space in a suburban office tower that also housed the FBI offices and rented an apartment about a ten-minute drive away. Fiske was inundated with résumés of lawyers volunteering for the staff, but Fiske chose either people he knew and had worked with, or those recommended by people he chose to consult, including Griffin Bell, attorney general during the Carter administration; and Frank Jones, former president of the American College of Trial Lawyers, in Atlanta; and Bob Mueller, the Bush criminal division head who'd handled the first Whitewater referral, now in private practice with a Boston firm. Fiske assembled a team of fifteen lawyers, most with experience as federal prosecutors. He also opened a Washington office, primarily to investigate Foster's death, and hired Rod Lankler, a respected New York trial lawyer who'd spent eight years prosecuting homicides in the Manhattan district attorney's office, to head it.

A grand jury was convened in Little Rock for the exclusive purpose of hearing Whitewater-related testimony. Whitewater not only now had a staff of full-time prosecutors, but they had all but unlimited access to the investigative resources of the FBI, whose ranks in Little Rock swelled to twenty-five agents. Almost immediately, the group made its presence felt in Arkansas.

In Flippin, Chris Wade, his ego already inflated by all the press attention, was "tickled," as he put it, when he first got a phone call from an FBI agent saying he wanted to chat about the Whitewater development. "It's about time I heard from you people," Wade said. "Come on up." The agent did, and Wade cheerfully walked him through the story of his involvement and made copies of many of the files for him. Two or three weeks later, the agent called again, saying he wanted copies of all the sales transactions for all the Whitewater lots. Wade made the copies and handed them over. But soon after, he was asked by Sam Heuer, McDougal's lawyer, to meet with them in Little Rock. McDougal was obviously a target of the Fiske probe, and Wade was happy to keep them apprised of what he was telling the FBI. Almost as an afterthought at the meeting, Wade asked Heuer, "Do I need an attorney?"

"Yeah," Heuer replied, "you probably do."

But Wade had emerged from bankruptcy proceedings in 1992, and the last thing he wanted was attorney's bills. He was just a witness; surely they wanted McDougal and people higher up, not a small-time real estate broker in the Ozarks. When the FBI called again, this time asking Wade to come to their offices in Little Rock, Wade arrived without a lawyer. He was stunned when they told him he was to be fingerprinted and that they wanted a handwriting sample.

Wade hired a lawyer at $150 an hour, a sum he found all but crippling. Within weeks it was obvious that he himself was a target, for what reason he couldn't fathom. Now, FBI agents descended on Flippin. The bankers at 1st Ozark were called before the grand jury. Other local people had to hire Little Rock lawyers. It seemed like half the population of Flippin was hiring lawyers and going before the grand jury. The once-friendly FBI agents suddenly turned stern, accusing Wade and his wife of stalling when they failed to produce masses of requested documents within three days. On one such occasion, Wade's wife, Rosalee, turned to the agent and said, "I'm sure you don't realize how rude you sound." But then an agent questioned one of Wade's salesmen, and asked him point-blank if he'd had an affair with Rosalee Wade. Wade's lawyer informed him that his wife was now a target as well.

The Wades wished they'd never heard of Whitewater—and had never met a politician.

At the White House, there was relief over the appointment of Fiske. Nussbaum wasn't a close friend of his, but he knew and respected Fiske's judgment. In particular, he had confidence in his exercise of prosecutorial discretion—the sometimes fine decision not to pursue criminal charges simply because some evidence might support a case. Nussbaum also felt that, at age sixty-three, with a distinguished career, Fiske wasn't out to further his own ambitions by filing charges to gain publicity. He wouldn't be angling for a judicial appointment from a Republican senator hostile to Clinton, nor would he be pursuing political ambitions of his own. Nussbaum was still opposed to the idea of an independent counsel, but he thought Fiske was as good a choice as the administration could hope for. Maybe it would gain them a reprieve from the relentless press investigations.

Fiske's appointment, however, had no immediate effect on the RTC investigation of Madison launched by Jean Lewis. Legislation extending the life of the RTC—and the statute of limitations for claims falling under its jurisdiction—had been passed by Congress and signed by Clinton late in the year. Pressure on the issue had been maintained by Senator D'Amato, who took to the Senate floor each day with his "countdown chart," showing the days remaining before the prior statute expired. Still, with the new statute of limitations on Madison Guaranty scheduled to expire on February 28, decisions on the latest referrals would have to be made quickly. With the most recent wave of publicity over Whitewater, Jean Hanson, the Treasury general counsel who'd been involved with earlier discussions of the RTC referrals at the White House, recommended that Roger Altman, who was still acting as head of the RTC, recuse himself. Given his relationship to the president and first lady, she believed his involvement would be politically damaging and look like a conflict of interest. At a meeting with Altman and Treasury Secretary Bentsen, Altman seemed to agree, and Bentsen recommended that they inform the White House of his decision to withdraw, so the president wouldn't learn about it in the press.

Hanson called Harold Ickes to schedule a meeting for the next day, February 2. Altman's decision had obvious implications that went well beyond an otherwise technical decision. The RTC investigation had the potential to do immense political damage to the administration and keep the Whitewater issue percolating, even if no charges were ever leveled directly against the president and first lady. If Altman withdrew from the case, oversight would fall to the RTC's deputy CEO, Jack Ryan, and its general counsel, Ellen Kulka. Ryan was a career official with no known loyalty to the president, and Kulka, while at the Office of Thrift Supervision, had

taken a hard line against Nussbaum's former client, the Kaye
Scholer law firm. Nussbaum had also read the clip on Kulka earlier
faxed to him by Altman, in which *Legal Times* had described her as
an "extremist" in her zeal to hold lawyers liable for S&L losses.

Ickes, Nussbaum, Maggie Williams, and one of Nussbaum's
assistants attended the meeting with Altman and Hanson. Altman
briefed the group on the impending statute of limitations deadline,
but then added that he was "considering" recusing himself,
"strongly inclined to do so," even though he'd been advised that
such a step wasn't mandated by any ethics laws. By withdrawing,
he'd leave the decisions to Ryan and Kulka, whose recommenda-
tions he'd be following in any event, he said.

The announcement drew an immediate storm of protest. Nussbaum was particularly worked up, because of his belief that government officials had an obligation to perform their jobs, not run for
cover every time they confronted a politically sensitive issue. As he
later testified, "Public officials should not have the option of
avoiding their responsibilities simply because they are difficult, or
inconvenient, or because the officials find it personally or politically
expedient to step aside. . . ." A public official "should do his or her
sworn duty." Anything less would be a "bad precedent," both for
Clinton's and future administrations, he argued. Nussbaum struck
Altman as "agitated" and "excited" over the issue. Nussbaum was
also alarmed by the prospect of letting Kulka make the decisions.
As Ickes later recounted, Nussbaum said he "questioned" Kulka's
"judgment and impartiality" in light of the tough stand she'd taken
against his client, the law firm Kaye Scholer.

Ickes and Williams also strongly opposed Altman's decision.
Williams chimed in, "You're a person of integrity, Roger. I mean,
why is it that you would have to recuse, plus you're going to take
the recommendation of staff anyway, so why bother?" But they all
agreed that the decision was ultimately Altman's, and he said he'd
think it over. By the next morning, he'd changed his mind, and told
Hanson he'd remain in charge of the case, at least for the time
being. Later that day, en route to a meeting on health care, he
dropped by Williams's office, who was meeting with Ickes, and told
them he'd agreed not to step down. They were relieved, and Williams said, "Good for you, Roger."

Minutes later, Hanson arrived, and Ickes told her Altman had just left. Then he asked, "How many people at [Treasury] know that you advised [Altman] to recuse himself?" Hanson mentioned only a few names. "That's good," Ickes continued. "Because if it gets out, it will look bad."*

Later that day, Altman told Bentsen that he'd decided not to step down, adding that the decision "made them happy." Bentsen had misgivings. He commented that he thought Altman would "take some political heat." Altman also spoke to Treasury chief of staff Joshua Steiner after both the White House meetings, and Steiner later described the events and the atmosphere in the White House in his diary:

"Every now and then you watch a disaster unfold and seem powerless to stop it. For weeks we have been battling over how RA [Altman] should handle the RTC investigation of Madison Guaranty S&L. Initially, we all felt that he should recuse himself to prevent even the appearance of a conflict. At a fateful WH mtg w/ Nussbaum, Ickes and Williams, however, the WH staff told RA it was unacceptable. RA had gone to brief them on the impending statute of limitations deadline and also to tell them of his recusal decision. They reacted very negatively to the recusal and RA backed down the next day and agreed to a de facto recusal where the RTC would handle this case like any other and RA would have no involvement. Were very concerned that at the RTC oversight hearings the GOP would hammer away at the recusal issue so we renewed discussions w/ the WH about what RA would do when his term expired on March 30. Once again they were very concerned about him turning the RTC [over to] people they didn't know so RA did not formally commit himself. . . ."†

Under the circumstances, Altman's expectations that Madison Guaranty was a case that could be "handled like any other" seems naive. Indeed, the same day of the first White House meeting to discuss Altman's decision to recuse himself, Kulka dispatched April

---

* Ickes later testified that he had no recollection of such a conversation. However, Hanson's account was confirmed by Neil Eggleston, a Nussbaum assistant who was present when the conversation took place.

† In later testimony that was widely ridiculed, Steiner disclaimed his diary, saying, "I think I was surmising something or giving my impressions based on the circumstances as I knew them." Still, his diary seems to be largely in accord with others' recollections of the events.

Breslaw, an official in the RTC's office of professional liability, to Kansas City to help review documents before the statute of limitations expired. She met with Richard Iorio, who took her to lunch and offered her a drink, which she found somewhat unprofessional. Then Iorio suggested she meet with Jean Lewis in Lewis's office. Breslaw was there to review documents, not talk to Lewis, but she thought it would be rude to say no. Lewis insisted Breslaw sit close to the desk, where, unbeknownst to Breslaw, Lewis had a tape recorder running. Convinced that the investigation was being hindered in Washington, Lewis was determined to gather evidence.

As the two began chatting, Breslaw remarked, "Whether under normal circumstances we would be so preoccupied about Whitewater, I don't know. But because that's the catchword and everything . . . they seem to ask and ask and ask."

"I think that's become the catchall phrase," Lewis replied.

"Yeah, but I think that somehow or other this group eventually is going to have to make a statement about whether or not there is any loss to Madison by reason of Whitewater. Because everybody realizes that they had no loan there, so that crosses off the most obvious choice. Obviously, Jean, you know better than I do, so many checks went in and out of there that it's hard to say exactly what happened in that checking account. . . ."

The two discussed the $30,000 "bonus" that McDougal put into the Whitewater account, then Breslaw volunteered, "I think, if they could say it honestly, the head people—Jack Ryan and Ellen Kulka—would like to be able to say Whitewater did not cause a loss to Madison. We don't know what you're going to find, and we don't offer any opinion on it. But the problem is, no one has been able to say to Ryan and Kulka, 'Sure, say that, that's fine.' "

Lewis showed the tape to no one, but deemed it so important that she kept it with her at all times, even while sleeping. She described the experience only to her father, the retired major general. Breslaw returned to Washington the same day, and never spoke again to Lewis. She soon forgot the conversation.

In Congress, there were continued rumblings about Altman's involvement in the RTC cases. Representative Leach issued a letter calling for an ethics ruling, and Senator D'Amato, concerned about whether there had been White House interference, indicated he would use routine RTC oversight hearings to examine the agency's handling of the Madison referrals. Meanwhile, D'Amato succeeded in his campaign to extend again the statute of limitations, removing the February 28 deadline.

On February 24, Altman, accompanied by Hanson, testified before the Senate committee. Senator Phil Gramm, a conservative Republican, turned to Altman's handling of the Madison case. "Mr. Altman," he began, reading a prepared question, "I want to ask you first. Have you or any member of your staff had any communication with the president, the first lady, or any of their representatives, including their legal counsel, or any member of their White House staff, concerning Whitewater or the Madison Savings and Loan?"

Altman replied, "I have had one substantive contact with White House staff, and I want to tell you about it." Altman proceeded to describe the February 2 meeting with Nussbaum at the White House, saying he had simply explained the process the RTC would follow to act on the Madison referrals before the February 28 deadline. "That was the whole conversation," he said, omitting any reference to his suggestion that he recuse himself. He also ignored entirely Gramm's question about whether any of his staff, such as Hanson, had had any White House contacts.

Hanson, seated just behind Altman, was startled by Altman's failure to mention the recusal issue, and thought about passing him a note to remind him of it. But when he said "that was the whole conversation," she thought she'd lost the opportunity.

Senator D'Amato followed up on Gramm's question, and Altman characterized the meeting at the White House as a "heads up."

"A heads up?" D'Amato asked. "In what connection would that 'heads up' be?" Altman again said he was simply explaining the internal processes of the RTC.

"Did anyone request this meeting?" D'Amato continued.

"I requested the meeting."

"Was there any other meeting that may have been requested?" "No."

"There was no other meeting that you are aware of that the White House counsel requested?"

"No."

"Or anyone else from the White House?"

"No."

Later, Senator Christopher Bond, a Missouri Republican,

asked how the White House had found out about the RTC referrals. "They were not notified by the RTC, to the best of my knowledge," Altman said.

"Nobody in your agency, to your knowledge, advised the
White House staff that this was going to be a major source of
concern?"

"Not to my knowledge."

At this point in the hearing, Altman turned to Hanson, asking,
"That's right, isn't it?" or something to that effect. Hanson shook
her head back and forth, which would ordinarily mean no, but she
and Altman both later said that she meant to confirm the accuracy
of his answer, and that's how Altman interpreted it. Hanson later
acknowledged she had had a "flash of remembering" about her fall
meetings at the White House, where she discussed the RTC referrals, and it may have been at that point in the hearings. But in any
event, she thought Bond was asking only about the RTC, and as
general counsel to the Treasury, she didn't consider herself an RTC
official. That would seem, at best, a tortured explanation—she was
passing on information she'd gotten directly from the RTC.

Hanson wasn't the only administration official concerned
about the testimony. Nussbaum's assistant Neil Eggleston left the
hearing and used a cellular phone to call John Podesta. He reached
Podesta's deputy, and said he was concerned about the accuracy of
the testimony.

But the mood inside the administration was generally self-
congratulatory. Joshua Steiner rode down in the elevator with Altman after the hearing, and told him he thought the hearing had
gone "reasonably well," though Altman's choice of the phrase
"heads up"—implying as it did some kind of tip-off—was "unfortu-
nate." Steiner again committed his thoughts to his diary: "At the
hearing, the recusal amazingly did not come up. The GOP did
hammer away at whether RA had any mtgs w/ the WH. He admitted to having had one to brief them on the statute deadline. They
also asked if the staff had met, but RA gracefully ducked the question and did not refer to phone calls he had had."

Any relief over Altman's testimony was short-lived. As Steiner
had anticipated, the press seized on Altman's "heads up" as though
some improper contact had occurred. The *New York Times* treated
it as a major story, running it on the front page. Then the same day,

Stephanopoulos learned that the RTC had hired Jay Stephens to conduct an independent investigation of Madison Guaranty for the RTC. Stephens, a former U.S. attorney in Washington who had conducted a vigorous investigation of Democratic representative Dan Rostenkowski, was not only a Republican appointee, but he'd been fired as part of Clinton's wholesale replacement of the nation's U.S. attorneys, and he'd been an outspoken critic of that action. Hiring Stephens confirmed Nussbaum's worst fears about Kulka. "It's so nonsensical," he told Eggleston, when Eggleston later told him the news, "and so ridiculous that they would go out and hire a, you know, bitter political opponent of the administration who accused the administration of railroading him out of office. . . . It's silly, it's funny in sort of a perverse way, but there is nothing we can or are going to do about it. We're not calling anybody up, we're not complaining, and we're not doing anything."

At about the same time this news was coursing through the White House, Howell Raines, the editorial page editor of the *New York Times*, called Altman. Altman's testimony had touched a raw nerve with Raines. He'd written a hard-hitting editorial criticizing Altman, and wanted to give him an opportunity to further explain his actions before deciding whether to publish it. "Tell me why we shouldn't have this view?" Raines asked. Altman gave what Raines considered a rambling, poorly thought out answer that did nothing to change his mind. He also thought Altman seemed tense and nervous. "We're going to criticize you and the way you've handled this," Raines continued. "Why don't you just recuse yourself?" But Raines was hardly prepared for the answer. "As a matter of fact, I am going to recuse myself," Altman said.

"Have you announced this?"

"No."

"I'm obliged to inform the news department," Raines said, suddenly aware that he had a scoop.

Altman issued a statement announcing his recusal and conceding he had exercised "bad judgment" in meeting with White House officials at all. When Steiner learned the news, he called Stephanopoulos—widely regarded as his mentor, who'd gotten Steiner his job—at the White House. Shortly after, Ickes and Stephanopoulos phoned Altman. The presidential aides were furious over Altman's decision and the fact that he'd told the *New York Times* before them. They said that Clinton was "upset as well." The conversation quickly turned into a shouting match. Altman said he'd already decided to step down when Raines called, and he thought it would help blunt the force of the editorial to go ahead and announce it. He planned to do it that afternoon anyway. And for his part, Altman was angry that the February 2 meeting had become such a point of controversy, and that the press was characterizing it as a "briefing" for the White House.

In another call, Stephanopoulos pressed Altman about the RTC's hiring of Stephens. Altman said he didn't even know who Stephens was. "He's an avowed political enemy of the president," Stephanopoulos shot back. Altman said it wasn't appropriate for him to clear the hiring of counsel in any event, and that if Stephens had been hired, it was final. Stephanopoulos tersely suggested that Altman write a letter to the president explaining his actions—a sure sign that Altman was in trouble.

Steiner described the events in his diary:

"We spent a tortured day trying to decide if he [Altman] should recuse himself. I spoke w/ Podesta to let him know of our deliberations. Very frustrating that he was chosen point of contact since he clearly was not in complete confidence of George and Harold. After Howell Raines from the NYT called to say they were going to write a brutal editorial, RA decided to recuse himself. Harold and George then called to say BC [Clinton] was furious. They also asked how Jay Stephens, the former USA [U.S. attorney], had been hired to be outside counsel on this case. Simply outrageous that RTC had hired him, but even more amazing when George then suggested to me that we needed to find a way to get rid of him. Persuaded George that firing him would be incredibly stupid and improper."*

In the midst of this controversy, Nussbaum returned from a Federal Bar Council meeting in Mexico. Another of his assistants, Cliff Sloan, mentioned to him that Altman had testified. "I know," Nussbaum said.

But there had been no mention of other meetings, no mention of the recusal issue, Nussbaum's assistants emphasized. It would look like the administration was hiding the recusal issue and the

---

* *Stephanopoulos later testified that he "did not remember" urging that Stephens be removed.*

earlier contacts, which would be politically explosive. As Ickes had indicated in his earlier comment to Hanson, if the press learned that Altman had wanted to recuse himself, and then had been talked out of it by White House officials, it would look terrible.

A flurry of meetings and memoranda ensued, including a summary prepared by Ickes and sent to the first lady, an indication that she was now following the controversy. A transcript of Altman's testimony was carefully reviewed by Nussbaum's staff. This activity culminated in a two-and-a-half-hour meeting on March 1 that included Nussbaum, Podesta, Lindsey, and Nussbaum's staff attorneys. However generously the group interpreted Altman's testimony, it concluded that it could be seen as "less than forthcoming." While the recusal discussion might be construed as a procedural issue, rather than a "substantive" one—the qualifier Altman had inserted in his testimony—it probably should be disclosed. The answer to Senator Bond's question was, in the group's view, a "serious" problem. Whether or not Hanson and Steiner were deemed RTC officials, the fall meetings and phone calls had to be disclosed to the committee.

Just as the group was reaching these conclusions, Podesta was called from the room. He returned with the news that a *Washington Post* reporter, Ann Devroy, had somehow learned of the October 14 meeting and was working on a story. If they didn't act quickly, Altman's incomplete testimony would be exposed in the press. Far better for the news to come from the Treasury Department.

Podesta contacted Altman, who seemed reluctant to discuss what had happened. Finally Podesta told him to "go talk to Hanson," his counsel. After doing so, Altman drafted the first of what would become four painfully worded "amendments" to his testimony.

Altman's effort to correct the record was swiftly overtaken by events. With the *Washington Post* pressing for an explanation, Stephanopoulos summoned Nussbaum, who described the earlier meetings with Hanson and Treasury officials. Stephanopoulos seemed appalled. Given the outcry over the February 2 meeting with Altman, this would generate a firestorm of criticism that the White House was interfering with the investigation of Madison Guaranty and the Clintons. The meetings "were wrong, and we should acknowledge it," Stephanopoulos said. "That will end the story."

Nussbaum was beside himself. "What are you saying?"

"You shouldn't have had the meetings," Stephanopoulos said. "Just say it was an appearance of impropriety."

Nussbaum was furious. He continued to believe there was nothing improper about those meetings. No one had interfered in the investigation. Now he was being urged to confess. It felt like the travel office all over again, and in Nussbaum's view it epitomized Stephanopoulos's instinct to appease the press: just keep apologizing, and it will stop. Well, he'd had enough of that. He stormed out of the meeting and went to see Podesta. "John, why don't we just construct a defense and stick by it?"

Podesta seemed weary. "Bernie," he said, "this White House is incapable of defending itself. Even if we did what you said, it would be undermined within twenty-four hours. A 'senior aide' to the president will say that the president doesn't support this view." Nussbaum had strong suspicions who the "senior aide" would be.

Nussbaum knew he had lost the argument when McLarty told him he was issuing a policy that all contacts between the White House counsel's office and the investigative agencies should go through Joel Klein, the deputy counsel, bypassing Nussbaum. "It'll calm things down if you step aside," McLarty told him.

The next morning, the *Washington Post* ran its story with a front-page headline, "Treasury Officials Told White House Status of S&L Probe." The story made the point that "RTC officials said yesterday that 'criminal referrals' are confidential legal documents that are virtually never discussed with those named in them. Without acknowledging that the discussions were in any way improper, White House Chief of Staff Thomas F. 'Mack' McLarty yesterday warned senior officials against contacts with officials from Treasury, the RTC or others outside the White House involved in the case," according to the *Post*. The story triggered a storm of publicity, led all the network news broadcasts, and triggered numerous editorials, all condemning the administration for the appearance of interfering with a criminal investigation.

In the next day's stories, the Stephanopoulos strategy was even more evident. Asked by reporters about the meetings between Nussbaum and Treasury officials, the president himself said, "I think it would be better if the meetings and conversations had not occurred." And there was far more ominous news for Nussbaum, now seen as the flash point for the growing controversy. The *Washington*

Post reported that "Some administration officials suggested yesterday that Nussbaum's involvement in what are seen as ethical breaches has caused him to consider resigning."

Nussbaum knew the writing was on the wall after such a public humiliation. He knew who the unnamed officials were: Stephanopoulos acknowledged that he had advised the president that Nussbaum had to go. "It's not fair," Stephanopoulos had said, but Nussbaum would have to resign. That week was the first since Nussbaum had taken the job that President Clinton didn't meet with him. He felt isolated and under attack, but he was too proud to beg to stay on. The president was his client, and if he wanted a new lawyer, so be it. But all he'd done was defend the president and the presidency. On a gut level, he thought Clinton would recognize that and defend him.

The next morning, Nussbaum went into the first lady's office to see Hillary. "I know a lot is going on," he said. "You and the president should act in his interest. Friendship and loyalty should not play that big a role. But, Hillary, I don't think it's in his interest to replace me."

The first lady seemed anguished. "Oh, Bernie, you did nothing wrong, but things look so bad," she said. "The press makes things look so bad."

Nussbaum didn't find her response very reassuring. "Well," he shrugged, "the president will have to decide." He left the office.

The next day, Friday, Nussbaum was startled when subpoenas from Fiske arrived for everyone involved in the RTC investigation of Whitewater. The independent counsel was now investigating whether there was criminal interference with the investigation and was acting swiftly to take testimony under oath. Suddenly everyone on his staff, and Nussbaum himself, had to hire criminal lawyers. It was a stark reminder that these matters were now out of the White House's control.

But Nussbaum had more pressing matters on his mind. At noon, McLarty called Nussbaum. "If the president asks you to resign, will you do so?"

"Of course," Nussbaum replied.

"There's no decision yet, Bernie, but we wanted to know."

Several hours later, the president called Nussbaum into his office. "Bernie, you've become so controversial," he began. "It's such a firestorm. If you'll just step aside. . . . There is some question whether [the meetings] were proper or improper. . . . "

"They were totally proper," Nussbaum insisted.

"I'm not arguing with you," Clinton hastily said, "I don't want to argue," but he reiterated that it would have been better if the meetings had never taken place.

"Yeah, if there were no newspaper stories," Nussbaum said.

"Whether right or wrong," the president continued, "I know you had my best interests at heart, but staying on will interfere with what we came to do, like pass health care. If you leave, it will be easier to get those things done."

"Look," Nussbaum replied, "I came down here to help you. Don't decide on friendship or loyalty. If I'm interfering, then I should go. I don't happen to think so. I won't tout my abilities. But you need someone who's strong, who's loyal, who will fight for your interests. If I go, there's nobody to fill that role. Anybody who replaces me will find it hard because of what happened to me. Especially in sensitive matters like Whitewater.

"Think what message you give to other people who are strong, loyal, and did nothing wrong," Nussbaum continued, becoming more impassioned. "Doesn't this say, 'Watch out for yourself'? Who's going to love you? I know it sounds like I'm trying to hold on to a job. No. I'm ready to go home. It's your judgment, but all this will do is feed the beast."

"I would like to think about this," Clinton concluded.

Two hours later, Nussbaum was alone in his office. He was reflecting on the advice he'd first given Bill and Hillary, how history had judged Lincoln and Truman, not the daily newspapers. He felt calm. If the administration succeeded, then historians would redeem them. Just then, Ickes and McLarty appeared. McLarty handed him a handwritten note. "Read this," he said. It was from Senator Carl Levin, a Michigan Democrat and a strong Clinton backer, addressed to the president.

"It pains me to write this note," the letter read, "but I believe your counsel has not served you well."

Nussbaum stared at it. What did Levin know? He, Nussbaum, knew what had happened.

"Bernie, the president just got this," McLarty said. "You really should resign."

Nussbaum knew it was over. The next day he drafted a brief letter of resignation and handed it to the president. In it he was unapologetic, saying he had performed his duties at all times "in an absolutely legal and ethical manner."

Sacrificing Nussbaum brought no reprieve. The bad news seemed to intensify. As a stream of White House officials began appearing before a grand jury—Maggie Williams and Lisa Caputo were among the first—a paralegal at the Rose Law Firm told the *New York Times* he'd shredded files belonging to Foster. Congressional calls for hearings on Whitewater intensified—even Henry Gonzalez, the Democratic chairman of the House Banking Committee capitulated, while still calling the whole thing a Republican "witch hunt." Congressman Leach released a tape recording of April Breslaw's conversation with Jean Lewis, which he obtained from Lewis after *Washington Post* reporter Sue Schmidt suggested Leach call Lewis's father, going so far as to give the congressman the major general's phone number. (In return, Schmidt was hoping Leach would tell her what Lewis said.) Lewis's father had put his daughter in touch with Leach. On the floor of the House, Leach said the tape demonstrated that the rule of law had been "flagrantly violated in an effort to protect a single American citizen."

Bill Kennedy, the White House lawyer involved in the travel office affair who handled background reviews for potential nominees, had to admit that he had his own ethical problem, the failure to pay Social Security taxes on the family's maid in Arkansas. Webster Hubbell abruptly resigned from the Justice Department, saying his dispute with the Rose firm over his billings—the matter raised at the meeting with Hubbell before Foster's death—was distracting him from his official duties. Though Hubbell publicly minimized the seriousness of the dispute, the amount of suspicious billings and client charges had now swelled to nearly $500,000, and the matter had been swept into the Fiske investigation, which was taking testimony about Hubbell before the grand jury. And for the Clintons, there was even more ominous news from the independent counsel. David Hale, the municipal judge who ran Capital Management Services and accused Clinton of pressuring him to make a loan, agreed to plead guilty to two felonies and to cooperate with the Fiske investigation. Hale had finally gotten what he wanted: a plea

bargain, albeit to two felonies. But Fiske had gained the cooperation of the first in what was likely to be a chain of witnesses that led
toward the White House.

After being battered in the press for weeks, Hillary Clinton
took the offensive, scheduling interviews with the three major news
magazines and appearing on all three Sunday morning network
interview shows on March 13. She dismissed the Whitewater controversy and the appointment of an independent counsel, saying it
will lead to "people spending millions and millions of dollars" to
"conclude we made a bad land investment." As she spoke, Jeff
Gerth was preparing to break yet another damaging story from her
days in Arkansas.

The *New York Times*'s managing editor, Joe Lelyveld, had convened a meeting in New York in January of all the paper's investigative reporters, the first such meeting any of them could recall.
Gerth had gone back over all his notes from his original Whitewater work and his early meetings with Susan Thomases. He came up
with about a half dozen items he'd never pinned down that he
thought warranted further investigation, which he circulated in a
memo to the other reporters. Among them was the source of the
down payment for the house the Clintons bought in 1980, the
money Thomases had characterized as "investments and savings."
Another was McDougal's early mention that Hillary had been looking for a tax shelter for her earnings in commodities. And, of course,
there was still the question of the missing 1978 and 1979 Clinton
tax returns, which had never been made public.

Gerth, now working with another investigative reporter who'd
been assigned to Whitewater, Dean Baquet, was again dispatched
to Arkansas. It didn't take them long to discover that there were
only a handful of successful commodities brokers in northwest Arkansas, and Red Bone was the most prominent, practically legendary. They were the first reporters to reach Bone—Baquet and
reporter Stephen Labaton tracked him down in rural northwest
Arkansas, knocking on doors during a snowstorm. Bone didn't even
remember that Hillary Clinton had been a client, but he certainly
did remember Jim Blair. That was the thread that led to the first
lady. As they pieced the story together over the next few weeks,
Gerth realized that the house down payment, the commodities
trading, and the tax returns had all merged into a single story. He

felt Thomases' earlier characterization had been extremely misleading, even if technically accurate. The down payment had come
from "savings" only in the sense that the commodities profits had
earned interest as they briefly passed through Hillary's bank account.

This time Gerth was determined not to be deflected. He called
Dee Dee Myers, explained the story, and said the *Times* wanted a
response within two days. Then Gerth called Lloyd Cutler, the
prominent Washington lawyer who replaced Nussbaum as counsel
to the president. "Look," Gerth said, "I think we have a story. This
is a substantive story. We've done a lot of reporting and we're
prepared to go forward with or without your involvement. I know
you're new on the job. You're not responsible for what happened in
the past."

Cutler was conciliatory, saying he'd do his best, and would get
back to Gerth. He asked for another day's time, which Gerth agreed
to, and Cutler arranged a meeting at 4 P.M. the following day at
David Kendall's office. Besides Kendall, the Clintons' personal lawyer, the meeting included Podesta and Lisa Caputo, the first lady's
press secretary. Cutler didn't attend. The reporters sensed they
were on to something significant. The White House group was
armed with records and notes that had been prepared for use in the
campaign had that proven necessary. They had copies of the actual
trading records for Hillary's account, which they said proved that
the first lady had her own account. Gerth hadn't yet pinned down
whether she had her own account or was sharing in the profits from
Blair's. But when he asked to see the trading records, he was refused. Finally they let him look at them briefly—only to verify that
the account was in her name—but wouldn't let him write anything
down or make copies. They told him the amount of her initial
investment, but not the amount of profit. Gerth and Baquet had an
estimate of about $100,000 for her profit, and they got the sense
that they weren't too far off the mark.

Gerth could see that they also had copies of the Clintons' 1978
and 1979 tax returns, but they wouldn't let him see them. Now he
realized why they hadn't released the returns: the commodities
profits would have been reported in the returns for those years.

Though they still didn't know the precise numbers, it seemed
obvious that Hillary had scored substantial gains in the notoriously

volatile commodities market, at a time when she had only recently
come to Arkansas and can't have known much about cattle futures.
How had she done it? Caputo seemed prepared for the question.
She said the first lady had done her own research, including "reading the *Wall Street Journal.*" She added that Hillary had consulted
"numerous people."

As the reporters put the final touches on the story, Kendall
issued a written statement: the first lady had traded "with her own
funds and assumed the full risk of loss. She did so through two
different trading accounts in her own name in Little Rock and
Springdale, Ark. Mrs. Clinton reported gains and losses on her tax
returns as appropriate." Podesta added, "Hillary and Jim [Blair]
were friends. He gave her advice. There was no impropriety. The
only appearance is being created by the *New York Times.*"

The story ran on the front page on March 18: "Top Arkansas
Lawyer Helped Hillary Clinton Turn Big Profit; Commodities
Trading in 70's Yielded $100,000." In addition to reporting the
trading itself and the White House responses, the story dwelled at
some length on the appearance of accepting assistance from Blair
at a time when he was a top lawyer for Tyson Foods, which was
obviously influenced by numerous decisions by Governor Clinton.
This aspect of the story particularly incensed Blair, who responded,
"Do they have to go weed their friends out and say they can only
have friends who are sweeping the streets? They have friends who
are high-powered lawyers. They have friends who write books, who
write poetry."

The commodities trading story set off a new storm of negative
publicity. By not telling the full story, the White House created a
fresh mystery, fueling more stories. Gerth alone received over a
hundred phone calls, more than had been generated by any of his
stories, most claiming that such returns by a neophyte commodities
trader were inexplicable. The White House, under a siege of questions, finally had to reveal that the first lady's initial investment had
been a mere $1,000, which meant her rate of return was strato-
spheric. No claim was more pilloried than the insistence that Hillary had made the decisions herself after consulting friends and
reading the *Wall Street Journal.* The *Journal* looked in its archives,
and produced a compendium of commodities stories that had run
in the paper during the period of Hillary's trading. It was obvious

that they would have been of scant value to any trader. Ultimately, in an impromptu news conference nearly a month after the story appeared—a press conference from which Gerth was banned—the first lady backed off the claim, acknowledging that it was Blair who had guided her trading.

Some weeks later, Gerth asked a White House official involved why he'd been given such a preposterous explanation in the first place. The official paused. "The first instinct from everybody from Arkansas," he said, "is to lie."

Whitewater was finally extracting a political toll. In late March, a poll placed Clinton's approval rating at 47 percent, down 11 points from February. His disapproval rating rose over the same period from 38 percent to 45 percent. And it was taking an emotional, personal toll.

The same day that Nussbaum resigned, the first lady sat down for a previously scheduled interview with Meryl Gordon, who was doing an article for *Elle* magazine. Gordon described her as looking "tired and a little reflective." The first lady plunged almost immediately into the Whitewater controversy, displaying flashes of anger at a vaguely defined "they," a coalition of press and other people determined to undermine her and her husband.

"Look, I know what this is about," she began. "This is a well-organized and well-financed attempt to undermine my husband and, by extension, myself, by people who have a different political agenda or have another personal and financial reason for attacking us. So taking it for what it is, which is pretty blatant, you can't take it seriously, and you have to keep doing what Bill and I do every day, which is remember why we did this—and work hard."

"How do you counter the constant attacks?" Gordon asked.

"You don't. Since I know, in the end, nothing bad happened—and that's what everybody's going to know eventually, because they have yet to come forward with anything other than the wildest kind of paranoid conspiracies—you just don't pay much attention to it. . . . I'm not interested in spending my days falling into the trap that the fomenters of all of this want us to, which is to become isolated and on the defensive and diverted. I'm not going to let that happen. Unfortunately, in today's climate, anyone can say anything about a person in public life, and it will get printed. I can't help that; it's not my problem."

Gordon asked about the *American Spectator* article about the troopers. "They'll try anything," Hillary responded. "What's so sad is that the so-called legitimate press—because of commercial pressures, as best I can figure out—gets sucked into it. I am stunned at the level to which malevolent, malicious, false gossip has been permitted to become newsworthy. . . ."

"Are you really able to blow it off?"

"I blow most of it off. I get angry. I get confused about why people are doing what they do. I don't get up every day thinking destructively about others. I don't spend my hours plotting for somebody else's downfall. My feeling is, gosh, there's more work that can be done, everybody ought to get out there and improve the health care system and reform welfare and get guns out of the hands of teenagers. That's real. This other stuff is not real to me, so why should I take stuff I consider foolish seriously?"

The answer to her rhetorical questions must have seemed all too obvious, as Altman's diary entry had made clear: "On Whitewater, Maggie told me that HRC was 'paralyzed' by it. If we don't solve this 'within the next two days,' you don't have to worry about her schedule on health care."

With the administration's legislative agenda—health care, law enforcement, welfare reform—clearly in peril, his approval ratings plummeting, the president held the second prime-time news conference of his presidency on March 24. With the commodities story still swirling (and all the damaging information essentially in the public domain), the president announced he would finally release his tax returns from 1977 to 1979 reporting the proceeds from the commodities trading. And he acknowledged that the Lyons report had been incorrect: he now conceded that the $20,744 check was a repayment of a personal loan he had taken out for the down payment on a lakefront home for his mother. He said his memory had been refreshed after he saw McDougal's appearance on ABC and read galleys of his mother's autobiography, which mentioned the house.

But more fundamentally, the press conference was Clinton's most serious effort yet to get Whitewater behind him. As it had been in so many comeback speeches before, his stance was both defiant and apologetic. Asked if he felt he made any mistakes in the Whitewater investment, the president responded:

"I certainly don't think I made a mistake in the initial investment. It was a perfectly honorable thing to do. And it was a perfectly legal thing to do. And I didn't make any money. I lost money. I paid my debts. And then later on, as you know, Hillary and I tried to make sure that the corporation was closed down in an appropriate way. . . . We were like a lot of people: we invested money and we lost." He also addressed the issue of contacts between the White House and the Treasury, acknowledging that "I think that we weren't as sensitive as we should have been, and I said before it would have been better if that hadn't occurred. But I think, you know, the one thing you have to say is you learn things as you go along in this business. None of this in the light of history will be remotely as important as the fact that by common consensus we had the most productive first year of a presidency last year of anyone in a generation."

Later, the president was asked, "Have you taken any lessons from this ordeal, whether it's about the presidency, about the process, about the city, or anything?" Clinton replied:

"Oh, I think I've learned a lot about it. I think one of the things I've learned about it is that it's very important to try to decide that the legitimate responsibility of the president is to be as forthcoming as possible and to do it.

"It's important for me to understand that there is a level here —and this is not a blame, this is just an observation—because of the experiences of the last several decades, of which I was not a part in this city, I think there is a level of suspicion here that is greater than that which I have been used to in the past. And I don't complain about it, but I've learned a lot about it. And that my job is to try to answer whatever questions are out there so I can get on with the business of the country. And I think I've learned a lot about how to handle that.

"I've also learned here that there may or may not be a different standard than I had seen in the past, not of right and wrong; that doesn't change, but of what may appear to be right or wrong. And I think that you'll see that, like everything else, this administration learns and goes on."

EPILOGUE

THE CLINTONS' 1994 press conferences were their last direct attempts to put Whitewater behind them. Susan Thomases' visit to me at about the same time was, presumably, part of the same strategy. And for at least a brief period, it seemed to work. As David Kendall, the Clintons' personal lawyer, confidently predicted, "Whitewater is evaporating." Clinton later told the *Los Angeles Times* that he would permit "no discussion of this in my household, no discussion of this in my office."

From the vantage point of the White House, the scandal might have been expected to run its course. The events in Arkansas during the 1980s had been pored over by the nation's media, and not much had surfaced beyond Jeff Gerth's first stories. The national media had largely vacated Arkansas. The Clintons' approach to the scandal—to brush it aside, promise full cooperation, then frustrate every inquiry—was put in place during the campaign and seemed to harden once the Clintons occupied the White House. However puzzling that strategy seemed to outsiders, it was routinely defended by those close to the Clintons in simple ends-justify-the-means terms: Bill and Hillary Clinton were the president and the first lady. The strategy had worked. Yet however effective in the short term, the strategy seemed to ignore the judgment of history that had so concerned Bernard Nussbaum.

In May, Paula Jones's lawyers, financed in part by the conservative Legal Affairs Council, had followed through on their threat and filed a sexual harassment and civil rights lawsuit against the president, the first such lawsuit against a sitting president. The complaint alleged "deprivation and conspiracy to deprive Plaintiff of her federally protected rights," and "intentional infliction of emotional distress, and for defamation." The filing of the suit generated a flurry of publicity, especially from news outlets that had been reluctant to carry the story when Jones surfaced months earlier. Worse, from the White House perspective, the complaint provided a graphic description of what Jones alleged transpired behind the closed doors of the hotel room, providing ample fodder for ridicule of the president. Through his lawyer, Robert Bennett, Clinton denied the claims, and asserted the president's immunity from prosecution. The case was soon embroiled in procedural issues that could take years to resolve (an appeals court recently ruled that Jones's suit could proceed while the president was in office, but that ruling was expected to be appealed by the White House). While delay seemed to be the White House's strategy, it meant that Jones's claims would still be pending during the 1996 presidential campaign.

In June Congress finally approved a new independent counsel law, which, like its predecessor, required that the counsel be appointed by members of the federal judiciary, not an attorney general beholden to the president. Given Reno's scrupulous effort to maintain the counsel's independence, she asked that a three-judge panel reappoint Robert Fiske.

On June 30, the same day that the president signed the new independent counsel law, Fiske issued a report on the death of Vincent Foster that was welcomed by the administration. The report concluded that "Vincent W. Foster, Jr. committed suicide by firing a bullet from a .38 caliber revolver into his mouth." It said that evidence "overwhelmingly supports" a suicide, and "there is no evidence to the contrary."

Fiske had not convened a grand jury dedicated to the Foster aspect of his probe, since he had not encountered any evidence of crime that would have justified the secrecy of a criminal probe. It isn't clear whether relevant documents, such as Foster's own handwritten notes that explicitly mention Whitewater, were made available to the Fiske investigators. For the report took pains to add, "We have learned of no instance in which Whitewater, Madison Guaranty, CMS (Capital Management Services) or other possible legal matters of the Clintons were mentioned. Moreover, in the spring and summer of 1993, Whitewater and Madison Guaranty related matters were not issues of concern either within the White House or in the press." A later passage adds that "we cannot conclusively rule out such a concern" (as Whitewater), but "there is no evidence he did have such a concern."

The report is also silent on the question of Webster Hubbell's irregular billing practices as a subject of concern to Foster, even though the Fiske lawyers were by then well aware of the problem, and were independently examining Hubbell's practices.

Given the partisan environment already swirling around Foster's death, predictably the report was attacked as incomplete and insufficiently skeptical. One of its most outspoken critics was Senator Lauch Faircloth, a conservative Republican from North Carolina, who called publicly for Fiske's replacement as soon as the independent counsel law was signed. In mid-July he had lunch with D.C. appeals court judge David B. Sentelle, also from North Carolina, and a member of the three-judge panel considering Fiske's reappointment, and Senator Jesse Helms, another North Carolina Republican. The three denied that they discussed Fiske or his possible replacement at the lunch. They had talked about "Western wear, old friends, and prostate problems," according to Helms.

In August, the three-judge panel announced that it was removing Fiske as independent counsel and replacing him with Kenneth Starr, a conservative Republican, former solicitor general in the Bush administration, and a former appeals court judge appointed by Ronald Reagan. Though Starr had been on the list of lawyers originally considered by Reno, his résumé had a far more partisan cast than had Fiske's.

People at the White House were dismayed, especially upset that Starr's law firm, Kirkland & Ellis, had considered submitting a brief supporting Paula Jones's claim that a president isn't immune from suit for sexual harassment. To the White House's further dismay, Starr reopened the investigation into the death of Foster, taking new testimony before a grand jury. Many members of the Fiske team resigned. From the viewpoint of the White House, the new independent counsel was independent only in the sense that his appointment had no taint of the executive branch.

But people who worked closely with Starr in the Bush administration say that Starr isn't so easily classified. They note that Starr's dream—to be nominated to the Supreme Court—was frustrated by even more conservative Republicans who had gained influence over the Reagan and Bush judicial selection process. Starr was deemed to have been too close to former Reagan solicitor general Rex Lee, whose moderate views offended conservative zealots. Both Lee and Starr were often derided by them as "country club" Republicans out of the George Bush mold. A more serious concern, these former colleagues say, is Starr's lack of experience in criminal prosecution.

Still, given the visibility of his conservative political ties, Starr appears to be one of the most partisan independent counsels or special prosecutors ever appointed, a factor that is sure to generate continuing debate over the wisdom of the independent counsel law. The *New York Times*, in an editorial, almost immediately called for Starr's resignation. That provided small comfort to the White House. The only possible silver lining, as the *Washington Post* editorialized, is that "If this counsel with these credentials finds he [Clinton] did no wrong, there will be no room for disbelief."

Starr vowed to be fair and impartial, but thorough. While his investigation is no doubt upending life for many in Arkansas—as would any criminal investigation as wide-ranging in scope—there hasn't been any public indication of prosecutorial misconduct or partisan zeal. On the contrary, had Starr been acting largely out of partisan motives, he would almost surely have sought more indictments than he has. Instead, he allowed the statute of limitations to run out with respect to various campaign financing matters under investigation.

However peripheral the Clintons tried to keep the Whitewater affair and other headaches, there was no doubt that these matters distracted them at a crucial time. Roger Altman's concern, expressed in his diary, that a fixation on Whitewater might derail health care reform proved prescient. In a humiliating defeat for the administration, the health care bill—the single most important piece of legislation scheduled for the president's first term—was repudiated by Congress in September 1994. Attacked for the secrecy in which it was conceived and as radical legislation that would threaten the quality of health care, the Democratic leadership couldn't muster enough votes to block a threatened Republican filibuster. Almost overnight, it seemed that Hillary Clinton went from being a groundbreaking, policy-making first lady likely to join ranks with her heroine Eleanor Roosevelt, to a political liability, an embarrassment who had to be kept out of the public eye. She suddenly seemed a shadow of her former self.

The midterm elections, in November, seemed to reflect the growing exasperation of voters with both the Democrat-controlled White House and with Congress. By campaigning against Congressman Newt Gingrich's "Contract with America," Clinton managed to transform the elections into a national referendum. In what could prove to be a historic shift, Republicans gained control of both houses of Congress for the first time in a generation.

In the previous Congress, the administration could, to a certain extent, count on the Democratic majority to keep any Whitewater inquiries within bounds. In May 1995, the Senate voted ninety-six to three to convene hearings into Whitewater and related issues, hearings to be presided over by one of Clinton's staunchest critics, Senator Alfonse D'Amato of New York. He scheduled fresh hearings, this time directed by aggressive and hostile Republicans. These began in the summer of 1995 and intensified toward the end of the year and into 1996. L. Jean Lewis, now being represented by the conservative Landmark Legal Foundation, found herself a star attraction, testifying to the obstacles she believed she'd encountered in her efforts to investigate Madison Guaranty.

At first the hearings seemed to attract scant public interest, with most major papers providing only dutiful coverage far inside, and the networks all but ignoring them. But as new evidence— phone records, internal memos, billing records from the Rose firm —surfaced from within the White House that seemed increasingly to contradict public assertions by the Clintons and their aides, the story took on greater momentum, and began moving to the front page. Faring especially poorly in the rounds of testimony before Congress in the fall of 1995 were Hillary's chief of staff, Maggie Williams, and her confidante Susan Thomases, whose memory lapses when confronted with records of phone calls made the morning after Foster's death were widely ridiculed. The president himself, having pledged full cooperation, had to resort to claims of executive privilege and attorney-client privilege in an attempt to protect from disclosure notes taken by Bill Kennedy of the November 5 meeting where White House lawyers and officials briefed David Kendall about Whitewater and related investigations. The notes, containing the puzzling reference to "vacuum," were ultimately produced to avert a constitutional showdown in the courts (a dispute most legal scholars predicted the White House would lose). The incident—as had so many before it—evoked memories of Richard Nixon's handling of Watergate and left many observers convinced that the White House had something to hide.

In other ways, however, the Republican Congress and especially the Newt Gingrich–led House proved a boon to the administration. The president, in opposition, was able to don the mantle of a strong leader. Casting himself as the champion of the elderly, the poor, and the ill, Clinton attacked the Republican budget cuts and gained new ground, shifting attention away from past troubles like Whitewater. At year-end 1995, his approval ratings moved over 50 percent for the first time since late 1993, just before the troopers' allegations surfaced and it was revealed that Foster's files had been removed. As before, the Clintons' popularity was almost immediately threatened by a fresh round of attacks on their candor, especially the first lady's. After long-missing billing records surfaced in the White House, Hillary Clinton was called before the grand jury investigating Whitewater, the first time a first lady had been subpoenaed in a criminal probe.

Others involved to varying degrees in aspects of the scandal have suffered much more. Despite his long friendship with the Clintons and his unfailingly polite, affable manner, Mack McLarty was replaced as chief of staff during the summer of 1994, relegated to a basement office in the White House and a vaguely defined role as liaison to the business community. Press secretary Dee Dee Myers, whose remark about the FBI investigation of the travel office caused such trouble, was also replaced, joining Republican political strategist Mary Matalin as co-host of a television talk show. Roger Altman drew such criticism for his seeming misstatements before Congress (he was investigated but not charged with perjury, and continues to maintain he was unaware of earlier Treasury contacts) that he was forced to resign. He, too, had a basement office for a time before returning to work as an investment banker in New York. Treasury officials Jean Hanson and Joshua Steiner, their credibility under attack in Congress, resigned as well.

David Gergen, his loyalty to the Clintons in question, left the White House to serve a stint as an advisor to Secretary of State Warren Christopher before leaving government to work at the Aspen Institute, teach at Duke University, and write at book on presidential leadership. As Nussbaum had unwittingly predicted at the Oval Office meeting about the independent counsel, Bruce Lindsey became a subject of Starr's probe into Clinton's campaign finances. The statute of limitations lapsed, however, and no charges were brought. Lindsey remains a close and trusted advisor to the president, as does George Stephanopoulos.

The "sport" decried by Vince Foster continued to claim its victims, with the Arkansas contingent in Washington faring especially poorly. In December 1994 Webb Hubbell pleaded guilty to felonies of income tax evasion and mail fraud. The billing issue first raised by the Rose partners in the months before Foster's death had led to Hubbell admitting that he defrauded Rose and its clients of $390,000. Offering no explanation for more than four hundred fraudulent bills to cover credit card purchases at such fashion outlets as Victoria's Secret and a fur salon, Hubbell said at his plea hearing that "I deeply regret the pain my actions have caused family, friends, and those who placed me in a position of trust." While the plea had nothing to do with anything involving the Clintons, Hubbell agreed to cooperate fully with independent counsel Starr, cooperation that may yet shed light on the handling of documents from the Rose firm. Hubbell was sentenced to twenty-one months in prison, where he has been working on a book, *Friends in High Places.*

David Watkins was forced to resign after an ill-considered helicopter reconnaissance mission to golf courses earmarked for prospective presidential use. He was told to repay the $13,000 cost of the helicopter ride. Billy Dale, who had run the travel office, was acquitted of all charges stemming from the travel office affair. Bill Kennedy, under continuing fire for failing to pay taxes for his family's nanny, resigned and returned to Arkansas and his partnership at the Rose firm. His activities in the travel office affair remained under scrutiny, and he was called before the grand jury. The Rose firm itself quietly closed its Washington office.

In Arkansas, Ozarks realtor Chris Wade pleaded guilty to two felonies—bankruptcy fraud and submitting a false loan application —and agreed to cooperate with the independent counsel. He was sentenced in December 1995 to a prison term of fifteen months. Wade claimed business losses and attorney's fees related to Starr's investigation had cost him $950,000. Steve Smith, Clinton's aide in the early days as governor and Jim McDougal's partner in the Bank of Kingston, also pleaded guilty to a misdemeanor and agreed to cooperate. David Hale, the head of Capital Management Services, pleaded guilty to two felonies and is still awaiting sentencing. While not technically in a witness protection program, he has been living in seclusion and is expected to be a key witness in any future trials.

Governor Jim Guy Tucker was indicted on eleven felony counts including misapplying funds and making false statements to a financial institution in connection with Castle Grande and other Madison Guaranty real estate developments. The indictment was thrown out by the federal judge in Little Rock presiding over the case as exceeding the jurisdiction of the independent counsel. The judge is a staunch Democrat and friend of the Clintons. Starr appealed the decision to the Eighth Circuit Court of Appeals, which seems almost certain to overrule the district court and reinstate the indictment.

Neither of the state troopers who spoke out against Clinton— Roger Perry and Larry Patterson—remain in the Arkansas governor's security detail. Patterson left the detail in July 1992. He remains on the state police force, working in the special services section overseeing used car dealers. He hopes to retire soon. Perry was further demoted from his narcotics job to highway patrolman. No book deals or other fees materialized. Danny Ferguson, who declined to speak to the press and is a likely witness in the Paula Jones case, was given a state job as liaison to the Bureau of Alcohol, Tobacco, and Firearms.

Paula Jones continues to live with her husband in California. Over her objections, nude photographs of her taken by a former boyfriend appeared in the January 1995 issue of *Penthouse* magazine. The accompanying article, "The Devil in Paula Jones," characterized her as "dedicated to snaring the attention of men." Her acting career has made no progress and she is estranged from her sister, Charlotte.

Among members of the media, Jeff Gerth remains a reporter in the Washington bureau of the *New York Times*. To the evident glee of those in the White House, his articles became the subject of an October 1994 cover story in *Harper's Magazine*, "Fool for Scandal: How the *Times* Got Whitewater Wrong" by Gene Lyons, an author and columnist for the *Arkansas Democrat-Gazette*. At a subsequent symposium at the National Press Club, Lyons further attacked Gerth (who was invited but didn't attend). *Harper's* editor Lewis Lapham introduced the discussion by saying that Lyons contended the Whitewater scandal "is based almost entirely on rumor, gossip, hearsay, flat-out fabrication and that there is no scandal there," and that "the evidence so far seems to support the argument made by Lyons."* The *Times* demonstrated its continuing support for Gerth by nominating his story on the first lady's commodities trading for a 1995 Pulitzer Prize. Gerth has moved on to stories other than Whitewater, though he has assisted other reporters covering the story.

At the *Los Angeles Times*, Bill Rempel remains a reporter in Los Angeles. Douglas Frantz carried out his threat to resign from the paper, and is now a reporter for the *New York Times* in New York. Ira Silverman retired from NBC News.

In the view of his editors at the *New York Post*, Christopher Ruddy became increasingly obsessed with conspiracy theories involving Foster and the Clintons. Ruddy ultimately resigned after he refused to work on any other topic. Still, *Post* editor Eric Breindel recommended Ruddy for a job as columnist at the *Tribune-Review* outside Pittsburgh, Pennsylvania, owned by Richard Mellon Scaife, the conservative philanthropist. Using his column there as a platform, Ruddy has continued to publicize such "scoops" as the claim that the Foster suicide note was a forgery. Scaife has also helped bankroll the Western Journalism Center, which has run full-page ads in major newspapers featuring Ruddy's work and seeking donations.

David Bossie resigned from Citizens United during the summer of 1995 to join the staff of Senator Faircloth, a member of the Banking Committee investigating Whitewater.

Lisa Foster was severely depressed after her husband's death,

---

* *Lyons's claims seem to involve issues best evaluated by confirmed Whitewater enthusiasts. For example, is it unfair and misleading, as Lyons claims, to describe McDougal as an "S&L operator," as Gerth did, when he became one only after the Whitewater investment began?*

and began seeing a psychiatrist. As she began to feel better, she began dating. She married a newly appointed federal judge in Little Rock at the end of 1995, and she told *The New Yorker*'s Peter Boyer in mid-1995 that she had come to terms with her husband's death. "I can't do anything about the fact that Vince is gone," she said. "The only thing I can do is try to make the best of what we have. I have found a wonderful man whom I love and who loves me, and who will be good to my children. And just because it's going to be an adjustment is no reason not to do it. The whole damned thing's been an adjustment. So we will adjust."

Apart from the Foster family, perhaps no lives have been more affected than those of Jim McDougal, who set the Whitewater affair in motion, and his wife, Susan. On August 17, both McDougals were indicted, Jim for nineteen and Susan for eight felony counts of conspiracy, mail fraud, bank fraud, and making or causing false statements to a financial institution.*

Both McDougals entered pleas of not guilty. "I would not be standing here if I had anything to say about President Clinton or his wife to the special counsel," Susan told the court. "I am not going to testify against anybody." Jim McDougal says he plans to repeat the bravura performance on the witness stand that proved so effective with the jury in his earlier trial. The McDougals' trials were scheduled for the spring of 1996, which means the independent counsel's investigation is almost sure to continue past the next presidential election.

The amount of money involved in Whitewater, though substantial to the average American, is minor compared to the S&L frauds, or the insider trading scandals on Wall Street. As the president and his lawyers have often emphasized, unlike Watergate or Iran-contra, the events that triggered the scandal—the Whitewater investment itself—did not occur while Clinton was president. There isn't any conclusive evidence that Clinton, as governor, bestowed undue favors on McDougal in return for being subsidized in Whitewater, or that he influenced Beverly Bassett to do so. Nor

---

*At the same time, Susan faces California state charges of embezzlement of nearly $200,000 stemming from her work as a financial manager for orchestra conductor Zubin Mehta and his wife. Susan pleaded not guilty. She said she had the Mehtas' permission to sign checks and called the dispute a misunderstanding.

is there any evidence that Madison Guaranty funds were siphoned from the S&L to Whitewater or the Clintons. Despite all the concerns in the Treasury Department and White House, the Resolution Trust Corporation concluded its investigation of Madison Guaranty at the end of 1995 and recommended that no action be taken against the president or first lady. Persistent allegations that Vince Foster was murdered, even that the Clintons may have been involved, are preposterous. The evidence is overwhelming that Foster committed suicide.

Yet the story of the Clintons' investment in Whitewater, Hillary Clinton's commodities trading, their lives in Arkansas, and their handling of these matters both during the presidential campaign and in the White House hardly shows the president and first lady in a flattering light. For reasons that seem rooted in their personalities, especially Hillary's, and in the dynamic of their marriage at the time, the Clintons seized what seemed to be opportunities to make easy money, even when that meant accepting favors or special treatment from people in businesses regulated by the state. Surely the Clintons, who went to such lengths to insulate Hillary Clinton from Rose firm income derived from state agencies, recognized the resulting possible conflicts of interest. The Rose firm's and Hillary's work for Madison, especially their involvement in the dubious Castle Grande transactions, raises serious questions of propriety.

Their handling of the Whitewater investment verges on reckless. Having instigated the investment, Bill Clinton largely abdicated responsibility, leaving to his wife the burden of complying with the minimal demands levied on them by the McDougals. While lack of knowledge about the investment has often been asserted by the Clintons as an excuse or defense, their ignorance seems willful. When finally asked, Susan McDougal was only too happy to turn over the Whitewater records to Hillary. Surely the Clintons could indulge in such a laissez-faire approach to what was their single largest financial asset only because they expected others to take care of them because of their power and prestige as the governor and his wife.

Once Hillary Clinton was actively managing the investment, after the McDougals moved to California in 1987, the Clintons' behavior seems even more questionable. Valuations of Whitewater on personal financial disclosure forms prepared by the Clintons seem inflated. In the case of 1st Ozark, such forms apparently weren't even submitted in 1988, despite efforts by the bank to obtain them. Yet despite its troubled status, the loan wasn't called —not with the bank's holding company seeking favorable legislation from the Arkansas government.

Still, nothing in the Clintons' past, on its face, seems to explain the pattern of evasions, half-truths, and misstatements that have characterized the Clintons' handling of the story, both during the campaign and in the White House. Advised repeatedly to fully disclose their roles, they declined. In the context of the campaign that may have seemed expedient, with Jeff Gerth's story coming at a time when a dreaded "third strike" seemed all too likely to cost Bill Clinton the nomination. Strikes one and two—the draft and Gennifer Flowers controversies—had been Bill Clinton's doing. But Whitewater focused on Hillary Clinton, which must have placed her under intense pressure to, as she had in the past, rescue her husband. Perhaps the full story would have cost the Clintons the election. The fierce effort to contain the story suggests that the Clintons thought it would.

In doing so, however, their dubious assertions took root, and grew to mythological proportion: The Clintons had virtually nothing to do with Whitewater and were simply "passive" investors. The McDougals didn't really absorb significantly more losses than the Clintons. Hillary wasn't responsible for Madison Guaranty becoming a client of the Rose firm. Her work for Madison before a state regulator was insignificant.

The pattern continued, especially after Vincent Foster's death: The first lady was only minimally involved in the travel office affair. Whitewater had nothing to do with Foster's state of mind. The first lady wasn't concerned about papers in Foster's office, and wasn't involved in their removal. Anyone who questioned the official version, even within the White House, was branded as disloyal. Others were accused of acting out of partisan hostility. Perhaps, as is so often the case, the official version of innocence and persecution took on a relentless logic of its own. It would have been relatively easy, early on, to disclose everything and correct the record. But as time passed, their drip-by-drip concessions gave credence to their critics and undermined their integrity.

The Clintons have enemies enough in a Republican Congress, in well-heeled think tanks, and in the conservative media. As they now surely recognize, there is a sophisticated, well-financed network, eager to exploit every false step and false statement, that has proven remarkably effective at keeping Whitewater and related scandals alive. But there is no sinister conspiracy, as the White House seems to envision. There is nothing linking the Arkansas troopers, Paula Jones, and the McDougals other than firsthand experiences that they have chosen, for better or worse, credibly or not, to make public. The Clintons needn't have reacted in ways that alienated the mainstream media and even many of their supporters.

The Clintons' and McDougals' activities in Whitewater, involving federally regulated banks, savings and loans, federal taxes, favors bestowed and accepted—not to mention political campaign financing—are areas covered by a network of criminal and civil laws. Factual issues of knowledge and intent loom large in whether any of these laws were broken. Whether there was obstruction of justice is also under investigation. Ultimately a grand jury and the independent counsel will make that decision, and decide whether, in their discretion, any further charges should be filed, against either the president or first lady, or others.

In November 1994, five months after he left Washington, Bernie Nussbaum was exercising on his treadmill when his wife called him to the phone. "It's Camp David."

It was President Clinton. The Republicans had just swept Congress. Hubbell was about to plead guilty, and Lindsey was under investigation. Whitewater wasn't going away.

"Hi, how are you?" the president asked.

"Fine."

Clinton began a monologue, blaming himself for the congressional defeat. He sounded uncharacteristically down, discouraged.

"Are you okay?" Nussbaum asked.

"Yes."

"You have to stay strong."

"The special counsel legislation, the whole institution," Clinton said. "We should have thought about it more. Can it be fair?"

"As you recall, we discussed that," Nussbaum answered, remembering almost reluctantly the pitched battle in the Oval Office.

"I know . . ." Clinton mused. "You're a good guy, Bernie. Your advice was good advice."

Clinton sounded like he wanted to keep talking, but Nussbaum felt like an old romance had ended.

"It was nice of you to call," he said.

"Yeah, let's talk some more," Clinton said.

"Maybe another time."

APPENDIXES

James B. McDougal
P. O. Box 1583
Little Rock, Ark. 72203-1583

November 27, 1984

Ms. Hillary Clinton
1800 Center Street
Little Rock, Ark. 72202

Dear Hillary:

I urgently need your personal financial statement
to renew the Whitewater note at Flippin.

Sincerely,

James B. McDougal

JBMcD/rm

12-17-84

FINANCIAL STATEMENT

WILLIAM J. CLINTON AND HILLARY RODHAM CLINTON

ASSETS

Cash on Hand	$ 90,000
Securities	40,000
Accounts, Loans, Notes Receivable	100,000
Cash Surrender Value - Life Insurance	4,000
Real Estate	100,000
Personal Property	35,000
TOTAL ASSETS	$ 369,000

LIABILITIES

Notes Payable	$ 200,000
Accounts and Notes Payable to Others	7,000
TOTAL LIABILITIES	$ 207,000
NET WORTH	$ 162,000

Bill Clinton

Security Bank

P.O. BOX 670 · PARAGOULD, ARKANSAS 72451

501-239-9571

March 5, 1987

<u>PERSONAL/CONFIDENTIAL</u>

Ms. Hillary Clinton, Attorney
Rose Law Firm
1200 East Fourth St.
Little Rock, AR 72201

Dear Hillary:

Enclosed is a new note in the amount of $14,117.59. This represents the principal and interest on the current note.

Upon receipt of the executed note, we will pay the present indebtedness and return the paid note to you.

It is my understanding that we will be receiving payments in the amount of $285.13. At present interest rates, this will retire the indebtedness in slightly over five years. Enclosed also are envelopes for the convenience of mailing the payments.

Please complete the enclosed financial statement and mail it to us in order that our records can be updated.

Give me a call if you have any questions.

Sincerely,

William B. Fisher
President & CEO

WBF:j1

CONFIDENTIAL

DKRT700351

PERSONAL FINANCIAL STATEMENT

IMPORTANT: Read these directions before completing this Statement.

☐ If you are applying for individual credit in your own name and are relying on your own income or assets and not the income or assets of another person as the basis for repayment of the credit requested, complete only Sections 1 and 3.

☐ If you are applying for joint credit with another person, complete all Sections providing information in Section 2 about the joint applicant.

☐ If you are applying for individual credit, but are relying on income from alimony, child support, or separate maintenance or on the income or assets of another person as a basis for repayment of the credit requested, complete all Sections, providing information in Section 2 about the person whose alimony, support, or maintenance payments or income or assets you are relying.

☐ If this statement relates to your guaranty of the indebtedness of other person(s), firm(s) or corporation(s), complete Sections 1 and 3.

TO:

These forms are intended for use in commercial lending transactions. Where any other use is contemplated it is suggested that a careful review be made with applicable laws and regulations.

SECTION 1 - INDIVIDUAL INFORMATION (Type or Print)		SECTION 2 - OTHER PARTY INFORMATION (Type or Print)	
Name	Hillary Rodham Clinton	Name	Bill Clinton
Residence Address	1800 Center St	Residence Address	1800 Center St.
City, State & Zip	Little Rock, Ark. 72206	City, State & Zip	Little Rock, Ark. 72206
Position or Occupation	Attorney	Position or Occupation	Governor
Business Name	Rose Law Firm	Business Name	State of Arkansas
Business Address	120 E. 4th	Business Address	State Capitol
City, State & Zip	Little Rock, Ark. 72201	City, State & Zip	Little Rock, Ark. 72202
Res. Phone 376-6884	Bus. Phone 375-9131	Res. Phone 376-6884	Bus. Phone 371-2345

SECTION 3 - STATEMENT OF FINANCIAL CONDITION AS OF March 24 19 87

ASSETS (Do not include Assets of doubtful value)	In Dollars (Omit cents)	LIABILITIES	In Dollars (Omit cents)
Cash on hand and in banks	50,000 00	Notes payable to banks - secured	84,000
U.S. Gov't. & Marketable Securities - see Schedule A	120,000	Notes payable to banks - unsecured	
Non-Marketable Securities - See Schedule B		Due to brokers	
Securities held by broker in margin accounts		Amounts payable to others - secured	
Restricted or control stocks		Amounts payable to others - unsecured	
Partial interest in Real Estate Equities - see Schedule C	50,000	Accounts and bills due	
		Unpaid income tax	
Real Estate Owned - see Schedule D		Other unpaid taxes and interest	
Loans Receivable	50,000	Real estate mortgages payable - see Schedule D	
Automobiles and other personal property	20,000	Other debts - itemize:	
Cash value-life insurance-see Schedule E			
Other assets - itemize:			
		TOTAL LIABILITIES	84,000
		NET WORTH	206,000
TOTAL ASSETS	290,000	TOTAL LIAB. AND NET WORTH	290,000

SOURCES OF INCOME FOR YEAR ENDED 12 31 19 86		PERSONAL INFORMATION
Salary, bonuses & commissions	$ 135,000	Do you have a will? Yes if so, name of executor Spouse
Dividends	20	
Real estate income	-	Are you a partner or officer in any other venture? If so, describe
Other income (Alimony, child support, or separate maintenance)		Partner in Rose Law Firm
Income need not be revealed if you do not wish to have it considered as a basis for repaying this obligation)		Are you obligated to pay alimony, child support or separate maintenance payments? If so, describe. NO
		Are any assets pledged other than as described on schedules? If so, describe NO
TOTAL	$ 155,000	
CONTINGENT LIABILITIES		Income tax settled through (date) 1985
Do you have any contingent liabilities? If so, describe		Are you a defendant in any suits or legal actions? NO
As indorser, co-maker or guarantor?	$	Personal bank accounts carried at:
On leases or contracts?	$	Worthen Bank
Legal claims	$	
Other special debt	$	Have you ever been declared bankrupt? If so, describe NO
Amount of contested income tax liens	$	

(COMPLETE SCHEDULES AND SIGN ON REVERSE SIDE)

SCHEDULE A - U.S. GOVERNMENTS & MARKETABLE SECURITIES

Number of Shares or Face Value (Bonds)	Description	In Name Of	Are These Pledged?	Market Value
400 sh	Wal-Mart	HR Clinton	NO	~20,000
16	Value Partners I	"	NO	-80,000
	Fidelity Mutual Funds	"	NO	-20,000

SCHEDULE B - NON-MARKETABLE SECURITIES

Number of Shares	Description	In Name Of	Are These Pledged?	Source of Value	Value

SCHEDULE C - PARTIAL INTERESTS IN REAL ESTATE EQUITIES

Address & Type Of Property	Title In Name Of	% Of Ownership	Date Acquired	Cost	Market Value	Mortgage Maturity	Mortgage Amount

SCHEDULE D - REAL ESTATE OWNED

Address & Type Of Property	Title In Name Of	Date Acquired	Cost	Market Value	Mortgage Maturity	Mortgage Amount

SCHEDULE E - LIFE INSURANCE CARRIED, INCLUDING N.S.L.I. AND GROUP INSURANCE

Name Of Insurance Company	Owner Of Policy	Beneficiary	Face Amount	Policy Loans	Cash Surrender Value

SCHEDULE F - BANKS OR FINANCE COMPANIES WHERE CREDIT HAS BEEN OBTAINED

Name & Address Of Lender	Credit In The Name Of	Secured Or Unsecured?	Original Date	High Credit	Current Balance
First National Bank of Ozark	HR + Bill Clinton + Jim + Susan McDougal	Secured	1979		29,000
Security Bank of Paragould	HR + B.H. Clinton	"	"		14,000

The information contained in this statement is provided for the purpose of obtaining, or maintaining credit with you on behalf of the undersigned, or persons, firms or corporations in whose behalf the undersigned may either severally or jointly with others, execute a guaranty in your favor. Each undersigned understands that you are relying on the information provided herein (including the designation made as to ownership of property) in deciding to grant or continue credit. Each undersigned represents and warrants that the information provided is true and complete and that you may consider this statement as continuing to be true and correct until a written notice of a change is given to you by the undersigned. You are authorized to make all inquiries you deem necessary to verify the accuracy of the statements made herein, and to determine my/our creditworthiness. You are authorized to answer questions about your credit experience with me/us.

Signature (Individual) Hillary Rodham Clinton
S.S. No. 353-40-2576   Date of Birth 10-26-47

Signature (Other Party) Bill Clinton
S.S. No. 429-92-9947   Date of Birth 8-19-46

Date Signed March 24 19 87

CONFIDENTIAL   DKRT700353

5·11

COMMERCIAL LOAN APPLICATION

Date: __January 8, 1987__ Loan Officer ____Ron Proctor____

Applicant: __Whitewater Development Company, Inc.__

Address: _____

_____

_____

Telephone:_____

Loan Amount: __$53,161.52__ Rate: ___10.50%___

Terms: DND; 12 month note; 60 month amort.;
monthly payments of $1143.00

Principals:_____
   Whitewater Development Company, Inc.
   By: James B. McDougal, President
   By: Susan H. McDougal, Secretary
_____

Guarantors:_____
   Ind. co-makers:
     James B. McDougal
     Susan H. McDougal
     Bill Clinton
     Hillary Rodham Clinton

Type of Business:

   Real Estate Development

___X___ Corp.
_____ Prop.
_____ Part.

Purpose of Loan:

   Renew loan 5885 originally for purchase and development of subdivision

Participation:

     Yes_____ No____

If yes. Name of Participant:_____
Total Loan Amount $_____

Insurance Agent:

Collateral:

Value: __$104,136__

   1st REM on lots in Whitewater Estates consisting of 57.80 acres
   at $750.00 acre average—$43,350.00
   Assignment of escrow funds on sold lots—Total performing receivables—$60,786

Disbursement Instructions:

   None

Comments. agreements and sources of repayment:

CONFIDENTIAL

   See file notes dated 1/6/'87.

   Receivables on sold lots total 1338.43 per month. All proceeds of these contracts
are to be deposited into escrow account and applied to note monthly. Any deficiencies
to be funded by co-makers.

- All Sales Proceeds (less Commissions) Applied to Note OKP
- All Contracts to be maintained here or RP
- All Financials in file before Renewal OKRP

Loan Officer _____ Granted - ~~Declined~~
      Ron Proctor

With the exceptions noted below, approved or declined.

DKRT700406

Approved by Officers Loan Committee 1/8/87

1st Ozark National Bank

P.O. BOX 250
FLIPPIN, ARKANSAS 72634
TELEPHONE (501) 453-2255

is now final acount

March 26, 1987

Susan McDougal
P.O. Box 7326
Little Rock, AR 72217

Dear Susan:

Enclosed please find the renewal note and guaranty forms for the renewal of the Whitewater Development loan number 5885. The interest to date was taken out of the Whitewater Account. The interest amounted to $385.66. The next payment on the loan will be due May 3, 1987 and will be in the amount of $1,143.00. Please sign the note and guaranty forms where indicated and return to me. I would appreciate receiving these documents before the end of the month, so please send them by overnight mail.

If you have any questions, please feel free to call.

Sincerely,

Ron Proctor
Vice President

TO BE DRAWN MONTHLY FROM EXISTING PAyment ON CONTRACTS IN ESCROW. SMc

RP/gw

Enclosures

CONFIDENTIAL

Dear Hillary:

Jim and I have executed the renewal note and our guaranty forms and returned them. Enclosed is the guaranty form and notice for you and Bill to sign. Please return them direct to Mr. Proctor. Thanks —

Susan 374-6464

DKRT700432

THE TWIN CITY BANK
ON   VERFRONT PLACE
NORTH LITTLE ROCK, ARKANSAS 72114
TELEPHONE (501) 372-4700

Personal Financial Statement

(NOTE: Any willful misrepresentation could result in violation of Federal Law.)

Name _Bill Clinton_   S.S. Number _429-92-9547_
(One Name if Statement for One Individual Only)
Name _Hillary Rodham Clinton_   S.S. Number _353-40-2536_
(Second Name if Statement is Joint)
Home Address _1800 Center St._   Zip _72206_ Telephone _501-376-6984_
Business Address _120 E. 4th St_   Zip _72201_ Telephone _501-375-9131_
Position or Occupation _Attorney_

STATEMENT OF CONDITION AS OF ___3/8___, 19_87_

ASSETS		DOLLARS		LIABILITIES		DOLLARS	
Cash	A	$ 50,000	00	Accounts & Bills Due		$	
Cash Value Life Insurance	B			Cash Value Insurance Loans	B		
Listed Securities	C	120,000	00	Secured Debt Due Banks	H		
Unlisted Securities	D	~~110,000~~		Unsecured Debt Due Banks	H		
Accounts/Notes Receivables	E	50,000	00	Accrued Taxes			
TOTAL CURRENT ASSETS				TOTAL CURRENT LIABILITIES			
Real Estate Owned	F			Real Estate Mortgages	F		
Real Estate - Partial Interest	G	50,000		Real Estate - Partial Interest	G		
Automobiles		10,000	00	Secured Debt Due Others		84,000	00
Personal Property		10,000	00	Unsecured Debt Due Others		~~20,000 00~~	
Other Assets - Itemize				Other Debts - Itemize			
				TOTAL LIABILITIES		$14,000 00	
				NET WORTH (total assets less total liabilities)		~~246,000~~ 206,000	
TOTAL ASSETS		$ 290,000 00		TOTAL LIABILITIES & NET WORTH		$ ~~~~ 290,000	

INCOME SOURCE				PERSONAL INFORMATION
Salary	$ 185,000	00		Date of Birth: 10/26/47 (Hrc) 8/19/46 (BC)
Bonus / Commissions				Do You Have a Will? Yes Executor:
Dividends / Interest	20,000	00		Have you been declared bankrupt? NO
Real Estate Income				Explain:
				Are you a defendant in legal action? No
TOTAL	$ 185,000	00		Explain:

CONTINGENT LIABILITIES AS COMAKER, ENDORSER, GUARANTOR

Debt Payable By	Debt Payable To	Amount Due

(BOTH SIDES OF THIS STATEMENT MUST BE COMPLETE   CBF 0399

For the purpose of procuring and maintaining credit, I/we submit the foregoing as a true and accurate statement of my/our financial condition.
Authorize... to obtain... to... against... or any other... on this statement... I/we agrees to
notify the Lender immediately in writing of any significant changes in such financial condition and also agrees to submit a current financial statement on an
annual...
The undersigned certifies that the information provided on both sides of this statement is true and correct.

___, 19_87_   _Hillary Rodham Clinton_
(Date)   (Signature)
Bill Clinton
(Second Signature if Joint Statement)

2-01-034

344   g= DDA 3175   CC-M   EC-50   . . . .   RENEWAL

Whitewater Development Company, Inc.	**1ST OZARK NATIONAL BANK** 4TH & MAIN, P.O. BOX 250 FLIPPIN, ARKANSAS 72634	Loan Number **R-5885** Date **March 26** 1987 Maturity Date **April 3** 1988 Loan Amount $ **52,135.80** Renewal Of **5885**
BORROWER'S NAME AND ADDRESS "I" includes each borrower above, jointly and severally.	**LENDER'S NAME AND ADDRESS** "You" means the lender, its successors and assigns.	

Note: I promise to pay to you, or your order, at your address above, the principal sum of:
Fifty-two thousand one hundred thirty-five and 80/100———————————— Dollars $ **52,135.80**
plus interest from **March 26, 1987** at the rate of **10.50** % per year until **April 3, 1988**
I will pay this amount as follows:

(a) ☐ on demand.   (b) ☐ on demand, but if none is made, on _____ , ___ .   (c) ☐ on _____
If (a), (b) or (c) is marked, I will pay accrued interest _____ and on the maturity date.
(d) ☒ In **11** installments of $ **1,143.00** each, beginning **May 3** **1987** and continuing on the same day of each ☒ month
☐ _____ thereafter, until **April 3** **1988** when a final payment of $ **44,763.68** will be due.
(e) ☐ (other) _____

PAYMENTS: Each payment when made shall be applied first toward accrued finance charges with the remainder of each payment being applied to reduce the principal balance. The final payment may be more or less than the amount scheduled depending upon my payment record.

PREPAYMENT: I may prepay this note in whole or in part at any time. However, any partial prepayment will not excuse any later scheduled payments until this note is paid in full.

DELINQUENCY AND DEFAULT: I agree to pay the costs you incur to collect this note in the event of my default, including your reasonable attorneys' fees.
☐ If checked, I agree to pay a finance late interest charge of $ _____ if I pay this loan off before you have earned this amount in interest.

☒ If checked, I agree to pay a late charge of $ **5.00** % of the amount of a payment which is not paid within **10** days of when it is due, up to a maximum of $ **10.00** .
☐ If checked, I agree to pay interest at the rate of **10.50** % per year on the balance of this note remaining unpaid after final maturity, including maturity by acceleration.

THE PURPOSE OF THIS LOAN IS: Renew loan #5885

ANNUAL PERCENTAGE RATE The cost of my credit as a yearly rate	FINANCE CHARGE The dollar amount the credit will cost me.	AMOUNT FINANCED The amount of credit provided to me or on my behalf.	TOTAL OF PAYMENTS The amount I will have paid when I have made all scheduled payments.	I have the right to receive at this time an itemization of the Amount Financed
10.50 %	$ **5,200.88**	$ **52,135.80**	$ **57,336.68**	X YES - I want an itemization ☐ NO - I do not want an itemization

My Payment Schedule will be:

Number of Payments	Amount of Payments	When Payments Are Due	
11	1,143.00	Monthly payments beginning May 3, 1987 and continuing until maturity date.	"e" means an estimate
1	44,763.68	Total payment of principal and interest due April 3, 1988.	$ ___ Filing Fees $ ___ Non-filing Insurance

☐ This note has a demand feature.   ☐ This note is payable on demand and all disclosures are based on an assumed maturity of one year.

Security: I am giving a security interest in:
☒ the goods or property being purchased.   ☒ (brief description of other property) **existing mortgage dated August 2, 1978**
☒ collateral securing other loans with you may also secure this loan.   **Assignment of escrow funds**
☒ my deposit accounts and other rights to the payment of money from you.

Late Charge: I will be charged **5.00** % of the amount of a payment which is more than **10** days late, up to a maximum of $ **10.00** .
Prepayment: If I pay off this loan early, I ☐ may ☒ will not   have to pay a penalty.
☐ may ☒ will not   be entitled to a refund of part of the finance charge.
I can see my contract documents for any additional information about nonpayment, default, any required repayment before the scheduled date, and prepayment refunds and penalties.

Insurance: Credit life insurance and credit disability insurance are not required to obtain credit, and will not be provided unless I sign and agree to pay the additional cost.

Type	Premium	Term	Signatures (or Initials)		Itemization of Amount Financed	
Credit Life			I want credit life insurance X ___	Name of Insured	Amount given to me directly	$ ___ (a)
Credit Disability			I want credit disability insurance X ___	Name of Insured	Amount XXXXXXXXXX RENEWED $52,135.80 (b) Amounts paid to others on my behalf: To Property Insurance Company $ ___ (c)	
Joint Credit Life			I want joint credit life insurance X ___	Name of Insured	To Credit Life Insurance Company $ ___ (d) To Disability Insurance Company $ ___ (e) To Public Officials $ ___ (f)	

I do not want: **X** Credit Life Ins ; **X** Credit Disability Ins ; **X** Joint Credit Life Ins.
Property Insurance: I may obtain property insurance from anyone I want that is acceptable to you. If I get the insurance from or through you I will pay $ ___ for ___ of coverage.

$ ___ (g)
$ ___ (h)
Prepaid Finance Charge $ ___ (i)
AMOUNT FINANCED (a through h - i) $ **52,135.80** (j)
Finance Charge (include prepaid) $ **5,200.88** (k)
Total of Payments (j + k) $ **57,336.68** (l)

Security - To secure the payment of the note total (defined on the reverse side).
(1) I acknowledge and agree that you have the right to set-off this note against any obligation you have (now or hereafter) to pay money to me.
(2) You may collect the proceeds (or rebates of unearned premiums) on any insurance policy insuring me (where you are named as loss payee) and on any policy insuring the property securing this note. You would apply this toward what I owe you.

(3) ☐ If checked, this note is not further secured by any contemporaneous agreement (except for (1) and (2) of this section).
(4) ☒ If checked, this note is secured by a separate **existing mortgage** dated **August 2, 1978**

(5) ☒ Security Agreement - If checked, I give you a security interest in the property described below. The rights I am giving you in this property, and the obligations this agreement secures are defined on the reverse side of this form.

. . . . Par. 349-343A. Marion

☐ If checked this security agreement (if filed) should be filed in the real estate records.
This property will be used for ☐ Personal ☐ Business ☐ Agricultural
☐ ___ purposes.
☐ If checked, this is a purchase money loan. You may include the name of the seller on the check or draft with this loan.

I agree to the terms and acknowledge receipt of at least one copy on today's date.
COSIGNERS SEE NOTICE ON REVERSE SIDE BEFORE SIGNING

Signatures:
X ___
X ___ Date ___
Signature for Lender - Advice necessary for filing this security agreement

Signature ___
Signature ___

GUARANTY

The undersigned _____ Bill J. Clinton and Hillary Rodham Clinton _____

_____ 1st Ozark National Bank _____

for value received, do hereby guarantee the payment to CITIZENS BANK OF FLIPPIN, ARK. of that certain negotiable promissory note dated the 26th day of March 19 87, in the principal sum of $ 52,135.80 , executed by Whitewater Development Company, Inc.

_____

to the order of said Bank at its maturity, and at all times thereafter, together with accrued interest thereon. Said Bank may extend the time of payment or grant one or more renewals of said note without notice to the undersigned, and the undersigned shall continue obligated under this guaranty until said original note or any extensions or renewals thereof, together with accrued interest, have been paid in full.

The acceptance of this guaranty is hereby waived, and the undersigned acknowledge that this guaranty is operating and binding without reference to whether it is signed by any other person or persons.

Notification of the default of the maker of said note is hereby waived, and after default it shall not be necessary for said Bank to first endeavor to collect from the maker of said note before proceeding against the undersigned for recovery of the full amount of the liability hereby assumed.

The undersigned hereby pledge to said Bank as security for the performance of this guaranty any and all stocks, bonds or other personal property belonging to the undersigned and in possession of the Bank, whether held as collateral or otherwise.

In the event of bankruptcy or insolvency of the maker of said note, said Bank shall not be required to attempt collection of said debt from said principal debtor, but shall be entitled to make immediate demand upon and proceed against the undersigned for the payment of the note evidencing said indebtedness, whether or not the same is then due in accordance with the tenor thereof.

This guaranty shall be binding upon the heirs, legal representatives, successors and assigns of the undersigned and shall inure to the benefit of said Bank, its successors and assigns.

The undersigned waive presentment for payment, notice of non-payment, protest and notice of protest and due diligence in enforcing payment of said note or any renewal thereof.

If this guaranty is signed by more than one guarantor, it is agreed that the liability of each of the undersigned is joint and several.

EXECUTED at Flippin, Arkansas, this 26th day of March, 1987

WITNESS TO SIGNATURE:

_____
Address

_____
Address

_____
Address

Hillary Rodham Clinton
1800 Center Street, LR, AR 72206
Address

Bill Clinton
1800 Center Street, LR, AR 72206
Address

_____
Address

1s. Ozark National Bank

P.O. BOX 250
FLIPPIN, ARKANSAS 72634
TELEPHONE (501) 453-2255

J. WESLEY STRANGE, PRESIDENT

April 12, 1988

Hillary Clinton
120 E. 4th Street
Little Rock, AR. 72114

Dear Mrs. Clinton:

As per our phone conversation, we have researched the transaction regarding the Whitewater Development Company, Inc. and they are enclosed. The loan and escrow data are for 1987 only and do not include any of 1988 transactions. Hope this will help you in preparing your tax returns and some type of balance sheet.

I have also enclosed a renewal note, hoping that you could help me in getting all the signatures on this and returning it as soon as possible.

In addition, we will be needing an updated financial statement on the personal, as well as the corporation.

Respectfully,

J. W. Strange

JWS/rjo

Enclosures

REQUEST FOR LOAN
DOCUMENTATION WAIVER

TO: CREDIT DEPARTMENT

FROM: RON PROCTOR

DATE: July 15, 1988

RE: DOCUMENTATION REQUIREMENT

BORROWER NAME: Whitewater Development Co., Inc.

NOTE NUMBER: R-5885

DOCUMENT: Personal Financial Statements of Guarantors and Financial Statement on

REASON FOR REQUEST: 1) Payments on loan are derived from escrow contracts Whitewater

                        .   controlled by FONB.

                     2) Collateral is sufficient to cover the loan.

THIS REQUEST IS EFFECTIVE FOR THE TIME STATED BELOW:

_____ Permanently.

____X_____ Term of this note only.

_____ Extension until_____only.

_____   _____
REQUESTING LOAN OFFICER   APPROVED BY

ROSE LAW FIRM

A PROFESSIONAL ASSOCIATION

ATTORNEYS

120 EAST FOURTH STREET

LITTLE ROCK, ARKANSAS 72201

TELEPHONE (501) 375-9131

TELECOPIER (501) 375-1309

———

U. M. ROSE

1834-1913

PHILLIP CARROLL
W. DANE CLAY
GEORGE E. CAMPBELL
HERBERT C. RULE, III
W. WILSON JONES
VINCENT FOSTER, JR.
WEBSTER L. HUBBELL
ALLEN W. BIRD II
WILLIAM E. BISHOP
HILLARY RODHAM CLINTON
C. BRANTLY BUCK
TIM BOE
M. JANE DICKEY
WILLIAM H. KENNEDY, III
KENNETH R. SHEMIN
RONALD M. CLARK
GARLAND J. GARRETT
JERRY C. JONES
THOMAS P. THRASH
CHARLES W. BAKER
DAVID L. WILLIAMS
CAROL S. ARNOLD

JACKSON FARROW JR.
LES R. BALEDGE
JIM HUNTER BIRCH
R. DAVIS THOMAS, JR.
KEVIN R. BURNS
RICHARD T. DONOVAN
RICHARD N. MASSEY
GARY N. SPEED
MICHAEL F. LAX
M. ELIZABETH GOFF
SARAH C. HOOD
MICHAEL B. JOHNSON
STEPHEN N. JOINER
B. MICHAEL BENNETT
THOMAS C. VAUGHAN, JR.
JAMES H. DRUFF
ELANA L. CUNNINGHAM
JAY F. SHELL
GORDON M. WILBOURN

J. GASTON WILLIAMSON
OF COUNSEL

July 27, 1988

Mr. J. W. Strange
President
1st Ozark National Bank
P. O. Box 250
Flippin, AR 72634

Dear Wes:

I am returning the note on Whitewater Development Company, Inc., signed by my husband and me, as you requested. Thank you for your assistance in this matter.

With best regards, I am,

Sincerely yours,

Hillary

HILLARY RODHAM CLINTON

HRC:ckp

Encl.

Lekcham contacted by Quast
& confirmed retainer paid to Rose firm

2/24 Tx w/ Webb Hubbell
① Preferred Stock offering 4/85
② Broker dealer Summer 1985
Massey had relationship w/ Lekcham & HC
had relationship w/ MacD. Rick will say he
had cl w/ Lekcham & had alot to do w/ getting
the client in. She did all the billing.

Sec. + others HC had numerous conf w/ Lekcham, Mackey +
rec McDougell on both transaction. She reviewed
some doc. She had one to in 4/85
at beginning of the deal w/ Bev.
Neither deal went through.
Broker dealer was opposed by staff but
approved by Bev under certain conditions
which they never met.
Preferred stock ?!
But for Massey it would not have been there.
Rose firm prohibited from using
Examiner's Report. Rose relied on
critiqued audit report.

RTC paid Rose law firm $240,000 in 1991

but HC was billing partner &
attended conferences. He has a
major role _____ has vs HC's _____ has.

1985 deeds 1/2 lots to Ozark Air Service's
with no revenue stamp. Wade's
recollection still had signif # of lots
Wade was given authority to sell them
& Wade assumed liability on
the loan balance. Partial releases
- on mortgage when lots are sold

WH Travel Office   6-2-93

- Hillary, ~~telephone~~ conversation with D. Watkins
  on Friday, May 14
  - "Harry says his people can
    run things better; save
    money, etc. And besides
    we need those people out —
    ~~we's~~ — We need our people in —
    — We Need the slots —

- POTUS, ~~real~~ relationships with Catherine Cornelius

- Travel Office Review HAs become an
  inquisition —
    Neel, Podesta, Gearan, McLarty
  Panatta —
    * NO TEAMWORK
    * Attitude of Guilty or stupidity
    * Need ~~corps~~ War Room to
      house — computers, etc.

- Is the real story to Be Told?

-

                                        CGE 001497

-Betsy Wright had those Records - Took em home
-Betsy Wright

WH retrieved - records from BW

Been at WH - Sent files related to WW

Make a more complete reconstruction

Charles James - subpoenaed w/SBIC matter
                Relate to $ going into WW

GJ indicted Hale ~ Press says that GJ continue investigation

    RTC - people trying to get BC and JGT

        - story of a referral by RTC regarding
          Indictment of JGT - Chuck Banks
          rejected

Vacuum   Rose Law files   WWDC Docs - subpoena

    *Documents - never know go out
                 Quietly(?)

NOTES ON SOURCES

MUCH OF THE INFORMATION in this book is based on hundreds of interviews with participants in the story conducted from March 1994, when I began my work, until January 1996. Every person named other than in passing was interviewed, asked for an interview, or given an opportunity to comment. Many other people with knowledge of aspects of the story were interviewed but not named. After a draft of the book was finished, they were again contacted as part of the fact-checking process and given the opportunity to hear what was said about them and make any additions or corrections.

Many of the interviews were conducted on a not-for-quotation basis, but with the understanding that the text would reflect the states of mind and conversations recalled by those being interviewed. States of mind come from the person identified, either directly, in an interview, or from sworn testimony or notes taken by lawyers. Quotations come from the speaker, someone who heard the remark, or from transcripts and notes of conversations. To the extent practicable, the substance of quotes provided by anyone other than the speaker was repeated to the speaker for comment or correction. Many sources not only demonstrated excellent memories, but kept extensive contemporaneous notes of their thoughts and remarks. Still, readers should bear in mind that remembered dialogue, particularly when years have elapsed, is rarely an exact reproduction of a conversation, as comparisons with actual recordings and transcripts often make clear.

President Clinton and Hillary Clinton declined to be interviewed (while never explicitly declining repeated interview requests). As it became clear the Clintons would not agree to the kinds of interviews I had originally envisioned, I offered numerous alternatives that might limit the time and effort required, even, near the end, offering the opportunity to discuss only matters not under investigation. All of these negotiations were with the Clintons' personal lawyer, David Kendall. None of my offers was accepted.

Kendall also declined to make available whatever documents relevant to Whitewater and related matters he has in his possession. However, he did make available copies of documents I specifically asked for, including some but not all of the Clintons' loan records from 1st Ozark. Extensive information about the Clintons was submitted for comment both to Kendall and to the White House press office, in some cases in written form. Kendall did contest some characterizations, which is reflected in the text or accompanying footnotes.

At the direction of the White House, other inquiries were referred to Mark Fabiani and Chris Lehane, who operate as press spokesmen but work in the office of the White House counsel. They made copies of documents available as they were released to the press, but they didn't provide any assistance in the fact-checking process, neither confirming nor denying specific facts. Nor did they help gain access to people in the White House who might be able to do so. Indeed, calls to these people were routinely referred to Fabiani. In keeping with standard policy toward all subjects of the book, I declined Kendall's and the press office's requests to review the manuscript before publication.

I do not know how I could have been any more accommodating of the Clintons consistent with accepted journalistic standards. The Clintons' version of events appearing in the text is based on their sworn, written responses to the Resolution Trust Corporation's interrogatories and those portions of their testimony before the independent counsel that have been made public. As for the extensive material in this book not covered by the Clintons' testimony, I relied on and corroborated the accounts of other firsthand participants, such as Jim and Susan McDougal. When the White House was told that the Clintons' lack of participation gave me no alternative, a spokesman responded that he had found that the McDougals were, by and large, accurate in their recollections, with the exception of Jim McDougal's acknowledged memory lapses after suffering his seizure, and his generally vague awareness of documents. In my experience, the McDougals, especially Susan, were meticulously careful, and much of what they said is corroborated by written records.

I did not rely on the accuracy of statements by David Hale. As described in the text, he was under the threat of indictment when he made them. He had an obvious incentive to implicate others, including Bill Clinton. He did not agree to be interviewed by me nor could I corroborate his crucial claims. Under the circumstances, I treated his assertions as allegations.

The White House remains vehement that the Arkansas state troopers who spoke out cannot be relied upon. This was not my experience. Nevertheless, I used only information for which they were a direct participant or eyewitness and which, in almost every case, could be corroborated by others. The primary purpose of including this is so that readers understand the troopers' states of mind and reasons for speaking out, matters on which they are the only reliable sources. Whatever the troopers' impressions, whether Bill Clinton did or did not have affairs is beyond the scope of this book.

Multiple witnesses to an event invariably provide inconsistent accounts of what happened. Usually the differences are minor, and accounts can be harmonized, as I tried to do in this book. Thus, future researchers will discover, as I did, numerous minor variations in the testimony of some participants. In some cases, versions cannot be reconciled. When I thought these discrepancies were significant, I have noted the instances in footnotes to the text.

I and my research assistants reviewed thousands of pages of documents and testimony. These included numerous depositions taken pursuant to subpoenas issued by the Senate and House committees, documents and other materials submitted to those committees and to the RTC, and FBI interview reports of people questioned by the independent counsel regarding the death of Vincent Foster. Among those people who were especially helpful in obtaining these materials were Carl Stern, head of public affairs for the Department of Justice; Jackson R. Sharman III, special counsel; Joe Reilly, David Runkel, and David Cohen of the House Committee on Banking and Financial Services; Eric Berman of the Democratic National Committee; James Jones, legislative assistant to Senator John F. Kerry, D.-Mass., on the Senate Banking, Housing and Urban Affairs Committee; Ed Amorosi, press secretary for the House Government Reform and Oversight Committee; Lynn Cutler and Tim Hackler of the Back to Business Committee; Alfred Thomas, library manager, and Monte Bemis, librarian, at the *Arkansas Democrat-Gazette;* and Dawn Grey-Eppes of the *Yellville Mountain Echo.*

Published accounts on which I relied are usually mentioned in the text. Following is a bibliography of the principal written source material.

BOOKS

Brummett, John. *High Wire: The Education of Bill Clinton.* New York: Hyperion Press, 1994.

Drew, Elizabeth. *On the Edge: The Clinton Presidency.* New York: Simon & Schuster, 1994.

Dumas, Ernest, ed. *The Clintons of Arkansas: An Introduction by Those Who Know Them Best.* Fayetteville, Ark.: University of Arkansas Press, 1993.

Flowers, Gennifer. *Passion and Betrayal.* Del Mar, Calif.: Emery Dalton Books, 1995.

Goldman, Peter, Thomas M. DeFrank, Mark Miller, Andrew Murr, and Tom Mathews. *Quest for the Presidency 1992.* College Station, Texas: Texas A&M Press/Newsweek, 1994.

Kelley, Virginia Clinton. *Leading with My Heart: My Life.* New York: Simon & Schuster, 1993.

Marannis, David. *First in His Class: A Biography of Bill Clinton.* New York: Simon & Schuster, 1995.

Radcliffe, Donnie. *Hillary Rodham Clinton: A First Lady for Our Time.* New York: Warner Books, 1993.

Woodward, Bob. *The Agenda.* New York: Simon & Schuster, 1994.

ARTICLES

On Hillary and Bill Clinton:

Bruck, Connie. "Hillary the Pol." *The New Yorker,* May 30, 1994.

Gordon, Meryl. "Hillary Rodham Clinton Talks Back." *Elle,* May 1994.

Nelson, Jack. "Angry Clinton Rebukes His Whitewater Critics." *Los Angeles Times,* December 21, 1995.

On the Whitewater investment:

Boyer, Peter J. "The Bridges of Madison Guaranty." *The New Yorker,* January 17, 1994.

Gerth, Jeff. "Clintons Joined S&L Operator in an Ozark Real-Estate Venture." *New York Times,* March 8, 1992.

Lyons, James M., with Patten, McCarthy & Associates. "Review of Whitewater Development Company, Inc." March 23, 1992 (the "Lyons Report").

Pillsbury, Madison & Sutro, with Tucker Alan Inc. "Madison Guaranty Savings & Loan and Whitewater Development Company, Inc.: A Preliminary Report to the Resolution Trust Corporation." April 24, 1995 (the "RTC Report").

———. "Madison Guaranty Savings & Loan and Whitewater Development Co., Inc." December 28, 1995.

Rothenberg, Mike. "Conflicts Surround Acreage." *Arkansas Democrat*, October 29, 1979.

Schneider, Howard. "Down the Whitewater Rapids; The McDougals Were on a Wild Ride, Then They Hit the Rocks." *Washington Post*, January 13, 1994.

Senate Committee on Banking, Housing and Urban Affairs. "Hearings Related to Madison Guaranty S&L and the Whitewater Development Corporation" (nine volumes to date).

On Hillary Clinton's commodities trading:

Cohen, Laurie P. "What *Journal* Said About Cattle Futures During 1978–79 Rally." *Wall Street Journal*, April 1, 1994.

Gerth, Jeff, with Dean Baquet and Stephen Labaton. "Top Arkansas Lawyer Helped Hillary Clinton Turn Big Profit." *New York Times*, March 18, 1994.

Gibson, Richard, and Jeffrey Zazlow. "Brash Trader, Thomas Dittmer Roils Commodities Markets with Clout, Timing." *Wall Street Journal*, August 13, 1984.

Glassman, James K. "Hillary's Cows: And What They Could Tell Us." *The New Republic*, May 16, 1994.

Taylor, Jeffrey, and Bruce Ingersoll. "Cash Cows: Red Bone's Business Was Wildly Profitable, and Profitably Wild." *Wall Street Journal*, April 1, 1994.

On Madison Guaranty Savings and Loan:

Barth, James R., and Dan R. Brumbaugh, Jr., Committee on Banking and Financial Services, U.S. House of Representatives. "The Condition and Regulation of Madison Guaranty Savings and Loan Association in the 1980s and Its Seizure in 1989." August 7, 1995.

Pillsbury, Madison & Sutro, with Tucker Alan Inc. "A Report on the Representation of Madison Guaranty Savings & Loan and Related Entities." December 28, 1995.

———. "General Report on the Investigation of Madison Guaranty Savings & Loan and Related Entities," December 28, 1995.

On Castle Grande:

Hargrove, Mark, Don Johnson, and Michael Whitely. "The Deal That Won't Die." *Arkansas Democrat-Gazette*, August 28, 1994.

On the death of Vincent Foster:

Blumenthal, Sidney. "The Suicide." *The New Yorker.* August 9, 1993.

Boyer, Peter J. "Life After Vince." *The New Yorker,* September 11, 1995.

Fiske, Robert B., Jr., Roderick C. Lankler, Mark J. Stein, and Carl J. Stich, Jr. "Report of the Independent Counsel in Re Vincent W. Foster, Jr." June 30, 1994.

Pollock, Ellen Joan. "Vince Foster's Death Is a Lively Business for Conspiracy Buffs." *Wall Street Journal,* March 23, 1995.

On the RTC investigation and contacts with the Treasury Department:

Schmidt, Susan. "U.S. Is Asked to Probe Failed Arkansas S&L; RTC Questions Thrift's Mid-80s Check Flow." *Washington Post,* October 31, 1993.

On the travel office affair:

Davis, Joseph R., and legal counsel division of the Federal Bureau of Investigation. "An Internal Review of F.B.I. Contacts with the White House as Related to the Investigation of the White House Travel Office." May 28, 1993.

Podesta, John. "White House Travel Office Management Review." July 2, 1993.

Shaheen, Michael E., Jr., counsel to Department of Justice, Office of Professional Responsibility. "Review of Conduct of the F.B.I." March 18, 1994.

United States General Accounting Office. "White House: Travel Operations." May 1994.

On the Arkansas state troopers and Paula Jones:

Blumenthal, Sidney. "The Friends of Paula Jones." *The New Yorker,* June 20, 1994.

Brock, David. "His Cheatin' Heart: Living with the Clintons." *American Spectator,* January 1994.

Maxa, Rudy. "The Devil in Paula Jones." *Penthouse,* January 1995.

Rempel, William C., and Douglas Frantz. "Troopers Say Clinton Sought Silence on Personal Affairs." *Los Angeles Times*, December 21, 1993.

On David Hale:

United States General Accounting Office. "Small Business Administration: Inadequate Oversight of Capital Management Services Inc.—An SSBIC." March 1994.

On the Rose Law Firm:

Adair, John J., RTC Office of the Inspector General. "Investigation and Audit Concerning the Rose Law Firm." August 10, 1995.
Duff, Audrey. "Is a Rose a Rose?" *American Lawyer*, July/August 1992.

On the media:

Boyer, Peter J. "The Howell Raines Question," *The New Yorker*, August 22, 1994.
Lieberman, Trudy. "Churning Whitewater." *Columbia Journalism Review*, May/June 1994.
Lyons, Gene. "Fool for Scandal: How the *Times* Got Whitewater Wrong." *Harper's Magazine*, October 1994.

ACKNOWLEDGMENTS

I AM DEEPLY GRATEFUL for the extraordinary efforts of my two research assistants, Anne Farris in Washington and David Kirkpatrick in New York. Anne previously lived in Little Rock, where she was a reporter for the *Arkansas Gazette* and a stringer for the *New York Times*. Her insights and sources in Arkansas were invaluable, and she did extensive additional research in Washington, gathering documents, attending hearings, and conducting interviews. David worked as a fact-checker at *The New Yorker* for two years, where he fact-checked most of my stories. His contributions to this book go far beyond fact-checking, and include research and interviewing. I came to rely on Anne and David unconditionally, and this book would not have been what it is without their work. I will miss our daily contacts.

Alice Mayhew, my editor at Simon & Schuster, was enthusiastic about this project from the outset and provided wise counsel as it developed. I am grateful for her outstanding editing, guidance, and support. Carolyn Reidy, president of Simon & Schuster, has also encouraged me from the beginning. I am grateful as well to Eric Rayman for his careful legal review. As my agent, Amanda Urban has been involved in every aspect of this project, and I have benefited from her advice and friendship. My colleague Steve Swartz, editor of *SmartMoney*, read the manuscript and provided continual advice, counsel, and friendship. My assistant, Julie Allen, was tireless and helpful.

I'm not sure how anyone can write a book without the love of family and friends. Anton Klusener provided daily support. My parents, Ben and Mary Jane Stewart; my sister, Jane Holden, and her family; and my brother, Michael, have been unquestioning in their backing. I wish also to thank Didier Malaquin, Kate McNamara, Elizabeth McNamara, Barbara Presley Noble, Joel Goldsmith, Jim Gauer, Jeffrey Khaner, Jane Berentson, Gene Stone, Edward Flanagan, Charles Kaiser, Arthur Lubow, David Hollander, Andrew Tobias,

James Cramer, Laurie Cohen, Jill Abramson, Connie Bruck, Jane Mayer, John Barnard, Mark Drummond, Stephen Henderson, and Susan Heilbron, all of whom, in ways they may not even realize, helped me report and write this book.

INDEX